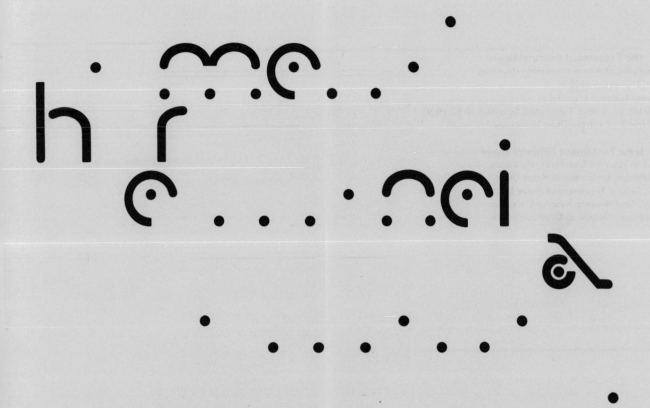

**Hermeneia
—A Critical
and Historical
Commentary
on the Bible**

The Song of Songs

A Commentary on the
Book of Canticles or
The Song of Songs

by Roland E. Murphy, O. Carm.

Edited by
S. Dean McBride, Jr.

**Fortress
Press**   Minneapolis

The Song of Songs

A commentary on the Book of Canticles or the
Song of Songs

© 1990 Augsburg Fortress

Scripture quotations are the author's own translation.

Excerpt from *Songs of Songs: A New Translation with
Introduction and Commentary* by Marvin H. Pope,
copyright © 1977 by Doubleday. Used by permission.
Excerpts from *The Harps That Once . . .: Sumerian Poetry
in Translation* by Thorkild Jacobsen, copyright © 1987
by Yale University Press. Used by permission. Excerpts
from *The Literature of Ancient Egypt: An Anthology of
Stories, Instructions, and Poetry,* edited by William Kelly
Simpson, copyright © 1972 by Yale University Press.
Used by permission.

Cover and internal design by Kenneth Hiebert
Typesetting on an Ibycus System at Polebridge Press

Library of Congress Cataloging-in-Publication Data

Murphy, Roland Edmund, 1917–
The Song of songs : a commentary on the Book of
  Canticles or the Song of songs / by Roland E.
  Murphy : edited by S. Dean McBride, Jr.
p. cm. — (Hermeneia—a critical and historical
  commentary on the Bible)
Includes bibliographical references.
ISBN 0-8006-6024-2
1. Bible. O.T. Song of Solomon—Commentaries.
I. McBride, S. Dean (Samuel Dean), 1937– .
II. Bible. O.T. Song of Solomon.
III. Title.
IV. Series.
BS1485.3.M87   1990
223'.9077–dc20   89–16891
                                                         CIP

The paper used in this publication meets the minimum
requirements of American National Standard
for Information Sciences—Permanence of Paper for
Printed Library Materials, ANSI Z329.48–1984.

Manufactured in the U.S.A.   AF 1–6024

94 93 92 91 90 1 2 3 4 5 6 7 8 9 10

IN MEMORIAM
MSGR. PATRICK W. SKEHAN

Contents
The Song of Songs

The name *Hermeneia*, Greek ἑρμηνεία, has been chosen as the title of the commentary series to which this volume belongs. The word *Hermeneia* has a rich background in the history of biblical interpretation as a term used in the ancient Greek-speaking world for the detailed, systematic exposition of a scriptural work. It is hoped that the series, like its name, will carry forward this old and venerable tradition. A second, entirely practical reason for selecting the name lies in the desire to avoid a long descriptive title and its inevitable acronym, or worse, an unpronounceable abbreviation.

The series is designed to be a critical and historical commentary to the Bible without arbitrary limits in size or scope. It will utilize the full range of philological and historical tools, including textual criticism (often slighted in modern commentaries), the methods of the history of tradition (including genre and prosodic analysis), and the history of religion.

Hermeneia is designed for the serious student of the Bible. It will make full use of ancient Semitic and classical languages; at the same time, English translations of all comparative materials—Greek, Latin, Canaanite, or Akkadian—will be supplied alongside the citation of the source in its original language. Insofar as possible, the aim is to provide the student or scholar with full critical discussion of each problem of interpretation and with the primary data upon which the discussion is based.

Hermeneia is designed to be international and interconfessional in the selection of authors; its editorial boards were formed with this end in view. Occasionally the series will offer translations of distinguished commentaries which originally appeared in languages other than English. Published volumes of the series will be revised continually, and eventually, new commentaries will replace older works in order to preserve the currency of the series. Commentaries are also being assigned for important literary works in the categories of apocryphal and pseudepigraphical works relating to the Old and New Testaments, including some of Essene or Gnostic authorship.

The editors of *Hermeneia* impose no systematic-theological perspective upon the series (directly, or indirectly by selection of authors). It is expected that authors will struggle to lay bare the ancient meaning of a biblical work or pericope. In this way the text's human relevance should become transparent, as is always the case in competent historical discourse. However, the series eschews for itself homiletical translation of the Bible.

The editors are heavily indebted to Fortress Press for its energy and courage in taking up an expensive, long-term project, the rewards of which will accrue chiefly to the field of biblical scholarship.

The editor responsible for this volume is S. Dean McBride, Jr., of Union Theological Seminary in Virginia.

Frank Moore Cross	*Helmut Koester*
For the Old Testament	For the New Testament
Editorial Board	Editorial Board

Biblical commentaries complement each other; each one has strengths and weaknesses, and can be used accordingly. Many examples of this complementarity could be cited. The most formidable recent commentary on the Song of Songs is that of Marvin H. Pope (1977). It embodies the author's massive erudition in linguistics and comparative materials, which will retain their value for a long time to come. But it offers more an attempt to discern a prehistory of the text than an interpretation of the biblical book as it now stands in the canon. Previously, André Robert's commentary (1963) presented incisive grammatical and textual observations, in the scholarly manner that characterized the work of that great French scholar. Despite his views favoring an allegorical understanding of the Song, his exegetical labors remain valuable for one who confronts the issues of the Hebrew text.

Like all commentaries, the present work rests on the labors of past scholars. It aims to explain the sense and meaning of the biblical text as adequately as possible. This has required that decisions be made where there are problems and ambiguities in the text, which in many cases have given rise to a plethora of varying interpretations. The reader should not be spared confrontation with difficulties that the text presents; but the myriad scholarly interpretations of specific passages is another matter. A certain parsimony is desirable here, because a detailed listing or exposition of views that differ with those proferred by the present author would be more distraction than help for most readers. The effort to provide a coherent and consistent commentary may be guilty of unintentional injustices to previous scholarship, but it has the advantage of clarity.

The author is indebted to more than commentaries. He is particularly grateful to his graduate students at Duke University, who were first exposed to this interpretation of the Song of Songs. Several of them aided in commenting on the growing manuscript, and helped in the expansion of references and bibliography. Special thanks are due to John B. White, Carole R. Fontaine, Claudia Camp, and Elizabeth Huwiler. Nancy Rosebaugh typed the manuscript handily and the secretarial pool of the Duke University Divinity School patiently reproduced many pages that had been disfigured by my revisions. Most of all, I am indebted to S. Dean McBride, Jr., the editor of the volume, for his wise suggestions, careful editing, and encouragement.

This work is dedicated to the memory of Msgr. Patrick W. Skehan, who was an inspiring example to me and to many others during his tenure in the department of Semitic languages at the Catholic University of America (1938–1981).

May 24, 1990

Roland E. Murphy, O.Carm.
G. W. Ivey Professor Emeritus
Duke University

1. Abbreviations

a / Sources, Secondary Literature, and General

AB	Anchor Bible (ed. William Foxwell Albright *et al.*)
ACW	Ancient Christian Writers
AfO	*Archiv für Orientforschung*
AHW	*Akkadisches Handwörterbuch*, 3 Vols. (ed. Wolfram von Soden; Wiesbaden: Otto Harrassowitz, 1959–81).
AJSL	*American Journal of Semitic Languages and Literatures*
Am	Amos
AnBib	Analecta Biblica
ANEP	*The Ancient Near East in Pictures Relating to the Old Testament* (ed. James B. Pritchard; Princeton: Princeton University, 1954).
*ANET*³	*Ancient Near Eastern Texts Relating to the Old Testament* (ed. James B. Pritchard; Princeton: Princeton University, ³1969).
AnOr	Analecta Orientalia
AOAT	Alter Orient und Altes Testament
AOS	American Oriental Series
ASTI	*Annual of the Swedish Theological Institute* (Jerusalem)
ATD	Das Alte Testament Deutsch (ed. Volkmar Herntrich and Artur Weiser).
AV	Authorized ("King James") Version (1611)
b.	Babylonian Talmud (followed by name of tractate)
Bar	Baruch
BASOR	*Bulletin of the American Schools of Oriental Research*
BAT	Die Botschaft des Alten Testaments
BC	Biblischer Commentar über das Alte Testament (ed. Carl Friedrich Keil and Franz Delitzsch)
B.C.E.	Before the Common Era (= B.C.)
BeO	*Bibbia e Oriente*
BET	Beiträge zur biblischen Exegese und Theologie
BETL	Bibliotheca Ephemeridum Theologicarum Lovaniensium
*BH*⁵	*Biblia Hebraica* (ed. Rudolph Kittel *et al.*; Stuttgart: Württembergische Bibelanstalt, ⁵1937).
BHS	*Biblia Hebraica Stuttgartensia* (ed. Karl Elliger and Wilhelm Rudolph; Stuttgart: Deutsche Bibelstiftung, 1967–77).
Bib	*Biblica*
BibOr	Biblica et Orientalia
BKAT	Biblischer Kommentar, Altes Testament (ed. Martin Noth *et al.*)
BLS	Bible and Literature Series
BMik	*Beth Mikra*
BOT	De boeken van het Oude Testament
BT	*The Bible Today*
BTB	*Biblical Theology Bulletin*
BTr	*The Bible Translator*
BVC	*Bible et vie chrétienne*
BZ	*Biblische Zeitschrift*
BZAW	Beihefte zur Zeitschrift für die alttestamentliche Wissenschaft
c.	*circa*, about
CAD	*The Assyrian Dictionary of the Oriental Institute of the University of Chicago* (ed. A. Leo Oppenheim *et al.*; Chicago: University of Chicago, 1956–).
Cant	Canticles/Song of Songs
Cant. Rab.	Midrash Rabbah to Canticles/Song of Songs
CBC	The Cambridge Bible Commentary, New English Bible (ed. Peter R. Ackroyd *et al.*)
CBQ	*Catholic Biblical Quarterly*
CCSL	Corpus Christianorum, Series Latina
C.E.	Common Era (= A.D.)
Cf.	Compare/consult with
CFS	Cistercian Fathers Series
CFTL	Clark's Foreign Theological Library
CHB	*The Cambridge History of the Bible*, 3 Vols. (Cambridge: University Press, 1970 [Vol. 1: ed. P. R. Ackroyd and C. F. Evans]; 1969 [Vol. 2: ed. G. W. H. Lampe]; 1963 [Vol. 3: ed. S. L. Greenslade]).
Chr	Chronicles
col(s).	column(s)

Com	*Commentary*	*GHG*	*Gesenius' Hebrew Grammar* (ed. E.
Cor	Corinthians		Kautzsch; tr. and rev. A. E. Cowley;
COT	Commentaar op het Oude Testament		Oxford: Clarendon, ²1910).
CRB	Cahiers de la Revue biblique	Hab	Habakkuk
CSCL	Corpus Christianorum, Series Latina	HAT	Handbuch zum Alten Testament (ed.
CSCO	Corpus Scriptorum Christianorum		Otto Eissfeldt)
	Orientalium	HB	Herder Bibelkommentar: Die Heilige
CTA	Ugaritic texts, cited according to:		Schrift für das Leben erklärt
	Andrée Herdner, *Corpus des tablettes en*	*HELOT*	*A Hebrew and English Lexicon of the Old*
	cunéiformes alphabétiques découvertes à		*Testament* (ed. Francis Brown, Samuel
	Ras Shamra—Ugarit de 1929 à 1939, 2		R. Driver, and Charles Briggs; Oxford:
	Vols. (Mission de Ras Shamra 10; Paris:		Clarendon, 1907).
	Imprimerie Nationale/Librairie Orien-	HK	Handkommentar zum Alten Testa-
	taliste Paul Geuthner, 1963).		ment (ed. Wilhelm Nowack)
d.	(year of) death	Hos	Hosea
Dan	Daniel	HS	Die heilige Schrift des Alten Testa-
DB	*Dictionnaire de la Bible,* 5 Vols. (ed. F.		mentes (ed. Franz Feldmann and
	Vigouroux and Louis Pirot; Paris:		Heinrich Herkenne)
	Letouzey et Ané, 1899–1928).	*HSyn*	Ronald J. Williams, *Hebrew Syntax: An*
DBSup	*Dictionnaire de la Bible, Supplément* (ed.		*Outline* (Toronto: University of
	Louis Pirot *et al.;* Paris: Letouzey et		Toronto, ²1976).
	Ané, 1928–).	*HTR*	*Harvard Theological Review*
DD	*Dor le Dor*	*HUCA*	*Hebrew Union College Annual*
Deut	Deuteronomy	*IDB*	*The Interpreter's Dictionary of the Bible,* 4
DJD	Discoveries in the Judaean Desert		Vols. (ed. George Arthur Buttrick *et*
Eccl	Ecclesiastes		*al.;* New York/Nashville: Abingdon,
ed(s).	editor(s)/edited by		1962).
e.g.	For example	*IDBSup*	*The Interpreter's Dictionary of the Bible,*
EncJud	*Encyclopaedia Judaica,* 16 Vols. (ed.		Supplementary Volume (ed. Keith
	Cecil Roth *et al.;* Jerusalem: Keter,		Crim *et al.;* Nashville: Abingdon,
	1971–1972).		1976).
esp.	especially	*IEJ*	*Israel Exploration Journal*
Est	Esther	*Int*	*Interpretation: A Journal of Bible and*
EstBib	*Estudios Bíblicos*		*Theology*
et al.	and others	Isa	Isaiah
ÉtB	Études bibliques	*JAAR*	*Journal of the American Academy of*
ETL	*Ephemerides theologicae lovanienses*		*Religion*
Exod	Exodus	*JAC*	*Jahrbuch für Antike und Christentum*
Ezek	Ezekiel	*JAOS*	*Journal of the American Oriental Society*
Ezr	Ezra	*JBL*	*Journal of Biblical Literature*
fig(s).	figure(s)	*JCS*	*Journal of Cuneiform Studies*
FOTL	The Forms of the Old Testament	Jdt	Judith
	Literature (ed. Rolf Knierim and Gene	*JE*	*The Jewish Encyclopedia,* 12 Vols. (ed.
	M. Tucker).		Isidore Singer *et al.;* New York/
GCS	Die griechischen christlichen Schrift-		London: Funk and Wagnalls, 1901–
	steller der ersten drei Jahrhunderte		1916).
Gen	Genesis	*JEA*	*Journal of Egyptian Archaeology*
GHB	Paul Joüon, *Grammaire de l'hébreu*	Jer	Jeremiah
	biblique (Rome: Pontifical Biblical	*JETS*	*Journal of the Evangelical Theological*
	Institute, ²1947).		*Society*

JPOS	*Journal of the Palestine Oriental Society*		OBO	Orbis Biblicus et Orientalis (ed. Othmar Keel *et al.*)
JQR	*Jewish Quarterly Review*		OBT	Overtures to Biblical Theology (ed. Walter Brueggemann and John R. Donahue)
JSOT	*Journal for the Study of the Old Testament*			
JSOTSup	Journal for the Study of the Old Testament, Supplement Series		OTM	Old Testament Message: A Biblical Theological Commentary
JSS	*Journal of Semitic Studies*		OTS	Oudtestamentische Studiën
JTS	*Journal of Theological Studies*		p(p).	page(s), of the present volume
Judg	Judges		*PAPS*	*Proceedings of the American Philosophical Society*
KAT	Kommentar zum Alten Testament (ed. Ernst Sellin *et al.*)			
KBANT	Kommentare und Beiträge zum Alten und Neuen Testament		par.	paragraph
			PEQ	*Palestine Exploration Quarterly*
KEH	Kurzgefasstes exegetisches Handbuch		*PG*	*Patrologiae cursus completus, Series Graeca* (ed. Jacques-Paul Migne)
Kgs	Kings			
KHC	Kurzer Hand-Commentar zum Alten Testament (ed. Karl Marti *et al.*)		pl(s).	plates(s)
			PL	*Patrologiae cursus completus, Series Latina* (ed. Jacques-Paul Migne)
KK	Kurzgefasster Kommentar zu den heiligen Schriften Alten und Neuen Testamentes (ed. Hermann Strack and Otto Zöckler)			
			PMLA	*Proceedings of the Modern Language Association*
			Prov	Proverbs
l(l).	line(s)		Ps	Psalm(s)
Lam	Lamentations		*RB*	*Revue biblique*
LBS	Library of Biblical Studies		*RCT*	*Revista Catalana de Teologia*
LCL	Loeb Classical Library		rev.	revision/revised by
LD	Lectio Divina		*RivB*	*Rivista Biblica*
LVTL	*Lexicon in Veteris Testamenti Libros* (ed. Ludwig Koehler and Walter Baumgartner; Leiden: E. J. Brill, ³1967).		*RGG³*	*Religion in Geschichte und Gegenwart*, 7 Vols. (ed. Hans F. von Campenhausen *et al.*; Tübingen: J. C. B. Mohr [Paul Siebeck], ³1957–1965).
LW	*Luther's Works* (ed. Jaroslav Pelikan *et al.*; Saint Louis: Concordia; Philadelphia: Fortress).			
			RHPR	*Revue d'histoire et de philosophie religieuses*
			Rom	Romans
m.	Mishnah (followed by name of tractate)		*RQ*	*Revue de Qumrân*
Macc	Maccabees		*RSO*	*Rivista degli Studi Orientali*
Matt	Matthew		*RSR*	*Recherches de science religieuse*
Mic	Micah		RSV	The Revised Standard Version (1952 [Old Testament]; 1957 [Apocrypha])
MGWJ	*Monatsschrift für Geschichte und Wissenschaft des Judentums*			
			RThom	*Revue thomiste*
MTZ	*Münchener Theologische Zeitschrift*		Sam	Samuel
NAB	The New American Bible (1970)		SAT	Die Schriften des Alten Testaments in Auswahl (ed. Hermann Gunkel *et al.*)
NEB	The New English Bible (1970)			
NEchB	Die Neue Echter Bibel (ed. Josef G. Plöger *et al.*)		SBLDS	Society of Biblical Literature, Dissertation Series
			SBS	Stuttgarter Bibelstudien
N.F.	Neue Folge		SC	Sources chrétiennes
NIV	The New International Version (1978)		*Scr*	*Scripture*
NJV	The New Jewish Publication Society Version (1982) [Kethubim])		Sir	Sirach (Ecclesiasticus)
			SJ	Studia Judaica
no(s).	number(s)		SH	Scripta Hierosolymitana
N.S.	New Series		SPIB	Scripta Pontificii Instituti Biblici
Num	Numbers			

t.	Tosephta (followed by name of tractate)	ZBAT	Zürcher Bibelkommentare, Altes Testament (ed. Hans Heinrich Schmid and Siegfried Schulz)
TB	Theologische Bücherei		
TBC	Torch Bible Commentaries	*ZDMG*	*Zeitschrift der deutschen morgenländischen Gesellschaft*
Tg.	Targum		
Tg. Onq.	Targum Onqelos	Zech	Zechariah
Tob	Tobit	*ZKT*	*Zeitschrift für katholische Theologie*
TOTC	Tyndale Old Testament Commentaries	*ZTK*	*Zeitschrift für Theologie und Kirche*
TQ	*Theologische Quartalschrift*		
tr(s).	translator(s)/translated by	**b / Textual Sigla**	
TRu	*Theologische Rundschau*		
TU	Texte und Untersuchungen zur Geschichte der altchristlichen Literatur	𝕲	Old Greek version (Septuagint)
		𝕲ᴬ	Codex Alexandrinus
TZ	*Theologische Zeitschrift*	𝕲ᴮ	Codex Vaticanus
UUÅ	*Uppsala Universitets Årsskrift*	𝕲ˢ	Codex Sinaiticus
UT	Ugaritic texts, cited according to: Cyrus H. Gordon, *Ugaritic Textbook* (AnOr 38; Rome: Pontifical Biblical Institute, 1965).	𝔏	Old Latin version
		𝔐	Masoretic Text of the Hebrew Bible
		𝔐ᴸ	Leningrad Codex
		Q	Qumran documents
Vol(s).	Volume(s)	1QapGen	"Genesis Apocryphon" from Qumran Cave 1
VT	*Vetus Testamentum*		
VTSup	Supplements to Vetus Testamentum	6QCant	Canticles scroll from Qumran Cave 6
WA	Weimarer Ausgabe = *D. Martin Luthers Werke. Kritische Gesamtausgabe* (Weimar: Hermann Böhlaus, 1883–)	𝕾	Syriac "Peshiṭta" version
		𝖁	Vulgate version
		α'	The Greek translation of Aquila
Wis	Wisdom of Solomon	*θ'*	The Greek translation of Theodotion
ZAW	*Zeitschrift für die alttestamentliche Wissenschaft*	*σ'*	The Greek translation of Symmachus

2. Short Title List

Albright, "Archaic Survivals"
William Foxwell Albright, "Archaic Survivals in the Text of Canticles," *Hebrew and Semitic Studies Presented to Godfrey Rolles Driver* (ed. D. Winton Thomas and W. D. McHardy; Oxford: Clarendon, 1963) 1–7.

Audet, "Le sens"
Jean-Paul Audet, "Le sens du Cantique des cantiques," *RB* 62 (1955) 197–221.

Audet, "Love"
Jean-Paul Audet, "Love and Marriage in the Old Testament" [tr. F. Burke] *Scr* 10 (1958) 65–83.

Bea
Augustinus Bea, *Canticum Canticorum Salomonis quod hebraice dicitur Šîr Haššîrîm* (SPIB 104; Rome: Pontifical Biblical Institute, 1953).

Broadribb, "Thoughts"
Donald Broadribb, "Thoughts on the Song of Solomon," *Abr-Nahrain* 3 (1961–62 [Leiden: E. J. Brill, 1963]) 11–36.

Budde
Karl Budde, "Das Hohelied erklärt" in *idem*, Alfred Bertholet, and D. G. Wildeboer, *Die fünf Megillot (Das Hohelied, Das Buch Ruth, Die Klagelieder, Der Prediger, Das Buch Esther)* (KHC 6; Freiburg/ Leipzig/Tübingen: J. C. B. Mohr [Paul Siebeck], 1898) IX–48.

Childs, *Introduction*
Brevard S. Childs, *Introduction to the Old Testament as Scripture* (Philadelphia: Fortress, 1979).

Delitzsch
Franz Delitzsch, *Commentary on the Song of Songs and Ecclesiastes* (tr. M. G. Easton; CFTL 4/54; Edinburgh: T. & T. Clark, 1891).

Eissfeldt, *Old Testament*
Otto Eissfeldt, *The Old Testament: An Introduction* (tr. Peter R. Ackroyd; New York/Evanston: Harper and Row, 1965).

Exum, "Analysis"
J. Cheryl Exum, "A Literary and Structural Analysis of the Song of Songs," *ZAW* 85 (1973) 47–79.

Feuillet
André Feuillet, *Le Cantique des Cantiques: Étude de théologie biblique et réflexions sur une méthode d'exégèse* (LD 10; Paris: Cerf, 1953).

Fox
Michael V. Fox, *The Song of Songs and the Ancient Egyptian Love Songs* (Madison: University of Wisconsin, 1985).

Fuerst
Wesley J. Fuerst, *The Books of Ruth, Esther, Ecclesiastes, The Song of Songs, Lamentations: The Five Scrolls* (CBC; Cambridge: Cambridge University, 1975).

Gerleman
Gillis Gerleman, *Ruth, Das Hohelied* (BKAT 18; Neukirchen-Vluyn: Neukirchener, 1965).

Ginsburg
Christian David Ginsburg, *The Song of Songs and Coheleth* (LBS; New York: Ktav, 1970 [reprinting *The Song of Songs, Translated from the Original Hebrew with a Commentary, Historical and Critical* (London: 1857)]).

Gordis
Robert Gordis, *The Song of Songs and Lamentations: A Study, Modern Translation and Commentary* (New York: Ktav, ²1974).

Greer, *Origen*
Rowan A. Greer, *Origen* (The Classics of Western Spirituality; New York: Ramsey; Toronto: Paulist, 1979).

Hanson, *Allegory*
R. P. C. Hanson, *Allegory and Event: A Study of the Sources and Significance of Origen's Interpretation of Scripture* (London: SCM; Richmond: John Knox, 1959).

Hermann, *Liebesdichtung*
Alfred Hermann, *Altägyptische Liebesdichtung* (Wiesbaden: Otto Harrassowitz, 1959).

Horst, "Formen"
Friedrich Horst, "Die Formen des althebräischen Liebesliedes" in *idem*, *Gottes Recht: Gesammelte Studien zum Recht im Alten Testament* (ed. Hans Walter Wolff; TB 12; München: Chr. Kaiser, 1961) 176–187.

Jacobsen, *Harps*
Thorkild Jacobsen, *The Harps That Once . . .: Sumerian Poetry in Translation* (New Haven/ London: Yale University, 1987).

Jacobsen, *Treasures*
Thorkild Jacobsen, *The Treasures of Darkness: A History of Mesopotamian Religion* (New Haven/ London: Yale University, 1976).

Joüon
Paul Joüon, *Le Cantique des Cantiques: Commentaire philologique et exégétique* (Paris: Gabriel Beauchesne, ²1909).

Keel
Othmar Keel, *Das Hohelied* (ZBAT 18; Zürich: Theologischer Verlag, 1986).

Keel, *Metaphorik*
Othmar Keel, *Deine Blicke sind Tauben: Zur Metaphorik des Hohen Liedes* (SBS 114–115; Stuttgart: Katholisches Bibelwerk, 1984).

Kramer, "Studies"
"Cuneiform Studies and the History of Literature: The Sumerian Sacred Marriage Texts," *PAPS* 107 (1963) 485–516.

G. Krinetzki
Günter Krinetzki, *Hoheslied* (NEchB; Würzburg: Echter, 1980).

L. Krinetzki
Leo Krinetzki, *Das Hohe Lied: Kommentar zu Gestalt und Kerygma eines alttestamentlichen Liebesliedes* (KBANT; Düsseldorf: Patmos, 1964).

Kuhn
Gottfried Kuhn, *Erklärung des Hohen Liedes* (Leipzig: A. Deichert [Werner Scholl], 1926).

Lauterbach, *Mekilta*
Jacob Z. Lauterbach, *Mekilta de Rabbi Ishmael*, 3 Vols. (Philadelphia: Jewish Publication of America, 1933).

Lawson
R. P. Lawson, *Origen: The Song of Songs. Commentary and Homilies* (ACW 26; Westminster, Maryland: Newman; London: Longman, Green, 1957).

Lichtheim, *Literature 2*
Miriam Lichtheim, *Ancient Egyptian Literature: A Book of Readings*, Vol. 2: *The New Kingdom* (Berkeley/Los Angeles/London: University of California, 1976).

Loewe, "Apologetic Motifs"
Raphael Loewe, "Apologetic Motifs in the Targum to the Song of Songs" in Alexander Altmann (ed.), *Biblical Motifs: Origins and Transformations* (Philip W. Lown Institute of Advanced Studies, Brandeis University, Studies and Texts 3; Cambridge: Harvard University, 1966) 159–196.

Loretz
Oswald Loretz, *Studien zur althebräischen Poesie 1: Das althebräische Liebeslied. Untersuchungen zur Stichometrie und Redaktionsgeschichte des Hohenliedes und des 45. Psalms* (AOAT 14/1; Kevelaer: Butzon & Bercker; and Neukirchen-Vluyn: Neukirchener, 1971).

Loretz, "Eros"
Oswald Loretz, "Zum Problem des Eros im Hohenlied," *BZ* N.F. 8 (1964) 191–216.

Lys
Daniel Lys, *Le plus beau chant de la création: Commentaire du Cantique des Cantiques* (LD 51; Paris: Cerf, 1968).

Meek
Theophile J. Meek, "The Song of Songs: Introduction and Exegesis" in George Arthur Buttrick *et al.* (eds.), *The Interpreter's Bible*, Vol. 5 (Nashville: Abingdon, 1956) 89–148.

Miller
Athanasius Miller, *Das Hohe Lied übersetzt und erklärt* (HS 6/3; Bonn: Peter Hanstein, 1927).

Murphy, *Wisdom Literature*
Roland E. Murphy, *Wisdom Literature: Job, Proverbs, Ruth, Canticles, Ecclesiastes, and Esther* (FOTL 13; Grand Rapids: William B. Eerdmans, 1981).

Nolli
Gianfranco Nolli, *Cantico dei Cantici* (La Sacra Bibbia; Torino/Roma: Marietti, 1968).

Ohly, *Studien*
Friedrich Ohly, *Hohelied-Studien. Grundzüge einer Geschichte der Hohenliedauslegung des Abendlandes bis um 1200* (Schriften der wissenschaftlichen Gesellschaft an der Johann Wolfgang Goethe-Universität Frankfurt am Main, Geisteswissenschaftliche Reihe 1; Wiesbaden: Franz Steiner, 1958).

Pope
Marvin H. Pope, *Song of Songs: A New Translation with Introduction and Commentary* (AB 7c; Garden City: Doubleday, 1977).

Ricciotti
Giuseppe Ricciotti, *Il Cantico dei Cantici: Versione critica dal testo ebraico con introduzione e commento* (Torino: Società editrice internazionale, 1928).

Ringgren
Helmer Ringgren, "Das Hohe Lied" in *idem* and Artur Weiser, *Das Hohe Lied, Klagelieder, Das Buch Esther: Übersetzt und erklärt* (ATD 16/2; Göttingen: Vandenhoeck & Ruprecht, 1958) 1–37.

Robert
André Robert; and Raymond Tournay, with André Feuillet, *Le Cantique des Cantiques: traduction et commentaire* (ÉtB; Paris: Librairie Lecoffre [J. Gabalda], 1963).

Rowley, "Interpretation"
Harold H. Rowley, "The Interpretation of the Song of Songs" in *idem, The Servant of the Lord and Other Essays* (Oxford: Basil Blackwell, ²1965) 195–245.

Rudolph
Wilhelm Rudolph, *Das Buch Ruth, Das Hohe Lied, Die Klagelieder* (KAT 17/1–3; Gütersloh: Gütersloher Verlagshaus [Gerd Mohn], 1962).

Scheper, *Spiritual Marriage*
  George L. Scheper, *The Spiritual Marriage: The Exegetic History and Literary Impact of the Song of Songs in the Middle Ages* (Ph.D. dissertation; Princeton University, 1971).
Segal, "Song"
  Morris [Moshe] Hirsch Segal, "The Song of Songs," *VT* 12 (1962) 470–490.
Simon
  Maurice Simon (tr.), "Song of Songs" in *Midrash Rabbah*, Vol. 9 (ed. H. Freedman and Maurice Simon; London: Soncino, 1930).
Simpson, *Literature*
  William Kelly Simpson (ed.), *The Literature of Ancient Egypt: An Anthology of Stories, Instructions, and Poetry* (New Haven/London: Yale University, 1972).
Smalley, *Study*
  Beryl Smalley, *The Study of the Bible in the Middle Ages* (Oxford: Basil Blackwell, 1952).
Sperber
  Aramaic text of the "Targum to Canticles" *(Tg. Šir haššîrîm)*, cited according to Alexander Sperber (ed.), *The Bible in Aramaic, Based on Old Manuscripts and Printed Texts*, Vol. 4A: *The Hagiographa: Transition from Translation to Midrash* (Leiden: E. J. Brill, 1968) 127–141.
Swete, *Introduction*
  Henry Barclay Swete, *An Introduction to the Old Testament in Greek* (Cambridge: University Press, 1900).
Tournay, *Études*
  Raymond Jacques Tournay, *Quand Dieu parle aux hommes le langage de l'amour. Études sur le Cantique des cantiques* (CRB 21; Paris: J. Gabalda, 1982).

Urbach, "Homiletical Interpretations"
  Ephraim E. Urbach, "The Homiletical Interpretations of the Sages and the Expositions of Origen on Canticles, and the Jewish-Christian Disputation" in Joseph Heinemann and Dov Noy (eds.), *Studies in Aggadah and Folk-Literature* (SH 22; Jerusalem: Magnes/Hebrew University, 1971) 247–275.
Vajda, *L'amour*
  Georges Vajda, *L'amour de Dieu dans la théologie juive du Moyen Age* (Études de Philosophie médiévale 46; Paris: Librairie philosophique [J. Vrin], 1957).
Verbraken
  Patricius Verbraken (ed.), *Sancti Gregorii Magni* (CCSL 144; Tyrnholti: Brepols, 1963) 3–46 [*Expositiones in Canticum canticorum*].
Wagner, *Aramaismen*
  Max Wagner, *Die lexikalischen und grammatikalischen Aramaismen im alttestamentlichen Hebräisch* (BZAW 96; Berlin: Alfred Töpelmann, 1966).
White, *Study*
  John Bradley White, *A Study of the Language of Love in the Song of Songs and Ancient Egyptian Literature* (SBLDS 38; Missoula: Scholars, 1978).
Würthwein
  Ernst Würthwein, "Das Hohelied" in *idem*, Kurt Galling, and Otto Plöger, *Die fünf Megilloth* (HAT 18; Tübingen: J. C. B. Mohr [Paul Siebeck], 1969) 25–71.

The English translation of the Song of Songs presented in this volume by Professor Murphy is new, representing his assessment of the Hebrew "Masoretic" textual tradition (𝔐) in the light of other ancient witnesses.

For assistance in editorial revision of the commentary proper, thanks are due to Steven S. Tuell. The indices for the volume were prepared by John T. Strong.

Displayed on the endpapers to this volume is a fragment of the Song of Songs from Qumran Cave 6 (6QCant) dating from the later Herodian period (mid-first century C.E.). The extant text, which exhibits portions of Cant 1:1–7, was originally published in DJD 3 (Maurice Baillet, J. T. Milik, and Roland de Vaux, *Les 'Petites Grottes' de Qumran: Exploration de la falaise. Les grottes 2Q, 3Q, 5Q, 6Q, 7Q à 10Q* [Oxford: Clarendon, 1962] Vol. 1: Textes 112–114; Vol. 2: Planches, pl. 23/6). The fragment is reproduced here with the permission of the Israel Antiquities Authority; the photographic plate was supplied through the courtesy of the Ancient Biblical Manuscript Center in Claremont, California.

Who is it whom your soul loves,
for whom you inquire?
Has he no name?
Who are you and who is he?
I speak like this because of the strange
style of speech and extraordinary
disregard for names, quite different from
the (usual) ways of Scripture.

But in this marriage song it is affections,
not words, that are to be considered.
Why is this, except that the holy
love which is the subject of the entire song
cannot be expressed by words or
language, but only in deed and truth.

Here love speaks everywhere!

If anyone desires to grasp these writings,
let him love! For anyone who does
not love, it is vain to listen to this song
of love—or to read it, for a cold heart
cannot catch fire from its eloquence.
The one who does not know Greek cannot
understand Greek, nor can one
ignorant of Latin understand another
speaking Latin, etc. So, too, the language
of love will be meaningless jangle,
like sounding brass or tinkling cymbal,
to anyone who does not love.

—Bernard of Clairvaux (*Sermon* 79.1)

1. Authorship, Date, and Canonicity

"The Song of Songs" is a literal translation of the Hebrew title, šîr haššîrîm,[1] which appears in the editorial superscription (1:1) together with an attribution of the work to Solomon. Whoever contributed the superscription presumably had in mind 1 Kings 5:12 [4:32] where Solomon is said to have authored more than a thousand songs as well as some three thousand proverbs. In the editor's view, the Song was thus a superlative work, either the greatest of all songs or the most sublime of Solomon's prosodic compositions. However, this traditional claim of Solomonic authorship finds little support in the work itself. Solomon is nowhere designated among the speakers, who are rather anonymous individuals (a woman and a man) and a collective entity (the "Daughters of Jerusalem"). No doubt the third-person references to Solomon in the poetry (1:5; 3:7,9,11; 8:11,12) were a primary reason why the composition came to be ascribed to him.

The question of authorship is complicated by the issue of the unity of the Song. Is the work a collection of disparate poems, variously authored over the course of several centuries, or should the individual units of poetry be attributed to a single author, with perhaps some later additions contributed by an editor? Our analysis of the Song allows for an oral or even written preexistence of some parts of the work. However, we have argued for a certain homogeneity of the poems and structural coherence to the larger composition as it has been received.[2] Although individual pieces can be distinguished (notably 3:6–11 and 8:5–14) which may suggest multiple author-

ship, the whole gives the impression of being a literary unity. To be sure, this unity may be contrived, reflecting the efforts of a later redactor or editor who is perhaps also responsible for the superscription in 1:1. But there is equal merit to the view that the poet who authored most if not all of the individual love poems preserved in the Song also designed the composition as a whole. While no certainty can be reached in such matters of authorship, the collection of poems within the Song is not haphazard. The individual poems themselves attest a world of imagery, a literary style and form, and a pathos that point in the direction of a unified composition rather than a mere anthology.

The date of the composition, as a whole or in its various parts, is equally problematic. The judgment of Pope is admirable for its clarity and conciseness: "The dating game as played with biblical books like Job and the Song of Songs, as well as with many of the Psalms, remains imprecise and the score is difficult to compute. There are grounds for both the oldest and the youngest estimates."[3] This apparent critical impasse exists because of conflicting and uncertain positions taken on three fundamental issues: the connection of the work with Solomon or his period; the import of certain geographical references within the Song; and assessment of the Song's linguistic profile. Here we will do no more than illustrate the types of argument which have been offered in these three areas.[4]

a) Obviously, if one accepts the tradition that Solomon authored the Song, the work must be dated to the mid-tenth century B.C.E. As we have noted, however, this

---

1 The Hebrew construction, which expresses the superlative, was idiomatically rendered by Luther, yielding the German title *Das Hohelied*, "The Finest Song" (*D. Martin Luthers Werke. Kritische Gesamtausgabe*, Die Deutsche Bibel 10/2 [Weimar: Hermann Böhlaus, 1957] 134–135). In the AV tradition, and so still the RSV, the book bears the title "The Song of Solomon." The work is also known in

English as "Canticle of Canticles" or briefly "Canticles," reflecting the Latin tradition (𝕍 *canticum canticorum*).

2 See below, pp. 62–67.

3 Marvin H. Pope, *Song of Songs: A New Translation with Introduction and Commentary* (AB 7c; Garden City: Doubleday, 1977) 27.

4 Pope (22–24) offers a relatively detailed review of

attribution is not sustained by the poetry itself. A rather abstract argument for the Song's composition in the Solomonic era (though not by Solomon himself) has been advanced by Gerleman.[5] He considers the style in which the Song depicts love and portrays the lovers to reflect a relatively early rather than later period in Israel's cultural history. He suggests specifically the appropriateness of associating the Song's literary themes and spirit with the period of Solomonic humanism (or the supposed Solomonic "Enlightenment" to which von Rad refers)[6] when Israelite culture pursued an interest in human beauty, under the influence of Egyptian art and literature. Although there are indeed striking similarities of style and literary topoi between the Song and Egyptian love lyrics,[7] decisive evidence for Gerleman's view is lacking. One may as easily posit a Persian period date, when pertinent cultural traditions were both reviewed and widely diffused throughout the ancient Near East.

b) The reference to Tirzah in 6:4 can serve as an example of the argumentation based upon geographical data. It has been suggested that the Song must have been composed during the era of Tirzah's prominence as the capital of the Northern Kingdom, and therefore before the building of Samaria by Omri in the first half of the ninth century B.C.E. (cf. 1 Kgs 14:17; 16:23–24).[8] This and similar arguments can be neutralized if they are seen as limited to the possible dating of particular verses òr poems within the Song. Moreover, such claims are in themselves inconclusive, since none of the geographical references in the Song betrays an interest in concrete political history; other associations may account for the places mentioned. In the particular case of Tirzah, the word may well have been chosen for the poet's simile because of its sound and semantic connotation (i.e., *rṣh* = "be pleasing").

c) Philological arguments for the Song's date of composition bristle with difficulties. On the one hand, certain lexical, grammatical, and literary parallels between the Song and Ugaritic texts have been adduced.[9] These might suggest an early, at least preexilic dating of the Song. On the other hand, composition in the postexilic period is suggested by the substantial number of alleged Aramaisms in the Song as well as by cases of what appear to be late foreign loan words: most notably Persian *pardēs* in 4:13, and *'appiryôn* in 3:9 (possibly reflecting Greek *phoreion*).[10] Although the present state of scholarly

---

scholarly positions and arguments regarding the date of the Song.

5 Gillis Gerleman, *Ruth. Das Hohelied* (BKAT 18; Neukirchen-Vluyn: Neukirchener, 1965) 63–77.

6 Gerhard von Rad, *Old Testament Theology*, Vol. 1: The Theology of Israel's Historical Traditions (tr. D. M. G. Stalker; New York: Harper and Row, 1962) 55, 425–432.

7 See below, pp. 45–48.

8 Robert Gordis, *The Song of Songs and Lamentations: A Study, Modern Translation and Commentary* (New York: Ktav, ²1974) 23.

9 See William Foxwell Albright, "Archaic Survivals in the Text of Canticles," *Hebrew and Semitic Studies Presented to Godfrey Rolles Driver* (ed. D. W. Thomas and W. D. McHardy; Oxford: Clarendon, 1963) 1–7; and, most recently, Pope (720–721, 742–743) who

provides a list of Ugaritic references.

10 See especially the nuanced expression of this position offered by Raymond Tournay in the commentary of André Robert, *Le Cantique des Cantiques* (ÉtB; Paris: J. Gabalda, 1963) 21: "Although it is always delicate to handle, the linguistic criterion orientates us also to the Persian period." He then lists the lexical items usually supposed to be Persian loan-words, such as *pardēs* ("paradise") in 4:13 and *karkōm* ("saffron") in 4:14, and claims that there are as well at least seventeen Aramaic terms used in the song: *šzp, nṭr* (1:6); *šlmh* (1:7); *ḥrwzym* (1:11); *brwt* (1:17); *ktl, ḥrkym* (2:9); *stw* (2:11); *pgh* (2:13); *šwq* (3:2); *'ḥz* (3:8); *ṭnp* (5:3); *'bb* (6:11); *mzg, swg* (7:3[2]); *rpg* (8:5); and probably also *lph* (4:4). Cf. Max Wagner, *Die lexikalischen und grammatikalischen Aramaismen im alttestamentlichen Hebräisch* (BZAW 96; Berlin: Alfred

discussion renders these arguments uncertain, most critical commentators do favor a postexilic date for the Song's composition.

Related to the issue of language is the question of the song's cultural provenance. Does the work represent folk poetry (*Volksdichtung*) or is it a sophisticated, elitist artistic composition (*Kunstdichtung*)? Those who favor associating the work with popular culture posit its origins in concrete social settings, such as ancient Israelite celebrations of betrothal and marriage. Those who view the Song as a refined literary creation attribute its composition and transmission to the educated elite of ancient Israel.[11] Again, such arguments are unconvincing. It is evident that love poetry in particular is at home in all strata of society, and at all times. There is, in any event, no compelling way of discriminating between what was "popular" and what was deemed courtly or "cultivated" in ancient Israel. It is noteworthy that the question of cultural provenance reflects the division of scholarly

opinion regarding "folk wisdom" and "school wisdom." Here, too, a doubtful distinction is sometimes drawn between the cultural lore generated and nurtured within the Israelite family or the general populace and the higher "wisdom" supposedly cultivated in courtly circles.[12]

In short, very little can be said with confidence about the authorship and date or social provenance of the Song. We are on only slightly firmer ground when we consider issues relating to the Song's acceptance into the canon of scripture.

The factors leading to the canonization of the Song remain obscure. Despite this, there has been no lack of assumptions regarding how the Song achieved canonical status—for example, as a result of its supposed Solomonic authorship, its cultic significance, or an alleged "allegorical" interpretation of it.[13] Whatever the precise

---

Töpelmann, 1966); and Avi Hurwitz, "The Chronological Significance of 'Aramaisms' in Biblical Hebrew," *IEJ* 18 (1968) 324–340, who lays out prudent conditions concerning the use of Aramaisms as a criterion of lateness in dating Hebrew literature. He allows the possibility that the Song was written in a northern dialect which shared with Aramaic a significant number of linguistic features unattested in the "standard Biblical Hebrew" of the classical Jerusalem dialect.

11 For example, Gerleman (71–72) considers parallels with Egyptian poetry to support an upper-class provenance for the work.

12 See the discussion in Roland E. Murphy, *Wisdom Literature: Job, Proverbs, Ruth, Canticles, Ecclesiastes, and Esther* (FOTL 13; Grand Rapids: William B. Eerdmans, 1981) 6–9, on the setting of wisdom literature.

13 E.g., Otto Eissfeldt, *The Old Testament: An Introduction* (tr. Peter R. Ackroyd; New York: Harper and Row, 1965) 485: "The fact that the Song of Songs was taken into the canon, and its use as festal scroll at

Passover . . ., are due probably to the allegorical interpretation of its chief characters." Cf. Max L. Margolis, "How the Song of Songs Entered the Canon," *The Song of Songs: A Symposium* (ed. Wilfred H. Schoff; Philadelphia: The Commercial Museum, 1924) 9–17; Wilhelm Rudolph, "Das Hohe Lied im Kanon," *ZAW* 59 (1942–43) 189–199; Aage Bentzen, "Remarks on the Canonization of the Song of Solomon," *Studia Orientalia Ioanni Pedersen* (Hauniae: Einar Munksgaard, 1953) 41–47; and André Lacocque, "L'insertion du Cantique des Cantiques dans le Canon," *RHPR* 42 (1962) 38–44. See also Roland E. Murphy, "Recent Literature on the Canticle of Canticles," *CBQ* 16 (1954) 10-11.

reasons and process, the fact of canonization is firmly supported by both ancient Jewish and Christian traditions.

There is no reason to think that Ben Sira (c. 175 B.C.E.) is referring specifically to the Song in his encomium of Solomon (Sir 47:15–17). The remarks of Josephus (c. 100 C.E.) on the twenty-two "justly accredited" books of Jewish scripture are unfortunately vague as regards the Song.[14] His classification includes four books which contain "hymns to God and precepts for the conduct of human life"; these are probably the psalter and the three wisdom books attributed to Solomon (Proverbs, Ecclesiastes, and the Song of Songs). The first certain comments on the Song's canonicity in Jewish tradition appear in the Mishnah and reflect some continuing debate among first-century sages regarding the full scriptural status of this book as well as Ecclesiastes.[15] Here the majority of rabbinic opinion declares both works to "defile the hands"; i.e., they are deemed canonical.

Particular weight is given to the judgment of Rabbi ʿAqiba (d. 135 C.E.) who opposes the view attributed to Rabbi Yose that the authority of the Song was disputed. ʿAqiba is purported to have said: "God forbid!—no man in Israel ever disputed about the Song of Songs [that he should say] that it does not render the hands unclean, for all the ages are not worth the day on which the Song of Songs was given to Israel; for all the Writings are holy, but the Song of Songs is the Holy of Holies."[16] Although it is not possible to determine how and exactly when the book entered the Jewish canon, it is reasonable to suppose that its position was secured by 100 C.E.

According to the Jewish division of the Bible, the Song belongs to the third section, the kĕtûbîm or "Writings."[17] Later rabbinic tradition further classified the Song as the first of five mĕgillôt, the "Scrolls" which were read during the great feasts of the Jewish liturgical year.[18] Association of the Song with the celebration of Passover accounts for its initial position in the collection.[19]

---

14 *Contra Apionen* 1.8 (Henry St. John Thackeray, tr., *Josephus*, Vol. 1 [LCL; Cambridge: Harvard University; London: William Heinemann, 1926] 178–179).

15 See *m. Yadayim* 3.5; *m. ʿEduyyot* 5.3. Cf. *t. Yadayim* 2.14; *b. Megillah* 7a; and also *Cant. Rab.* 1:1.10 (Maurice Simon, tr., "Song of Songs" in *Midrash Rabbah*, Vol. 9 [ed. H. Freedman and Maurice Simon; London: Soncino, 1939] 18–19). For discussion of the relevant data, see Sid Z. Leiman, *The Canonization of Hebrew Scripture: The Talmudic and Midrashic Evidence* (Transactions of the Connecticut Academy of Arts and Sciences 47; Hamden: Archon, 1976) 120–126, 132.

16 Herbert Danby, tr., *The Mishnah* (London: Oxford University, 1933) 782. With this may be compared the remark attributed to ʿAqiba in midrash *ʾAggādat šîr haššîrîm:* "Had not the Torah been given, Canticles would have sufficed to guide the world" (Ephraim E. Urbach, "The Homiletical Interpretations of the Sages and the Expositions of Origen on Canticles, and the Jewish-Christian Disputation," *Studies in Aggadah and Folk-Literature* [SH 22; Ed. Joseph

Heinemann and Dov Noy; Jerusalem: Magnes/ Hebrew University, 1971] 250). Elsewhere ʿAqiba is reported to have excluded from the world to come anyone who would recite or sing the Song in a profane way in a banquet house (*t. Sanhedrin* 12.10).

17 In *b. Baba Batra* 14b–15a, the order of books in the Ketubim is given as Ruth, Psalms, Job, Proverbs, Ecclesiastes, Song of Songs, Lamentations, Daniel, Esther, Ezra-Nehemiah, and Chronicles. The Song is thus grouped with the other two books (Proverbs and Ecclesiastes) traditionally ascribed to Solomon, though a subsequent comment in the section attributes the "writing" (redaction, collection, transmission?) of these works as well as the book of Isaiah to "Hezekiah and his colleagues" (I. Epstein, tr., *The Babylonian Talmud*, Seder Nezikin 3/Baba Bathra 1 [London: Soncino, 1935] 71). Cf. also the rabbinic discussion on the order of Solomonic composition of the three books attributed to him, in *Cant. Rab.* 1:1.10 (Simon, 17).

18 Cf. Ludwig Blau, "Megillot, The Five," *JE* 8, 429–431; and Ismar Elbogen, *Der jüdische Gottesdienst in*

In specifically Christian tradition, the Song is first mentioned in the so-called Bryennios list of canonical works, which has been dated to the end of the first century C.E.[20] Here, as well as in the somewhat later lists of Melito and others, the books attributed to Solomon are listed in the order Proverbs, Ecclesiastes, and the Song of Songs.[21]

2. Hebrew Text and Traditional Versions

To the extent that it can be accurately reconstructed from available data, the textual history of the Song poses few difficulties. Major witnesses exhibit a narrow range of significant variants, most of which are attributable to differences in interpreting a Hebrew text closely resembling the consonantal base preserved in the medieval "Masoretic" version ($\mathfrak{M}$). While the non-Hebrew versions shed welcome light on semantic and syntactical issues, they provide only minimal help in repairing damage which the Song may have suffered in transmission prior

to the consolidation of the text-form underlying $\mathfrak{M}$. In short, the extant evidence preserves little if any trace to suggest that more than a single Hebrew recension or edition of the Song ever existed.

The Hebrew text of the Song in $\mathfrak{M}$[22] appears to be in good repair, relative especially to the condition of the traditional Hebrew text of Job or even Proverbs. The only verse in the Song which seems to defy cogent decipherment is 6:12, where the problems are attested in $\mathfrak{M}$ and the other versions alike. Occasionally departures from the vocalizations and strict versification of $\mathfrak{M}$ yield preferable sense, sometimes with versional support.[23] Only rarely does conjectural emendation of the Hebrew consonantal text seem either necessary or useful.[24] Rather than possible errors in transmission, it is the large number of hapax legomena and other words of uncertain meaning in the $\mathfrak{M}$ version which challenges the modern critic; here, as already suggested, the readings of the

seiner geschichtlichen Entwicklung (Hildesheim: Georg Olms, 1965 [= Frankfurt, ⁴1931]) 184–186.

19 Rabbinic interpretation found allusion to the exodus from Egypt especially in the reference of 1:9 to "Pharaoh's chariots." See the Targum to this verse (Pope, 342, provides an English translation) and also *Cant. Rab.* 1:9.4–6 (Simon, 68–72). Connection of the Song with the Passover season was also suggested by the references to spring in 2:1–13 and 7:12[11] (see the comments of Tournay, and the literature cited, in Robert, 429). Additional but less obvious associations between exodus-passover events and imagery of the Song are suggested already in the tannaitic midrash *Mekilta de Rabbi Ishmael:* e.g., Pisha 7.83–86; 13.147–149; 14.23–27; Beshallah 3.89–94; Shirata 1.136–139; 6.99; 10.4 (references are to the edition of Jacob Z. Lauterbach, *Mekilta de Rabbi Ishmael*, 3 Vols. [Philadelphia: Jewish Publication Society of America, 1933]).

20 See Jean-Paul Audet, "A Hebrew-Aramaic List of Books of the Old Testament in Greek Transcription," *JTS* N.S. 1 (1950) 135–154, especially 149. See

also *idem*, "Le sens du Cantique des cantiques," *RB* 62 (1955) 202 n.2.

21 The canonical enumeration of Melito, Bishop of Sardis in the later second century, is preserved in Eusebius' *Ecclesiastical History*, 4.26.12–14. For additional data on the position of the Song in Jewish and Christian canonical traditions, see Henry Barclay Swete, *An Introduction to the Old Testament in Greek* (Cambridge: University Press, 1900) 198–214, 228.

22 Unless specific note to the contrary is made, readings and citations of $\mathfrak{M}$ are based on Codex Leningradensis (early eleventh century) as published in the standard edition of *BHS*.

23 See, e.g., the Notes to the translation on 3:11 (incorporation of [*m*]*bnwt yršlym* from the end of the preceding verse) and 5:13 (*mĕgaddĕlôt* for *migdālôt*). In 7:10[9] $\mathfrak{M}$ *śipĕtê yĕšēnîm* ("lips of sleepers"?) makes little sense; $\mathfrak{G}$, V, and $\mathfrak{S}$ support a reading *śĕpātay wĕšinnāy* ("my lips and my teeth").

24 See the Notes to 5:12 (conjectural restoration of *šinnāw* ["his teeth"]).

ancient non-Hebrew versions can provide valuable assistance.

The Song is attested, but only minimally so, among the fragmentary Hebrew manuscripts recovered since 1947 from sites in the Judaean wilderness. Four Hebrew exemplars of the Song are included in Skehan's count of the Qumran biblical finds.[25] Three of these belong to the small fragments of scrolls recovered from Qumran Cave 4 and are as yet unpublished.[26] The fourth exemplar, from Qumran Cave 6 (6QCant), consists of a single scrap from a narrow parchment scroll which has been dated paleographically to the later Herodian period (mid-first century c.e.); the initial two columns of the Song are partially preserved, exhibiting portions of 1:1–7.[27] The text offers no real surprises. In orthographic detail it represents the tradition promulgated in 𝔐. Several legible readings are in minor disagreement with 𝔐 and one of these, which provides the Hebrew construction apparently underlying a Vulgate rendering,

merits critical attention.[28] In sum, 6QCant seems to be a close congener of the transmission which eventuated in 𝔐.

A contemporary, full-scale critical edition of Septuagintal and other early Greek witnesses to the Song is unfortunately not yet available. In the meantime, the manual edition of Rahlfs,[29] supplemented with the hexaplaric data compiled by Field,[30] provides serviceable access to the Old Greek evidence, but it does not enable us to speak with much confidence about possible pre-hexaplaric recensional complexities in the Greek transmission.[31] Caution is thus necessary with regard to Barthélemy's suggestion that the version of the Song preserved in the traditional "Septuagint" (𝕲) is a first-century c.e. revision, bringing an Old Greek translation into closer agreement with a (late) Palestinian Hebrew text-tradition considered authoritative in Pharisaic circles.[32] At all events, the "Septuagintal" text of the Song presented in Rahlfs' preliminary reconstruction

25 Patrick W. Skehan, "Littérature de Qumran.—A. Textes bibliques," *DBSup* 9/51, 806.

26 Cf. Frank M. Cross, Jr., "Le Travail d'édition des Fragments manuscrits de Qumrân," *RB* 63 (1956) 57.

27 Maurice Baillet, J. T. Milik, and Roland de Vaux, *Les 'Petites Grottes' de Qumrân: Exploration de la falaise. Les grottes 2Q, 3Q, 5Q, 6Q, 7Q à 10Q*, Vol. 1: Textes (DJD 3; Oxford: Clarendon, 1962) 112–114; Vol. 2: Planches, pl. 23/6.

28 See Notes to 1:3 (*šmnym ṭwbym* for 𝔐 *šĕmānêkâ ṭôbîm*).

29 Alfred Rahlfs, ed., *Septuaginta. Id est Vetus Testamentum Graece iuxta LXX interpretes*, Vol. 2: Libri poetici et prophetici (Stuttgart: Württembergische Bibelanstalt, 1935 [and subsequent reprint editions]). For the Song, as generally elsewhere, Rahlfs' eclectic text of 𝕲 is based primarily on collation and critical evaluation of readings in the three major fourth-fifth century uncial manuscripts Vaticanus (𝕲ᴮ), Sinaiticus (𝕲ˢ) and Alexandrinus (𝕲ᴬ). Still useful is the "Shorter Cambridge Septuagint" (Henry Barclay Swete, ed., *The Old Testament in Greek according to the Septuagint*, Vol. 2: I Chronicles-Tobit [Cambridge:

University Press, ²1896]; the 𝕲 text of the Song is represented by Vaticanus while the apparatus lists variants attested in Alexandrinus, Sinaiticus, and "Codex Ephraemi Syri rescriptus Parisiensis" (= 𝕲ᶜ, a fifth-century uncial, only partially intact).

30 Fridericus Field, *Origenis Hexaplorum quae supersunt sive veterum interpretum Graecorum in totum Vetus Testamentum Fragmenta*, Vol. 2: Jobus—Malachias (Hildesheim: George Olms, 1964 [= Oxford, 1875]) 407–424.

31 On recensional developments in the early history of the Greek transmission, see the following survey of the recent and extensive critical discussion: Kevin G. O'Connell, "Greek Versions (Minor)," *IDBSup*, 377–381 (with bibliography).

32 Dominique Barthélemy, *Les Devanciers d'Aquila* (VTSup 10; Leiden: E. J. Brill, 1963), especially 33–34, 49, 67. Although the presence or influence of a putative "Kaige Recension" in other parts of the Greek Old Testament need not be challenged, the lexical criteria for recognizing it, initially proposed by Barthélemy and subsequently enlarged by other

presupposes a Hebrew original closely affiliated with but not identical to the consonantal base of 𝔐.[33] The 𝔊 text, for example, exhibits some harmonistic and expansionistic readings[34] which may already have been present in its Hebrew *Vorlage*.[35] Not infrequently, 𝔊 and 𝔐 offer differing interpretations of the same consonantal base. In 1:2, for example, Hebrew *ddyk* is rendered in 𝔊 as *mastoi sou* ("your breasts"), which presumes a vocalization *daddêkâ* or the like, rather than 𝔐, *dōdêkâ* ("your love").[36] Similarly, in 4:8 𝔊 *deuro* (cf. 𝔙 *veni*) construes Hebrew *'ty* (= 𝔐 *'ittî* ["with me"]) as a Qal feminine singular imperative of the root *'th* (= *'ĕtî* ["come hither"]). An interesting mistranslation which occurs several times in 𝔊 (4:1,3; 6:7) is the rendering of consonantal *ṣmtk* as *siōpēseōs sou* ("your silence"), apparently

deriving the rare Hebrew term from the root *ṣmt*; the 𝔐 reading *ṣammātēk* ("your veil") has *ṣmm* as its ostensible root.[37] Such philological disagreements, even when 𝔐 offers the more plausible or clearly superior interpretation, should not obscure the fact that the 𝔊 translation of the Song attempted to represent scrupulously the Hebrew *Vorlage*. Indeed, the results are sometimes faithful to a fault, sacrificing Greek idiom in favor of a woodenly literal approach to the Hebrew. Thus at the beginning of 3:4, the rendering *hōs mikron hoti parēlthon* makes scant sense in Greek, except as a mechanical approximation of the Hebrew construction (*km'ṭ š'brty*). The same awkward literalness, though differently manifest, best accounts for the translation of Hebrew *r'š 'mnh* (= 𝔐 *rō'š 'ămānâ* ["Mt. Amana"]) as *archēs pisteōs*

---

scholars, are not sufficiently attested in the Song to make the identification convincing. Thus in the Hebrew text of the Song, the particle *gam* appears only twice, represented in 𝔊 once by *pros* (7:14[13]) and once by *kaige* (8:1). We have, in any case, no clear evidence that the Old Testament Hagiographa, in whole or major part, circulated in Greek translation before Herodian times; certain features supposed to be "Theodotionic" or "proto-Theodotionic" may indeed have been employed in the earliest Greek translations of some biblical books.

33 See the analysis of Gerleman (77–81) who characterizes 𝔊 as exhibiting "almost slavish fidelity" to a Hebrew *Vorlage* which is "very close to the Massoretic Text" (77).

34 E.g., the initial colon of 1:3 in 𝔊 is harmonized with the similar but simpler expression in 4:10; the final colon in the 𝔊 text of 3:1 is apparently an addition, taken from 5:6. Cf. also in 𝔊 5:8 with 2:7, and 8:2 with 3:4.

35 A tendency toward harmonization and expansion, based especially on parallel passages, is characteristic of the Hebrew textual tradition (now well attested in Qumran manuscripts as well as the Samaritan Pentateuch) which Cross has identified as "Palestinian." He notes further that books of the Writings among the Qumran scrolls witness to a text-type

which may be considered both "proto-Masoretic" and "Palestinian" (Frank M. Cross, "The Evolution of a Theory of Local Texts," *Qumran and the History of the Biblical Text* [ed. Frank Moore Cross and Shemaryahu Talmon; Cambridge: Harvard, 1975] 308). This may aptly describe not only 6QCant but also the Hebrew texts of the Song underlying both 𝔊 and 𝔖.

36 𝔊 exhibits the same interpretation of Hebrew *ddyk/ddy* in 1:4; 4:10 (bis); and 7:13[12]. In all these instances, 𝔊 is followed by 𝔙: *ubera/um* (1:2,4; 4:10b; 7:13[12]) and *mammae* (4:10a). 𝔖 distinguishes contextually between references to "love" (1:2,4; 4:10b) and to the woman's "breasts" (4:10a; 7:13[12]).

37 Elsewhere in the Hebrew Bible the feminine noun appears only in Is 47:2, where 𝔊 translates correctly: *katakalymma* ("veil"). 𝔙 in each case gives an abstract rendering of the noun but apparently presupposes the 𝔐 derivation from *ṣmm*, with a meaning "to hide" or the like.

(= *rō'š 'ĕmūnâ* ["top of faith"]) in 4:8. There is no reason, in any case, to take this rendering as evidence that the translator was familiar with an allegorical interpretation of the Song.

Brief note should be taken of a secondary feature which makes its appearance already in some of the older 𝔊 uncials. Specifically, in both Alexandrinus and Sinaiticus rubrics have been introduced into the Song to interpret the supposed dialogue or dramatic action.[38] 𝔊^A supplies simple designations, identifying the speaking parts of *hē nymphē* ("the bride") and *ho nymphios* ("the bridegroom"). The notations in 𝔊^S are considerably more elaborate, for example, assigning words to "the maidens" and typically identifying those being addressed as well as the speakers. There is no doubt that this type of scribal elaboration reflects unusual Christian interest in the interpretation of the Song, stimulated especially by Origen's influential commentary.[39]

The Old Syriac translation of the song, preserved in the so-called Peshiṭta version (𝔖),[40] is also a literal rendering but a more fluent one than exhibited in 𝔊. Most of the expansions found in 𝔊 are lacking in 𝔖 (but see 8:12), indicating that its Hebrew *Vorlage* was even more closely related than the parent text of 𝔊 to the line of transmission which eventuated in 𝔐.[41] It is not unusual, however, for 𝔖 to join 𝔊 and sometimes 𝔙 in an interpretation of the consonantal Hebrew text, against the vocal-ization of 𝔐. Thus in 4:8 𝔖 also understands *'ty* to be a feminine singular imperative and renders *ddyk* in 4:10a as "your breasts."[42] Such instances may suggest direct or indirect influence of 𝔊 on the Peshiṭta version of the Song, but it is easier to explain them as common reflection of early Jewish interpretive tradition. Certainly there are enough cases where each translation of the Song goes its own way to discount wholesale dependence of 𝔖 on 𝔊.[43] One curious example of this appears in 4:11: consonantal *klh* (= 𝔐 *kallâ* ["bride"] is rendered correctly in 𝔊 as *nymphē* but is represented in 𝔖 by *kul* ("all").

Illustrations included in the preceding remarks are sufficient to indicate that the Song in its Latin "Vulgate" version (𝔙)[44] occasionally presupposes Hebrew consonantal readings and philological interpretations which differ with the vocalized text of 𝔐. These differences are relatively few and of minor consequence for criticism of the Hebrew text itself. In the case of the Song, as generally elsewhere, the chief text-critical significance of 𝔙 is the witness it provides to consolidation by the fourth century of the "proto-Masoretic" Hebrew transmission. It may be added that the 𝔙 version of the Song well attests to Jerome's impressive skills as a translator.

Only passing note need be taken here of other ancient and medieval versions. The extant Aramaic Targum to the Song[45] is less an expansive translation of the Hebrew

---

38   The pertinent data are given in an addendum to Rahlfs' edition of the Song. Cf. also Swete, *Introduction*, 360.

39   See below, pp. 16–21.

40   A critical edition, prepared by John A. Emerton and D. J. Lane, has appeared in the "Leiden Peshiṭta": *The Old Testament in Syriac According to the Peshiṭta Version*, Vol. II/5 (Leiden: E. J. Brill, 1979).

41   For a detailed study of the 𝔖 version of the Song, see Joshua Bloch, "A Critical Examination of the Text of the Syriac Version of the Song of Songs," *AJSL* 38 (1921–22) 103–139. Cf. also Sebastian Euringer,

"Die Bedeutung der Peschitto für die Textkritik des Hohenliedes," *Biblische Studien*, Vol. 6 (ed. O. Bardenhewer; Freiburg im Breisgau: Herder, 1901) 115–128.

42   See above, n. 35.

43   See the discussion in Gerleman, 82–83.

44   Robert Weber, ed., *Biblia Sacra iuxta Vulgatum Versionem*, Vol. 2 (Stuttgart: Württembergische Bibelanstalt, 1969) 997–1002.

45   Alexander Sperber, ed., *The Bible in Aramaic, Based on Old Manuscripts and Printed Texts*, Vol. 4A: The Hagiographa: Transition from Translation to

text than an extended homiletical midrash. It gives important testimony to the crystallization in the earlier Middle Ages of Jewish "allegorical" interpretation of the Song.[46] The Old Latin (𝔏) and other "daughter" versions of 𝔊 have little independent text-critical significance, though they are, of course, valuable as witnesses to the broader history of the Song's transmission and interpretation.[47]

3. History of Interpretation

Over the course of the centuries study of the Song of Songs has generated an enormous quantity of expository literature, and yet the exegetical history so attested would appear at first sight to be a rather cut and dried affair. It is well known that the dominant traditions of interpretation, in Judaism and Christianity alike, have understood the Song to portray the relationship between God and the people of God—more specifically, the bond of mutual love between Israel and her divine Lord in

Jewish exegesis or between the Church as bride and Christ as the bridegroom in Christian exposition. Except for the departures of a few individual interpreters, these basic views of the book held sway from late antiquity until relatively modern times and they continue even today to find some support.

There are available detailed surveys of this history of interpretation, many of them treating expositors in chronological sequence with comments on items of particular interest.[48] Rather than plowing the same ground here, it seems preferable to offer a representative sounding in major periods of the Song's exegetical history, in order to help the reader to grasp the broad shape of this history as well as to become acquainted with some of the most outstanding interpreters.[49] Particular attention will be given to the hermeneutical principles operative in the development of Jewish and Christian exposition. Whether these principles are true or false from a modern perspective is not the primary issue. If

Midrash (Leiden: E. J. Brill, 1968) 127–141. Cf. also Raphael Hai Melamed, "The Targum to Canticles according to Six Yemen MSS. Compared with the 'Textus Receptus' (Ed. de Lagarde)," *JQR* N.S. 10 (1919–20) 377–410; N.S. 11 (1920–21) 1–20; N.S. 12 (1921–22) 57–117.

46 See below, pp. 30–31.

47 For pertinent bibliographical information, see especially Pope, 233–236, and Robert, 29–30.

48 Helpful overviews of the history of the Song's interpretation can be found in a number of commentaries, especially the following: Christian David Ginsburg, *The Song of Songs and Coheleth* (LBS; New York: Ktav, 1970 [= London, 1857 and 1861]) 20–126; Gerleman, 43–51; Pope, 89–229. The following surveys may also be noted: Isaäk Brot, *De Allegorische Uitlegging van het Hooglied voornamelijk in Nederland* (Zuijderduijn-Woerden, 1971); Curt Kuhl, "Das Hohelied und seine Deutung," *TRu* 9 (1937) 137–167; David Lerch, "Zur Geschichte der Auslegung des Hohenliedes," *ZTK* 54 (1957) 257–277; Roland E. Murphy, "Recent Literature on the Canticle of

Canticles," *CBQ* 16 (1954) 1–11; Friedrich Ohly, *Hohelied-Studien. Grundzüge einer Geschichte der Hohenliedauslegung des Abendlandes bis um 1200* (Schriften der wissenschaftlichen Gesellschaft an der Johann Wolfgang Goethe–Universität Frankfurt am Main Geisteswissenschaftliche Reihe 1; Wiesbaden: Franz Steiner, 1958); Harold H. Rowley, "The Interpretation of the Song of Songs," *The Servant of the Lord and Other Essays* (Oxford: Blackwell, ²1965) 195–245; Alberto Vaccari, "Il Cantico dei Cantici nelle recenti publicazioni," *Bib* 9 (1938) 433–457; Ernst Würthwein, "Zum Verständnis des Hohenliedes," *TRu* 32 (1967) 177–212.

49 Portions of the following review were previously published: Roland E. Murphy, "Patristic and Medieval Exegesis—Help or Hindrance?" *CBQ* 43 (1981) 505–516.

such judgments are to be made, they should be preceded by an effort to understand the why and the how of our exegetical forebears. Moreover, the course of this history underscores an important lesson: the effect of theological presuppositions and cultural assumptions on the work of every interpreter, even a contemporary one who may take pride in a strictly literal and historical-critical approach.

A selective review of the expository literature frees us from attending to all the vagaries which have led some writers to label the Song's history of interpretation a "collection of curiosities" (Raritätenkabinett) or even a "tale of woe" (Leidensgeschichte).[50] It bears repeating that only when we understand the social and intellectual provenances of earlier commentators can we perhaps extend a sympathetic ear to their expositions. When one realizes, for example, that most of the Christian exegesis on the Song until the Reformation was produced by clerics and monks, it becomes understandable that a mystical interpretation thrived. This social reality in combination with an entrenched hermeneutical position —that the Old Testament must have a specifically Christian meaning and that the scriptural word of God should deal directly with the religious aspirations of the individual believer and the community of faith—made the spiritual interpretation of the Song in patristic and medieval Christian exposition virtually inevitable.

A. Early Jewish Interpretation of the Song and the Emergence of Christian Allegorical Exposition

The earliest stages in the interpretation of the Song are far from certain. The relative poverty of our knowledge in this regard needs to be emphasized, if only to counter the common assumption that the "history" of interpretation begins with a firm Jewish tradition of allegorical or spiritualizing exposition, in which the Song was understood to celebrate the love between God and Israel, and that this tradition was simply taken over with slight adaptation by the early church.[51]

The fact is, however, that we know very little about early Jewish readings of the Song, apart from the quite literal renderings of it preserved in the Greek and Syriac translations. Neither do we have reliable evidence to establish when and why the book was originally included in the corpus of Jewish scripture. Solomonic authorship, claimed for the book in its superscription, is often alleged

---

50 So, respectively, David Lerch, "Hoheslied, II. Auslegungsgeschichtlich," *RGG*[3] 3, 431, and Samuel Oettli, "Das Hohelied," *Die Poetischen Hagiographen* (KK A/7; Nordlingen: C. H. Beck, 1889) 167. For the Christian reader, such pejorative assessments can be amply justified by examining the work of Richard Frederick Littledale, *A Commentary on the Song of Songs From Ancient and Medieval Sources* (London: 1869). Despite this compiler's good intentions, his *florilegium* of sources is rather bewildering, if not defeating, for the modern student of the Song.

51 Cf. Wilhem Riedel, *Die Auslegung des Hohenliedes in der jüdischen Gemeinde und der griechischen Kirche* (Leipzig: Deichert, 1898); and also the summary remarks of Robert, 45; Rowley, "Interpretation," 202; Ohly, *Studien*, 13; and Gordis, 2–3. Audet ("Le sens," 199–200) rightly calls this widely held

assumption into question. It should be emphasized that the issue here is interpretation of the Song in particular, not the wider impact of Jewish exegetical theory and practice on early Christian exposition of scripture. For discussion of the latter, with appropriate attention especially to the influence of Philo on the development of patristic allegorical methodology, the following surveys may be consulted: R. P. C. Hanson, "Biblical Exegesis in the Early Church," *CHB* 1, 412–453; *idem, Allegory and Event: A Study of the Sources and Significance of Origen's Interpretation of Scripture* (London: SCM; Richmond: John Knox, 1959) 97–129; Beryl Smalley, *The Study of the Bible in the Middle Ages* (Oxford: Basil Blackwell, 1952) 1–36; and especially Henry Austryn Wolfson, *The Philosophy of the Church Fathers: Faith, Trinity, Incarnation* (Cambridge: Harvard University, [3]1970) 24–72.

to explain the Song's canonical status. Attribution to Solomon of this work, Proverbs, and Ecclesiastes no doubt bears witness to the notion that Solomon was the chief patron of biblical "wisdom." Audet has underscored this point and suggested that it indicates an early sapiential interpretation in which the contents of the Song were understood to portray the bond of love between man and woman.[52] What may have been a literal or even bawdy interpretation of the Song, as well as profane usage, was apparently condemned by Rabbi ʿAqiba (c. 100 C.E.).[53] ʿAqiba's personal testimony to the Song's superlative

sanctity is elsewhere cited in rabbinic sources to dispel any continuing doubt regarding the canonical authority of the work.[54] Although his specific views on the overall meaning of the Song simply cannot be determined, it seems likely that he favored a symbolic rather than a literal interpretation.[55]

Historical control is lacking for other data cited by critics to support the antiquity of Jewish allegorization of the Song. The metaphorical references to Israel as "lily," "dove," and "bride" in 2 Esdras 5:24–36 and 7:26 may

---

52 Audet, "Le sens," 202–203 and 216–217; see further below, pp. 98–99.

53 The remark is preserved in *t. Sanhedrin* 12.10: "Rabbi ʿAqiba says, 'Whoever sings the Song of Songs with tremulous voice in a banquet hall and (so) treats it as a sort of ditty *[dĕmîn zemer]* has no share in the world to come" (cf. *b. Sanhedrin* 101a, where a similar rebuke is cited anonymously). Possibly relevant here also is the dictum attributed to Rabbi Simeon ben Gamaliel in *m. Taʿanit* 4.8, which seems to connect Cant 3:11 with festivities during the season of grape harvest (even though the present mishnaic context interprets "the day of his marriage" as the law-giving at Sinai and "the day of the joy of his heart" with the completion of the Solomonic temple). Cf. Urbach, "Homiletical Interpretations," 247–248; and Michael V. Fox, *The Song of Songs and the Ancient Egyptian Love Songs* (Madison: University of Wisconsin, 1985) 252.

54 See above, p. 6 nn. 15 and 16.

55 The most substantive but still cryptic remarks on the Song attributed to ʿAqiba are cited in the *Mekilta de Rabbi Ishmael*, Shirata 3.49–63 (commenting on Ex 15:2): "Rabbi Akiba says: Before all the Nations of the World I shall hold forth on the beauties and splendor of Him Who Spake and the World Came to Be! For, lo, the Nations of the World keep asking Israel, 'What is thy Beloved more than another beloved, that thou dost so adjure us' (Cant. 5:9), that for His sake you die, for His sake you let yourselves be slain, as it is said, 'Therefore do the maidens (ʿlmwt) love Thee' (Cant. 1:3)—they love Thee to the

point of death (ʿd mwt)!—and it is written, 'Nay, but for Thy sake are we killed' etc. (Ps. 44:23). Look you! You're attractive, look you! you're brave. Come merge with us!

But Israel reply to the Nations of the World: Have you any notion of Him? Let us tell you a little bit of His Glory: 'My beloved is white and ruddy' etc. (Cant. 5:10ff.).

And when the Nations of the World hear but a little bit of the Glory of Him Who Spake and the World Came to Be, they say to Israel, Let us go along with you, as it is said, 'Whither is thy Beloved gone, O thou fairest among women? Whither hath thy Beloved turned Him, that we may seek Him with thee' (Cant. 6:1)?

But Israel reply to the Nations of the World: You have no part of Him; on the contrary, 'My beloved is mine, and I am His' (Cant. 2:16), 'I am my Beloved's and my Beloved is mine' etc. (Cant. 6:3)" (tr. Judah Goldin, *The Song at the Sea, being a Commentary on a Commentary in Two Parts* [New Haven and London: Yale University, 1971] 115–117 [cf. Lauterbach, *Mekilta* 2, 26–27]. Similar remarks are cited anonymously in *Cant. Rab.* 5:9.1 (Simon, 238) and midrash *Sipre Deut.* 343 (Louis Finkelstein, ed., *Siphre ad Deuteronomium* [Corpus Tannaiticum 3/3; Berlin: Jüdischer Kulturbund in Deutschland, 1939] 399; cf. Hans Bietenhard, tr., *Sifre Deuteronomium: Übersetzt und erklärt* [Judaica et Christiana 8; Bern: Peter Lang, 1984] 833–834).

directly reflect language of the Song.[56] Even so, this neither suffices to establish a first-century exegetical *tradition* among the Jews nor sheds significant light on motives for the Song's canonization.[57] While the Targum and the Midrash Rabbah to the Song amply attest Jewish symbolical exposition, these sources in their received forms date only to the Middle Ages, even if some elements in them may plausibly be associated with second-century circumstances.[58] In short, the classical Jewish interpretation of the Song came to be "allegorical," but we are unable to trace the roots of this interpretation with any certainty or even to be sure that it began in pre-Christian times.

No less obscure is the meaning which may have attached to the Song in earliest Christianity. The New Testament and other Christian writings that antedate the third century offer nothing which suffices to establish the beginnings of a Christian expository tradition for the Song.[59] The earliest extant Christian exposition of the book was authored by Hippolytus of Rome (d. 235). Written in Greek and transmitted also in other languages, his work as preserved is fragmentary, covering only 1:1—3:8.[60] It exhibits throughout the style of a spirited address to an audience, while the treatment of 3:1–4 is particularly suggestive of an Easter homily.[61]

Little direct echo of Hippolytus' specific points of interpretation can be heard in later Christian commentaries, but his perspective on the biblical text well illustrates important features of patristic exegesis. Hippolytus does not suggest that the Song is concerned with the

56 It should be noted, though, that the same metaphors are more explicitly connected with "Israel" in the prophecy of Hosea: "lily" *(šôšān)* Hos 14:6[5]; "dove" *(yônâ)* Hos 7:11 and 11:11; "bride" *(kallâ)* Hos 4:13–14 (and also Jer 2:32, etc.). Cf. André M. Dubarle, "La femme couronnée d'étoiles *(Ap., 12)*," *Mélanges Bibliques rédigés en l'honneur de André Robert* (Travaux de l'Institut Catholique de Paris 4; Paris: Bloud et Gay, 1957) 518 n. 2.

57 Otherwise, e.g., Gordis, 2, and Pope, 92. Cf. also Hanson, *Allegory*, 33–34; and Raphael Loewe, "Apologetic Motifs in the Targum to the Song of Songs," *Biblical Motifs: Origins and Transformations* (Studies and Texts 3; ed. Alexander Altmann; Cambridge: Harvard University, 1966) 161. A still useful summary of older rabbinical views on the Song may be found in Joseph Bonsirven, *Exégèse rabbinique et exégèse paulinienne* (Paris: Beauchesne, 1939) 215–235. He emphasizes that the various comments on the Song attributed to tannaitic sages (first and second centuries C.E.) attest several types of symbolical readings but do not comprise an allegorical interpretation per se, because there is yet no unified or systematic exposition of the kind that "allegory" properly calls for.

58 The same reservation applies even more strongly to mystical interpretations of the Song reflected in the *Zohar* and other Jewish Qabbalistic literature. Supposed connections between these sources and early Jewish interpretation are summarized at length by Pope, 99–101 and 153–179 (where the discussion of Raphael Patai, *The Hebrew Goddess* [New York: Ktav, 1967] is cited extensively). See also Loewe, "Apologetic Motifs," 184–193; Gershom Scholem, *Jewish Gnosticism, Merkabah Mysticism and Talmudic Tradition* (New York: Jewish Theological Seminary of America, ²1960) 36–42 (and especially the "Appendix D" contribution of Saul Lieberman); *idem, Ursprung und Anfänge der Kabbala* (SJ 3; Berlin: Walter de Gruyter, 1962) especially 17, 331–342; and *idem, On the Kabbalah and Its Symbolism* (tr. Ralph Manheim; New York: Schocken, 1965) 33–35, 138–142.

59 For a different opinion, see M. Cambe, "L'influence du Cantique des cantiques sur le Nouveau Testament," *RThom* 62 (1962) 5–26; and Brian McNeil, "Avircius and the Song of Songs," *Vigiliae Christianae* 31 (1977) 23–34. Cf. also Jacques Winandy, "Le Cantique des Cantiques et le Nouveau Testament," *RB* 71 (1964) 161–190.

60 Only a small portion of the Greek text is accessible in the Migne edition (*PG* 10, 627–630). Major fragments of the work preserved in various languages are treated in the following: Gottlieb Nathanael Bon-

relationship between God and the individual human soul (which line of interpretation emerges clearly in Origen's work). Rather his approach is broadly salvation-historical. Thus the Song is taken to be Solomonic prophecy of the end of the "old" covenant and the beginning of the "new"; Israel is replaced by the church as the object of God's love. If one remembers that this work was most likely designed for sermonic purposes, it is easy to grant Hippolytus his right to adapt the biblical text to the situation of his Christian audience. The homiletical stance is, in any case, familiar from the New Testament and other early Christian writings: Old Testament traditions are applied to contemporary issues and the identity of biblical "Israel" is typically transferred to the church. In light of this, it is not surprising that Hippolytus interprets the (male!) "breasts" in 1:2 as the two testaments.[62] The symbolical reading here need not be viewed as an effort to salvage some spiritual meaning from an otherwise sexually provocative reference but rather flows logically from Hippolytus' understanding of the basic unity and profound significance of the two-part Christian canon of scripture. Chappuzeau's description of this approach is apt. "The hermeneutics of Hippolytus is very concise: 'Through the earthly one must view the heavenly, and through the symbolic understand the spiritual, and through the temporal hope for the eternal.' It is the task of those 'who love knowledge' to reach this understanding of the Scripture. The symbols of the Bible are 'symbols of truth,' that is to say in the Song, symbols of the truth proclaimed by Solomon and fulfilled in Christ, the 'new grace of God.'"[63]

Nowhere does Hippolytus discuss allegory per se, yet his method of interpreting the Song is the first manifestation of a Christian allegorizing tradition which comes to classical expression in the work of Origen and his medieval successors. Before examining Origen's extraordinarily influential treatment of the Song, brief consideration of the underlying motive for Christian allegorical exegesis is in order.

To moderns steeped in the "plain sense" of scripture and historical-critical methodology, allegorical exposition as practiced by patristic and medieval commentators may appear to be merely arbitrary, amusing, and even devious. In the particular case of the Song, it has been supposed that the physical language and explicitly amorous content were a major embarrassment to early

---

wetsch, *Studien zu den Kommentaren Hippolyts zum Buche Daniel und zum Hohenliede* (TU 16/2 [N.F. 1]; Leipzig: J. C. Hinrichs, 1897); *idem, Hippolyts Kommentar zum Hohenlied auf Grund von N. Marrs Ausgabe des grusinischen Textes* (TU 23/2c [N.F. 8]; Leipzig: J. C. Hinrichs, 1902); *idem* and H. Achelis, eds., *Hippolytus Werke*, Vol. 1: Hippolyts Kommentar zum Buche Daniel und die Fragmente des Kommentars zum Hohenliede (GCS: Leipzig: J. C. Hinrichs, 1897). A Latin translation of the Georgian text is available: Gérard Garitte, *Traités d'Hippolyte* (CSCO 264; Louvain: Secretariat du CorpusSCO, 1965).

61 See Gertrud Chappuzeau, "Die Auslegung des Hohenliedes durch Hippolyt von Rom," *JAC* 19 (1976) 45–81, especially 46 where she characterizes the work as follows: "Bei dem Kommentar Hippolyts handelt es sich zweifellos um einen Predigttext, wahrscheinlich um eine Osterpredigt." Cf. also Ohly, *Studien*, 15.

62 See above, p. 9 n. 36. Other examples of Hippolytus' allegorization of the Song are discussed briefly by Hanson, *Allegory*, 116–117, 315.

63 Gertrud Chappuzeau, "Die Exegese von Hohelied 1, 2a.b und 7 bei den Kirchenvätern von Hippolyt bis Bernhard," *JAC* 18 (1975) 131.

Christian sensitivities and that the device of allegory, by which Hellenistic authors had reinterpreted earlier Greek mythology, was ready at hand to provide a solution. Pope gives vivid testimony to this view. "Thus from the early days of the Church, Solomon's salacious Song, which at first blush tended to appeal to the pernicious pruriency of men, women, and children, had to be interpreted in a way that would eliminate the evil impulse and transform and spiritualize carnal desire into praise of virginity and celibacy and sexless passion of the human soul and/or the Church for God, and of God's response in kind. This was accomplished by means of allegorical interpretation in much the same way that the Greek philosophers had managed to change the lusty gods of Homer and Hesiod into spiritual ideals. Celibate Christian theologians were thus able by allegory to unsex the Sublime Song and make it a hymn of spiritual and mystical love without carnal taint. *Canticum Canticorum* thus became the favorite book of ascetics and monastics who found in it, and in the expansive sermons and commentaries on it, the means to rise above earthly and fleshly desire to the pure platonic love of the virgin soul for God."[64] Such account of the matter is unfortunately one dimensional. A preoccupation with eroticism is rather boldly projected onto the ancient church, while allegory is reduced to a sort of exegetical alchemy for transmutation or spiritualization of the Song's ostensibly objectional sexual themes. There is no reason to deny that the values and goals of Christian asceticism contributed to and were significantly nurtured by a "spiritual" understanding of the Song. But the actual course of Christian interpretation—from the complex exegetical achievement of Origen in the third century through the appreciative elaboration of it which continued for more than a millennium thereafter—cannot adequately be explained as an exercise in pathological rejection of human sexuality.

Allegory served a much broader purpose in patristic and medieval Christianity: it facilitated construction and maintenance of a Christian worldview, providing the intellectual mechanism to effect a synthesis between Old Testament witnesses to God's providential love for humankind and what was confessed to be the preeminent display of that love in the Christ event. Already in Hippolytus' treatment of the Song, soteriology is the dominant concern; allegory supplied a hermeneutical technique which enabled him to read the erotic lyrics attributed to Solomon as a prophetic vision of the love that united God and the church through Christ. Although much more elaborately developed, Origen's approach to the Song is quite similar.[65]

B. Origen on the Song of Songs

Unfortunately, only a part of Origen's work on the Song has survived.[66] His masterpiece was a ten-volume commentary, written during the period 240–245.[67] A few quotations of the original Greek text are found in the writings of later exegetes and theologians; otherwise the initial three volumes are preserved in a Latin translation made by Rufinus. The extant portion includes Origen's extensive prologue as well as his consecutive exposition of 1:1—2:15. In addition, we have two homilies of

---

64   Pope, 114. See also William E. Phipps, "The Plight of the Song of Songs," *JAAR* 42 (1974) 86–94.

65   Origen was a younger contemporary of Hippolytus and may have been acquainted with the latter's interpretation of the Song, but there is no clear evidence to support this. Cf. Hanson, *Allegory,* 115–116 and 251 n. 5.

66   The extant Latin translations of Origen's two homilies on the Song and the initial three (or, in variant tradition, four) volumes of his commentary are published in *PG* 13, 35–198 (with Jerome's translation of the homilies reappearing in *PL* 23, 1173–1196); for the surviving Greek fragments and Origen's scholia, see *PG* 13, 197–216 (Procopius excerpts) and *PG* 17, 253–288. The standard critical edition of the evidence is W. A. Baehrens, ed.,

Origen on the Song, together covering 1:1—2:14; these have survived in a Latin translation made by Jerome, who added a preface in praise of the superb quality and thoroughness of Origen's treatment in the commentary.[68] In the homilies themselves, Origen develops the declarations of love made by the Song's male and female protagonists (or "the Bridegroom" and "the Bride" as he refers to them) into a portrait of the nuptial relationship between Christ and the church; here the female figure is only rarely identified as the individual human soul espoused to Christ. The commentary gives much closer

scrutiny to details of the biblical text and presents Origen's complex soteriological analysis at length, expounding both the ecclesial and the psychic (individual soul) interpretations of "the Bride."[69] It must suffice here to remark on some specific aspects of Origen's hermeneutics as exhibited in the commentary.

One might easily gain the impression from the terse summaries of his work offered by modern critical commentators that Origen quickly passed over the "plain sense" of the Song and wielded allegory with a heavy hand to craft an esoteric interpretation which suited his

---

Origenes Werke, Vol. 8 (GCS 33; Leipzig: J. C. Hinrichs, 1925). On the homilies, see also O. Rousseau, *Origène: Homélies sur le Cantique des cantiques. Introduction, traduction et notes* (SC 37; Paris: Cerf, 1954 ²1966). In the discussion which follows, Origen's work is quoted from the English translation of R. P. Lawson, *Origen: The Song of Songs. Commentary and Homilies* (ACW 26; Westminster, Maryland: Newman; London: Longman, Green and Co., 1957). The prologue to the commentary is also available in a new English translation: Rowan A. Greer, *Origen* (The Classics of Western Spirituality; New York: Ramsey; Toronto: Paulist, 1979) 217–244.

67 The work was completed while Origen was a resident of Caesarea in Palestine, where he would have had opportunity to engage in dialogue and debate with Jewish scholars on hermeneutical issues. Yet the extent to which Origen's work on the Song is indebted to specific features of rabbinical exegesis remains uncertain, as does the possibility that rabbinical sources include responses to his views. An intriguing case for concrete mutual influence has been made by Reuven Kimelman, "Rabbi Yoḥanan and Origen on the Song of Songs: A Third-Century Jewish-Christian Disputation," *HTR* 73 (1980) 567–595. See also Gustave Bardy, "Les traditions juives dans l'oeuvre d'Origène," *RB* 34 (1925) 237; Loewe, "Apologetic Motifs," 169–175; Urbach, "Homiletical

Interpretations," 251–270; Y. Baer, "Israel, the Christian Church, and the Roman Empire, from the time of Septimus Severus to the Edict of Toleration of A.D. 313," *Studies in History* (SH 7; ed. A. Fuks and I. Halpern; Jerusalem: Magnes/Hebrew University, 1961) 99–106; and, more generally, Nicholas Robert Michael de Lange, *Origen and the Jews: Studies in Jewish-Christian Relations in Third-Century Palestine* (Cambridge: University Press, 1976).

68 Jerome remarks that while Origen's writings, in comparison with those of other authors, are generally superlative, in his commentary on the Song of Songs Origen excelled even himself. The homilies, Jerome acknowledges, were composed in a popular vein and are of lesser substance; he has translated them into Latin to provide ". . . a sample of his [Origen's] thinking, so that you may reflect how highly his great thoughts should be esteemed, when even his little ones can so commend themselves" (Lawson, 265).

69 On this, see Ohly, *Studien,* 19–21; Lawson, 10–16; and the expansive discussion in Jacques Chênevert, *L'église dans le commentaire d'Origène sur Cantique des cantiques* (Studia, Travaux de recherche 24; Paris: Brouwer; Montréal: Bellarmin, 1969).

mystical predilections.[70] On the contrary, the ostensible character of the text on a mundane literary level was the foundation for Origen's analysis. In the initial remarks of the methodological prologue to his commentary, Origen characterizes the biblical work as ". . . a marriage-song [epithalamium] which Solomon wrote in the form of a drama [dramatis in modum]. . . ."[71] By "drama" he means ". . . the enaction of a story on the stage, when different characters are introduced and the whole structure of the narrative consists in their comings and goings among themselves."[72] With comparative reference to Greek literature, he notes too that, as in the case of the Song, drama may be composed primarily of ". . . dialogue between the characters."[73] Consistent with this view of the genre, he establishes the *dramatis personae* whose verbal reflections and direct exchanges comprise the overt content of the work: "the Bride" and "the Bridegroom" hold center stage, but each of them also interacts with companions, the "maidens" (the "Daughters of Jerusalem") who accompany the woman and the "friends" of the groom.

Origen's consideration of the work as a drama in dialogue form is by no means confined to the opening paragraphs of his prologue. Throughout the extant sections of the commentary he gives constant attention to supposed aspects of dramatic structure and plot, often venturing to suggest specific scenarios only implied at best by the biblical script.[74] A particularly interesting example of this is found in his exposition of 2:9b–14, which includes a review of the drama's *mise-en-scène*. The central theme to this point has been the presence and absence of the male lover. The action has focused on the woman as she stands at a crossroad just outside her house, awaiting with great longing the return of her husband (who, it seems, is often away from home). Sometimes in conversation with her handmaids, she has declared aloud her intense desire for the man and has recalled particular assignations with him. Finally in 2:8 she sees him returning ". . . overtopping the crests of the nearby mountains with great leaps, and so descending to the house, where the Bride is yearning and burning for His love."[75] Origen continues to explore details of scene and staging as he comments on the reunion of the lovers in the following verses. With regard to 2:12–13 he says: "The statements that the flowers have appeared on the earth, and that the trees have budded, tell us further that the season of spring is now with us. Therefore He calls upon the Bride, who has doubtless sat indoors all winter, to come forth as at a fitting time."[76] Yet having proffered such an elaborate dramatic reconstruction or "historical" reading of the text, Origen immediately adds a formidable qualification: "But these things seem to me to afford no profit to the reader as far as the story goes; nor do they maintain any continuous narrative such as we find in

---

70   E.g., Theophile J. Meek, "The Song of Songs: Introduction and Exegesis," *The Interpreter's Bible*, Vol. 5 (ed. George Arthur Buttrick *et al.*; Nashville: Abingdon, 1956) 92. Cf. also Gerleman, 44; and Gordis, 3.

71   Lawson, 21. From the outset, to be sure, Origen emphasizes that the drama is essentially concerned with spiritual matters (rather than, for example, one of Solomon's actual marriages or love affairs). He immediately identifies the Song's male and female protagonists as, respectively, the divine "Word" (*Verbum = Logos*) and "the soul made in his image" or

"the Church."

72   Lawson, 22. See below, p. 58.

73   Lawson, 23.

74   See, e.g., Lawson, 58, 62–63, 91, 159, 205–206.

75   Lawson, 231.

76   Lawson, 247.

other Scripture stories. It is necessary, therefore, rather to give them all a spiritual meaning."[77]

These last remarks of Origen clearly point to the controlling purpose of his exegesis. Appropriately understood as a part of scripture, the Song should address the spiritual needs of its audience. His chief concern is for theological relevance. Nevertheless, the allegorical method which enables him to pursue this goal is not arbitrarily adopted but rather proceeds from a conscientious assessment of the literary character of the text itself.

In the prologue, Origen also formulates his approach to the Song in consideration of its canonical position as the third of the books of wisdom authored by Solomon.[78] He avers that this arrangement of the works is not gratuitous; it rather corresponds to and inspired the tripartite philosophical curriculum of the Greeks.[79] "Wishing, therefore, to distinguish one from another those three branches of learning, which we called general just now—that is, the moral, the natural, and the inspective, and to differentiate between them, Solomon issued them in three books, arranged in their proper order. First, in Proverbs he taught the moral science, putting

rules for living into the form of short and pithy maxims, as was fitting. Secondly, he covered the science known as natural in Ecclesiastes; in this, by discussing at length the things of nature, and by distinguishing the useless and vain from the profitable and essential, he counsels us to forsake vanity and cultivate things useful and upright. The inspective science likewise he propounded in this little book that we have now in hand—that is, the Song of Songs. In this he instills into the soul the love of things divine and heavenly, using for his purpose the figure of the Bride and Bridegroom, and teaches us that communion with God must be attained by the paths of charity and love."[80] In effect, the setting of the Song in the larger corpus of divinely inspired wisdom is taken by Origen as a mandate for reading the work as an advanced course in spirituality.[81]

It is easy to recognize in Origen's exposition of the Song, as generally elsewhere in his writings, the influence of Hellenistic intellectual currents which also shape Neo-

---

77   Lawson, 247. This illustrates an important feature of Origen's exegetical method; see especially his discussion in *De Principiis*, Book 4 Chapter 2, where he argues that the *lack* of "logically coherent narrative meaning" in biblical passages indicates or necessitates spiritual interpretation (cf. Greer, *Origen*, 183).

78   See above, pp. 6–7 and n. 17.

79   "The branches of learning by means of which men generally attain to knowledge of things are the three which the Greeks called Ethics, Physics and Enoptics; these we may call respectively moral, natural, and inspective" (Lawson, 39–40). Origen cites 1 Kings 5:9–10[4:29–30] to support his claim ". . . that all the sages of the Greeks borrowed these ideals from Solomon, who had learnt them by the Spirit of God at an age and time long before their own . . ."

(Lawson, 40).

80   Lawson, 41. See also the remarks of Greer, *Origen*, 23.

81   A similar contextual argument is found in Origen's discussion of the book's title, which he understands to express the superlative in relation to six earlier (i.e., pre-Solomonic) hymnic compositions in Hebrew scripture: the "Song of the Sea" in Ex 15; the "Song of the Well" in Num 21:17–18; the "Song of Moses" in Deut 32; the "Song of Deborah" in Judg 5; the "Song of David" in 2 Sam 22; and the hymn of the Asaphites in 1 Chr 16. These songs he takes to mark the progress of the Bride's advance in spiritual understanding, culminating in her introduction through marriage into the "perfect mystery" of God's love (Lawson, 46–50; cf. Loewe, "Apologetic Motifs," 169–170).

Platonism and Christian Gnosticism.[82] A prime example of this is the dualistic anthropology that sustains his quest for the spiritual significance of a work whose erotic "plot" and imagery he does not deny. At least in part, the anthropology is grounded in scripture. Especially in the creation accounts of Genesis and the Pauline epistles, Origen finds support for the view that every individual human is comprised of two persons: the inner, which is the "soul," created in the image and likeness of God; and the outer, the physical body, secondarily fashioned by God from the dust of the earth.[83] Since these two persons are counterparts, coexisting in earthly life, scripture generally uses the same terminology to describe their various attributes and activities. What is said literally about the outer, physical person should, if properly understood, apply in a figurative sense to the inner person, promoting the spiritual growth of the soul in its desire for communion with God (i.e., salvation). It is in this context that Origen acknowledges the Song to pose an unusual danger for immature readers. Anyone still living only in accord with the outer person of flesh ". . . not [yet] knowing how to hear love's language in purity and with chaste ears, will twist the whole manner of his hearing of it away from the inner spiritual man and on to the outward and carnal; and he will be turned away from the spirit to the flesh, and will foster carnal desires in himself, and it will seem to be the Divine Scriptures that are urging and egging him on to fleshly lust!"[84] On the other hand, those who possess the maturity to hear the Song correctly, as addressed to the deepest needs of their inner selves, are taught that among the varieties and objects of human desire ". . . the only laudable love is that which is directed to God and to the powers of the soul."[85]

Closely related to Origen's ontology of human personhood is a complex epistemological rationale for his hermeneutics. This too is part of a broader cosmology which is conspicuously indebted to Platonic thought. For example, in consideration of Wisdom 7:17–21 Origen writes: "Since, then, it is impossible for a man living in the flesh to know anything of matters hidden and invisible unless he has apprehended some image and likeness thereto from among things visible, I think that He who made all things in wisdom so created all species of visible things upon earth, that He placed in them some teaching and knowledge of things invisible and heavenly, whereby the human mind might mount to spiritual understanding and seek the grounds of things in heaven. . . ."[86] Just as the outer person of flesh is an imperfect counterpart of the soul, so all phenomena of this world in some measure correspond to and hence may symbolize perfect, spiritual forms existing in the heavenly realm. For Origen, scripture is no exception, somehow exempt from this equation. Scripture is revelatory precisely because it epito-

---

82 Origen's indebtedness to Platonic thought is well known; see especially Harry Austryn Wolfson, *The Philosophy of the Church Fathers: Faith, Trinity, Incarnation* (Cambridge: Harvard University, ³1970) 270–280 and 571–573. Greer calls Origen a "Christian Platonist" and observes that he ". . . as well as Plotinus, must be regarded as one of the founders of Neoplatonism" (*Origen*, 5; see also 9–12, 25–28).

83 For this, Origen specifically cites Gen 1:26 (the inner person) and Gen 2:7 (the fleshly creature), and develops the distinction on the basis of various Pauline statements, notably Rom 7:22; 1 Cor 3:1–2;

13:11; and 2 Cor 4:16 (Lawson, 24–27).

84 Lawson, 22. Origen also refers here to a tradition among the Jews ". . . to allow no one even to hold this book in his hands, who has not reached a full and ripe age" (Lawson, 23). Cf. Urbach, "Homiletical Interpretations," 252 and n. 14.

85 Lawson, 36.

86 Lawson, 220.

mizes the conjunction of visible and invisible matters, disclosing heavenly mysteries while cloaking them in the language, events, and diverse physical manifestations of earthly reality.[87] When viewed from this perspective, allegory is much less a "method" that Origen brings to the text in order to explicate it than a metaphysical presupposition: his exegesis assumes that "spiritual" meaning is an inherent dimension of the biblical text itself. His method is, rather, disciplined attention to issues of literary context and semantics; for however imaginative or overly ingenious his symbolical interpretations may seem to modern readers, his exegetical practice in the commentary on the Song is consistent with his hermeneutical theory that only by first grasping the outer, "literal" meaning may human minds perceive or at least glimpse the "spiritual" sense hidden within.[88]

Origen's commentary on the Song of Songs is an intellectual achievement of monumental proportions, a grand synthesis of exegetical reasoning, philosophical reflection, and theological vision. Yet to understand the extraordinary impact of the work on subsequent generations of interpreters, it is equally important to stress that the whole is imbued with the excitement of a scholar who considered himself, first and foremost, a spiritual pilgrim and who wrote to convince others that the Song charted the final, sublime stages of life's journey into communion with God.

C. Christian Interpretation in the Middle Ages

During the later patristic period and the rest of the Middle Ages, Christian interpreters wrote more works on the Song of Songs than on any other individual book of the Old Testament. To be sure, the great majority of these writings as known to us are homiletical and devotional expositions rather than systematic commentaries. Many of them were never completed or treat only small portions of the biblical text, and none rivals the exegetical scope and hermeneutical sophistication of Origen's commentary. While it is clear, too, that medieval Christian interpretation of the Song consists largely of variations on Origenist themes, some particular developments merit attention.[89]

By the end of the fifth century, Origen's quest for the spiritual meaning of the Song was an established tradition, especially in western Christendom, having won the

---

87 Cf. Lawson, 74, 218–221. Origen's incarnational view of the inspiration of scripture is fully presented in his *De Principiis,* Book 4. Note especially the following formulation (Chapter 1.7; Greer, *Origen,* 177): "But just as divine providence is not refuted, especially for those who are sure of its existence, because its works or operations cannot be comprehended by human capacities, so neither will the divine inspiration that extends through the entire body of sacred Scripture be called into question because the weakness of our understanding is not strong enough to discover in each different verse the obscure and hidden meanings. This is because the treasure of divine wisdom is hidden in the baser and rude vessel of words . . . (citing 2 Cor 4:7)."

88 For example, the comparison of the man to a "young stag" or "hart" in 2:9 leads Origen into a lengthy consideration of other biblical passages where the term appears, for the purpose of discerning the spiritual reality both hidden by and revealed through the mundane images (Lawson, 216–228).

89 Detailed surveys of the relevant evidence may be found in the following special studies: F. Cavallera, A. Cabassut, and M. Olphe-Galliard, "Cantique des cantiques. II: Histoire de l'interprétation spirituelle," *Dictionnaire de Spiritualité,* Vol. 2 (ed. Marcel Viller *et al.;* Paris: Beauchesne, 1953) 93–109; Rosemarie Herde, *Das Hohelied in der lateinischen Literatur des Mittelalters bis zum 12 Jahrhundert* (Münchener Beiträge zur Mediavistik und Renaissance-Forschung [Estratto da "Studi medievali" 3/8 (1967) 957–1073]; Spoleto: Centro italiano di studi sull' alto medioeva, 1968); Helmut Riedlinger, *Die Makellosigkeit der Kirche in den lateinischen Hoheliedkom-*

enthusiastic endorsement of such influential patristic authors as Gregory of Nyssa, Jerome, Ambrose, Theodoret, and Cyril of Alexandria.[90] We cannot pass over this era, however, without mentioning an alternative approach to the Song which came to be associated almost exclusively with the views of Theodore, bishop of Mopsuestia in Cilicia from 392–428. As the intellectual figurehead of the so-called Antiochene school of exegesis and theology, Theodore epitomized resistance to the allegorical emphasis of Alexandrian hermeneutics in general and Origen's exegetical work in particular.[91] As far as we know, Theodore never authored a comprehensive study of the Song, but his perspective on the biblical work seems to be cogently represented in the extracts of a letter he had written to a friend, preserved as part of the evidence brought against Theodore when he was posthumously condemned by the Second Council of Constantinople in 553.[92] According to these extracts, Theodore vigorously rejected the notion that the Song should be understood as Solomonic prophecy of the spiritual relationship between Christ and the church. Rather, he suggested, for the contemporary Christian reader the Song had only limited didactic and apologetic

relevance, the work being comprised of love poetry that Solomon had apparently written in response to popular criticism of his marriage to the dark-skinned daughter of pharaoh. While this example of Theodore's "literal" exegesis was only peripheral to the charge that he was "the father of Nestorianism," his condemnation by the Second Council was unfortunately to cast a long shadow over the subsequent history of the Song's interpretation.

Gregory the Great (540–604), a Benedictine monk who became pope, played a major part in shaping medieval Christian interpretation of the Song along Origenist lines. As an exegete, Gregory was neither erudite nor particularly innovative, but there is a clarity and provocative eloquence to his style that no doubt contributed to the popularity of his writings. Most of his extant reflections on the Bible, including his treatments of the Song, are explicitly homiletical compositions, written during an era when the Roman empire was under severe attack; Gregory sensitively addressed his expositions to audiences in need of encouragement, enlightenment, and spiritual fortitude.[93] His influence was far-reaching, especially because the later *florilegia* drew extensively on his work, making it accessible to

mentaren des Mittelalters (Beiträge zur Geschichte der Philosophie und Theologie des Mittelalters. Texte und Untersuchungen 38/3; Münster: Aschendorf, 1958); and George L. Scheper, *The Spiritual Marriage: The Exegetic History and Literary Impact of the Song of Songs in the Middle Ages* (Ph.D. dissertation; Princeton University, 1971).

90 Scheper, *Spiritual Marriage*, 404–452, provides an excellent treatment, especially of the views of Gregory of Nyssa, Jerome, Ambrose, and Augustine.

91 An insightful discussion of Theodore's exegetical methods and hermeneutical emphases, in comparison with those of Origen, is provided by Rowan A. Greer, *Theodore of Mopsuestia: Exegete and Theologian* (Westminster: Faith, 1961) 86–131. On Theodore's work as exegete, see also Smalley, *Study*, 14–20; and Maurice F. Wiles, "Theodore of Mopsuestia as

Representative of the Antiochene School," *CHB* 1, 489–510.

92 *PG* 66, 699–700 *[Expositio in Canticum canticorum]*. For discussion of Theodore's remarks on the Song and their import in the proceedings of the Second Council of Constantinople, see Louis Pirot, *L'oeuvre exégétique de Théodore de Mopsueste, 350–428 après J.-C.* (Scripta Pontificii Instituti Biblici; Rome: Pontifical Biblical Institute, 1913) 131–137; and J. M. Vosté, "L'oeuvre exégétique de Théodore de Mopsueste au IIᵉ concile de Constantinople," *RB* 38 (1929) 394–395.

93 Smalley (*Study*, 33) succinctly relates the character of Gregory's expository work to his historical context: "St. Gregory was preaching at a moment when civilization seemed to be condemned. He finished his homilies on Ezechiel with a barbarian army at the

such notable commentators of the following centuries as Bede and William of Saint Thierry.

Gregory dealt with the Song in two homilies, together consisting of a hermeneutical overview of the book and expository comments on its initial eight verses.[94] His introductory remarks sketch a succinct rationale for allegorical exposition in relationship to the fallen state of humankind. Allegory, which is defined by Gregory as "a kind of machine" (*quasi quandam machinam*), may serve to elevate to God the soul that, after the expulsion of the primal human couple from the garden of Eden, is otherwise cut off from intimate knowledge of divine realities. Although the resulting viewpoint is similar to Origen's, it is quickly established, without recourse to philosophical arguments: "In the things we know, out of which allegories are made, the divine sentences are clothed, and by recognizing the outer words we arrive at the inner understanding."[95] Moreover, far from being an exercise in human exegetical ingenuity or psychic self-illumination, allegorical method is consistent with Gregory's understanding of God as the initiating and continuing agent of biblical revelation. Thus, with reference to Habakkuk 3:3, Gregory compared expository insight

with the experience of epiphany, because sacred scripture could be likened to ". . . a kind of mountain from which the Lord comes, to be understood in our hearts."[96] This perspective enabled Gregory to expound the spiritual significance of the Song, but without hesitating in the least to acknowledge the erotic character and conspicuously physical language of the work. Accordingly, he underscored the fact that ". . . in this book are mentioned kisses, breasts, cheeks, thighs . . ." in order to make the point that ". . . by the words of love that is below, the soul may be moved to love that which is above."[97] It is due to divine mercy that the Song's exuberant celebration of physical love becomes a call, inviting the human soul to burn all the more intensely with the sublime love of God.

At many specific points in these homilies, Gregory is directly indebted to Origen's work.[98] Like Origen, he understood the Song to be comprised essentially of speeches describing the experiences of two lovers, a bride and a groom, whom he identified allegorically as the perfect church and her divine Lord. The secondary parts of the maidens associated with the bride and the friends of the groom were also, in his view, ultimately to

---

gates of Rome, when men returning with their hands chopped off told him that some were prisoners, others dead. Spiritual instruction was what his audience needed, simple for the clergy and people, more advanced for the religious. The problems of biblical scholarship did not concern him."

94 *PL* 79, 471–492. The remainder of the *Expositio super Cantica canticorum* attributed to Gregory (*PL* 79, 492–548) has been identified as an eleventh century contribution of Robert of Tombelaine; cf. Ohly, *Studien*, 60 and the literature there cited. In the notes which follow, references are to the newer critical edition of Gregory's homilies on the Song: Patricius Verbraken (ed.), *Sancti Gregorii Magni* (CCSL 144; Tyrnholti: Brepols, 1963) 3–46 *[Expositiones in Canticum canticorum]*.

95 *Expositiones*, par. 2 (Verbraken, 3–4): *Rebus enim nobis*

notis, per quas allegoriae conficiuntur, sententiae diuinae uestiuntur et, dum recognoscimus exteriora uerba, peruenimus ad interiorem intellegentiam.*

96 *Expositiones*, para. 5 (Verbraken, 7): *Scriptura enim sacra mons quidam est, de quo in nostris cordibus ad intellegendum dominus uenit.*

97 *Expositiones*, par. 3 (Verbraken, 4): . . . *per uerba amoris, qui infra est, excitetur ad amorem, qui supra est. Nominantur enim in hoc libro oscula, nominantur ubera, nominantur genae, nominantur femora. . . .*

98 E.g., Gregory followed Origen in speaking of the "Sabbath of Sabbaths" by analogy with the "Song of Songs": *Expositiones*, par. 6 (Verbraken, 8); cf. Origen, *First Homily*, par. 1 (Lawson, 266).

be identified with the ecclesial bride.[99] Perhaps the most distinctive features of Gregory's exposition reflect his devotion to monastic spirituality and contemplation.[100] In commenting on the fervent wish in 1:2a, for example, he interpreted the lover's "kiss" to be a symbol of divine colloquy. Gregory quoted Numbers 12:6–8, which uses the expression "mouth to mouth" to convey the peculiar intimacy of God's conversations with Moses, and concluded that "the Lord as it were kissed Moses with the kiss of his mouth . . ."; this reading yielded in turn the figurative sense that Gregory sought for 1:2a: "To speak mouth to mouth is as it were to kiss, and to touch the mind by inner understanding."[101] The interpretation so adumbrated was to be expansively developed in the *Sermones* of Bernard of Clairvaux.

The Venerable Bede (d. 735) is another influential link in the chain of exegetes who transmitted the classical view of the Song to the later Middle Ages. Bede did not have direct access to Origen's work, but he drew selectively on the expositions of other predecessors, including the homilies of Gregory the Great, to produce a thorough and coherent commentary, albeit one that broke little new ground.[102] It is noteworthy that while Bede understood the Song along traditional lines—as Solomonic prophecy of Christian mysteries—he employed allegory in restrained fashion to develop the presumed textual portrait of the nuptial relationship between Christ and the church; only rarely did he refer to the individual soul interpretation of the "bride." Bede's strong ecclesial emphasis set the tone for later medieval commentaries and sermons which celebrated the Song's female protagonist as the unblemished church of the saints *(sine macula)*, in contrast to or in disregard of the sinners who comprised its temporal membership.[103] The Song thus came to serve increasingly as scriptural warrant for viewing the church as the actualization of a sort of platonic ideal, the pristine bride of Christ garbed in spiritual splendor. To be sure, there were some, such as William of Auvergne, who offered very sharp criticism of the ecclesial situation in the high Middle Ages, but it was all too easy for Christians to become enraptured by the vision which the Song was supposed to project.

The patristic heritage of interpretation yielded a rich harvest of exegetical and homiletical reflection on the Song throughout the twelfth and early thirteenth centuries. At the beginning of this period, Rupert of Deutz

99 *Expositiones*, par. 10 (Verbraken, 13): *Sponsa enim ipsa perfecta ecclesia est; sponsus, dominus; adulescentulae uero cum sponsa sunt inchoantes animae et per nouum studium pubescentes; sodales uero sponsi sunt siue angeli, qui saepe hominibus ab ipso uenientes apparuerunt, seu certe perfecti quique uiri in ecclesia, qui ueritatem hominibus nuntiare nouerunt.*

100 Cf. Henri de Lubac, *The Sources of Revelation* (tr. Luke O'Neill; New York: Herder & Herder, 1968) 50: "Gregory is a monk, and his is a monastic exegesis. He popularizes the conception of the Bible as a mirror of human activity or of the inner man. But above and beyond the tropology which he zealously cultivates, as a conscientious shepherd of souls, he still searches for the 'spiritual allegory' which will allow him to unfold the 'wing of contemplation.'"

101 *Expositiones*, par. 15 (Verbraken, 17–18): *Quasi osculo oris sui osculabatur Moysen dominus,. . . . Os quippe ad os loqui quasi osculari est et interna intellegentia mentem tangere.*

102 *PL* 91, 1065–1236 *[Expositionis in Cantica canticorum].* On the character and significance of Bede's expository work, cf. Smalley, *Study*, 35–36.

103 Cf. Helmut Riedlinger, *Die Makellosigkeit der Kirche in den lateinischen Hoheliedkommentaren des Mittelalters* (Beiträge zur Geschichte der Philosophie und Theologie des Mittelalters. Texte und Untersuchungen 38/3; Münster: Aschendorf, 1958) 400–403.

(d. 1129) developed an approach already suggested in the writings of Ambrose and became the first medieval scholar to apply a thoroughgoing Marian exegesis to the Song.[104] His identification of the woman with the Blessed Virgin, as the figure most representative of the church in her true colors, gave new form and impetus to the idealization of the church noted above. Among the numerous contributions from the period, one can observe interesting differences between the expository work issuing from cathedral schools on the one hand and that which reflects the revival of monastic spirituality on the other.[105] The academic approach known as *sacra pagina,* which understood scripture to be the inspired repository of doctrinal and ethical wisdom, is exemplified in the Song commentary of Anselm of Laon (d. 1117).[106] Conversely, the exposition of William of Saint Thierry (d. about 1148) well illustrates renewed monastic devotion to *lectio divina,* in which the Song is much less a source of revealed knowledge about the relationship

between Christ and the church than an instrument of spiritual illumination.[107] In general, while the scholastic commentaries expound the text in systematic fashion, the monastic expositions have an affective character and are typically incomplete or unfinished. As Leclercq has remarked, when the monks felt they had said what they wanted to say about love, they had the right to put down the pen.[108]

Those who are acquainted with the forceful role that Bernard of Clairvaux played in the ecclesiastical politics of his age, especially his advocacy of the Crusades and his part in the affairs of Peter Abelard and Peter ("the Venerable") of Cluny, may be tempted to tread warily into the realm of his expository work.[109] Yet Bernard's *Sermones in Canticum* are widely recognized to be at once the crowning achievement of the approach to the Song initiated by Origen and the superlative contribution of monastic theology to Christian spirituality.[110] Two preliminary points are pertinent to an assessment of this

104 *PL* 168, 837–962 *[Commentaria in Cantica canticorum].* Cf. Gustave Bardy, "Marie et le Cantique chez les Pères," *BVC* 7 (1954) 32–41; and Henri de Lubac, *Méditation sur l'Église* (Collection "Theologique," Études publiées sous la direction de la Faculté de Théologie S.J. de Lyon-Fourvière 27; Paris: Montaigne, 1953) 273–324.

105 For discussion, see Jean Leclercq, "From Gregory to Saint Bernard," *CHB* 2, 183–197, especially 189–193; and the full treatment in Smalley, *Study,* 37–263.

106 *PL* 162, 1187–1228 *[Enarrationes in Cantica canticorum].* Cf. Ohly, *Studien,* 112–120.

107 *PL* 180, 473–546 *[Expositio altera super Cantica canticorum].* The following translations, with introductory comments, may be noted: J.-M. Déchanet and M. Dumontier, *Guillaume de Saint-Thierry: Exposé sur le Cantique des cantiques* (SC 82; Paris: Cerf, 1962); and Columba Hart, tr., *The Works of William of St. Thierry,* Vol. 2: *Exposition on the Song of Songs* (CFS 6; Spencer, Massachusetts: Cistercian Publications, 1970).

108 Jean Leclercq, *The Love of Learning and the Desire of God: A Study of Monastic Culture* (tr. Catherine Misrahi; New York: Fordham University, 1961) 107.

109 Cf. Pope, 123–124.

110 *PL* 183, 799–1198; now superseded by the critical edition: Jean Leclercq, Henri M. Rochais, and Charles H. Talbot, eds., *Sancti Bernardi opera,* Vols. 1–2 (Rome: Editiones Cistercienses, 1957, 1958). A new English translation of the *Sermones,* based on the critical edition, has appeared: Kilian Walsh and Irene M. Edmonds, trs., *[The Works of] Bernard of Clairvaux: On the Song of Songs,* 4 Vols. (CFS 4, 7, 31, 40; Spencer, Massachusetts/Kalamazoo, Michigan: Cistercian Publications, 1971–80) [cited below as CFS with vol. number].

remarkable effort. First, the work is a product par excellence of monastic *lectio divina* and exhibits virtually no interest in scholastic *Sic et Non*. It is neither an exegetical commentary nor even a consecutive homiletical exposition but a series of eighty-six sermons based—at times quite loosely—on selected verses and themes, most of them from the initial two chapters of the Song. The repetitive elaboration of key texts[111] reflects Bernard's understanding of their import but also in part the fact that the sermons were delivered and redacted over a period of about eighteen years (1135–1153). Second, although the sermons in their published form quickly reached a wider public, the majority of them directly attest their origin in addresses which Bernard delivered to conferences of the Cistercian monks of Clairvaux.[112] It should be noted that those who comprised this order were not all men who had lived the hot-house existence one might associate with a monastery. Many in Bernard's monastic audiences were undoubtedly worldly figures, among them former knights who had served in the armies of the Crusades and who knew what life was about. We can only admire the temerity and insight of Bernard to choose the Song as the scriptural basis for his prolonged and wide-ranging instructions on the discipline of Christian spirituality.[113]

Throughout the sermons, one is struck by Bernard's thorough acquaintance with the Old and New Testaments. Not only does he make frequent use of scriptural quotations, especially from the Pauline epistles, to illustrate and establish his points, but his reflections are suffused with biblical allusions. In particular, the language of the Psalms had clearly become second nature to him, and it is this which he skillfully uses to construct a universe of meaning around the Song. At the same time, however, Bernard rarely attends to the kinds of semantic issues which occupied many of his predecessors, most notably Origen, nor does he self-consciously rely on allegorical method to make the literal text yield an appropriately spiritual sense. As he says apologetically on one occasion, pausing in the midst of an unusually extended inquiry into the significance of the number seven, "it is not so much my desire to explain words as it is to influence hearts."[114] This affective purpose, rather than an exegetical technique or hermeneutical stance as such, is eloquently announced in Bernard's introductory sermon. Here he offers a bare sketch of the Solomonic provenance of the sublime Song, yet his apparent aim in doing so is less to inform than to whet the appetite of his audience.[115] Instruction on the Song, he suggests, has a sacramental analogy: Solomon's inspired poetry is like a loaf of bread, which is to be broken open through sensitive exposition and fed to those who are prepared to receive its spiritual nourishment.[116] In short, Bernard is a mystic, and his sermons are immediately addressed to

---

111 E.g., Bernard returns again and again to the sense and significance of the "kiss" in 1:2.
112 On the compositional history of the work, see especially the introductory essay of Jean Leclercq in CFS 7, vii–xxx.
113 Cf. Jean Leclercq, *Monks on Marriage: A Twelfth-Century View* (New York: Seabury, 1982) 73–86. Leclercq points out very effectively how the language of (nuptial) sexual union is much to the fore in Bernard's *Sermones*. Even when Bernard enters fully into the metaphor of the spiritual marriage of the human soul with God, sexual references are never

taboo, or the object of repression. The boldness of the erotic imagery is, of course, based on the explicit language of the Song. Cf. also *idem, Monks and Love in Twelfth-Century France: Psycho-Historical Essays* (Oxford: Clarendon, 1979) especially 16–23.
114 *Sermon* 16.1 [author's tr.]: *sed nec studium tam esse mihi ut exponam verba, quam ut imbuam corda.*
115 *Sermon* 1.6–8, with the final paragraph as follows: "We must conclude then it was a special divine impulse that inspired these songs of his [Solomon] that now celebrate the praises of Christ and his Church, the gift of holy love, the sacrament of

of works composed for singing.[268] Such interpretations are too specific and speculative, especially given the paucity of our knowledge about musical scores, composition, and performance in ancient Israel.[269] Already in antiquity the poetry of the Song may have been chanted or sung,[270] but there is no concrete evidence to indicate that it was originally composed for this purpose.

Attempts to identify the work as an *epithalamium* or book of wedding songs suffer from additional difficulties. A presumed institutional *Sitz im Leben* of the Song or its major components is supposed to be determinative of genre (even though various kinds of poems and songs might be featured in a wedding celebration). Form is defined by hypothetical social function rather than by a configuration of literary features per se.

Interpreting the Song as a collection of marriage songs is particularly associated with Karl Budde, who called it a "textbook of a Palestinian-Israelite wedding."[271] Positing a seven-day celebration, in which bridegroom and bride assumed roles of king and queen, Budde attempted to discern in the text a detailed scenario of communal festivities, involving choruses of male and female singers as well as the "sword dance."[272] A more cautious approach is taken by Ernst Würthwein, who contends that twenty-four literary units (out of a total of twenty-nine he recognizes in the Song) refer to aspects of an Israelite wedding.[273]

---

268 E.g., Morris Jastrow considered the Song to be a loosely structured anthology of twenty-three or more disparate love ballads and "folk songs" (*The Song of Songs, Being a Collection of Love Lyrics of Ancient Palestine: A New Translation Based on a Revised Text, together with the Origin, Growth, and Interpretation of the Songs* [Philadelphia: J. B. Lippincott, 1921]). More recently, Ernst Würthwein ("Das Hohelied" in *idem,* Kurt Galling, and Otto Plöger, *Die fünf Megilloth* [HAT 18; Tübingen: J. C. B. Mohr (Paul Siebeck), 1969] 25) speaks of "love songs" (*Liebeslieder*) and "antiphonal singing" (*Wechselgesänge*). Cf. also Michael D. Goulder, *The Song of Fourteen Songs* (JSOTSup 36; Sheffield: JSOT/University of Sheffield, 1986).

269 For a useful, succinct survey of available data, see J. H. Eaton, "Music's Place in Worship: A Contribution from the Psalms," *Prophets, Worship and Theodicy: Studies in Prophetism, Biblical Theology and Structural and Rhetorical Analysis and on the Place of Music in Worship* (OTS 23; ed. A. S. van der Woude; Leiden: E. J. Brill, 1984) 85–107. Cf. also Alfred Sendrey, *Music in the Social and Religious Life of Antiquity* (Cranbury: Associated University Presses, 1974) 77–278, esp. 136–37 and 160–62.

270 For references in rabbinical literature, see above, p. 13 n. 53; cf. Würthwein, 31–32, and Fox, 247–50.

Some modern choral works based on the Song are noted by Peter Gradenwitz, *The Music of Israel: Its Rise and Growth Through 5000 Years* (New York: W. W. Norton, 1949) 201, 207, 209, 269.

271 Budde, xix.

272 As suggested by J. G. Wetzstein, "Die syrische Dreschtafel," *Zeitschrift für Ethnologie* 5 (1873) 270–302. It is surprising how influential Wetzstein's study has remained, in view of the problem stated succinctly by Wesley J. Fuerst: "The most serious objection to the 'wedding cycle' theory stems from the fact that nineteenth-century Syrian customs cannot illuminate very well the situation in Old Testament Israel" (*The Books of Ruth, Esther, Ecclesiastes, The Song of Songs, Lamentations: The Five Scrolls* [CBC; Cambridge: Cambridge University, 1975] 166).

273 Würthwein, 32; cf. also Eissfeldt, *Old Testament,* 486–88.

While it is reasonable to suppose that portions of the Song were used in ancient Israelite wedding festivities,[274] there is no solid basis for identifying marriage rites as either the *primary* setting of the entire work or the purpose for which most of the individual poetic units were composed. The Song's only explicit reference to marriage appears in 3:11, though in 4:8–12 and 5:1 the woman is indeed called "bride" (*kallâ*). Any number of other possible settings, associated with the manifold interactions and reflections of lovers, could account for the rest of the poetic units preserved in the Song.

Love Poems. Because it involves fewer presuppositions, *poems* is a more neutral term than *songs* to describe the literary contents of the Song. While *love poems* is a very general classification, rather than a specific *Gattung*, it has the advantage of emphasizing the themes and motifs that are not only the common stock of the Song's poetry but are expressive of universal human experiences of love.

B. Component Genres

Friedrich Horst initiated contemporary discussion of the specific literary genres of love poetry that comprise the Song. He differentiated and described such categories as "songs" of yearning (*Sehnsuchtslieder*), self-descriptions (*Selbstschilderung*), tease (*Scherzgespräch*), admiration (*Bewunderungslied*), description of experience (*Erlebnis-schilderung*), description of the beloved's physical charms (*Beschreibungslied*, the Arabic *wasf*), boasting (*Prahllied*), and the like.[275] Following Horst's lead, the present commentary will give attention to specific formal features of individual poetic units.[276] The sequence of genres and sub-genres recognized in this commentary is as follows:

1:1	Superscription.
1:2–4	A poem of yearning, spoken by the woman.
1:5–6	A self-description, spoken by the woman.
1:7–8	A "tease," in the form of dialogue between the man and the woman.

---

274 Audet ("Le sens," 211–14) plausibly suggests that choral singing of wedding songs is meant by the repeated reference in Jeremiah to "the voice of the bridegroom and the voice of the bride" (Jer 7:34; 16:9; 25:10; 33:11). Cf. Roland de Vaux, *Ancient Israel: Its Life and Institutions* (tr. John McHugh; New York/Toronto/London: McGraw-Hill, 1961) 33–34.

275 Friedrich Horst, "Die Formen des althebräischen Liebesliedes," *Orientalistische Studien, Enno Littmann zu seinem 60. Geburtstag überreicht* (Leiden: E. J. Brill, 1935) 43–54 (reprinted in *idem, Gottes Rechte: Gesammelte Studien zum Recht im alten Testament* [ed. Hans Walter Wolff; TB 12; München: Chr. Kaiser, 1961] 176–87). Cf. Roland E. Murphy, "Form-Critical Studies in the Song of Songs," *Int* 27 (1973) 413–22. Form-critical analysis, with close attention to rhetorical patterns, is a particular strength of Leo Krinetzki's earlier commentary: *Das Hohe Lied: Kommentar zu Gestalt und Kerygma eines alttestamentlichen Liebesliedes* (KBANT; Düsseldorf: Patmos, 1964). His recent commentaries treat form-critical

issues more succinctly: Günter Krinetzki, *Hoheslied* (NEchB; Würzburg: Echter, 1980); *Kommentar zum Hohenlied: Bildsprache und Theologische Botschaft* (BET 16; Frankfurt am Main/Bern: Peter D. Lang, 1981). In accord with the format of the BKAT series, Gerleman's commentary offers a discussion of "Form" for each pericope of the Song.

276 See also the overview in Murphy, *Wisdom Literature*, 98–124. With this analysis may be compared the eleven *Gattungen* in the Song recognized by G. Krinetzki (3–5):
1. "Songs of Admiration" (*Bewunderungslieder*), which generally begin with a simile or metaphor and conclude with a wish, proposal, or request: 1:9–11, 15–17; 2:1–3; 4:10–11; 6:4–5b, 10; 7:7–10[6–9].
2. "Image Songs" (*Bildlieder*), exhibiting three sub-types: (a) metaphorical: 1:13–14; 4:12; (b) comparative: 4:13–15; (c) allegorical: 1:12; 2:15–17; 6:3; 7:14[13] (cf. also 8:14 and 6:2).
3. "Songs of Description" (*Beschreibungslieder*): 3:6–8, 9–10; 4:1–7, 8–9; 6:5c–7; 7:1–6[6:13—7:5]; 8:5a–b (cf. 5:10–16), the first two of which are identified

1:9–11	A poem of admiration (adornment), spoken by the man.
1:12–14	A poem of admiration (comparison to exotic perfumes), spoken by the woman.
1:15—2:3	Poems of admiration, united by dialogue.
2:4–7	A poem of yearning (?); cf. 8:1–4.
2:8–13	A "description of an experience," including a "song of yearning" (vv 10–13), in which the man invites the woman to a love tryst.
2:14–15	A "tease."
2:16–17	An invitation issued to the man by the woman. (The *inclusio*—formed by repetition of the "gazelle/young stag" simile in 2:9, 17—supports the view that the entire unit in 2:8–17 is a reminiscence.)
3:1–5	A "description of an experience" (which many interpreters regard as a dream).
3:6–11	A mixed unit, exhibiting elements of the genres of description and admiration.
4:1–7	A classical example of the *wasf*, or description of the physical charms of the woman.
4:8	An invitation issued by the man to the woman (which is perhaps to be joined with 4:9—5:1).
4:9—5:1	A poem of admiration (4:9–15), which ends in a dialogue (4:16—5:1a) and a concluding address to the lovers (5:1b).
5:2–8	A description of an experience (perhaps a

dream; cf. 3:1–5).

5:9	A question, posed by the Daughters to the woman.
5:10–16	In response to the preceding question, the woman utters a *wasf* describing the man.
6:1–3	A dialogue, comprised of a question posed by the Daughters concerning the whereabouts of the man (6:1) and the woman's answer (6:2–3), in which she speaks of the pleasure the man finds in her.
6:4–7	A mixed unit, with a poem of admiration and a *wasf* (repetition of 4:1–3), spoken by the man.
6:8–10	A poem of praise, in which boast is also present.
6:11–12	A description of an experience, spoken by the woman.
7:1–7 [6:13–7:6]	A *wasf*, in praise of the woman's beauty, preceded by a two-part introduction mentioning "the Shulammite" (7:1).
7:8–11 [7–10]	A poem of admiration and yearning, which ends in a dialogue, as the woman interrupts (7:10b), and concludes with the formula of mutual possession (cf. 2:16; 6:3).
7:12–14 [11–13]	A poem of yearning.
8:1–4	A poem of yearning.

more precisely as "Wedding Songs" (*Hochzeitslieder*).
4. "Self-Descriptions" (*Selbstschilderungen*), spoken by the young woman in 1:5–6 and by the brothers in 8:8–10.
5. "Boast Songs" (*Prahllieder*), setting the young woman's triumph over against the possessions of an oriental monarch: 6:8–9; 8:11–12.
6. "Tease" (*Scherzgespräche*), found only in 1:7–8.
7. "Dialogues" (*Wechselgespräche*), which are primarily a redactional creation, combining individual elements of various genres: 4:16—5:1d; 5:8–16; 6:1–2; 8:13–14.

8. "Descriptions of Experience" (*Erlebnisschilderungen*): 2:8–9, 10–13; 3:1–4; 5:2–7.
9. "Songs of Yearning" (*Sehnsuchtslieder*): 1:2–4; 2:4–5; 2:14; 7:12–13[11–12]; 8:1–2, 6–7 (cf. 2:10b–c, 13c–d; 4:16).
10. "Adjuration Song" (*Beschwörungslied*): 2:7=3:5=8:4 (cf. 5:8).
11. "Summons to Joy" (*Aufforderung zur Freude*): 3:10e–11 and 5:1e–f.

8:5	A poem of admiration (?).
8:6–7	A poem in praise of love, spoken by the woman.
8:8–10	A poem of self-description, or perhaps a boast, spoken by the woman.
8:11–12	A boast.
8:13–14	A dialogue expressing yearning.

C. Structural Integrity

Is there a coherent arrangement of the individual poetic units that comprise the Song?

Although the work in its received form does not exhibit an overt literary structure, such as one would expect to find in an integrated collection of poetic discourses (cf. the books of Job and Ecclesiastes), ostensible dialogue between the primary male and female speakers does suggest at least a contrived unity. It is uncertain whether the dialogical arrangement of poetic units was the work of an original author or was contributed secondarily by a collector of the poems or an editor. Similarly, whether or not some substantial units are later additions to the work must remain an open question.[277]

Commentators who have attempted to discern structural coherence to the Song have usually identified a smaller number of poems within it than the twenty-five or more typically distinguished by critics who consider the work to be an anthology or loose collection of love poetry.[278] Those who defend the view that the Song is a drama attempt to identify a limited number of scenes as providing overall structure, but here no agreement prevails, as we have already noted. The stoutest proposals for the Song's unity have been based on rhetorical analysis, identifying features that are supposed to conjoin major poetic units or otherwise to indicate an artful literary arrangement of individual poems.

Joseph Angénieux, for example, has argued that the Song consists of only eight poems, which he distinguishes on the basis of primary (e.g., 2:7) and secondary refrains (1:4; 2:4; etc.), but a hypothetical reconstruction of the sequence of the text greatly weakens his case.[279] A more detailed stylistic and structural analysis has been presented by J. Cheryl Exum. Her methodology ". . . consists of the isolation of poetic units, the examination of the form and stylistic characteristics of each poem, and the establishment of parallels among the poems."[280] Refrains and repetitions provide the major criteria she uses to identify six individual poems, which form three paired sets: 1:2—2:6 with 8:4–14; 2:7—3:5 with 5:2—6:3; and 3:6—5:1 with 6:4—8:3. In her view, such a sophisticated structure rules out the possibility that the Song can be considered a haphazard collection of love poetry. Whether or not Exum has correctly identified the larger structure of the work, the strength of her analysis is a perceptive description of the Song's literary artistry,

---

277 E.g., 3:6–11 and 8:6–14 seem problematic in context, though they do exhibit some thematic links with other segments of the Song.

278 Eissfeldt (*Old Testament,* 489–90) considers approximately twenty-five separate songs or poems to be the "right assumption"; Franz Landsberger, on the other hand, is persuaded that the number is "far, far greater" than this ("Poetic Units Within the Song of Songs," *JBL* 73 [1955] 215–16).

279 Joseph Angénieux, "Structure du Cantique des Cantiques en chants encadrés par des refrains alternants," *ETL* 41 (1965) 96–112. Cf. also *idem,*

"Les trois portraits du Cantique des Cantiques. Étude de critique littéraire," *ETL* 42 (1966) 582–86; and "Le Cantique des Cantiques en huits chants à refrains alternants. Essai de reconstitution du texte primitif avec une introduction et des notes critiques," *ETL* 44 (1968) 87–140.

280 J. Cheryl Exum, "A Literary and Structural Analysis of the Song of Songs," *ZAW* 85 (1973) 49.

involving such devices as repetition, paronomasia, and chiasmus. A brief review cannot do justice to the cumulative effect of her arguments, but attention to two important parts of her case for structure will suffice to indicate the possibilities and limitations of the approach.

Recognition of parallelism between 2:7—3:5 and 5:2—6:3 is the starting point for Exum's determination of the Song's literary architecture.[281] These textual segments are indeed the most convincing examples of larger, composite poems within the work.[282] Both of them feature a call to the woman (2:8–14; 5:2–6a) and they share the predominant theme of seeking/finding (3:1–5; 5:6b—6:3). Exum understands the adjuration in 2:7 to be a distinct unit, forming an *inclusio* with 3:5. However, it seems difficult to separate 2:7 from what precedes it, and so also when the lines are repeated in 8:3–4 (where Exum again assigns the verses to different units). She considers 2:6 and 8:3 to be a concluding refrain, whereas the adjuration in 2:7 and 8:4 is deemed an opening refrain. Moreover, in the section 5:6b—6:3, only the initial part (5:6b–8) is thematically parallel to 3:1–5. The question that follows in 5:9 is contrived, providing opportunity for the woman to praise the man's physical charms (the *wasf* in 5:10–16), while a second question enables her to respond that she has never really lost her lover (6:1–3).

On the basis of supposed parallelism between 2:7—3:5 and 5:2—6:3, Exum proposes to identify another pair of parallel poems in 3:6—5:1 and 6:4—8:3.[283] The first of these poems is basically comprised of three sub-units: a description of the procession of Solomon (3:6–11); a *wasf*

describing the woman (4:1–11); and an extended "garden" simile that forms the poem's climax (4:12—5:1). Already here it is difficult to discern a unified poem: the juxtaposition of the vision of Solomon's procession with the *wasf* and similes is simply too jarring. The supposed components of the parallel poem are even more difficult to comprehend as a unity: a song of admiration, spoken by the man (6:4–10, borrowing from the *wasf* in 4:1–3) is followed by some enigmatic verses (6:11–12), a *wasf* about the woman (7:1–7[6:13—7:6]), an announcement of the man's desire for her (7:8–10a[7–9a]), and a concluding response from the woman (7:10b[9b]—8:3). These disparate elements do not form a convincing sequence in themselves, nor are they conspicuously parallel to the units identifiable in 3:6—5:1. Such judgment admittedly emphasizes form-critical considerations and thematic development, rather than the rhetorical features that are the chief signals in Exum's discernment of coherent literary structure.

These remarks by no means refute the case Exum makes for the Song's artistic design, but they do illustrate the difficulties encountered in detailed rhetorical analysis. The problem is to determine whether or not minute stylistic features are sure signs of structure, assessing them in light of other factors, such as seemingly incongruous content and lack of coherent sequence, which weigh against literary unity.

Another noteworthy attempt to discern an overall literary design in the text of the Song has been offered by William Shea.[284] His analysis is based on two key observations: an A:B:A arrangement of material in

281 Exum, "Analysis," 49–59.

282 The present commentary understands 5:2—6:3 to form a major unit, created by dialogue between the woman and the Daughters.

283 Exum, "Analysis," 61–70.

284 William H. Shea, "The Chiastic Structure of the Song of Songs," *ZAW* 92 (1980) 378–95. Cf. the chiastic arrangement of balanced pairs of poems

proposed by Edwin C. Webster, "Patterns in the Song of Songs," *JSOT* 22 (1982) 73–93.

biblical literature; and supposed chiastic relationship between the two halves of the Song (with 1:2—2:2 corresponding to 8:6–14; 2:3–17 to 7:11[10]—8:5; and 3:1—4:16 to 5:1—7:10[9]). As Shea understands it, the A:B:A pattern may be represented by the sequence prose, poetry, prose (as in Job); or by a content sequence of instructions, proverbs, instructions (as in Proverbs, but omitting three appendices in 8:6–14). In Shea's treatment of the Song, however, the A:B:A pattern must be identified solely on the basis of the *quantity* of lines in major poetic segments. It is difficult to see how so many diverse literary phenomena in different works can usefully be comprehended by such a general scheme or, in any case, what support this scheme provides for the literary coherence of the Song. The chiastic arrangement posited by Shea is also problematic. For example, he supposes 1:2—2:2 to have 8:6–14 as its chiastic counterpart; within these two larger segments, 1:2–7 is said to correspond to 8:12–14. But what are the specific links between these internal units? In both, the woman is speaking and expressing a "desire." The term ḥăbērîm ("companions") appears in 1:7 and 8:13, while 1:6 and 8:11 refer to a "vineyard." Finally, the reference to "Daughters" of 1:5 is supposed to have a counterpart in "the feminine plural participle" of 8:13, although 𝔐 attests a singular form (hayyôšebet ["dweller, inhabitant"]).[285] These data seem much too thin and loosely related to support a claim of intentional chiastic correspondence between the units in which they appear. There are similar problems with the remainder of Shea's analysis. Chiastic relationships are strained; alleged correspondences seem to lack the thematic and verbal links needed to sustain a viable sense of literary structure.

Several factors contribute to the diversity of views among critics who argue that the Song exhibits a dramatic structure based upon dialogue. There is, first, disagreement regarding the number of speakers and the specific lines that are to be assigned to them. The present commentary recognizes only two main characters who speak, a woman and a man; other speaking parts, such as the "Daughters of Jerusalem," are minor.[286] By and large, context suffices to identify the lines spoken by the man and the woman (especially since Hebrew differentiates gender in second and third person pronouns and verb forms), but difficulties remain. The most questionable passages are the following: 1:2–4 (where an abrupt change of speakers occurs); 8;8 (probably spoken by the woman rather than the Daughters); the refrain in 2:7, 3:5, and 8:4 (probably spoken by the woman); 3:6–11; 5:1b; 6:10; 6:11–12 (with an obviously corrupt text in v 12); 7:1–6[6:13—7:5] (in which a group addresses the Shulammite); and 8:5. Allowing for uncertainties, a substantially larger number of lines must be attributed to the woman than to the male speaker.[287]

A more serious difficulty in arguing for a dialogical structure of the Song is posed by apparent lack of continuity at several points in the text, where there are sudden shifts of scene, topic, and ostensible speaker. For example, it is not clear how the lines describing Solomon's procession in 3:6–11 link up with the woman's account of her search for her lover in 3:1–5. Again, in

285 Shea presumably revocalizes to read *hayyōšĕbôt* (cf. 𝕾), but he gives no account of other departures from the text of the verse in 𝔐, which this reading would necessitate.

286 See the remarks on literary fiction and characterization in the Song, pp. 80–85.

287 Donald Broadribb ("Thoughts on the Song of Solomon," *Abr-Nahrain* 3 [1961–62] 18) attributes to the woman 118 of the 207 poetic lines he counts in the Song.

2:8–13 the woman describes the visit of the man to her house and his invitation to a tryst; but this is followed in 2:14 by his address to her as if she were hidden in a rocky mountain area (cf. 4:1–7 with 4:8). Sequence is particularly dubious in 8:8–14, which may comprise three fragments (vv 8–10, 11–12, 13–14).[288] Difficulties of this kind have led many commentators to claim that the Song is an anthology of many disparate love poems, written by several hands and in different historical periods.

Although it seems perilous to argue that an intricate compositional design can be recognized in the Song, conspicuous elements of dialogue may be used to distinguish major literary divisions. A fuller justification for dialogical structure is given in the sections of commentary, but a sequential sketch of the Song's contents is appropriate here.

1:1. Superscription.

1:2–6. Here the woman is the key figure and apparent speaker; the subject is her yearning for her absent lover. In referring to the man, she switches from third person to second person (enallage) and perhaps associates others with herself ("we," the "maidens" of 1:3?). In vv 5–6 she offers an apology for herself to the Daughters of Jerusalem, explaining why she has been darkened by the sun. This explanation introduces the theme of the "vineyard" (i.e., the woman herself and her disposition of her own person). There is only a loose connection between vv 2–4 and 5–6.

1:7—2:7. The woman is still speaking in 1:7, but now to the man who is certainly present. He answers her inquiry (v 8) and bursts into a song of admiration (vv 9–11), which in turn evokes from her lines describing him, in the third person, as the source of her pleasure (vv 12–14). Then the two lovers participate in a dialogue of mutual admiration (1:15–17; 2:1–4); at the end of the dialogue, the woman again refers to the man in the third person, as she describes their tryst. She now proclaims her love-sickness, asking for sustenance (2:5). The unit concludes with her description of their embrace and an adjuration to the Daughters of Jerusalem (which becomes a refrain; cf. 8:3–4 and also 3:5 and 5:8).

2:8–17. The dialogue in this section does not run smoothly, but there appears to be a deliberate *inclusio* ("gazelle or young stag") in vv 9 and 17.[289] Hence the whole can be considered a unit, a reminiscence by the woman of her lover's visit. She recalls his animated arrival at her home, his invitation (the poem on spring in vv 10–13), his request and her coquettish reply (vv 14–15), and her welcome to his visit (vv 16–17).

3:1–11. A new section begins with two units that have very little connection with each other, except that both end with an address to the Daughters (vv 1–5 and 6–11). The first unit forms a doublet with 5:2–8; the theme is the presence/absence of the man, and the search made for him by the woman. She finds him in 3:4, but in chapter 5 the door is opened to further dialogue (contrast 3:5 with 5:8). A second unit combines a description of a procession of Solomon's litter "on the day of his marriage" with an invitation to the Daughters to gaze upon him. It is not clear who speaks these lines (vv 6–11), which give the impression of being a separate poem. In

288 Cf. Robert (308), who aptly termed these verses "appendices."
289 See Roland E. Murphy, "Cant 2:8–17—A Unified Poem?" *Melanges bibliques et orientaux en l'honneur de M. Mathias Delcor* (ed. André Caquot et al.; AOAT 215; Kevelaer: Butzon & Bercker; Neukirchen: Neukirchener, 1985) 305–10.

the context, the mention of Solomon is to be interpreted in line with the fiction of the lover as "king" (cf. 1:4, 12; 6:8–9; 7:6).

4:1—5:1. The section begins with a *wasf*, in which the man describes the physical charms of the woman (4:1–7). This is followed, first, by the man's invitation to her to come from her inaccessible place ("Lebanon," v 8), and then by a poem of admiration, in praise of her (vv 9–16a). She replies to his invitation with an invitation of her own, picking up on the theme of the "garden" (v 16b); his response is an affirmation that he has indeed come to his garden (5:1a). The section closes with an address, by an unidentified voice, urging the lovers to enjoy themselves (5:1b). (Catchwords that unite the lines of this section are noted in the commentary. However, it must be confessed that the dialogical structure here seems somewhat contrived; 4:1–7, 8, 9–11, and 12–16 could originally have been separate poems.)

5:2—6:3. Poems representing several different genres comprise this section, but they make good sense in terms of a sequence of dialogue between the woman and the Daughters. She begins by recounting to them a nocturnal experience with her lover; the theme is finding/not finding (5:2–8; cf. 3:1–5). Appropriately, the Daughters reply by asking for a description of the lost lover (v 9), and she launches into a *wasf* about him (vv 10–16). The interest of the Daughters is quickened by her description; they wish "to seek him with you" (6:1). But to this the woman gives triumphant response that he is in his "garden"—i.e., he is not really "lost" but always with her (6:2–3; cf. 2:16 and 7:11[10]). The small refrain of mutual possession in 6:3 closes the section.

6:4–12. The man is the speaker in the initial unit (vv 4–10). He begins with an expression of his admiration for the woman (v 4), which develops into a *wasf* (vv 5–7,

borrowing from 4:1b–3b), and concludes by boasting that even "queens and concubines" of the royal harem acknowledge the woman's unique beauty (vv 8–10). The expression "awe-inspiring as visions" in vv 4b and 10b may form an *inclusio.* The lines in 6:11–12 are a problem: they do not seem to have any obvious connection with what precedes, and the identity of the speaker is unclear; but it is no easier to associate them with the following section.

7:1[6:13]—8:4. Dialogue between bystanders and the woman in 7:1–2a[6:13—7:1a] serves to introduce a *wasf* about the woman (vv 2b–7[1b–6]). It is reasonable to identify the man, rather than the bystanders, as speaking the *wasf*, because he clearly expresses his yearning for the woman in the following lines (vv 8–10a[7–9a]). She apparently interrupts him in v 10b[9b] with her positive response and then recites the formula of mutual possession (v 11[10]; cf. 6:3). Next she issues him an invitation and a promise (7:12[11]—8:2). The section concludes in 8:3–4 with a repetition of the refrain of 2:6–7, addressed to the Daughters of Jerusalem. After the passionate exchange between the lovers that precedes it, the refrain seems somewhat anticlimactic and artificial.

8:5–14. These verses exhibit little coherence and lend support to the claim that the Song is simply a collection of disparate love poems.[290] Echoes of earlier lines can be noted: for example, v 5a repeats 3:6a. Verses 8–10 apparently hearken back to 1:6b ("sons of my mother"), giving the woman's response to the plans her brothers have made for her. Verses 13–14 may preserve a snatch of conversation between the man and the woman.

In sum, elements of dialogue seem to provide the strongest evidence of sequential arrangement of poetic units within the Song and thus also suggest the work's overall coherence. Our emphasis on dialogical structure

---

290 Cf. Robert, 308; his characterization of 8:8–14 is also
applicable to 8:5–7.

intends only to comprehend the text in its received form, leaving largely unresolved questions of original composition (i.e., authorship, dates, settings, and functions of individual poems within the corpus).

6. Aspects of Composition and Style

Form-critical analysis, as we have seen in the preceding section, sheds significant light on the genres of love poetry that comprise the Song but provides little help in addressing issues of overall literary structure and compositional integrity. Rhetorical criticism brings these issues into sharper focus, enabling us to discern a remarkable coherence of literary style and language throughout the Song. An argument in favor of common authorship of most, if not all, of the poetry included in the work is especially advanced when we look at the Song's characteristic perspective on human love, as well as to its peculiar imagery, vocabulary, and thematic topoi.

A. Language

With the partial exception of Psalm 45, which celebrates a royal marriage and is presumably the work of a court poet, the Hebrew Bible has not preserved any composition with which the content of the Song can be closely compared.[291] There are indeed some interesting similarities of vocabulary and theme between these two works.[292] However, Psalm 45 cannot really be classified as love poetry. The psalm's protagonists, a king and a queen, are extolled and instructed by the poet; they do not address each other with words of praise, delight, and yearning as do the male and female speakers in the Song. Nor for all of its richness of imagery does Psalm 45 touch on the subjective feelings and aspirations of the royal couple. Their emotions can at best be inferred from the external portraits the poet sketches.

One would expect Hebrew love poetry to have a distinctive style and its own characteristic vocabulary. The Song's uniquely vivid depictions of a loving relationship between a man and a woman supports such a view. The distinctiveness of this poetry can be appreciated by comparing its emphases with the more familiar perspectives and language of biblical wisdom literature.

Love and the Natural Order. Biblical sages and the love poetry of the Song share an intense interest in the created order. However, the former generally looked at their physical environs in an objective manner, while the poetry of the Song relishes the subjective dimensions of

---

291 Cf. the assessment of Oswald Loretz, who claims that an allegorical reading of Psalm 45 is already indicated by textual glosses in vv 7 and 12 (*Studien zur althebräischen Poesie 1: Das althebräische Liebeslied. Untersuchungen zur Stichometrie und Redaktionsgeschichte des Hohenliedes und des 45. Psalms* [AOAT 14/1; Kevelaer: Butzon & Bercker; Neukirchen-Vluyn: Neukirchener, 1971] esp. 69–70). A messianic interpretation is given by Raymond Jacques Tournay, "Les affinités du Ps. xlv avec le Cantique des Cantiques et leur interprétation messianique," *Congress Volume, Bonn 1962* (VTSup 9; Leiden: E. J. Brill, 1963) 168–212.

292 Cf. Broadribb ("Thoughts," 24–25), who identifies some twenty-four points of contact, including the following: šîr ("song") is used in the titles of both works; Cant 3:11 attests to a "conjunction of coronation and wedding," which is the focus of the entire psalm; ʾîš ḥarbô ʿal-yĕrēkô ("each with his sword upon his thigh") in Cant 3:8 and ḥăgôr-ḥarbĕkâ ʿal-yārēk ("Gird your sword upon [your] thigh") in Ps 45:4; and shared attestation of relatively uncommon terms such as ʾăhālôt ("aloes"), ḥăbērîm ("companions"), keṭem ("gold"), and šôšān ("lily").

nature.[293]

For example, the elaborate divine speeches in Job 38—41 invoke dramatic natural imagery to depict the preeminent wisdom and providence of God, the creator: the raging sea, kept within bounds by divine decree; the cosmic sources of light and meteorological phenomena; the fixed orders of the constellations; and a bestiary that includes not only the fleet-footed ostrich but the monstrous forms of Behemoth and Leviathan.[294] What count here are divine power and design, so splendid that they dwarf the capacity of humankind to understand fully its environment or to control it. The phenomena of nature provoke amazement, but they also contain valuable—though not always welcome—theological lessons that human beings can deduce through diligent scrutiny. Similarly, the sage known as Qohelet is presented as an astute observer of the natural order. In the marvelous poem that begins the book, he directs attention to the endless succession of human generations and to the relentless movements of sun, wind, and water, although only to support his contention that all human industry is futile, "vanity" (Eccl 1:2–11; cf. 3:10–15, etc.).[295] It is typical of Qohelet's melancholic wisdom to warn that even observation of nature can be overdone (Eccl 11:4), thereby offering an implicit critique of more traditional practitioners of the sapiential approach to life. The latter delighted in articulating what they learned from nature:

the extraordinary diligence of the ant, for example (Prov 6:6–8), or the insight that small, if not beautiful, is at least not a handicap to becoming wise (Prov 30:24–28).

The Song does not scrutinize nature in this scholastic manner.[296] Lessons from the natural order are still heard and appreciated, but more as musical accompaniment to the inner stirrings of a human heart. The difference is between knowing about and feeling, between diligently analyzing and sensually participating in the texture of life. The Song's side of this perspectival contrast is illustrated by the poem in 2:10–13. The observations that winter's grip has been broken, that the sights and sounds of nature have signaled the onset of spring, are made to embellish an invitation: the season when love beckons most urgently has arrived.

Throughout the Song, references to the physical world abound. Indeed, the poetry presents a far more detailed onomasticon of natural phenomena than any work of traditional wisdom preserved in the canonical and deuterocanonical scriptures. Here are invoked a panoply of trees, fruits, flowers, and exotic spices (e.g., 1:17; 2:1–3, 13, 15; 4:13–14; 5:13; 6:2–3, 11; 7:9[8], 13–14[12–13]); birds and beasts (e.g., 1:9, 15; 2:9, 12, 17; 4:1–2, 5, 8; 5:11–12); stones, wind, and water (e.g., 4:15–16; 5:2, 14–15; 8:7); times, seasons, and places (e.g., 1:7; 2:11; 4:6; 5:2; 6:4, 10; 7:5[4]). But what comes to the fore is the sensory delight that such varied phe-

---

293 Cf. Roland E. Murphy, "The Hebrew Sage and Openness to the World," *Christian Actions and Openness to the World* (ed. Joseph Papin; Villanova: Villanova University, 1970) 219–44.

294 An illuminating discussion of the nature imagery in these chapters of Job is offered by Robert Alter, *The Art of Biblical Poetry* (New York: Basic Books, 1985) 85–110.

295 Cf. Edwin M. Good, "The Unfilled Sea: Style and Meaning in Ecclesiastes 1:2–11," *Israelite Wisdom: Theological and Literary Essays in Honor of Samuel Terrien* (ed. John G. Gammie *et al.*; Missoula:

Scholars, 1978) 59–73; and, in the same volume, Hans-Jürgen Hermisson, "Observations on the Creation Theology in Wisdom," 43–57.

296 Cf. Angel Gonzáles, "El lenguaje de la naturaleza en el Cantar de los Cantares," *EstBib* 25 (1966) 242–82.

nomena provide and how experiencing them illuminates the intimate pleasures of love. Hence emphasis falls not only on beauty that the eye beholds (e.g., 1:10–11; 6:4, 10) but on the joys of tasting (e.g., 2:3; 4:16; 5:1; 7:10[9]; 8:2), smelling (e.g., 1:3; 4:10–11; 7:14[13]), hearing (2:14; 8:13), and touching (5:5; 7:9[8]; 8:3).

Contrasting attitudes toward natural existence are also evident, of course, in the ways that wisdom literature and the Song deal with matters of human sexuality. In the book of Proverbs, as generally elsewhere in biblical literature, women play secondary roles and are usually depicted against a moral background that represents masculine values.[297] The point is well-illustrated by the acrostic poem in Prov 31:10–31, which portrays "the good wife" who is hard to find. She is idealized, but in terms that bear no resemblance to the subjective idealizations of the woman's charms in the Song (e.g., 4:1–16). What matters to the sage is neither the wife's gracefulness nor her beauty, apparently not even in the eye of her husband: "Charm is deceptive, and beauty is an illusion" (v 31a). Praise for her is rather elicited on account of her sagacity in business affairs, her industriousness at home and in the marketplace, her skill in managing the household, and the acts of charity she performs—all of which she does to enhance the wealth and reputation of her husband. There are no innuendos of sexual enjoyment here, nor is "love" mentioned. The measure of the "good wife" is "her net worth" (mikrāh); for the man who is able to find and wed her, she is like having an unlimited line of credit at the bank (v 10a). A husband can expect to gain "wind-fall profits" (šālāl,

literally "spoil, plunder") if he puts his trust in such a wife (v 11).

Language similar to that employed in the Song does appear in the early chapters of Proverbs, but the contrast is scarcely diminished. Physical allure and skill in lovemaking are traits of the "alien woman" (zārâ, nŏkriyyâ) caricatured in Prov 7:5–27 (cf. also 5:20).[298] The words of entrapment that she speaks (7:14–20) seem to echo themes and motifs of the Song, but here, interestingly, the erotic subtlety of the Song's language is lost. Like a common harlot (cf. vv 10–13), she has come out to "search for" and "find" a lover (v 15; cf. Cant 3:1–4; 5:6). Her bed has already been prepared for the tryst, perfumed with "myrrh, aloes, and cinnamon" (v 15; cf. Cant 4:14; 5:5). She promises a night-long bout of intoxicating love (v 18; cf. Cant 7:12–13[11–12]), because—as we only learn at the end of her speech (vv 19–20)—her husband is out of town on a business trip. In short, her interest in sex is lascivious; it is an invitation to adultery and the way to perdition (vv 21–27). In Prov 5:18–19, to be sure, marital sex is commended in somewhat similar terms; the wife is even described as "a lively hind, a graceful doe," which reminds us of language in the Song (e.g., 4:5), though in this case the primary concern is to praise her fidelity to the husband and to encourage him to remain faithful to her.

In the poetry of the Song there is no such moralizing. Human sexual love is treated as something beautiful and desirable in itself. Perhaps the sages eventually learned this lesson, too, if the aphorisms in 8:6–7 ("Strong as

---

297 Cf. the fine overview provided by Phyllis Bird, "Images of Women in the Old Testament," *Religion and Sexism: Images of Woman in the Jewish and Christian Traditions* (ed. Rosemary Radford Ruether; New York: Simon and Schuster, 1974) 41–88.

298 Cf. Roland E. Murphy, "Wisdom and Eros in Proverbs 1–9," *CBQ* 50 (1988) 600–603.

death is love . . .") are to be attributed to them.[299] But nowhere else in the Hebrew Bible does the intimate pleasure—at once exquisitely naive and profound—of mutual love between man and woman come to expression as in the Song.

Gillis Gerleman makes an interesting observation in this regard, to support his characterization of the Song as lyric poetry that expresses the emotions of the poet.[300] He notes that adjectives appear in the text only about forty times, a proportional representation generally in accord with biblical Hebrew style. But contrary to the norm in biblical Hebrew literature, relatively few of the adjectives employed in the Song are impersonal (such as terms for size, shape, color, and number). Most carry affective meanings and are used quite sparingly elsewhere: *yāpeh / yāpâ*, "beautiful," with eleven occurrences (1:8, 15, 16; 2:10, 13; 4:1, 7; 5:9; 6:1, 4, 10); *nā'weh / nā'wâ*, "lovely, pleasant," used four times (1:5; 2:14; 4:3; 6:4); *ṭôb / ṭôbîm [min]*, "goodly, better, more pleasing [than]," attested three times (1:2, 3; 7:10[9]; cf. 4:10); *'ăyūmmâ*, "awe-inspiring," appearing twice (6:4, 10); as well as single occurrences of *nā'îm*, "pleasant, delightful" (1:16), *mātôq*, "sweet" (2:3), and *'ārēb*, "pleasant" (2:14).

So strongly marked is the Song's perspective in comparison with views attested elsewhere in scripture that one is pressed to ask if the author may have been a woman; and surely she was, at least in part.[301] It is the female protagonist, rather than the male, who speaks the majority of the lines, and she reveals her feelings more fully than does he.[302]

Metaphorical Description, Comparison, and Allusion. Nothing is more characteristic of the Song's exuberant portrait of human love than the wealth of metaphorical imagery it draws upon to depict the physical charms, delights, and desires of the lovers themselves. Nor has any other aspect of the poetry given more enjoyment or presented greater challenge to interpreters, ancient and modern alike.

Not infrequently, comparisons take the form of simple juxtaposition of subjects and metaphorical predicates, as in the following examples: *šemen tûraq šĕmekā*, "flowing perfume, your name" (1:3); *'ênaik yônîm*, "your eyes [are] doves" (1:15; 4:1); *'ănî ḥăbaṣṣelet haššārôn šôšannat hā'ămāqîm*, "I [am] a flower of Sharon, a lily of the valleys" (2:1); *śip(ĕ)tôtāw šôšannîm not(ĕ)pôt môr 'obēr*, "his lips, lilies that drip flowing myrrh" (5:13). Somewhat more common, though, is the simile proper, which prefixes the prepositional comparative *kĕ-* to the predicate: *kĕpelaḥ hārimmôn raqqātēk mibba'ad lĕṣammātēk*, "Like a cut of pomegranate, your cheek behind your veil" (4:3); *'ênāw kĕyônîm*, "his eyes, like doves" (5:12); and, more elaborately, *kĕšôšannâ bên haḥôḥîm kēn ra'yātî bên habbānôt*, "As a lily among thorns, so is my friend among women [daughters]" (2:2). This formal differ-

---

299 Cf. Nicolas J. Tromp, "Wisdom and the Canticle. Ct 8,6c–7b: text, character, message and import," *La Sagesse de l'Ancien Testament* (ed. Maurice Gilbert; BETL 51; Gembloux: J. Duculot, 1979) 94.
300 Gerleman, 53.
301 Cf. Phyllis Trible, *God and the Rhetoric of Sexuality* (OBT 2; Philadelphia: Fortress, 1978) 145; and Athalya Brenner, *The Israelite Woman: Social Role and Literary Type in Biblical Literature* (The Biblical Seminar; Sheffield: JSOT Press/University of Sheffield, 1985) 46–50.
302 See above, p. 64 n. 287. Fox's observation is cogent (309): "The Song is *her* song, and there is no scene from which she is absent. . . . All events are narrated from her point of view, though not always in her voice, whereas from the boy's angle of vision we know little besides how he sees her."

ence, it should be noted, does not enable us to distinguish between literal (e.g., 'ănî šĕḥarḥōret, "I am blackish" [1:6]) and metaphorical descriptions. In a number of instances, generally where the metaphor is further developed, forms of the verb dāmâ ("to be like, resemble" [Qal], "to compare" [Pi'el]) are used to make the object of the comparison explicit: lĕsusātî bĕrik(e)bê par'ōh dimmîtîk ra'yātî . . . , "To a mare of Pharaoh's chariots I compare you, my friend . . ." (1:9); dômeh dôdî liṣ(ĕ)bî 'ô lĕ'ōper hā'ayyālîm . . . , "My lover is like a gazelle, or a young stag . . ." (2:9); sōb dĕmēh-lĕkâ dôdî liṣ(ĕ)bî . . . , "Turn, my lover; be like a gazelle . . ." (2:17; cf. 8:14); zō't qômātēk dāmĕtâ lĕtāmār . . . , "Your very stature is like a palm tree . . ." (7:8[7]). Extensions may also be attached to the basic metaphor by use of the preposition 'im ("with"), as in 4:13–14.

In most of the Song's metaphors and similes, the basis of comparison (tertium comparationis) between the subject or referent and the selected image seems straightforward but not necessarily or even typically one-dimensional. Color and form are involved in many instances.[303] For example, the man likens the woman's lips to a "scarlet thread" and her veiled cheeks to slices of pomegranate (4:3); she in turn describes his hair as "black as a raven" (5:11) and compares his legs to alabaster columns (5:14). Even in essentially representational comparisons, however, a poetic playfulness is often evident, nuancing realism with suggestions of voluptuousness, unusual vitality, gracefulness, and the like.[304] When the woman compares herself to the "tents of Qedar" and Solomon's "pavilions" (1:5) she takes advantage of the color of her sun-darkened skin to emphasize her own unusual beauty. The comparison of her hair to a flock of goats apparently has in view both color (black) and texture or flowing movement (4:1). Perhaps for ancient oriental as well as modern western ears the similitude between the ordered whiteness of the woman's teeth and rows of newly washed sheep intends to sound a pleasant note of whimsy (4:2). Her exotic, ornamented splendor certainly comes to the fore in playful fashion when the man likens her to "a mare of Pharaoh's chariots," outfitted with beads and golden pendants (1:9–10). The metaphor of the palm with date-clusters is intelligible enough as a representation of the woman's full-bosomed stateliness, but the sense becomes more explicitly erotic when the man

---

303 Especially so in the waṣfs (poems of descriptive praise of a lover's physique): 4:1–7; 5:10–16; 6:4–7; 7:1–7 [6:13—7:6]. Although Gillis Gerleman recognized the affective character of the Song's metaphors in these texts, he argued that the specific imagery of the waṣfs reflects the particular artistic traditions of form and color used in ancient Egyptian statuary ("Die Bildersprache des Hohenliedes und die altägyptische Kunst," ASTI 1 [1962] 24–30; and his commentary, esp. 53–59 and 224–27). An important response, emphasizing the "presentational" rather than "representational" character of the imagery, was offered by Richard N. Soulen, "The Waṣf of the Song of Songs and Hermeneutic," JBL 86 (1967) 183–90. Cf. Fox, 274: ". . . since the Egyptian love poets themselves did not take their imagery from Egyptian art, it is most unlikely that the poet of Canticles would have

turned to it as a prime source of imagery."

304 Cf. Morris [Moshe] Hirsch Segal, "The Song of Songs," VT 12 (1962) 480: "[The Song] abounds in playfulness, in gentle raillery and fun, mingled with touching sentiments of love and tenderness." Recently, Enrica Salvaneschi (Cantico dei Cantici: Interpretatio ludica [Genova: Melangolo, 1982]) has moved beyond literal analysis of the Song's metaphorical terminology in an effort to identify the "metalanguage" of the poetry; she subjects several terms to a "playful analysis" (interpretatio ludica) within the biblical range of meanings.

expresses his intention to climb the tree and take hold of its branches in order to enjoy its choice fruits (7:8–9[7–8]).[305]

In more than a few instances, however, the *tertium comparationis* is not immediately obvious or seems to involve likenesses that strike the literal-minded modern reader as comical, even grotesque. An often noted case in point is the overburdened metaphor for the woman's neck in 4:4:

> Like David's tower, your neck,
>> built in courses;

A thousand shields hang upon it,
>> all the weapons of warriors.

Such exaggerated simile fueled allegorical interpretation in earlier times.[306] Some recent critics have supposed that the comparison means to portray not the visual appearance of the woman's garlanded neck but her proud and pure inaccessibility;[307] others suggest that the physical proportions of the metaphor are mythological and hence only intelligible if the female in question is a goddess.[308]

Similitudes using natural imagery are not always

---

305 Descriptions in the Song's *waṣfs* of the lower human torso and genitalia use subtle imagery that seems to heighten the erotic effect. The pertinent region of the female anatomy is described as follows (7:3[2]):

> Your valley, a round bowl
>> that is not to lack mixed wine.
> Your belly, a heap of wheat,
>> surrounded with lilies.

For comparable, but more explicit, imagery in the Sumerian love poems, see above, pp. 54–55. The Song's terse depiction of the male genital region in 5:14b employs some difficult terminology: *mēʿāw ʿešet šēn měʿullepet sappîrîm*. The first term usually refers in biblical Hebrew to internal organs of digestion and procreation; its use here for external anatomy seems to mean "belly" or more specifically "loins" (cf. Pope, 543). While *ʿešet* is a hapax in biblical Hebrew (cf. the verb, connoting "smoothness," in Jer 5:28), rabbinic sources understood the term to refer to a smooth "bar," "pillar" or "column," e.g., comparable to the shape of a scroll (cf. *Cant. Rab.* 5:14.2 [Simon, 246]; and Marcus Jastrow, *A Dictionary of the Targumim, the Talmud Babli and Yerushalmi, and the Midrashic Literature* [New York: Pardes, 1950] 1128). Rather than "covered with sapphires" or the like, the final two words may be literally rendered "ensconced in lapis lazuli." With the translation that these readings yield ("His loins, a shaft of ivory, ensconced in lapis lazuli") one may compare the following praise of male virility in one of the Sumerian love poems (Jacobsen, *Harps*, 98 ["Tavern Sketch"]):

> O my pure pillar, my pure pillar
> sweet are your charms
> Pillar of alabaster set in lapis lazuli
> sweet are your charms.

306 E.g., *Cant. Rab.* 4:4.9 (Simon, 196): "Just as a man's neck is the highest part of him, so the Temple was the highest part of the world. And just as most ornaments are hung round the neck, so the priests were attached to the Temple, the Levites were attached to the Temple." Recent literary criticism may be in process of "rediscovering" and appreciating anew the affective, allusive aspects of the Song's language and rich poetic imagery which gave rise to early Christian and Jewish allegorical readings. In this regard, see Albert Cook, *The Root of the Thing: A Study of Job and the Song of Songs* (Bloomington/London: Indiana University, 1968) 99–151, with appreciative attention given to the work of Paul Claudel. See now also Harold Fisch, *Poetry with a Purpose: Biblical Poetics and Interpretation* (Bloomington/Indianapolis: Indiana University, 1988) 80–103 (with the section entitled, interestingly, "Song of Solomon: The Allegorical Imperative"); note esp. 95: "It seems that there is no way to avoid interpretation and that interpretation—especially in a poem so dreamlike in its symbolism—will tend to partake of the nature of allegory. This is true of all poetry and of all interpretations of poems. It is more compellingly true of the Song of Solomon. If the ancients had not already taken this path, modern literary critics would certainly have felt obliged to do so."

307 For the development of this approach, see Thorlief Boman, *Hebrew Thought compared with Greek* (tr. Jules

transparently representational in meaning. The "garden" and "vineyard" metaphors for the woman (e.g., 4:12–16) convey a sense of her blossoming sexuality and, at least in part, are euphemistic. Comparison of the man to a "gazelle or a young stag" suggests his youthful beauty and swiftness but also perhaps his untamed freedom as far as the woman is concerned (2:8–9; 8:14).

Hans-Peter Müller discerns what he calls "semantic dissonance" between referent and physical imagery in many such cases; he argues that the *tertium comparationis* is aesthetic rather than literal, with the poetic language having a magical function that seeks to affirm the illusive spiritual bond between the realms of natural and human beauty.[309] In similar fashion, Othmar Keel has recently proposed a "dynamic interpretation" of the Song's metaphorical comparisons, requiring functional analysis of both the referents and the natural images invoked.[310] For example, to grasp how human "eyes" are comparable to "doves" (1:15; 4:1; 5:12) one must recognize that in

biblical usage the eye is not simply a static organ of sight but a mode of emotional communication, here connoting "glance." Moreover, since "doves" are associated with love goddesses in ancient Near Eastern iconography, Keel argues that they function metaphorically here as vehicles of ardor, which yields his paraphrastic translation: "Your glances are messengers of love."[311] Similarly, while comparison of the woman's "nose" (*'ap*) to a "(fortified) tower of Lebanon, looking toward Damascus" (7:5[4]) seems "grotesque" if taken literally,[312] Keel argues that the simile has to do not with the woman's unusually large or misshapen snout but her prideful carriage, haughtiness, teasing petulance, or the like.[313] A considerably more elaborate decoding is needed to understand how her breasts are comparable to "two fawns, the twins of a gazelle, browsing among the lilies" (4:5). According to Keel, this complex metaphor pertains to the graceful movement of her young bosom but also evokes iconographic images of gazelles and lilies, which

---

L. Moreau; Philadelphia: Westminster, 1960) 76–84. Keel (*Metaphorik*, 33–39 and esp. 38) pursues the same line and paraphrases the sense of the simile as follows: Unzugänglich wie der Davidsturm ist deine stolze Haltung ("Inaccessible as David's tower is your proud bearing").

308 Pope, 465: "The size of the damsel's neck stretches poetic hyperbole a bit as applied to a peasant lass or any earthly creature. . . . If the lady is divine, her proportions would not be abnormal."

309 Hans-Peter Müller, *Vergleich und Metapher im Hohenlied* (OBO 56; Freiburg Schweiz: Universitätsverlag; Göttingen: Vandenhoeck & Ruprecht, 1984). Cf. also Fox (274–77 and 328–30) who draws upon the hermeneutical work of Colin Martindale and Paul Ricoeur, invoking the principle of "metaphoric distance" in his analysis of the Song's more exaggerated comparisons (e.g., 7:3–5[2–4]). According to this approach, the incongruent distance between the anatomical referent and the image emphasizes the image itself; the cumulative effect of such images is ". . . to form a cohesive picture of a

self-contained world . . ." in which expressions of human love become transcendently real (329–30). Cf. now also Daniel Grossberg, *Centripetal and Centrifugal Structures in Biblical Poetry* (SBLMS 39; Atlanta: Scholars, 1989) 61–68.

310 Keel, *Metaphorik;* although he makes important use of Egyptian, Syrian, and Mesopotamian artistic evidence to illuminate the Song's imagery, Keel argues that a Palestinian provenance for the composition is supported by its use of geographical terms and references to Palestinian arts and crafts (textiles in 1:5; 4:3; 7:6[5]; jewelry in 1:10–11; cf. also 5:14–15 and 7:2[1]).

311 Keel, *Metaphorik*, 53–62 and 142–52 (figs. 36–55).

312 So, e.g., Rudolph, 173.

313 Keel, *Metaphorik*, 33.

together symbolize renewal of life, the triumph of natural and human vitality over the power of death.[314] Even if the recent approaches of Müller, Keel, and others are not always convincing in their specific interpretations, they encourage modern critics to move beyond banal or woodenly literalistic interpretations of the Song's enchanting images.

Peculiarities of Grammar and Lexicon. The Song displays an unusual profile of grammatical and lexical features. It may be noted that these features are distributed fairly evenly throughout the poetry; hence they provide no firm basis either for making distinctions among the individual poems—e.g., as regards provenance, date of composition, and authorship—or for identifying likely editorial accretions to the corpus. Moreover, while individual features of the profile have counterparts in "earlier" biblical Hebrew literature, their cumulative effect is to suggest postexilic composition, and possibly as late as the end of the Persian period.[315]

The Song's most striking grammatical peculiarity is regular use of the proclitic particle *še-/šel* and, conversely, absence of the relative *'ăšer*, except for a singular occurrence in the editorial superscription of 1:1. Among the books of the Hebrew Bible, the total of thirty-two occurrences of this proclitic in the Song is exceeded only by the sixty-seven attestations in Ecclesiastes (where, however, *'ăšer* is also and even more extensively employed as a relative marker). Earlier criticism seized upon the usage as an indication of Aramaic influence and a sign of late composition or editing, especially since the particle is also well attested in "Mishnaic Hebrew."[316] Such judgments are rendered problematic by the ostensibly early testimony to the particle in the "Song of Deborah" (Judg 5:7) and by comparative Semitic evidence, which may point to the presence in both the Song and Ecclesiastes of a north-Israelite dialect influenced by Phoenician.[317] In general, however, the Song's nimble use of *še-/šel* finds its closest parallels in postexilic Hebrew literature. In terms of function, the specific occurrences of the particle in the Song may be classified as follows.[318]

a) In combination with the preposition *lě*, *šel* is used to express possession (i.e., functioning as does *'ăšer lě* in the superscription, 1:1): *karmî šellî*, "My vineyard *which is* mine" = "My own vineyard" (1:6; 8:12); *miṭṭātô šelliš(ě)lōmōh*, "his litter *which is* Solomon's" = "Solomon's litter" (3:7).

b) The particle appears as a relative pronoun to introduce clauses serving as descriptive modifiers: *še'iṭṭěrâ-lô 'immô*, "*with which* his mother crowned him" (3:11); *šeggālěšû mēhar gil'ād*, "*that* stream down from Gilead" (4:1; 6:5); *še'ālû min-hāraḥṣâ*, "*that* come up from the washing" (4:2a; 6:6a); *šekkullām mat'îmôt*, "all of them in pairs" (4:2b; 6:6b); *bayyôm šeyyědubbar-bāh*, "on the day *that* she will be spoken for" (8:8).

c) When attached directly to nouns and pronouns, the particle may have a causal or resultative sense (in either case functioning like the particle *kî* in general Hebrew usage): *'al-tir'ûnî še'ănî šěḥarḥōret šeššězāpatěnî haššāmeš*, "Do not stare at me *because* I am blackish, *for* the sun has burned me" (1:6); *šerrō'šî nimlā'-ṭāl*, "*for* my head is wet with dew" (5:2); *šekkākâ hišba'tānû*, "*that* you adjure us so"

---

314 Keel, *Metaphorik*, 81–88 and 168–72 (figs. 83–93).

315 Cf. Broadribb, "Thoughts," 29–33.

316 Segal, "Song," 478 and 484–85; and also Wagner, *Aramaismen*, 110–11.

317 Cf. Mitchell J. Dahood, "Canaanite-Phoenician Influence in Qoheleth," *Bib* 33 (1952) 44–45.

318 Cf. Broadribb, "Thoughts," 31–32 (but there is a disconcertingly large number of errors in the biblical citations); and Ronald J. Williams, *Hebrew Syntax: An Outline* (Toronto/Buffalo: University of Toronto, ²1976) 76–78.

(5:9); *šehēm hirhîbūnî*, *"for* they disturb me" (6:5).

d) Related to the category above is a particular "recitative" usage, to introduce a quotation (cf. *'ăšer*, 1 Sam 15:20): *šeḥolat 'ahăbâ 'ănî*, *"that* I am sick with love!" (5:8b).

e) In a set expression, used by the woman to designate her lover, the particle is employed with quasi-demonstrative force to nominalize or substantivize a verbal construction: *še'āhăbâ napšî*, *"the one whom* my soul loves" (1:7; 3:1, 2, 3, 4).

f) Finally, in a significant number of cases the particle is construed with *'ad* (cf. Aramaic *'ad-dî* [Dan 7:4, 9, 11; etc.]) in temporal statements: *'ad-šehammelek bim(ě)sibbô*, *"While* the king was in his enclosure" (1:12); *'ad šettehpāṣ*, *"until* it [love] be ready" (2:7; 3:5; 8:4); *'ad šeyyāpûaḥ hayyôm*, *"until* the day breathes" (2:17; 4:6); *kim(ě)'aṭ še'ābartî mēhem 'ad šemmāṣā'tî 'ēt še'āhăbâ napšî*, "I had *hardly* left them *when* I found him whom my soul loves" (3:4a); *'ad-šehăbê'tîw 'el-bêt 'immî*, *"until* I brought him to the house of my mother" (3:4b).

Especially when one considers its modest length and repetitious character, the Song exhibits an extraordinarily large number of uniquely attested terms (hapax legomena), as well as many other words and forms that make only rare appearances elsewhere in biblical Hebrew literature. Statistics Frederick Greenspahn compiled in a recent study indicate that among all books of the Hebrew Bible the Song has the highest percentage of its total vocabulary comprised of "absolute hapax legomena" (i.e., terms that are not only unique but apparently represent verbal roots otherwise unattested in biblical Hebrew).[319]

Greenspahn identifies a total of thirty-seven hapax legomena in the Song; in the sequential list that follows, the fourteen forms built on terms that he classifies as "absolute hapax legomena" are prefixed with asterisks: *šěharhōret* (1:6); *nihărû* (1:6); *gědiyyōtaik* (1:8); *lěsūsātî* (1:9); **hărûzîm* (1:10); *něquddôt* (1:11); *raḥîtēnû* (1:17); **běrôtîm* (1:17); **kŏtlēnû* (2:9); *hahărakkîm* (2:9); **hassětāw* (2:11); *hanniṣṣānîm* (2:12); *hazzāmîr* (2:12); **paggêhâ* (2:13); *'abqat* (3:6); **'appiryôn* (3:9); *rěpîdātô* (3:10); *rāṣûp* (3:10); *hătūnnātô* (3:11); **talpiyyôt* (4:4); *miṣṣawwěrōnaik* (4:9); **karkōm* (4:14); **'ăṭanněpēm* (5:3); *taltallîm* (5:11); *millē't* (5:12); *merqāḥîm* (5:13); *'ešet* (5:14); **'ěgôz* (6:11); *hammûqê* (7:2[1]); *'ammān* (7:2[1]); *hassahar* (7:3[2]); **hammāzeg* (7:3[2]); *sûgâ* (7:3[2]); **sansinnāw* (7:9[8]); *dôbēb* (7:10); *hāreqaḥ* (8:2); **mitrappeqet* (8:5). At least reasonable sense can be made of the majority of these hapax legomena, using internal evidence supplied by immediate context of usage (e..g, congruity of theme and parallelism) together with renderings in the ancient versions and data from cognate Semitic languages and literatures. In a few cases, however, translation remains very uncertain or merely approximate; prime examples are: *hărûzîm* ("beads"?) in 1:10; *talpiyyôt* ("courses [of a tower built of stones]"?) in 4:4; and *taltallîm* ("palm fronds"?) in 5:11.

The vocabulary of the Song also includes a significant number of items that cannot formally be classified as hapax legomena but that apparently have unique senses or nuances in comparison with usage elsewhere in biblical Hebrew. Among such cases may be noted use of the root *qpṣ* with the sense of "leaping" in 2:8 (*měqappēṣ*)

---

319 Frederick E. Greenspahn, *Hapax Legomena in Biblical Hebrew: A Study of the Phenomenon and Its Treatment Since Antiquity with Special Reference to Verbal Forms* (SBLDS 74; Chico: Scholars, 1984) esp. 23–29 and 183–99. Note, however, the following corrections to his survey of the data: *rpydh* appears in Cant 3:10 rather than 3:20 (197); the citation of *rhyt* for Cant 1:10 is erroneous (197; but correctly listed as *rhyt*, 186); the calculation of the Song's deviation from the biblical norm should be based on thirty-seven rather than thirty-six "actual hapax legomena" (199).

and the Puʿal participle of *qṭr* in 3:6 to refer to the fragrance of myrrh and frankincense (*mĕquṭṭeret*). Similarly, while the noun *degel* ("standard, banner") is reasonably well attested (cf. *diglô* in 2:4), the cognate forms *dāgûl* ("outstanding, conspicuous") in 5:10 and *nidgālôt* ("visions"?) in 6:4, 10 are unique. Or again, the rare verbal root *ḥnṭ* is used in 2:13 (*ḥānĕṭâ*) to connote the fragrant ripening of figs on the tree; the two other attestations of the root in biblical Hebrew refer specifically to embalming of corpses (Gen 50:2, 26). An interesting example of metaphorical nuance is the use of the root *šzp* (to "look upon" with the eye in Job 20:9 and 28:7) in 1:6 to describe how the woman has been affected by prolonged exposure to the sun: i.e., she is black or darkly tanned because the sun has "looked upon" her (*šĕzāpatĕnî*).

Among terms that appear two or more times in the Song, but rarely or not at all elsewhere in biblical Hebrew, the following may be noted: the repeated epithet *raʿyātî*, "my friend" (1:9, 15; 2:2, 10, 13; 4:1, 7; 5:2; 6:4); *ṭôrîm / ṭôrê*, "pendants" (1:10, 11); *kōper / kĕpārîm*, "henna" (1:14; 4:13); *sĕmādar*, "bloom, blossoms" (2:13, 15; 7:13[12]); *ʿōper / ʿŏpārîm* to connote "young" stags (2:9, 17; 4:5; 7:4[3]; 8:14); *raḥṣâ*, "washing [of sheep]" (4:2; 6:6); and the verb *gālĕšû* (from *glš*, "stream, flow") in 4:1 and 6:5.

There are also cases in the Song where translation of

terms is possible, but the precise sense remains elusive— for example, *hārê bāter* ("mountains of separation"?) in 2:17.

B. Literary Topoi

If the grammatical and lexical profile of the Song suggests common authorship of the poetry, the impression of homogeneity is considerably strengthened by the presence throughout the work of formulae and other literary topoi. With the exception of Ecclesiastes, no other book of the Bible so amply displays verbal and thematic repetitions. Here we will observe several broad categories of usage summarizing the primary evidence.[320]

Refrains. There are five notable refrains in the Song.[321] These can be recognized as instances of simple reprise, in which a significant expression or cluster of terms occurs two or more times. Functionally, the refrains underscore important themes and, in most cases, serve conspicuously as literary structure-signals.[322]
a) The lengthy first-person adjuration about the awakening of love, addressed by the woman to the "Daughters of Jerusalem," appears identically in 2:7 and 3:5, and a third time with only minor variations in 8:4:

> *hišbaʿtî ʾetekem bĕnôt yĕrûšālaim . . .*
> *ʾim/mah-tāʿîrû wĕʾim/mah-tĕʿôrĕrû ʾet-hāʾahăbâ ʿad šettehpāṣ*

---

320 The discussion in this section draws upon an earlier study: Roland E. Murphy, "The Unity of the Song of Songs," *VT* 29 (1979) 436–43; cf. also *idem*, "Towards a Commentary on the Song of Songs," *CBQ* 39 (1977) 482–96. For another approach to the unity of the Song, emphasizing "the rhythm of recurrence of association," see Francis Landy, "Beauty and the Enigma: An Inquiry into Some Interrelated Episodes of the Song of Songs," *JSOT* 17 (1980) 55–106; and *idem, Paradoxes of Paradise: Identity and Difference in the Song of Songs* (BLS; Sheffield: Almond, 1983).

321 With the following enumeration of the Song's refrains may be compared the analytical chart of Loretz, 60. He identifies eight refrains, though several are fragmentary or otherwise questionable (esp. no. 1, comprised of references to the "Daughters of Jerusalem," and no. 6, attested only by 5:1e-f). Specific correlations are: refrain a) below = Loretz no. 3; b) = no. 2; d) = no. 4; e) = nos. 5, 7, 8; refrain c) is not represented in Loretz's chart. Cf. also Feuillet, 38–87, who attempts to connect the Song's refrains to thematic topoi attested in other scriptural sources.

I adjure you, O Daughters of Jerusalem, . . .

Do not arouse, do not stir up love, until it be ready!
Each of these occurrences marks what many commentators have judged to be the conclusion of a major poetic unit in the Song. Closely evocative of this particular refrain is a fourth adjuration, also addressed by the woman to the Daughters, in 5:8:

hišbaʿtî ʾetekem běnôt yěrûšālāim

ʾim-timṣěʾû ʾet-dôdî mah-taggîdû lô

šeḥôlat ʾahăbâ ʾānî

I adjure you, O Daughters of Jerusalem:
If you find my lover, what shall you say to him?
That I am sick with love!

b) A refrain on the motif of embracing occurs twice, in 2:6 and 8:3:

śěmōʾlô taḥat (lě)rōʾšî wîmînô těḥabběqēnî

His left hand is under my head,
  and his right hand embraces me.

Significantly, each instance immediately precedes an occurrence of the adjuration refrain noted above. Although the embracing refrain per se is not found before the adjuration in 3:5, it may be observed that 3:4 does express a comparable notion, as the woman speaks of taking hold of the man and not letting him go until she has brought him into her mother's house and bedchamber.

c) The interrogative expression *mî zōʾt* ("Who is this?") is attested three times in the Song (3:6; 6:10; 8:5). In 3:6 and 8:5 it serves to announce or hail a party "coming up from the desert"—more specifically, Solomon's splendid litter, accompanied by a contingent of warriors (3:6–8), and the woman "leaning upon her lover" (8:5). In these cases the refrain seems to mark the beginning of poetic units, and it is perhaps significant that both are preceded by occurrences of the adjuration refrain. The third

instance, in 6:10, introduces a cry of admiration for the woman, apparently voiced by a host of "maidens," "queens," and "concubines" (6:8–9).

d) There are three occurrences of a "possession refrain," in each case spoken by the woman (2:16; 6:3; 7:11[10]). The first two are found at the end of poetic units and exhibit slight variation in wording, apparently for emphasis:

dôdî lî waʾănî lô

My lover is mine and I am his (2:16);

ʾănî lědôdî wědôdî lî

I am my lover's, and my lover is mine (6:3).

The third occurrence has a more interesting variation, making reference to the man's "desire" (*těšûqâ*, cf. Gen 3:16):

ʾănî lědôdî wěʿālay těšûqātô

I am my lover's, and toward me is his desire
  (7:11[10]).

e) A more complex refrain, involving collocations of a number of key words and motifs, can be identified in 2:17 (cf. 2:8b–9a!); 4:6; and 8:14, the concluding verse of the Song:

ʿad šeyyāpûaḥ hayyôm wěnāsû haṣṣělālîm

sōb děmēh-lěkâ dôdî liṣ(ě)bî ʾô lěʿōper hāʾayyālîm

ʿal-hārê bāter

Until the day breathes and the shadows flee,
Turn, my lover; be like a gazelle or a young stag,
upon the mountains of Bether (2:17);

ʿad šeyyāpûaḥ hayyôm wěnāsû haṣṣělālîm

ʾēlek lî ʾel-har hammôr wě ʾel-gibʿat hallěbônâ

Until the day breathes and the shadows flee,
I shall go to the mountain of myrrh and the hill of
  incense (4:6);

běraḥ dôdî ûd(ě)mēh-lěkâ liṣ(ě)bî ʾô lěʿōper hāʾayyālîm

---

322 Fox (209–10) prefers the looser term "repetends" to "refrains"; but the latter designation seems justified by indications that the formulae are instructive of literary design and boundaries within the Song.

'al harê bĕśāmîm

Flee, my lover; be like a gazelle or a young stag,
upon the mountains of spices! (8:14).

The movement in the three variant forms of the refrain
is to the "mountain(s)" (har/harê); in the first and third
cases (2:17; 8:14), the metaphor of movement is the
"gazelle/young stag" (sĕbî/'ōper hā'ayyālîm); and the
time, "day/shadow" (yôm/sĕlālîm) is specified in the first
two instances (2:17; 4:6).

Themes and Motifs. There are other literary topoi that
lack the formulaic character of the refrains but attest to
important continuities and parallels in the Song. Among
such topoi, three may be identified as having thematic
significance, while the rest constitute more loosely-
related motifs.

a) The Garden of Love's Delights. Central to the poem
of admiration in 4:9–16a is comparison of the woman to
a luxuriant "garden" (gan) that produces choice fruits
and spices (vv 12–16a):

gan nā'ûl 'ăhōtî kallâ
ga⟨n⟩ nā'ûl ma'yān hātûm
šĕlāhaik pardēs rimmōnîm
'im pĕrî mĕgādîm
. . . . .
'ûrî ṣāpôn ûbô'î têmān
hāpîhî gannî yizzĕlû bĕśāmāw

A garden enclosed, my sister, bride,
a ⟨garden⟩ enclosed, a fountain sealed!
Your shoots, a paradise of pomegranates
with choice fruits:
. . . . .
Arise, north wind, and come south wind!
Blow upon my garden, that its spices may flow.

Immediately following this extended simile is an invitation, spoken by the woman (4:16b):

yābō' dôdî lĕgannô wĕyō'kal pĕrî mĕgādāw

Let my lover come to his garden
and eat its choice fruits.

This elicits a quick response from the man (5:1a):

bā'tî lĕgannî 'ăhōtî kallâ
'ārîtî môrî 'im-bĕśāmî
'ākaltî ya'rî 'im-dibšî
šātîtî yênî 'im-hălābî

I have come to my garden, my sister, bride!
I gather my myrrh with my spices.
I eat my honeycomb with my honey;
I drink my wine with my milk.

The garden theme is echoed twice more, and somewhat
enigmatically, in the Song, in words perhaps spoken
respectively by the woman and the man:

'el-ginnat 'ĕgôz yāradtî
lir'ôt bĕ'ibbê hannahal

To the nut-garden I came down
to see the fresh growth of the valley (6:11a);

hayyôšebet baggannîm
hăbērîm maqšibîm
lĕqôlēk hašmî'înî

You who dwell in the gardens,
friends are listening;
let me hear your voice! (8:13)

b) The Woman as Vineyard. Allied to the garden theme
is the imagery of vines and vineyards that appears
throughout the Song (1:6b, 14; 2:13, 15; 6:11; 7:9[8],
13[12]; 8:11–12). At least a number of these passages
comprise a theme (rather than simply a cluster of motifs)
because in the initial reference the woman refers to her
brothers' plans for her and then clearly refers to herself
as an untended vineyard (1:6b):

bĕnê 'immî niharû-bî
śāmūnî nōtērâ 'et-hakkĕrāmîm
karmî šellî lō' nātārtî

The sons of my mother were angry with me;
they assigned me as keeper of the vineyards—
my own vineyard I have not kept.

The woman may be making an implicit reference to
herself in 1:14, when she speaks of the "vineyards of

Engedi" (*karĕmê ʿên gedî*); and so also in 7:13[12], when she invites her lover to go with her "early to the vineyards," to discover "if the vines have budded" (cf. also 6:11). Though the sense of 2:15 remains enigmatic, "our vineyards in bloom" (*kĕrāmēnû sĕmādar*), which are being devastated by the little foxes, could be similarly interpreted. Finally, in 8:11–12 there can be no doubt that the woman is contrasting her own self (*šellî*) with Solomon's "vineyard."

c) The Theme of "Seeking/Finding." Two remarkably parallel units in 3:1–5 and 5:2–8 suffice to establish this theme, but other references can be related to it as well. The key passages describe nocturnal experiences, or possibly dreams, in which the woman rises from her bed to search in the city for her missing lover. In the first episode, her "seeking" (Piʿel of *bqš*) is mentioned four times (3:1–2), followed twice with the remark that she "did not find him" (*wĕlōʾ mĕṣāʾtîw*). Watchmen, making their rounds of the city, "find" her and she asks if they have seen the man; she then abruptly "finds" him and leads him to the bedchamber of her mother's house. In the second episode, the watchmen who "find" her during her futile search for the lover abuse her physically and remove or tear her outer garment (5:6–7). In 6:1, the Daughters volunteer to assist the woman in searching for the man:

   ʾānâ pānâ dôdēk ûnĕbaqĕšennû ʿimmāk

   Where has your lover turned, that we may seek him with you?

Her teasing response to this suggests that she needs no help from them or that the man is not really missing,

since he has gone down to browse in his garden and to gather lilies (6:2). The woman's request to know where her lover rests at midday and his instructions on how to find him (1:7–8a) may be connected with the broader theme. Finally, in 8:1–2 the woman expresses the wish that the lover were her "brother," so that if she "found" him in public she could greet him with a kiss and lead him to her mother's house, there to be instructed by him in love.

In addition to these three themes, there are four noteworthy motifs.

a) Love-sickness is mentioned twice, both times referring to the woman's intoxication with the man: *ḥôlat ʾahăbâ ʾānî*, "I am sick with love" (2:5; 5:8).

b) Twice the man invites the woman to come away with him: to witness the renewal of nature in the springtime (2:10–13);[323] and to visit the Lebanon (4:8). She invites him to come to "his garden and eat its choice fruits" (4:16b) and, later, to accompany her into the "field" and the "vineyards" to witness nature's blossoming and receive her love (7:12–13[11–12]). Her invitation is also implied in the refrain of 2:17 and 8:14.

c) "Lilies" (*šôšannîm*, singular *šôšān / šôšannâ*) figure prominently in the Song's metaphorical epithets and similes, apparently with a range of euphemistic and symbolical meanings.[324] In 2:1 the woman describes herself as "a lily of the valleys," an idea the man takes up immediately thereafter in praising her superlative beauty: "As a lily among thorns, so is my friend among women" (2:2). "He who browses among the lilies" is used as an epithet of the man in connection with the posses-

---

323 See further Norman H. Snaith, "The Song of Songs: The Dances of the Virgins," *AJSL* 50 (1933–34) 129–42, for a discussion of the poetic language appropriate to the Autumn and Spring passages which he identifies in the Song. His observations about the language and imagery are more important than the hypothesis concerning the origins of the poems. Cf. also Segal, "Song," 485–88.

324 For detailed discussion of the evidence, see Keel, *Metaphorik*, 63–78 and related illustrations.

sion refrain (2:16; 6:3), while in 6:2 he is said to have gone down to his garden "to gather lilies." In 7:3[2] the woman's lower abdomen is described as "surrounded with lilies," but in 4:5 (= 7:4[3]) her breasts are compared to twin fawns that "browse among the lilies." On the other hand, she describes his lips as "lilies that drip flowing myrrh" (5:13).

d) Although it seems hardly to constitute a significant motif in itself, "houses" are referred to frequently enough to merit mention here. The woman's maternal house appears twice as the place where she wishes to bring her lover (3:4; 8:2).[325] The house of the lovers is mentioned in 1:17; the woman also refers to a "house of wine" where the man took her for a tryst (2:4; cf. 1:4).

Characterizations and Principal Epithets. The case for the Song's essential unity hinges in no small measure on the consistency with which both major and significant minor characters are portrayed throughout the poetry. Our analysis recognizes only two chief protagonists, an unnamed young woman and her anonymous lover, who is apparently sketched in the guise of king as well as shepherd. A choruslike group of other women, referred to as the "Daughters of Jerusalem," also speaks on occasion; the only personage specifically named in the Song, "Solomon," appears to be peripherally related to the dialogic scenario and exchanges of the two lovers.

A woman, still in her youth, is the Song's focal character. It is she who speaks the great majority of the lines, initiates most of the verbal exchanges and activities depicted, and with whom the other major and minor protagonists interrelate. Moreover, as Fox has ob-

served,[326] while we learn very little about her lover's life and identity, even from what she tells us, some specific information is supplied regarding her own social context: she has worked as a vineyard-keeper, and hence her skin is burned black by the sun (1:5–6); she still resides in her maternal home (3:4; 8:2); and she must contend with overbearing brothers (1:6; 8:8–10). Few as they are, these details establish a persona for her that is independent of the way she is seen by the man.

The Song's literary portrait of this "young woman" may, of course, be composite, fashioned from originally independent units of love poetry. But that is less important than indications of coherent design in the various sketches offered of her by the poet or editor responsible for the received text. Such design is evident in the two extended *wasf*s praising her attributes (4:1–7; 7:2–7[1–6]): almost identical imagery is employed here to describe her "neck" (4:4; 7:5[4]) and "breasts" (4:5; 7:4[3]). Similarly, an insertion in 6:5–7 appears to be a quite deliberate reprise of segments of the *wasf* in 4:1–7, taking note of her "hair" (6:5 = 4:1), "teeth" (6:6 = 4:2), and "cheeks" (6:7 = 4:3).

Somewhat more ambiguous but interesting results are obtained when attention is specifically focused on distribution of the eleven epithets used in the Song with reference to the woman.[327] Order of the frequency of attestation is observed in the following review; secondary designations—i.e., those that only appear as parallels in subordinate position—are noted in connection with the primary epithets to which they are attached. Seven categories emerge.

---

325 Cf. also references to the woman's mother (1:6; 6:9; 8:1), to Solomon's mother (3:11), and, apparently, to the man's mother (8:5).

326 Fox, 308.

327 Though the study is not easily accessible, an important analysis of the Song's epithets and other rhetorical features was published by R. Kessler, *Some*

Poetical and Structural Features of the Song of Songs (Leeds University Oriental Society Monograph Series 8; Leeds, 1957) esp. 1–9; see the useful summary in Pope, 47–51.

a) The man most often refers to the woman as "my friend" (ra'yātî), a term of collegiality or, here, endearment whose feminine form is otherwise unattested in biblical Hebrew. The nine attestations of this epithet are spread fairly evenly throughout the poetic units of 1:2—6:3, but none appears after the occurrence in 6:4. The epithet is used alone six times: 1:9, 15; 2:2; 4:1, 6; 6:4. In two additional cases, 2:10 and 13, it is immediately followed by the parallel "my beautiful one" (yāpātî).[328] In the final instance, 5:2, "my friend" is the second in a grand series of four epithets—invoked by the man in his urgent plea for the woman to open the door of her (mother's) house.

b) "Bride" (kallâ) is attested six times, always in direct address of the man to the woman: 4:8, 9, 10, 11, 12; 5:1. The epithet appears alone in 4:8 and 11; it follows "my sister" (see below) in the remaining four instances. These occurrences obviously form a tight cluster, in a section of poetry that begins with an invitation of the man to the woman (4:8) and concludes with his acceptance of her invitation to partake of fruits of the "garden" (5:1a, followed in v 1b by an anonymous exhortation to the two of them to enjoy the banquet of love's delights).[329]

c) While the epithet "my sister" ('ăḥōtî) is never used alone, it appears in initial position in each of its five attestations; once again, these are tightly clustered: 4:9, 10, 12; 5:1, 2. In the first four cases the "sister" epithet is followed by "bride" as noted above; in the final case it introduces the consecutive series of four epithets ("my sister, my friend, my dove, my perfect one").

d) The man three times addresses the woman as "my dove" (yônātî): 2:14, where the epithet appears alone; 5:2, as the third in the series of four epithets, followed by "my perfect one" (tammātî); and 6:9, followed by the only other occurrence of "my perfect one."

e) The woman is also referred to three times as "(the) most beautiful of women" (hayyāpâ bannāšîm); it is used alone in each instance. The man introduces this epithet in 1:8, which is the first time he speaks in the Song. Later, in 5:9 and 6:1, the "Daughters" employ the epithet—apparently as an intentional echo of the man's words—when addressing inquiries to the woman concerning the uniqueness and whereabouts of her lover.

f) In 7:1[6:13] the enigmatic epithet or title "the Shulammite" (ha/baššûlammît) is twice associated with the woman, first when she is so addressed by an unspecified

---

328 Note that the combination of these epithets here forms part of an obvious *inclusio* (2:10b, 13b): *qûmî lāk ra'yātî / yāpātî ûl(ĕ)kî-lāk* ("Arise, my friend / my beautiful one, and come!"). There are close resemblances to this construction elsewhere. Another *inclusio* is apparent in 4:1, 7: *hinnāk yāpâ ra'yātî / hinnāk yāpâ* ("Ah, you are beautiful, my friend, / ah, beautiful"); *kullāk yāpâ ra'yātî* . . . ("You are all beautiful, my friend . . ."). Note also the exchange of compliments in 1:15–16, spoken by the man and the woman respectively: *hinnāk yāpâ ra'yātî / hinnāk yāpâ* . . . ("Ah, you are beautiful, my friend; ah, you are beautiful . . ."); *hinnĕkā yāpeh dôdî 'ap nā'îm* ("Ah, you are beautiful, my lover, most pleasing!"). Echoes may be discerned in 6:4, 10: *yāpâ 'att ra'yātî kĕtirṣâ* ("Beautiful are you, my friend, as Tirzah"); *yāpâ kallĕbānâ* ("beautiful as the moon"). Cf. the related

epithet in category e) below, "(the) most beautiful of women" (*hayyāpâ bannāšîm*), with occurrences in 1:8; 5:9; and 6:1; and also the verbal idiom, "How beautiful . . .!," that is used three times with reference to the woman: *mah-yyāpû dôdaik* (4:10); and, forming yet another *inclusio*, *mah-yyāpû pĕ'āmaik* (7:2[1]) and *mah-yyāpît* (7:7[6]).

329 The themes of this segment, as well as the repetition of the epithet "bride," strongly suggest its use as an epithalamium, and perhaps its origin in a wedding context. Cf. Keel, 173, who argues that this unit builds to a high point of the Song in 5:1.

group and then in her own questioning response.[330]
g) Each of the three additional epithets for the woman is attested only once. All of them appear in the *wasf* of 7:2–7[1–6], which is apparently introduced by the "Shulammite" exchange noted immediately above: "noble daughter" (*bat-nādîb*) in v 2[1]; "loved one" (*'ahăbâ*) in v 7[6]; and "beautiful daughter" (*bat ta'ănûgîm*), also in v 7[6]. Thus another tight cluster is formed by the final four epithets.

The more widely distributed of these epithets—comprising categories a), d), and e)—serve as semantic markers or threads, stitching together sections of dialogue through 6:10. The clustered designations in categories b) and c) suggest the isolation of 4:8—5:1; yet the occurrence of "my sister" heading the series in 5:2 creates at least a secondary bond between all of the epithets used for the woman in the first five categories. On the other hand, these epithetical threads are conspicuously absent in 6:11—8:14.[331] Indeed, the peculiar cluster of designations in categories f) and g) directs attention to the singularity of the sketch in 7:1–7[6:13—7:6]. While other literary topoi, already noted, indicate that this is supposed to involve the same woman who speaks and is addressed in earlier parts of the Song, we see her here from a different viewpoint, perhaps that of bystanders rather than her lover per se (cf. 7:8–9[7–8]).

The portrait of the Song's chief male protagonist is drawn almost entirely from the woman's perspective. When he speaks it is always about her and usually in direct address to her;[332] at least twice we hear his voice because she quotes him (2:10–14; 5:2a). His words reveal the depth of his passion for her, but little else about himself.

We glimpse his idealized physical charms through her adoring eyes in the *wasf* of 5:10–16. This she offers in response to a reduplicated question from the Daughters (5:9; cf. 6:1): "How does your lover differ from any lover . . .?" (*mah-dôdēk middôd*). Here the general term *dôd*—rendered "lover" but perhaps more literally having a quasi-passive sense, "one who is loved"—identifies him only in relationship to her (cf. also 8:5). It forms the base of the epithet "my lover/beloved" (*dôdî*), used by the woman throughout the poetry in speaking to and about the man.[333] Only once, in concluding the *wasf* addressed to the Daughters (5:16), does she append to this another designation—"my friend" (*rē'î*)—that has a counterpart among the more vivid and varied terms of endearment he employs with reference to her.

There are, however, two other repeated expressions used by the woman that function as more interesting appellatives for the man. In the Song's initial report of dialogue between the couple, she addresses him as "[you] whom my soul loves" (*še'āhăbâ napšî* [1:7]). This striking idiom[334] later reappears four times in close succession through the first of the "seeking/finding" episodes narrated by the woman (3:1–4). Twice, in connection with the "possession" refrain, she characterizes him as "[the one/he who] browses among the lilies" (*hārō'eh baššôšannîm* [2:16; 6:3]). "Lilies" here is presumably a metaphor for the woman herself (cf. 2:1–2), while the participial form rendered "browses" (*rō'eh*) alludes not

---

330 For discussion of the epithet's possible meaning and significance, see below, p. 181.

331 This provides another indication of the problem already noted of discerning dialogic structure and coherence in the final segments of the book; see above, pp. 66–67.

332 The brief address to "Solomon" in 8:12 may be a partial exception, if this concluding segment is to be assigned to the man.

333 There are twenty-six occurrences: 1:13, 14, 16; 2:3, 8, 9, 10, 16, 17; 4:16; 5:2, 4, 5, 6[bis], 8, 10, 16; 6:2, 3[bis]; 7:10[9], 11[10], 12[11], 14[13]; 8:14.

334 See above, p. 75.

only to the man's love-making but to his role or guise as shepherd.

Other than this allusive reference, the term "shepherd" is never used directly to characterize the man, though it is strongly implied in the couple's initial exchange of dialogue (1:7–8): "Tell me," she asks him, "where you pasture *[tirʿeh]*, where you rest (the flock) *[tarbîṣ]* at midday . . ."; "If you do not know," he replies, "follow the tracks of the flock and pasture *[ûr(ĕ)ʿî]* your kids near the tents of the shepherds *[hārōʿîm].*" The tenor of the exchange is playful. While the issue is obviously the prospect of a noontime tryst, it is not necessary to interpret literally the pastoral setting and roles of either party. Here, as elsewhere in the Song where the couple's liaisons come into view (e.g., 4:6–8; 5:1; 7:11–13[10–12]), the rustic, naturalistic imagery may be essentially metaphorical.

More frequent are depictions of the woman's lover as "king" (*melek*) as well as statements that otherwise seem to associate royal motifs with the man and the woman. The clearest instance occurs in the Song's initial unit, where a female voice either tersely describes, invites, or imagines an experience of majestic love-making (1:4):

Draw me after you! Let us run!
The king has brought me to his chambers.
Let us exult and rejoice in you!
Let us extol your love beyond wine!

What context there is for this suggests youthful enchantment of the speaker and other young women (the *ʿălāmôt* of v 3, who are possibly to be identified with the "Daughters of Jerusalem" first expressly mentioned in v 5) with a lordly swain. The second representation of the image is equally isolated and even more cryptic (1:12):

While the king was in his enclosure
my nard gave forth its fragrance.

Does the woman here represent herself as palace servant or entertainer, royal consort or concubine? Royal imagery is twice adumbrated in celebrations of the woman's beauty. In 6:8–10 the man boasts of her uniqueness, which is supposed to be obvious even to hosts of "queens" (*mĕlākôt*), "concubines" (*pîlagĕšîm*), and "maidens" (*ʿălāmôt,* again!). Finally, in the *waṣf* that follows the "Shulammite" exchange there is a difficult reference to her majestic hair (royal "purple" is the metaphor) in whose tresses "a king is caught" (7:6[5]).

Although proponents of the cultic-mythological interpretation, no less than historicists and allegorists before them, have extensively mined these textual veins, the yield is too small to repay the speculative labor. It is easier to maintain that the royal imagery belongs to the realm of popular romance and erotic fantasy, in which the lovers pay extravagant homage to each other.[335] In her ardor, the woman sees her lover in the guise of king; he, in turn, avows that she is superior to the varied delights of a royal harem (cf. 8:11–12). Even so, this "literary fiction" has thematic significance in the Song, constituting another thread that links disparate poetic units.

The appellation "Daughters of Jerusalem" (*bĕnôt yĕrûšālaim*) is introduced *ex abrupto* in 1:5 and invoked six additional times in the course of the Song, always in direct address (2:7; 3:5; 3:10;[336] 5:8, 16; 8:4). The

---

335 On "literary fictions" in the Egyptian love songs, see above, p. 47.

336 Here *bĕnôt yĕrûšālaim* is best understood as a vocative and connected with 3:11, paralleling *bĕnôt ṣiyyôn* ("Daughters of Zion"); see below, p. 150 (Notes *ad loc.*). Since the woman in all other instances is the one who addresses them, she may be the speaker here as well but this remains very uncertain.

group of women so designated might be associated with the "maidens" (*ʿălāmôt*) mentioned in 1:3 (cf. 6:8), but it is hardly necessary to do so in an intentional way. Nor is there sufficient reason to discern a dramatic "plot" in which the Daughters play a principal role, either as the rivals of the Song's female protagonist or, conversely, as her bridal party or cultic devotees.[337] To be sure, when she first speaks to them there is suggestion of a story *in medias res:* she offers a brief account of herself, apparently in response to their fascination with her black complexion and striking beauty (1:5–6). Perhaps, as the appellation itself suggests, they are a covey of Jerusalemite city-girls, while she is a maiden from the countryside, "the Shulammite" of 7:1[6:13], whose skin has been darkly tanned from working in the vineyards under the stare of the sun. Although this initial perception of difference between the woman and the Daughters does not have to be adversarial, it is important. It establishes her unique identity, preparing us for the man's testimony to her superlative beauty: "As a lily among thorns, so is my friend among women [literally 'the daughters,' *habbānôt*]" (2:2); "When women *[bānôt]* see her, they praise her . . ." (6:9).

From the outset, then, the Daughters function primarily as a foil for the woman's own reflections. They may be likened to an on-stage audience or chorus, perhaps present throughout but only rarely speaking, to whom she relates her experiences of love and the lessons she has learned.[338] Four times she adjures them. Three of these are fixed refrains (2:7; 3:5; 8:4), which follow her reports of particular encounters with her lover; the literary pattern suggests that while the woman has been speaking to the Daughters all along, she invokes them directly to underscore her conclusion about the overwhelming power of love aroused. The fourth adjuration (5:8) immediately follows her second account of a nocturnal search for her lover, which ends with the watchmen abusing her. Now she invokes the Daughters to convey her message of love-sickness to the man, should they "find" him. Her invitation for them to become directly involved in the affair provokes their questions in 5:9 and 6:1, to which she responds respectively with a *waṣf* describing the man's unique beauty (5:10–16) and what seems to be a smug admission that further search for him is not really necessary (6:2–3). Even here, where the role of the Daughters is most active, they neither

---

337 Proposed identifications of the "Daughters" represent the history of the Song's interpretation *in nuce.* Origen, citing Rom 11:28, takes them to be the Jewish community, ". . . the daughters of this earthly Jerusalem who, seeing the Church of the Gentiles, despise and vilify her for her ignoble birth; for she is baseborn in their eyes, because she cannot count as hers the noble blood of Abraham and Isaac and Jacob, for all that she forgets her own people and her father's house and comes to Christ" (*Commentarium in Canticum canticorum*, Book Two, 1:5 *ad loc.* [Lawson, 92]). They are generally identified as the "assembly of Israel" (*knśt' dyśr'l*) in the Targum (e.g., at 2:7 [Sperber, Vol. 4a, 130]). Joüon, 79 (citing in support Rashi's interpretation), considers them to represent the gentile nations, coming as proselytes to Zion. For proponents of the historicizing and dramatic

interpretations they become harem-women (e.g., Delitzsch, 24: "ladies of the palace"); the wedding-rites theory makes them the bride's cortege (Budde, 3: die weiblichen Hochzeitsgäste). In Meek's cultic interpretation they are "female votaries of the fertility goddess" (105).

338 Commenting on 1:5, Robert (70) remarks that the appearance of the daughters is a "dramatic trait." Whereas the woman seemed to be alone, soliloquizing, she suddenly appears to be involved in a kind of dialogue with the daughters, which enables her to express her feelings more fully. This recalls the function of the chorus in ancient Greek tragedy, and is a simple literary process. Cf. also the remarks of Fox, 302–303.

describe themselves nor reveal their own feelings and values; they are present solely to promote what the woman wishes to say.

Apart from the superscription (1:1), the name "Solomon" is mentioned six times in the Song. Although nothing warrants identifying Solomon as the woman's lover, the references to him appear to have thematic significance, especially in connection with the royal "literary fiction" noted above. That is, Solomon's proverbial wealth, splendor, and love-life comprise part of the allusive backdrop (along with the nature imagery) against which the Song's portraits of two young lovers are sketched. In the initial reference (1:5), the woman likens herself to "the pavilions of Solomon" (*yěrî'ôt šělōmōh*),[339] apparently as regards both color and exotic beauty. It is possible that her enigmatic epithet "the Shulammite" (7:1[6:13]) involves a deliberate wordplay on the name "Solomon," and so too her puzzling statement in 8:10b: "Then I have become in his (the lover's) eyes as one who finds peace *[šālôm]*." Solomon comes into direct view only in 3:6–11 (especially vv 7, 9, 11), where the procession of his splendid litter on his wedding day is described.[340] Finally, 8:11–12 seems to narrate a short parable about Solomon's "vineyard in Baal-hamon," with an appended remark addressed to Solomon, boasting that the speaker's own vineyard (*karmî šellî*) is both more accessible and valuable; apparently the woman herself is meant, whether the words are to be attributed to her or to her lover.

C. Prosody

In addition to the broader patterns of verbal and thematic repetition noted above, individual poetic units of the Song exhibit exquisitely crafted designs, often involving both formal (stichometric) and semantic (parallelistic) repetitions. The prosodic devices encountered—such as alliteration, paronomasia, chiasmus, and *inclusio*—are varied enough to constitute a virtual textbook of Hebrew prosody. Yet here too the sense that emerges from close analysis is one of great stylistic homogeneity, suggesting common authorship of most if not all of the major units.

Critical approaches to Hebrew prosody differ widely, with many matters remaining under intensive debate.[341] There is little agreement, for example, on the extent to which fixed rhythms can be considered a crucial factor

---

339 Following the suggestion of Hugo Winckler and Julius Wellhausen, many modern commentators (e.g., Ricciotti, 200–202; Miller, 26; Rudolph, 123; Gerleman, 99; and Pope, 320; cf. also NAB and NEB) emend the vocalization of 𝔐, which is fully supported by the ancient versions in this instance (e.g., 𝔊 δέρρεις Σαλωμων and 𝔙 *pelles Salomonis*) to read "Salmah" here rather than "Solomon." This reading may be "correct," providing a closer parallel to the preceding "tents of Qedar," but given other references to "Solomon" in the text, it seems preferable to retain 𝔐 in 1:5, while recognizing the possibility of an intentional wordplay.

340 It may be observed that one of the few obvious links between this puzzling unit and other parts of the Song is the reference in 3:10()11) to the "Daughters of Jerusalem."

341 For recent comprehensive discussions, though representing the particular approaches of the authors to ancient northwest Semitic prosody, see the following: David Noel Freedman, "Prolegomenon" to G. B. Gray, *The Forms of Hebrew Poetry* (New York: Ktav, 1972) vii–lvi (reprinted in *idem, Pottery, Poetry, and Prophecy: Studies in Early Hebrew Poetry* [Winona Lake: Eisenbrauns, 1980] 23–50); Marjo C. A. Korpel and Johannes C. de Moor, "Fundamentals of Ugaritic and Hebrew Poetry," *The Structural Analysis of Biblical and Canaanite Poetry* (JSOTSup 74; ed. Willem van der Meer and Johannes C. de Moor; Sheffield: Sheffield Academic Press, 1988) 1–61; and Wilfred G. E. Watson, *Classical Hebrew Poetry: A Guide to its Techniques* (JSOTSup 26; Sheffield: JSOT, 1984). Approaches to the prosody of the Song in recent commentaries are quite varied. Relatively full

and, if they are deemed fundamental, how to measure and describe them.[342] Larger prosodic structures—such as stanzas and strophes within poems—are another vexed issue, though some commentators have suggested that strophic arrangement is the most conspicuous literary feature of the Song's poetry.[343] While even the character of "parallelism," once considered the *sine qua non* of Hebrew poetry, has been subjected to recent redefinition,[344] it continues to provide the most helpful approach to prosodic analysis. In the following paragraphs, we will do no more than illustrate how such an approach facilitates recognition of the Song's artistic design.

Basic Units of Stichometry. Patterned lineation or

---

342 discussion is offered by Robert, whose sections of "critique litteraire" include metrical analysis for each poem he recognizes. On the other hand, while Gerleman offers a fine treatment of the Song's language and style, he avoids altogether discussion of metrical issues. Especially detailed is the treatment of L. Krinetzki (50–75 and *passim*) who addresses the whole range of the Song's literary and stylistic features, in the tradition of Luis Alonso Schökel (*Estudios de Poética Hebrea* [Barcelona: Flors, 1963]; and *Hermenéutica de la palabra,* Vol. 2: *Interpretación literaria de textos bíblicos* [Academia christiana 38; Madrid: Ediciones Cristiandad, 1987] = *A Manual of Hebrew Poetics* [tr. with Adrian Graffy; Subsidia Biblica 11; Rome: Pontificio Instituto Biblico, 1988]). For example, Krinetzki (59) argues that intentional use of assonance can be discerned in many cases: weak consonants may in his view express ecstatic admiration (1:15–17), or a feeling of happiness (2:16); repetition of the consonant *b* in *haššōbĕbîm bāʿîr* (3:3) suggests the noise of footsteps; *harʾînî . . . hašmîʿînî ʾet-qôlēk* (2:14) is supposed to imitate the sound of a shrill cry.

342 Stanislav Segert ("Die Versform des Hohenliedes," *Charisteria Orientalia praecipue ad Persiam pertientia: Ioanni Rypka sacrum* [ed. Felix Tauer *et al.;* Prague: Československé Akademie, 1956] 285–99) has made use of three metric schemes in his analysis of the Song's poetic rhythms: "Wortmetrik," in which the basic unit of measurement is each accented word of two or more syllables; accentual meter (a modification of the approach to accent-counting developed by E. Sievers and Max Haller), involving textual emendation and reconstruction of pristine cola; and alternating meter (as proposed especially by Gustav Hölscher), in which the criterion of measurement is the regular alternation of stressed and unstressed syllables. Loretz (55–56 and *passim*) settles for indicating basic patterns of symmetry between cola by giving consonant counts.

343 Esp. Rudolph, 99–100; in the sections of commentary proper, Rudolph's remarks on prosody consist only of noting the number of lines that comprise the supposed strophes. Cf. also Broadribb ("Thoughts," 16–17) who divides the Song into five major sections of poetry and counts some thirty-five strophes, averaging six lines each: I. 1:2—2:3 (1:2–4, 5–6, 7–8, 9–14; 1:15—2:3); II. 2:4–17 (2:4–6, 7, 8–10a, 10b–13, 14–17); III. 3:1—5:1 (3:1–4+5, 6–10; 4:1–3, 4–7, 8–11, 12–15; 4:16—5:1); IV. 5:2—7:14[13] (5:2–3, 4–6, 7–8, 10–13, 14–16; 6:1–3, 4–7, 8–9, 10–12; 7:1–3[6:13—7:2], 4–6[3–5], 7–10[6–9], 11–14[10–13]); V. 8:1–14 (8:1–4, 5–7, 8–10, 11–14).

344 So James L. Kugel, *The Idea of Biblical Poetry: Parallelism and Its History* (New Haven/London: Yale University, 1981) esp. 1–58. Kugel's argument that even in so-called synonymous parallelism the secondary segments do not simply repeat but emphasize, extend, and complete the poetic image is cogent. His use of / and // to represent partial and full pauses in clause structures is adopted below. However, as regards analysis of prosodic lineation and distinction between structures of prose and poetry, a more useful approach is outlined by Stephen A. Geller, *Parallelism in Early Biblical Poetry* (Harvard Semitic Monographs 20; Missoula: Scholars, 1979) esp. 5–52.

segmentation is evident throughout the Song. The great majority of these segments (cola) vary in length from five to ten syllables, according to the vocalization of 𝔐. Those in the lower range generally bear two stressed or tonic syllables, while those in the upper range have three or sometimes four such accents, with the cantillation of 𝔐 supplying the data.

Isolated segments (monocola) are rare in the Song.[345] Although these segments appear to be "prosaic," they can be functionally identified in relationship to prosodic units.[346] For example, the line "My lover responded to me" in 2:10a is an introductory rubric to the poem on Spring that follows in vv 10b–13.[347] Again, in 1:3b and the final two-word clause of v 4 the isolated lines— "therefore the maidens love you" and "Rightly do they love you"—are concluding formulae that themselves comprise a pair of cola (bicolon). In such cases, it is likely that we can discern editing meant to link originally discrete poetic units into larger structures.

Paired segments or couplets (bicola) are the building-blocks of the Song's poetry, though as will be seen below triplets (tricola) and more elaborate patterns are also quite common. The couplets sometimes exhibit only formal (nonparallelistic) linkage. That is, the segments together form a coherent two-part statement, characterized by syntactical enjambment. More often, however, semantic correlations ("parallelism") are evident between the segments of each couplet, as also between those of triplets and the like. In the examples of both formal and parallelistic lineation cited below, each Hebrew segment (colon) will be followed by either a single (/) or double (//) stroke; these indicate, respectively, minor and major stops that correspond approximately to comparable degrees of punctuation in the English translations.[348] Moreover, in the righthand margin a double notation is provided in parentheses to indicate the character of the relationship between the Hebrew lines and their compo-

---

345 The assessment of Segal ("Song," 479) is puzzling: "The parallelism, so characteristic of biblical poetic literature, is not frequent in the Song. Only occasionally does the rhythmic prose of the Song rise into parallelistic versification." He apparently counts only twenty-eight genuinely parallelistic cola in the entire Song. This minimalist approach should be compared with the analysis of Loretz, esp. 57–58.

346 Relative absence of prosaic syntax and particles is one of the major criteria urged by David Noel Freedman in recognizing poetic literature in the Hebrew Bible (e.g., "Another Look at Biblical Hebrew Poetry," *Directions in Biblical Hebrew Poetry* [ed. Elaine R. Follis; JSOTSup 40; Sheffield: Sheffield Academic Press, 1987] 11–28). In this regard it may be observed again that the relative ʾăšer never occurs in the Song after the superscription (see above pp. 74–75 on use of še-/šel). The definite object marker ʾet appears only sixteen times in the text of 𝔐, and at least in some cases its presence does seem to identify more prosaic statements (1:6; 2:7, 14; 3:1–5; 5:3, 7, 8; 7:13[12]; 8:4, 7bis, 12). There are two possibly

prosaic uses of conjunctive *waw* with cohortative (subjunctive) verb forms to express purpose: ʾāqûmâ(-n)nāʾ waʾăsôbĕbâ bāʿîr, "Let me arise *that I may make the rounds* of the city" (3:2); ûn(ĕ)baqĕšennû ʿimmāk, "*that we may seek him* with you" (6:1). There are also two attestations of *waw* consecutive with imperfect, both in 6:9: rāʾûhā bānôt wayĕʾaššĕrûhā mĕlākôt ûpîlagĕšîm wayĕhalĕlûhā, "When women see her, they praise her; queens and concubines, they bless her."

347 It seems gratuitous to consider the familiar Hebrew idiom "answer and said" to represent a parallelistic bicolon, *contra* Wilfred G. E. Watson, *Classical Hebrew Poetry: A Guide to its Techniques* (JSOTSup 26; Sheffield: JSOT, 1984) 368, though his analysis of the poem "Love in Spring" (2:10–13) is generally instructive.

348 See note 344 above. In the examples below, the translation used elsewhere in this commentary has occasionally been modified to represent Hebrew word order more closely; hyphens are used to link words that correspond to elements identified in the marginal notations.

nents. Capital letters (A,A′,B,B′, etc.) represent the basic relationship between segments (i.e., A/B indicates enjambed or non-parallelistic cola, while A/A′ signals semantic congruity). Lowercase letters (a,a′,b,b′, etc., separated by :) in square brackets identify the primary semantic and grammatical-syntactical elements that comprise the individual segments (with each lettered element usually bearing a single tonic stress).

Generally there are other features, besides syntax, that demonstrate both the segmentation and congruence of non-parallelistic couplets. Alliteration of sibilants is prominent in the following enjambed bicolon of 1:6a:

> ʾal-tirʾûnî šeʾănî šĕḥarḥōret / (A [a:b:c])
> šeššĕzāpatĕnî haššāmeš / / (B [d:e])
> Do-not-stare-at-me because-I-am blackish,
>   for-(it)-has-burned-me the-sun.

Enjambment is common especially in the *waṣfs* (which, in any case, should be considered a peculiar genre of poetry). Often, as in the following example from 4:2a, the basic metaphor or simile is stated in the initial line, with an elaborated indication of the *tertium comparationis* appearing in the second:

> šinnaik kĕʿēder haqqĕṣûbôt / (A [a:b:c])
> šeʿālû min-hāraḥṣâ / / (B [d:e])
> Your-teeth (are) like-a-flock-of-sheep to-be-shorn,
>   that-comes-up from-the-washing.

In the instance of 8:5a the terse, enjambed couplet appears to be an intentional echo (of the lengthier form of the refrain in 3:6):

> mî zōʾt ʿōlâ min-hammidbār / (A [a:b:c])
> mitrappeqet ʿal-dôdāh / / (B [d:e])
> Who-(is)-this (that)-comes-up from-the-desert,
>   leaning upon-her-lover?

Two basic lineation patterns can be distinguished in parallelistic couplets: balanced (symmetrical); and echoing, typically with ellipsis of one grammatical-syntactical element in the second line. Several examples of balanced couplets may be cited.

a) In 1:4:

> nāgîlâ wĕniśmĕḥâ bāk / (A [a:b:c])
> nazkîrâ dōdêkā miyyayin / / (A′ [a′–b′:c′:d])
> Let-us-exult and-rejoice in-you!
>   Let-us-extol your-love beyond-wine!

b) In 2:13:

> hattĕʾēnâ ḥānĕtâ paggêhā / (A [a:b:c])
> wĕhaggĕpānîm sĕmādar nātĕnû rêaḥ / / (A′ [a′:b′:c′])
> The-fig-tree yields its-figs;
>   and-the-vines, in-bloom, give-forth-fragrance.

c) In 8:3 (an example of the "embracing" refrain):

> šĕmōʾlô taḥat rōʾšî / (A [a:b:c])
> wîmînô tĕḥabbĕqēnî / / (A′ [a′:b′–c′])
> His-left-hand (is) under my-head
>   and-his-right-hand embraces-me.

Two examples of couplets with echoing parallelism will suffice (in each case with the "a" verbal element omitted but implied in the second segment).

a) In 8:2:

> ʾašqĕkā miyyayin hāreqaḥ / (A [a:b:c])
> mēʿăsîs rimmōnî / / (A′ [b′:c′])
> I-would-give-you-to-drink some-wine (that is) spiced,
>   some-juice of-my-pomegranate.

b) In 8:6:

> śîmēnî kaḥôtām ʿal-libbekā / (A [a:b:c])
> kaḥôtām ʿal-zĕrôʿekā / / (A′ [b:c′])
> Place-me as-a-seal on-your-heart,
>   as-a-seal on-your-arm.

In triplet lineations, two of the three segments usually display close parallelism, while one—often the first—is differentiated by syntactical and semantic elements. A number of examples may be cited to indicate characteristic as well as more unusual types.

a) In 1:5, interestingly, the appellative invocation—which is the initial reference in the Song to the "Daughters of Jerusalem"—seems to be a supplemental or extrametrical feature (and is not indicated in the marginal notation of elements):

šĕḥôrâ ʾănî wĕnāʾwâ (bĕnôt yĕrûšālāim) /   (A [a:b:c])
kĕʾohŏlê qēdār /   (B [d:e])
kîrîʿôt šĕlōmōh / /   (B′ [d′:e′])

Black am-I, and-beautiful, (O Daughters of Jeru-
    salem,)
      like-the-tents of-Qedar,
      like-the-pavilions of-Solomon.

b) In 1:6b the pattern is also A/B/B′:

bĕnê ʾimmî niḥărû-bî /   (A [a:b:c])
śāmūnî nōṭērâ ʾet-hakkĕrāmîm /   (B [c′:d:e])
karmî šellî lōʾ nāṭārtî / /   (B′ [e′:b′:d′])

The-sons of-my-mother were-angry-with-me;
    they-assigned-me as-keeper of-the-vineyards—
      my-vineyard which-is-mine I-have-not-kept.

c) Another example of the same pattern, here in 2:12, is
noteworthy because it seems to pivot around a wordplay
in the second segment.[349] The term *hazzāmîr* is homo-
nymic: representing *zāmîr*, "pruning" (from *zmr*[II]), it
echoes the "blossom" imagery of segment A; representing *zāmîr*, "song, singing" (from *zmr*[I]), it is proleptic,
introducing the imagery of sound/hearing in the final
segment (A″).

hanniṣṣānîm nirʾû bāʾāreṣ /   (A [a:b:c])
ʿēt hazzāmîr higgîaʿ /   (A′ [a′:b′])
wĕqôl hattôr nišmaʿ bĕʾarṣēnû / /   (A″ [a″:b″:c′])

The-blossoms appear in-the-land,
    the-time for-pruning/singing has-arrived;
      and-the-voice-of-the-turtledove is-heard in-our-
      land.

d) In 6:8 a triplet exhibiting numerical progression is
noteworthy.

šiššîm hēmmâ mĕlākôt   (A [a:b:c])
ûš(ĕ)mōnîm pîlagĕšîm   (A′ [a′:c′])

waʿălāmôt ʾên mispār   (A″ [c″:a″])

Sixty are the-queens,
    eighty (are) the-concubines
    and-maidens without-number.

Prosodic Design. If couplets and triplets are basic
features of the Song's poetry, there are delightfully
varied ways in which lineation segments and the grammatical-syntactical and semantic elements that comprise
them can be structured in both external and internal
patterns of repetition.

One example may be given to indicate that even when
the external linkage between segmented sets of cola is
essentially formal, other features may demonstrate
bonding. Here, in 1:2–3a, the non-parallelistic cola are
interconnected especially by word-repetition ("pleasing"
in segments two and three), onomatopoeia (imitative
sound, "kiss/kisses" in segment one), alliteration (particularly the sibilants in the first, third, and fourth cola),
and paronomasia (wordplay on "perfume(s)" [*šemen*] and
"name" [*šēm*] in segments three and four):

yiššākēnî minnĕšîqôt pîhû /   (A [a:b:c])
kî-ṭôbîm dōdêkā miyyāyin /   (B [d:e:f])
lĕrêaḥ šĕmānêkā ṭôbîm /   (B′ [g:h:d′])
šemen tûraq šĕmekā / /   (B″ [h′:i:j])

Let-him-kiss-me with-the-kisses of-his-mouth!
    Truly,-more-pleasing is-your-love than-wine.
    The-fragrance of-your-perfumes (is) pleasing,
      perfume flowing (is) your-name.

In the following case, two couplets are semantically
interlinked, especially by the catchword element designated "c" (1:10–11):

nāʾwû lĕḥāyayik battōrîm /   (A [a:b:c])
ṣawwāʾrēk baḥărûzîm / /   (A′ [b′:c′])
tôrê zāhāb naʿăśeh-llāk /   (B [c:d:e])
ʿim nĕquddôt hakkāsep / /   (B′ [c′:d′])

---

349 As observed by Cyrus H. Gordon, Review of Marvin
    Pope's *Song of Songs, JAOS* 100 (1980) 356.

Lovely (are) your-cheeks in-pendants,
    your-neck in-beads;
Pendants of-gold we-will-make-for-you,
    along-with-ornaments of-silver.

Semantic connections between sets of couplets in 1:13–14 are forged out of explicit repetitions and more allusive metaphors, apparently anatomical:

ṣĕrôr hammōr dôdî lî /	(A [a:b:c])
bên šāday yālîn //	(B [d:e])
ʾeškōl hakkōper dôdî lî /	(A' [aʹ:bʹ:c])
bĕkarĕmê ʿên gedî //	(B' [dʹ:f])

A-sachet of-myrrh (is) my-lover-to-me;
    between-my-breasts he-lies.
A-cluster of-henna (is) my-lover-to-me,
    in-the-vineyards of-Engedi.

A fine example of parallelistic cola that build to a climax is exhibited in 1:15–16a. This concatenation of segments is also interesting because it links lines A and A', spoken by the man, with the A'' line, spoken by the woman (whose address, it may be noted, continues in a following parallelistic triplet not cited here).

hinnāk yāpâ raʿyātî /	(A [a:b:c])
hinnāk yāpâ ʿênaik yônîm /	(A' [a:b:d:e])
hinnĕkā yāpeh dôdî ʾap nāʿîm //	(A'' [aʹ:bʹ:cʹ:cʹʹ])

Ah,-you (are) beautiful, my-friend;
    ah,-you (are) beautiful, your-eyes (are) doves.
Ah,-you (are) beautiful, my-lover, most-pleasing!

Three couplets are interconnected in the segments of 2:14; the design is particularly noteworthy because it exhibits a chiastic arrangement of elements in the B/B'//C/C' cola. In the initial line, the epithet seems to be extrametrical and is not indicated in the marginal notation.

(*yônātî*) *bĕḥagwê hasselaʿ* /	(A [a:b])
bĕsēter hammadrēgâ //	(A' [aʹ:bʹ])
harʾînî ʾet-marʾaik /	(B [c:d])
hašmîʿînî ʾet-qôlēk //	(B' [cʹ:dʹ])
kî-qôlēk ʿārēb /	(C [dʹ:e])
ûmarʾêk nāʾweh //	(C' [d:eʹ])

(My dove,) in-the-clefts of-the-rock,
    in-the-recesses of-the-cliff,
Let-me-see your-face,
    let-me-hear your-voice;
For-your-voice (is) pleasant
    and-your-face lovely.

A series of four terse segments is tightly interlocked by word-repetitions in 2:15:

ʾeḥĕzu-lānû šûʿālîm	(A [a:b])
šûʿālîm qĕṭannîm	(A' [b:c])
mĕḥabbĕlîm kĕrāmîm	(B [d:e])
ûk(ĕ)rāmênû sĕmādar	(B' [e:f])

Catch-for-us foxes,
    the foxes (which are) little,
(that) damage the-vineyards,
    when-our-vineyards (are) in-bloom.

What has variously been called climactic or "step/staircase" parallelism—in which the cola build to closure—is well illustrated in the Song. Although one example has already been given above, two more with different designs may be noted.[350]

a) A series of six segments, perhaps three couplets, is conjoined in 4:8:

ʾittî millĕbānôn kallâ	(A [a:b:c])
ʾittî millĕbānôn tābôʾî	(A' [a:b:d])
tāšûrî mērōʾš ʾămānâ	(B [dʹ:e:f])
mērōʾš śĕnîr wĕḥermôn	(B' [e:fʹ:fʹʹ])
mimmĕʿōnôt ʾărāyôt	(C [eʹ:g])
mĕharĕrê nĕmērîm	(C' [eʹʹ:gʹ])

With-me from-Lebanon, O-bride,

---

350 See also 4:1, 9, 10, 12; and 5:9. Cf. now the discussion of this prosodic design in Daniel Grossberg, *Centripetal and Centrifugal Structures in Biblical Poetry* (SBLMS 39; Atlanta: Scholars, 1989) 77–81.

> śĕmōʾlô taḥat (lĕ)rōʾší wîmînô tĕḥabbĕqēnî

> ʾănî lĕdôdî wĕʿalay tĕšûqātô

> ʿad šeyyāpûaḥ hayyôm wĕnāsû haṣṣĕlālîm
> sōb dĕmēh-lĕkâ dôdî liṣ(ĕ)bî ʾô lĕʿōper hāʾayyālîm
> ʿal-hārê bāter

> ʿad šeyyāpûaḥ hayyôm wĕnāsû haṣṣĕlālîm
> ʾēlek lî ʾel-har hammôr wĕʾel-gibʿat hallĕbônâ

> bĕraḥ dôdî ûd(ĕ)mēh-lĕkâ liṣ(ĕ)bî ʾô lĕʿōper hāʾayyālîm

gan nāʿûl 'ăḥōtî kallâ
ga⟨n⟩ nāʿûl maʿyān ḥātûm
šělāḥaik pardēs rimmônîm
ʿim pěrî mĕgādîm

ʿûrî şāpôn ûbô'î têmān
hāpîḥî gannî yizzĕlû běśāmāw

bā'tî lĕgannî 'ăḥōtî kallâ
'ārîtî môrî ʿim-běśāmî
'ăkaltî yaʿrî ʿim-dibšî
šātîtî yênî ʿim-ḥălābî

běnê 'immî niḥărû-bî
śāmūnî nōṭērā 'et-hakkěrāmîm
karmî šellî lō' nāṭārtî

hanniṣṣānîm nir'û bā'āreṣ /   (A [a:b:c])
'ēt hazzāmîr higgîa' /   (A' [a':b'])
wĕqôl hattôr nišma' bĕ'arṣēnû / /   (A''
                                   [a'':b'':c'])

nā'wû lĕḥāyayik battōrîm /   (A [a:b:c])
ṣawwā'rēk baḥărûzîm / /   (A' [b':c'])
tôrê zāhāb na'ăśeh-llāk /   (B [c:d:e])
'im nĕquddôt hakkāsep / /   (B' [c':d'])

ṣĕrôr hammōr dôdî lî /	(A [a:b:c])
bên šāday yālîn //	(B [d:e])
'eškōl hakkōper dôdî lî /	(A′ [a′:b′:c])
bĕkarĕmê 'ên gedî //	(B′ [d′:f])

(*yônātî*) *bĕhagwê hassela'* /	(A [a:b])
bĕsēter hammadrēgâ //	(A′ [a′:b′])
har'înî 'et-mar'aik /	(B [c:d])
hašmî'înî 'et-qôlēk //	(B′ [c′:d′])
kî-qôlēk 'ārēb /	(C [d′:e])
ûmar'êk nā'weh //	(C′ [d:e′])

'ittî millĕbānôn kallâ	(A [a:b:c])
'ittî millĕbānôn tābô'î	(A′ [a:b:d])
tāšûrî mērō'š 'ămānâ	(B [d′:e:f])
mērō'š śĕnîr wĕhermôn	(B′ [e:f′:f″])
mimmĕ'ōnôt 'ărāyôt	(C [e′:g])
mēharĕrê nĕmērîm	(C′ [e″:g′])

with-me from-Lebanon shall-you-come!
Come-down from-the-top of-Amanah,
    from-the-top of-Senir and-Hermon;
From-dens of-lions,
    from-ramparts of-leopards.

b) The final example, a triplet from 6:9a, is selected because it displays interesting verbal repetitions and semantic parallels:

ʾaḥat hîʾ yônātî tammātî /	(A [a:b:c:c′])
ʾaḥat hîʾ lĕʾimmāh /	(A′ [a:b:d])
bārâ hîʾ lĕyôladtāh	(A″ [a′:b:d′])

Unique (is) she, my-dove, my-perfect-one!
    Unique (is) she of-her-mother,
        chosen (is) she of-(the one who)-bore-her.

In sum, the multifaceted rhetorical structures of the Song contribute in substantial measure to its aesthetic beauty as well as to a strong sense of its literary coherence. If this is the craft of an editorial compiler of diverse poems, she—or whoever did the work of "Solomon" named in the superscription—deserves to be recognized as a superlative poet in her own right.

7. Meaning and Theological Significance

Cogent interpretation of any literary work, whether ancient or modern, involves a hermeneutical perspective as well as a methodology. In the preceding sections of Introduction, it has been argued that application of established comparative, philological, and literary-critical methods of analysis renders the text of the Song intelligible: It is a crafted work of poetic imagination that portrays the profound emotions of physical love between a man and a woman. There is nothing novel in this understanding. Traditional Jewish and Christian expositions acknowledged that the Song's overt language, characterizations, themes, and erotic imagery identify it as love poetry. Historical-critical methodologies have certainly illuminated this literal sense of the Song, enabling us to discern more sharply not only what the text says but how it is constructed. Still, important hermeneutical questions remain. Does the text "mean" only what it seems to say? Is meaning significantly affected if the astute interpreter can detect reverberations in the poetry of earlier usage? Should meaning be considered a function of individual poetic units and their likely social settings in the life of ancient Israel; or of the whole in its final, edited form, claiming Solomonic authorship; or of the finished work as ultimately included in the canon of sacred Scripture? To what extent, if any, should the foreground of the text—the way it has been read by the Jewish and Christian communities that treasured it—influence the perspective of the modern interpreter? If questions such as these have no definitive answers, neither can they be ignored altogether.

A. Contemporary Interpretations: Review and Assessment

Among works of biblical literature, the Song is without peer, like the woman of superlative beauty whose experiences of love it describes. Such judgments, however, are always relative to the context of comparison, and this is what differentiates the major views of the Song's meaning advocated by contemporary interpreters.

Divine-Human Marriage. Traditional Jewish and Christian views of the Song as a portrait of the love between God and God's people, Israel, or between Christ and his ecclesial bride, have not lacked defenders until the present day.[351] While the authority and intrinsic value of tradition per se have remained important factors

---

351 For a recent sympathetic restatement of the traditional Jewish perspective, see Gershon D. Cohen, *The Song of Songs and the Jewish Religious* *Mentality* (The Samuel Friedland Lectures; New York: Jewish Theological Seminary of America, 1966); reprinted in *The Canon and Masorah of the*

in such expositions,[352] other grounds recognize that the Song must have an intentional meaning beyond its literal sense. How, it is often asked, can we account for the Song's canonization unless we suppose that it had a spiritual significance from the outset? The question is moot, in any case, but it is usually posed to urge that poetry concerned with human sexual love would be unworthy of canonical status; this is a bias that must be challenged. However, more objective literary matters are adduced as well. Do not the Song's hyperbolic language, its striking metaphors, and the carefully preserved anonymity of its male protagonist indicate that the "literal" imagery has figurative import? The implication is that the text is designed to point the perceptive reader beyond the surface sense to a more profound theological meaning, which can be discovered when the Song is read in the light of other scriptural sources.[353]

The salvation-historical drama of covenant making between God and Israel at Sinai, comprehended through the metaphor of human marriage, provided the obvious point of reference for early and medieval Jewish exposition of the Song.[354] The same metaphor has continued to function as principal warrant in defenses of traditional Christian views. However, proponents have emphasized the metaphor's presence in prophetic contexts, such as Hosea 1—3 and Isaiah 62:3–5, more so than in pentateuchal sources.[355] This has the effect of identifying the Song's portrait of the ideal covenantal union as proleptic: it is supposed to portend a messianic consummation in which the bride is the new or repristinated "Israel,"

Hebrew Bible (ed. Sid Z. Leiman; New York: Ktav, 1974) 262–82.

352 See esp. the commentaries of Bea, 5, 13; and Miller, 6–7, who regards exegetical tradition and ecclesiastical decision (the condemnation of Theodore of Mopsuestia posthumously at the Fifth Ecumenical Council = Second Council of Constantinople in 553 c.e.) as the "theological" grounds for advocating the primacy of the Song's "typical" sense. As many scholars have pointed out, however, one cannot infer from the episode of Theodore that the Church condemned interpretation of the Song along the lines of human sexual love: see esp. André-Marie Dubarle, "L'amour humain dans le Cantique des cantiques," *RB* 61 (1954) 68–89; and Achille M. Brunet, "Théodore de Mopsueste et le Cantique des cantiques," *Études et recherches* 9 (1955) 155–70.

353 Cf. Geza Vermes, *Scripture and Tradition in Judaism: Haggadic Studies* (Studia Post-Biblica 4; Leiden: E. J. Brill, 1973) 37–39.

354 See above, p. 13, n. 55, and pp. 28–33. On the general scope and significance of the marriage metaphor in biblical traditions, see André Neher, "Le symbolisme conjugal: expression de l'histoire dans l'Ancien Testament," *RHPR* 34 (1954) 30–49.

355 E.g., Joüon, 73–76; André Feuillet, "Le Cantique des Cantiques et la tradition biblique," *Nouvelle Revue Theologique* 74 (1952) 92–102; and, recently, *idem,* "Le drame d'amour du Cantique des cantiques remis en son contexte prophétique," *Nova et Vetera* 62 (1987) 81–127; 63 (1988) 81–136. Two general problems with this approach may be noted. First, the metaphor appears in prophetic sources primarily to portray the broken covenant (i.e., Israel's harlotry, as in Hos 1—3; 4:12; 9:1; Jer 3:1–5; and Ezek 16, 23) rather than Israel's youthful or future devotion to God (so Jer 2:2; cf. Isa 54:5–8); in the Song, of course, there is no hint of the woman's infidelity. Second, when the marriage/divorce metaphor appears in prophetic literature there is no ambiguity regarding its interpretation; conversely, the Song never offers specific warrant for a transferred identification of either the man or the woman. The basic question thus remains: On what basis does one establish that the Song was composed with the prophetic theme of covenantal marriage specifically in view? Cf. the terse critical response to Feuillet's position given by Jean-Paul Audet, "Love and Marriage in the Old Testament" [tr. F. Burke] *Scr* 10 (1958) 80–81 n. 2; and the more extensive review in Jacques Winandy, *Le Cantique des Cantiques: Poème d'amour mué en écrit de sagesse* (Bible et vie chrétienne; Tournai: Castermann [Maredsous], 1960) 17–26.

espoused to Christ.

In recent times, the most thoroughgoing, sophisticated effort to interpret the Song as an allegory of divine-human love and covenantal marriage has been made by André Robert, and elaborated further by André Feuillet and Raymond Tournay.[356] According to Robert's view, the Song is a relatively late postexilic composition whose anthological style (*style/procédé anthologique*) demonstrates the allegorical intention of its author. This style is supposed to be a Jewish midrashic technique, in which words and image are carefully chosen from earlier biblical sources and artfully collocated so as to suggest a symbolic level of meaning.[357] Each textual segment is thus comparable to a tessera in a grand mosaic, valuable in itself but contributing to the greater richness of the broad design. Robert claims that context of usage provides a check on arbitrary parallelism in identifying significant semantic correlations and congruent literary themes that unlock the allegorical sense. In the case of *hārê bāter* (2:17), for example, he argues that the textual referent for the latter, unusual term is the covenant ceremony narrated in Genesis 15, where Abram "cut in half" (*wayĕbattēr*, Piʿel preterite of *btr*) several sacrificial

animals and arranged the severed parts in parallel rows, each "half" (*bitrô*) opposite the other (v 10; cf. v 17).[358] Hence, while the literal meaning of *hārê bāter*, "mountains of separation," yields little sense, the transferred contextual meaning intended by the poet is "mountains of the covenant" (*hārê bĕrît*), referring to the Palestinian hill-country God promised to grant to Abram's descendants. In the case of 7:4[3], the woman's anatomy becomes Israelite geography, when her "breasts" are supposed by Robert to represent the mountains of Ebal and Gerizim.[359] Great ingenuity is displayed in application of this method, and that is part of the problem; the textual data adduced are too precarious to bear the weight of interpretation placed on them.[360] Despite the pretense of exegetical precision, exaggeration and uncontrolled fantasy seem to be flaws endemic to allegorical exposition.

Some defenders of traditional Christian exposition have urged that the genre of the Song is parable rather than allegory.[361] A parable is an extended or complex metaphor with a didactic purpose; the details that comprise the metaphor are not meant to be deciphered in *ad hoc* fashion, as though each has a specific transferred

356 Robert's French translation of the Song, together with notes, first appeared in *Le Cantique des Cantiques* (La sainte Bible 18; Paris: Cerf, 1951, ²1953). It is worth noting that there has been a drastic revision of this treatment in the *revised* one volume edition, *La Bible de Jérusalem* (Paris: Cerf, 1974) 945–62; according to Pope (17), Roland de Vaux was responsible for this. The "Études bibliques" commentary, with contributions from Tournay and Feuillet, provides the fullest expression of Robert's position. For other pertinent studies of these authors, see above, n. 187.

357 On "anthological style" see André Robert, "Littéraires (Genres)," *DBSup* 5, 410–11; Renée Bloch, "Midrash" in *DBSup* 5, 1263–1281; and the remarks of Raymond Tournay in Robert, 10–17.

358 Robert, 128–29.

359 Robert, 261–62.

360 See Loretz, "Eros," esp. 204–11. Loretz argues against the claims of Robert and others for presence in the Song of obscure transferred meanings of terms by pointing out how contrastingly conspicuous is the transposition of sexual imagery to Lady Wisdom in Proverbs 2—9 (cf. also Sir 14:20–23 and 24:17–22). See also Roland E. Murphy, "Recent Literature on the Canticle of Canticles," *CBQ* 16 (1954) esp. 5–8.

361 Cf. already the positions of Bossuet and Lowth, summarized above, pp. 37–38. This position has been developed during the past generation especially by Denis Buzy: "La composition littéraire du Cantique des cantiques," *RB* 49 (1940) 169–94; "L'allégorie matrimoniale de Jahvé et d'Israël et le Cantique des cantiques," *RB* 52 (1944) 77–90; "Le Cantique des Cantiques. Exégèse allégorique ou

meaning distinguishable from others that form the overall design. As the methodological dictum of Maldonatus puts it, "persons are not compared with persons, nor parts to parts, but the whole affair is the burden of the comparison."[362] In this view, the Song is generally constructed to suggest the covenantal union of God with the people of God. The various scenes and segments of poetic dialogue illustrate the depth of divine-human love, but it is the literal text that supports this theological sense. While this approach avoids the pitfalls of detailed allegorical exposition, it still fails to establish any firm literary grounds for reading the biblical text as a parable. The genre is imputed to the Song rather than demonstrated on the basis of overt content.

Typology has provided a third approach adopted by some expositors in defense of traditional Christian interpretation of the Song.[363] Although there are variations in the understanding of typological method, it has generally demonstrated correspondences between Old and New Testament texts. A person, thing, or event in the Old Testament is correlated with something similar in the New (as, for example, when Adam and Christ are depicted as type and antitype in Romans 5). Typological interpretation affirms that the Song in its literal sense refers to love between a man and a woman, but claims that a broader canonical context also establishes a more sublime "typical" meaning, which portrays the love that unites God and God's chosen people. Thus the commentary of Athanasius Miller offers a twofold exposition: literal explanation of the Song is followed, in a register at the bottom of the page, by elaboration of the putative typical sense, based especially on the nuptial themes (Christ and the church) of Ephesians 5.[364] Here, too, the problem is one of control. No one has convincingly shown that Ephesians 5 or any other New Testament text intends to exegete the Song, either in whole or in part; hence the typological relationship remains a hermeneutical presupposition without solid literary foundation.

In sum, recent critics have been unable to establish an objective exegetical basis for decoding the Song along the lines of patristic and medieval Christian exposition. While this does not negate the value of the expository tradition in its own right, it leaves us without empirical criteria by which to assess the possible connection between "original" authorial intent and subsequent creations of hermeneutical imagination.

Cultic-Mythological Interpretation. Attempts during the present century to comprehend the Song's literary prehistory in relationship to ancient Near Eastern traditions of "sacred marriage" share certain premises with recent defenses of allegorical, parabolic, and typological readings. Here, too, peculiarities of language and theme, as well as the eventual canonization of the

---

parabolique?" *RSR* 39 (1951) 99–114; and *Le Cantique des Cantiques* (Paris: Letouzey et Ané, 1950) esp. 19. Cf. also Alberto Vaccari, "La Cantica," *I Libri Poetici* (La Sacra Bibbia 5/2; Firenze: Salani, 1950) 112: "Since the Canticle is a parable, it should be understood and explained according to the basic laws of the parable."

362 *In Mattheum,* 11:16: *non personae personis, nec partes partibus: sed totum negotium toti negotio comparatur* (Joannis Maldonati, *Commentarii in Quatour Evangelistas,* Vol. 1 [ed. Franciscus Sausen; Moguntia: Kircheim, Schott & Thielmann, 1840] 334).

363 E.g., Delitzsch; and Vincenz Zapletal, *Das Hoheslied kritisch und metrisch untersucht* (Freiburg, 1907). Cf. Joüon, 26–27. For an assessment of the typological approach to the Song, see G. Lloyd Carr, *The Song of Solomon: An Introduction and Commentary* (TOTC; Leicester/Downers Grove: InterVarsity, 1984) 24–32.

364 Miller, esp. 7–14 for discussion of his typological method.

work, can best be explained if the poetry originated as religious rather than secular literature. Although specific cultic associations and rites, which constituted the formative *Sitz im Leben,* seem to have receded in the transmission of the text,[365] traditional Jewish and Christian allegories are, in this view, supposed to give accurate witness to a significant continuity of theological meaning: They correctly recognized the divine persona of the Song's male protagonist, but remythologized his heavenly bride, casting her in the secondary guise of personified Israel or the church.

If the premises of allegorical and cultic-mythological approaches are similar, so too are their basic weaknesses. Because the biblical text in its received form gives no overt indication that it rehearses a theological drama or comprises a liturgy, hypothecated original meaning must be reconstructed from a skein of putative allusions to sacral personages and affairs.[366] For example, the effusive greeting that is said to befit the woman's appear-

ance in 6:10 is usually taken to be the strongest evidence for her possible divinity: "Who is this that comes forth like the dawn, beautiful as the moon? Pure as the sun, awe-inspiring as visions?"[367] It cannot be denied that the language here has a decidedly theophanic cast and may derive ultimately from hymnic tradition.[368] But does this isolated bit of poetic hyperbole provide sufficient reason to identify the female protagonist herself as an astral goddess (Ishtar, Astarte, or the like)? The text only indicates that her unique beauty merits such praise, not that her persona is divine. Similarly, although the epithet *dôdî* ("my lover/beloved") has a divine referent in Isaiah 5:1, as the context itself makes explicit, when it is used in the Song to refer to the man there is nothing to suggest

---

365 Meek, 95: "In course of time, however, the early connections of the book were forgotten, and it became so secularized that it appears today as a simple anthology of love poems without any religious connotation other than its connection with Passover and its inclusion in the canon." For an attempt to reconstruct the Song's origins in a Spring "New Year's Festival," associated with Israelite rites of Passover and Unleavened Bread, see Wilhelm Wittekindt, *Das Hohe Lied und seine Beziehungen zum Ištarkult* (Hannover: Orient-Buchhandlung [Heinz Lefaire], 1926) esp. 187–92; cf. also Ringgren, 3–4.

366 The problem is admitted by Meek, 96: "On separate items the evidence may be slight, but the critics fail to note that it is cumulative, and the theory does help to solve problems that were previously insoluble." Cf. Pope, 17–18. The most elaborate attempt to reconstruct the Song as a liturgical drama of hieros gamos remains that of Hartmut Schmökel, *Heilige Hochzeit und Hoheslied* (Abhandlungen für die Kunde des Morgenlandes 32/1; Wiesbaden: Deutsche Morgenlandische Gesellschaft [Franz Steiner], 1956) esp.

45–47. Schmökel's restructuring of the text is more radical even than restorations suggested by proponents of the secular drama theory; he posits three original ritual "scenes," comprised of the following rearranged textual segments: (Scene I.) 8:13; 6:10, 5a; 1:5–6; 6:1, 2, 11–12; 3:1–2; 5:7; 3:4; 5:2–6; 3:3; 5:8, 9, 10–16; 1:7, 8; 8:1–2; (Scene II.) 4:8; 8:5a, 5b–7; 7:7–10[6–9]; 2:10b–14, 17; 4:9–11; 2:16; 6:4, 5b–9, 3; 4:1—5:7; 7:11[10]; (Scene III.) 3:6–11; 7:1–6[6:13—7:5]; 1:9–14; 2:1–3; 4:12—5:1; 2:8–9; 7:12–14[11–13]; 2:6–7; 1:2–4; 3:5; 2:4–5; 8:3–4; 1:16–17.

367 This text and other references in the Song have been supposed to reflect Akkadian Ishtar in her double capacity as goddess of love and war: see Franz X. Kugler, "Vom Hohen Lied und seiner kriegerischen Braut," *Scholastik* 2 (1927) 38–52. Cf. also Hans-Peter Müller, "Die lyrische Reproduktion des Mythischen im Hohenlied," *ZTK* 73 (1976) esp. 24–26; Müller attempts to chart a middle course between literalistic and cultic-mythological readings of the Song.

368 See above, p. 51.

that the sense is theophoric.[369] Alleged allusions in the Song to mythological scenarios are even more difficult to control. Can adumbration of the shepherding motif in 1:7 support the claim that the male lover was originally Dumuzi/Tammuz?[370] Is the role of the city "watchmen" in 3:3 and 5:7 illuminated by that of the gatekeepers Inanna/Ishtar encountered in the myth of her descent into the netherworld?[371] Does 4:8 preserve a distant echo of Astarte's annual descent from the Lebanon range to the Adonis river?[372] Such parallels are simply too tenuous; even if some of them could be secured by new data, they are too isolated to provide a convincing or useful context for interpreting the Song.

One cannot refute the cultic theory by claiming that those who designed the canon of Hebrew Scriptures would never have included in it a work of heterodox origins. Conceivably, the actual derivation of the poetry may have been forgotten long before the period of the Song's canonization, though such argument considerably weakens the case for continuity with later Jewish and Christian traditions of symbolic interpretation. A greater difficulty is posed by the paucity of our knowledge about Canaanite-Phoenician and early Israelite cultic practices,

orthodox or otherwise. Polemics in biblical sources against pagan and paganizing cults do not, understandably enough, provide very detailed accounts of the objectionable rites themselves and how they were performed. The infamous orgiastic fertility religion of ancient Canaan—at best implied by such texts as Numbers 25:1–8, Deuteronomy 23:17–18, Amos 2:7, Jeremiah 3:6–10, and Ezekiel 16:15–34—is impossible to reconstruct with any specificity.[373] Was the Canaanite goddess Asherah sometimes worshipped as Yahweh's consort? Were rites of hieros gamos, thought to effect the annual renewal of nature, introduced into the Yahwistic cultus by such censured rulers as Solomon (1 Kgs 11:5), Ahab (1 Kgs 16:30–34), and Manasseh (2 Kgs 21:3–7; cf. 23:4–8)? Available evidence does not allow us either to affirm or to deny these possibilities.[374] What can be said, however, is that nothing in the Song shows the clear imprint of cultic performance. Certainly the poetry gives no hint of sexual licentiousness, secular or sacred, nor is there a discernible trace of funerary rites usually associated with the cults of Tammuz and Adonis.[375] The vitality of nature comes into view in the Song but only as the accompaniment of sexual love, not

---

369 *Contra* Meek, 96, who also cites the theophoric personal name *Dōdāwāhû* ("Yahu is beloved"?) in 2 Chron 20:37. A recently discovered Phoenician epigraph from the temple of Astarte at Kition in Cyprus may attest "beloved" (*dd*) as an epithet for Adonis, in association with communal rites of lamentation; for the text and pertinent discussion, see Brian Peckham, "Phoenicia and the Religion of Israel," *Ancient Israelite Religion: Essays in Honor of Frank Moore Cross* (ed. Patrick D. Miller, Jr. *et al.*; Philadelphia: Fortress, 1987) esp. 84–87.

370 Cf. Samuel Noah Kramer, *The Sacred Marriage Rite: Aspects of Faith, Myth, and Ritual in Ancient Sumer* (Bloomington/London: Indiana University, 1969), 90, 98–103.

371 So Meek, 118. For the Sumerian and Akkadian texts in translation, see Samuel Noah Kramer, *ANET*³, 52–

57 ("Inanna's Descent to the Nether World"); and Ephraim A. Speiser, *ANET*³, 106–109 ("Descent of Ishtar to the Nether World"). Cf. also Kramer, "Studies," 491–92.

372 Meek, 123; cf. Ringgren, 21.

373 For influential and representative attempts at such reconstruction, see Herbert G. May, "The Fertility Cult in Hosea," *AJSL* 48 (1931–32) 73–98; and Hans Walter Wolff, *Hosea* (tr. Gary Stansell, ed. Paul D. Hanson; Hermeneia; Philadelphia: Fortress, 1974) 13–16. See the critical remarks and studies cited by Robert A. Oden, Jr., *The Bible Without Theology: The Theological Tradition and Alternatives to It* (San Francisco: Harper & Row, 1987) 131–53, 187–92.

374 See the judicious assessment of the evidence, including the Kuntillet ʿAjrud epigraphs that refer to "Yahweh and his Asherah," offered by P. Kyle

as its outcome.

As our earlier survey of Egyptian and Sumerian sources indicated, there is no reason to doubt that the biblical Song is indebted, at least indirectly, to older traditions of Near Eastern love poetry. Nor need one quarrel with the likelihood that some of these antecedent traditions had specifically sacral significance or that they otherwise witness to the reciprocity of imagery depicting divine and human love. However, in the final analysis, the cultic-mythological approach—like its allegorical counterpart—proves to be inadequate because it too quickly shifts the focus of expository attention to a reconstructed level of "meaning." It is a contribution of sound historical-critical method to insist that the literary character and thematic content of the received text of the Song not be overwhelmed by detailed exploration of either ancient Near Eastern background or the foreground of traditional Jewish and Christian interpretation.[376]

Eros and Wisdom. What distinguishes the Song most sharply from other works of biblical literature is not the fact that it takes human sexuality seriously but rather the exuberant, thoroughly erotic, and nonjudgmental manner in which it depicts the love between a man and a woman. Here, the emotions of the two young lovers—their yearnings and pleasure in each other—occupy the textual foreground, almost blotting out conventions to which romance and sexual relations are generally subordinated elsewhere in scriptural sources. But it is important to notice that a social context is not entirely absent. The "Daughters of Jerusalem" may have significance in this regard (2:7; 3:5; 8:4) and possibly also the enigmatic "watchmen" (3:3; 5:7). Twice the young woman refers to constraints her elder brothers try to impose on her activities (1:6; 8:8–10). And she acknowledges that it would be indiscreet to greet her lover in public with a kiss (8:1). These touches alone suffice to indicate why the Song should not be described as a treatise on "free love."[377] The cultural setting is one that encouraged strict standards of sexual morality and marital fidelity (e.g., Deut 22:13–29). What this poetry celebrates is not eroticism for its own sake, and certainly not ribaldry or promiscuous sex, but rather the desires of an individual woman and man to enjoy the bond of mutual possession (2:16; 6:3; 7:10[9]).[378] It is all the more striking, therefore, that even when nuptial motifs come into view (3:11;

McCarter, Jr., "Aspects of the Religion of the Israelite Monarchy: Biblical and Epigraphic Data," *Ancient Israelite Religion: Essays in Honor of Frank Moore Cross* (ed. Patrick D. Miller, Jr. *et al.*; Philadelphia: Fortress, 1987) 137–55.

375 On the Phoenician cult of Adonis, see Noel Robertson, "The Ritual Background of the Dying God in Cyprus and Syro-Palestine," *HTR* 75 (1982) 313–59. The evidence accumulated by Pope (210–29) to suggest a connection between the Song and a Canaanizing mortuary cultus—featuring the *marzēaḥ,* a love feast "celebrated with wine, women, and song" (228)—is fascinating, but the specific thematic links are unconvincing as regards *Sitz im Leben* and literary character; the Song simply does not portray sexual revelry as a means of overcoming the power of death. Cf. the remarks of Fox, 243.

376 Although addressed to proponents of the allegorical approach, the following remarks of Audet ("Love," 80–81 n. 2) are equally applicable to cultic-mythological interpretations of the Song: "In any problem the most detailed solution is not necessarily the most accurate. I would even go so far as to say that in the present case, any temptation to enter too soon into detailed examination may very easily conceal a retreat from the much more serious problem raised by the text as a whole. For in such a situation detailed analysis is only possible on a basis of assumptions, and in the nature of things, with every move it sinks deeper into erroneous details. So it is with the assumptions themselves that one must quarrel."

377 *Contra* Rudolph, 105–106.

378 The individuality of the Song's lovers, within a particular socio-cultural context, is correctly stressed

4:8—5:1) no reference is made to the important familial "business" of Israelite marriage—contractual arrangements, dowries, child-bearing, inheritance, and the like.[379] The poetry allows us to suppose that these are matters for others to attend to and on other occasions. For the moment we, as audience, are invited by the poet to appreciate the qualities of tenderness, joy, sensual intimacy, reciprocal longing and mutual esteem, all of which are socially desirable and beautifully mysterious dimensions of human sexual love.

As suggested earlier, it is not unlikely that at least some of the poems that comprise the Song in its received form were originally discrete compositions.[380] One thinks in this regard of the major *wasf*s in 4:1–5 and 5:10–16 and of the beautiful "Spring Song" in 2:10–14. We can only speculate on the basis of genre, imagery, and theme as to the possible settings and functions of such units, were they indeed once independent poems. Courtship, in preference to wedding rites per se, generally commends itself as a context for the composition and use of love poetry. But specific occasion for and social interest in amatory lyrics obviously need not be limited to private interactions between young lovers themselves—as works of the Greek bucolic poets, Elizabethan love sonnets, and popular ballads of our own day attest, no less than the extant examples of Egyptian and Sumerian love poetry. Artful entertainment, whether of

a folkish or courtly sort or both, cannot be ruled out as a factor in the writing and transmission of poetry that was eventually incorporated into the literary text of the Song.

However, if one does seek a more formal preliterary setting for the Song's poems, Jean-Paul Audet may be correct in pointing to popular rites of betrothal (somewhat comparable, perhaps, to modern "engagement").[381] It is his suggestion that Hosea 2:17 alludes to lyrical declarations of love that belong to a prenuptial stage of espousal: "and there she (Israel) shall respond [*wě'ānětâ*] as in the days of her youth." Similarly, the "voice of the bride and the voice of the bridegroom" (Jer 7:32–34; 16:5–9; 25:10–11) in his view refers to semipublic avowals of love between a betrothed man and woman (cf. Gen 29:18–30). In such a putative setting the poetry testifies to an "état de conscience," as Audet calls it—the emphatically positive attitude that ancient Israel had toward human sexual love, love whose physical and emotional profundity was assumed to be fully consummated in the partnership of faithful marriage and would in due course perpetuate family and renew society. Moreover, at least implicitly this consciousness paid homage to God's design of creation: It acknowledged that human beings, as male and female, were expected to participate joyfully in the ordained sacral order of life.[382] Hence the intensely heightened awareness of

---

by Fox (308), this in response to Leo Krinetzki's psychological treatment of them along Jungian lines as male (*Animus*) and female (*Anima*) sexual archetypes ("Die erotische Psychologie des Hohen Liedes," *TQ* 150 [1970] 404–16).

379   For the legal-institutional dimensions of ancient Israelite betrothal and marriage, see the following useful surveys: Roland de Vaux, *Ancient Israel: Its Life and Institutions* (tr. John McHugh; New York/Toronto/London: McGraw-Hill, 1961) 24–38; and Ze'ev W. Falk, *Hebrew Law in Biblical Times: An Introduction* (Jerusalem: Wahrmann, 1964) 123–53.

380   See above, pp. 62–67.

381   Audet, "Le sens," 211–216; and *idem,* "Love," 79.

382   Cf. André-Marie Dubarle, "L'amour humain dans le Cantique des cantiques," *RB* 61 (1954) esp. 67, where he observes that a major problem in the history of the Song's interpretation has been an inability of many commentators to distinguish between "profane" (theologically humanistic) and "profaned" (licentious or corrupted) love. Along the lines suggested by Audet and Dubarle, a provocative discussion of the Song's view of human love as at once sexually erotic and implicitly sacral is offered by

nature's delights, so abundant in the Song's metaphorical portraits of the two lovers and their love-making, should not be described as indicative of merely "naturalistic," "secular," or "profane" interests. Ancient Israel perceived the wonders of human sexuality, fulfilled in marital love, to be a divine blessing.

Granted that the social provenance of Israelite love poetry may be envisioned along these lines, how are we to understand the literary compilation and promulgation of the Song itself? Audet ascribes this secondary level of work to postexilic sages, whose literary efforts otherwise bear the closest formal, semantic, and thematic resemblances to the Song.[383] Their attribution of the finished composition to "Solomon" (1:1) Audet takes to be less a claim regarding historical authorship than an appreciative expression of the text's superlatively sapiential significance.[384] Although more traditional wisdom lore exhibits a predominantly moralizing stance toward sexual matters, nowhere evident in the Song,[385] it is not even necessary in this view to suppose that the later sages misunderstood or drastically reinterpreted the original meaning of the erotic poetry. It remained for them what it had always been—a powerful affirmation of human sexual love, compatible with their intellectual curiosity about natural phenomena (cf. Prov 30:18–19) as well as their pragmatic recognition of what contributed to ideal connubial bliss and marital fidelity (Prov 5:18–19). Still, the sages seem to have added their own generalizing, self-consciously didactic signature in 8:6b–7:[386] "love" (ʾahăbâ) is not deified here but it is declared to be a force "as strong as Death" (ʿazzâ kammāwet), an unquenchable flame in human experience, and a value beyond material price. Interestingly, later sapiential theologizing developed these and similar themes in praising the incomparable joys and benefits of human love for personified Wisdom.[387]

the French Protestant scholar Daniel Lys, the title of whose commentary indicates the theological perspective adopted: *Le plus beau chant de la création: Commentaire du Cantique des Cantiques* (LD 51; Paris: Cerf, 1967) esp. 50–55; an extensive English summary of Lys' view is provided by Pope, 201–205. See, more recently, Daniel Lys, "Le Cantique des cantiques: Pour une sexualité non-ambiguë," *Lumière et Vie* (1979) 39–53. Cf. also Oswald Loretz, "Die theologische Bedeutung des Hohenliedes," *BZ* N.F. 10 (1966) 29–43.

383 Audet, "Le sens," 202–11, 216–21; and *idem,* "Love," 79–83. Audet's position is developed in the commentary of Jacques Winandy (with the sub-title suggesting his perspective): *Le Cantique des Cantiques: Poème d'amour mué en écrit de sagesse* (Bible et vie chrétienne; Tournai: Castermann [Maredsous], 1960). Cf. Würthwein, 34.

384 Audet, "Love," 81–83. This view is developed by Brevard S. Childs into the "canonical context," which he understands to be the theologically appropriate one for interpreting the Song: *Introduction to the Old Testament as Scripture* (Philadelphia: Fortress, 1979) 573–79. On the other hand, Gordis (13–16) seems to understand the attribution of the work to Solomon and the connection with "Wisdom" to be limited to technical aspects of prosody and music.

385 See above, pp. 69–70.

386 Audet, "Le sens," 216–17. On the connections of these lines with sapiential thought, see also: Nicolas J. Tromp, "Wisdom and the Canticle. Ct 8,6c–7b: text, character, message and import," *Le Sagesse de l'Ancien Testament* (ed. Maurice Gilbert; BETL 51; Gembloux: J. Duculot, 1979) 88–95; and M. Sadgrove, "The Song of Songs as Wisdom Literature," *Studia Biblica 1978, I: Papers on the Old Testament and Related Themes* (ed. E. A. Livingstone; JSOTSup 11; Sheffield: JSOT, 1979) 245–48. See below, p. 197.

387 The ardent "search" for and possession of personified Wisdom is depicted with erotic overtones, e.g., in Wis 6:12–20; 7:8–14; 8:2–21; Sir 51:13–22; and Bar 3:15—4:4. Metaphorical imagery, comparable to that of the Song, is used to describe Wisdom in Sir 1:16–20 and 24:13–22. On the rewards of "love" for

B. The Quality of Love, Human and Divine

It is a striking fact that the Song of Songs has largely been neglected in studies of biblical theology. This may be so because major contributors to the contemporary discussion have held views of the Song's original meaning that leave little room for theological development, either in relationship to salvation-historical traditions usually supposed to be central to ancient Israel's religious thought[388] or to modern social and spiritual concerns. Perhaps recognition that the Song is comprised of erotic poetry has meant for some an absence of religious or theological significance.[389] But such a perspective is surely too narrow, even within the boundaries imposed by a rigorously historical-critical interpretation.

While the Song is not designed to elaborate theological doctrine or to teach ethics, its unapologetic depiction of rapturous, reciprocal love between a man and a woman does model an important dimension of human existence, an aspect of life that ancient Israel understood to be divinely instituted and sanctioned. We need look no further than Genesis 1 to find express warrant for this view: the whole of God's creation is "good . . . indeed very good," specifically including the sexual differentiation of humankind (vv 26–31). In this passage, to be sure, procreation immediately comes to the fore as God's purposive blessing in relationship to human sexuality. But it fulfills rather than diminishes the extraordinary affirmation that the divine image itself is incarnated in male and female counterparts, which only together are granted sovereignty in God's world. Even more poignant, perhaps, are the familiar lines of Genesis 2:18–25, a text Karl Barth has called the "Old Testament Magna Carta of humanity" because, in his view, it epitomizes the creaturely co-existence that God intends for all humankind by focusing on the most basic and intimate of human unions, the physical bond formed between a man and a woman.[390] If, as some critics have argued,[391] the Song's humanistic viewpoint represents an Israelite

---

personfied Wisdom, see already Prov 4:7–9 and esp. 8:1–36; note also Prov 7:4, where embrace of knowledge is commended using epithets—"my sister" (*'ăḥōtî*) and "intimate one" (*mōdā'*)—reminiscent of the appellatives for the Song's lovers. Cf. the illuminating discussion of "love-language" in wisdom traditions offered by Gerhard von Rad, *Wisdom in Israel* (tr. James D. Martin; London: SCM, 1972) 166–76.

388 In this regard, of course, the Song has shared the fortunes of the more traditional books of Israelite wisdom with which it is most closely associated in the canon. For the contemporary reassessment of wisdom's significance, applicable at least in part to the Song, see Gerhard von Rad's already classic study, cited in the preceding note, and Roland E. Murphy, "The Theological Contributions of Israel's Wisdom Literature," *Listening* 19 (1984) 30–40; and *idem*, "Religious Dimensions of Israelite Wisdom," *Ancient Israelite Religion: Essays in Honor of Frank Moore Cross* (ed. Patrick D. Miller, Jr. *et al.*; Philadelphia: Fortress) 449–58.

389 See Gordis, 16; and Gerleman, 83–85, whose commentary deliberately omits the "Ziel" section, which is otherwise a regular feature of volumes in the BKAT series. Cf. Fuerst, 199–200.

390 Karl Barth, *Church Dogmatics*, Vol. 3: *The Doctrine of Creation* (ed. Geoffrey W. Bromiley and Thomas F. Torrance; Edinburgh: T. & T. Clark, 1958–61) esp. Part 1, 288–329; Part 2, 291–324; and Part 4, 116–240. In these contexts, Barth considers the Song to be a "second Magna Carta" that develops the view briefly adumbrated in Gen 2 ". . . although here in a form which is almost terrifyingly strong and unequivocal" (3/1, 312). But while he specifically rejects a symbolical interpretation of the Song and maintains that its literal "primitive sense" as human love poetry is profound, he supposes that the attribution to Solomon is intended to give the work an essentially eschatological significance, i.e., to identify it as a portrait of the messianic fulfillment of human sexual love (3/1, 312; 3/2, 294–95).

391 Gerleman, 84; cf. Rudolph, 105–109.

poet's self-conscious attempt to "demythologize" ancient Near Eastern concepts of sacred sexuality—manifest in fertility rites of sympathetic magic—the broader vision sketched in Genesis 1—2 calls into question the notion that male-female sexual relationships were thereby completely desacralized, secularized, or set loose from constraints of moral decision making. Neither in the Song nor elsewhere in Scripture is human sexual love celebrated as "its own legitimation."[392] It is to be diligently sought after and treasured when found, because it is a vital part of God's gracious design for human life; it is a "good" gift to be enjoyed and yet, like others, capable of being twisted by human perversity.[393]

The Hebrew Bible thus provides a coherent framework within which one can interpret the Song as expressing a theology of human sexuality. Moreover, although Israelite culture and the broader scope of scriptural witnesses understand marriage to be the institutional context in which sexual love is rightly fulfilled, what the Song itself encourages us to appreciate are the emotional experiences of love. Several key elements merit summary attention.

a) Prominent throughout the Song are themes of presence and absence in the poetic portraits of the woman and her lover. The joy of physical presence is obvious, of course, when the man and woman directly address each other with words of praise and, especially, when they embrace, sharing the intense pleasures of love (2:6; 8:3). But in the Song as in life the loved one is not always physically present, nor is absence necessarily the antithesis of passion's fulfillment. If the beloved other's absence is intolerable, it is also creative of more intense emotions: the ardent yearning to reunite (2:6–7, 17; 4:16; 8:14), a compulsive seeking that is not satisfied until the other is found again (3:1–5; 5:2–8; 6:1); and the "sickness" of love (2:5; 5:8) that, paradoxically, the lover's physical presence will only deepen, never cure. Sometimes the line between presence and absence is thin, even illusory perhaps. When the woman arises to greet her lover in 5:5–6, he has "gone" but is still somehow there with her ("flowing myrrh"). The question asked by the Daughters in 6:1 indicates that the woman's lover remains to be found, but her response (vv 2–3) suggests that he is not really lost; he has gone to enjoy his "garden." Absence, in a sense, defines presence, makes it more palpable and pleasing, more excruciating and joyous; it creates space for reflection within which the full impact of love's desire can be profoundly experienced.

b) Another striking feature of human sexual love as depicted in the Song is the mutuality of the feelings that draw together the man and the woman. As many episodes show, their admiration of and yearning for each other is both reciprocal and comparably intense: each

---

392 *Contra* Helmut Gollwitzer, *Song of Love. A Biblical Understanding of Sex* (Philadelphia: Fortress, 1979) 30. While Gollwitzer's reading of the Song from the point of view of modern culture is in many respects provocative, it also illustrates the danger of too quickly bypassing the ancient social and canonical contextualization of the poetry.

393 Cf. Brevard S. Childs, *Old Testament Theology in a Canonical Context* (Philadelphia: Fortress, 1985) 188–95. The comments that follow were presented in preliminary form in two essays: Roland E. Murphy, "Towards a Commentary on the Song of Songs," *CBQ* 39 (1977) 494–96; and *idem*, "A Biblical Model of Human Intimacy: The Song of Songs," *The Family in Crisis or in Transition: A Sociological and Theological Perspective* (ed. Andrew Greeley; Concilium 121 [141 in the international edition]; New York: Seabury, 1979) 61–66.

considers the other to be unrivalled, superlative (2:1–3); in the *wasf*s they exuberantly praise each other's physical charms (4:1–7; 5:10–16; 7:2–7[1–6]); and they exchange without embarrassment equally passionate invitations to love-making (1:2–4, 7–8; 2:13–14; 4:8, 16; 7:11–12[10–11]; 8:14). There is no sense here of masculine dominance and mere submission or subordination of the female; it is indeed the woman's voice that resounds most loudly in the poetry, eager to initiate as well as to respond to affirmations of love. Whereas in Genesis 2:23 we hear only the man's declaration of delight—"This one now (she) is bone of my bones and flesh of my flesh"—in the Song the woman announces the genuinely reciprocal wholeness of identity discovered in mutual enjoyment of physical love: "My lover is mine and I am his" (2:16); and conversely, "I am my lover's and he is mine" (6:3).[394] Significantly, too, while Genesis 3:16 refers only to thê sexual attraction that binds woman to man ("to your husband will be your desire [*tĕšûqātēk*]") in the Song she can relish his ardor as completion of her own sense of intimate belonging to him: "I am my lover's, and towards me is his desire [*tĕšûqātô*]" (7:11[10]). This biblical witness should not be taken lightly in a contemporary theology of human sexuality: "desire" relentlessly pursues its goal, strives to acquire, seeks its own fulfillment; but it can only nourish a love that is freely given and returned, a partnership that acknowl-edges the joy of being possessed by the beloved as well as the need to possess. Perhaps that is the message of the woman's repeated admonition: "Do not arouse, do not stir up love, until it be ready!" (2:7; 8:4).

c) Eroticism gets full play in the Song. From the outset there is nothing inhibited or tentative about the woman's desire for sexual fulfillment in the arms of her lover: "Let him kiss me with the kisses of his mouth! . . . Draw me after you! Let us run! . . . Let us exult and rejoice in you! Let us extol your love beyond wine!" (1:2, 4). Nor are the man's physical intentions disguised: "I will climb the palm tree, I will take hold of its branches. Let your breasts be like the clusters of the vine and the fragrance of your breath like apples" (7:9[8]). When the lovers offer praise of each other, their eyes neither pass over intimate parts of anatomy nor dwell on them (5:14; 7:2–3[1–2]). Although the poetry is explicitly erotic in its appreciation of sexual love, it never becomes prurient or pornographic.[395] What the poet depicts for us so vividly are the emotions of love, not clinical acts of love-making. Every sense is involved, indeed highlighted, in this rapturous portrait of love's delights. The man is like a fragrant "sachet of myrrh," lying between the woman's breasts (1:13), whose "fruit is sweet" to her taste (2:3). She relishes his ardent embrace (2:6; 8:3); even when he has departed, she feels his presence still, like flowing myrrh on her fingers (5:5). For his part, the man yearns

---

394 Cf. Karl Barth (n. 390 above), who stresses the import of the Song in completing the thought in Gen 2: "It is to be noted that in this second text we hear a voice which is lacking in the first. This is the voice of the woman, to whom the man looks and moves with no less pain and joy than she to him, and who finds him with no less freedom . . . than she is found. Implicitly, of course, this voice is heard in Genesis as well. But it now finds expression in words. And what words!" (3/2, 294). For interpretation of the Song in relationship to Gen 2—3, see also Phyllis Trible, *God and the Rhetoric of Sexuality* (OBT 2; Philadelphia:

Fortress, 1978) 144–65.

395 At times reference is made in the commentary to shades of meaning that attach to certain words or actions. This may be termed double entendre in the best sense of the term. The language of love is precisely that by its very nature. But it is important to preserve the double entendre, and not destroy it by a clinical translation or paraphrase; see the cautions of Jack M. Sasson, "On M. H. Pope's Song of Songs [AB 7c]," *Maarav* 1 (1979) esp. 182. Cf. also Fox, 310–15; and Benjamin J. Segal, "Double Meanings in the Song of Songs," *DD* 16 (1987–88) 249–55.

to see her lovely face and to hear her lyrical voice (2:14), to enjoy the rich tastes of her mouth and the exotic fragrances of her garments and body (4:11–14), and to cling to her shapely form (7:9[8]). The intensely sensual fascination of the lovers with each other finds poetic expression through the use of natural imagery: colors, perfumes and spices, flowers and fruits, fields, budding vineyards, and luxuriant gardens. Yet the experience of love not only draws upon the textures of nature for its metaphors, it opens the eyes of the lovers themselves to the beauty of the world around them—to its varied terrain and places of human abode (1:5, 16–17; 2:8; 3:6; 4:8; 6:4, 11; 8:5), to its seasons and the natural forces of wind and water that shape it (2:11; 4:15–16), and to other animate creatures that inhabit it with them (2:7–8; 4:1–2, 8; 8:14). In passion's true embrace the world is not recreated but reexperienced with heightened senses. In the intensity of committed love, mutually shared between man and woman, there is no transforming deification of humankind, but sexual servility and alienation may be overcome (cf. Gen 3:16–19); through such love there is no self-salvation from the forces of sin and death, but a vision of God's creation become whole again (cf. Gen 3:5–7).

Human sexual fulfillment, fervently sought and consummated in reciprocal love between woman and man: Yes, that is what the Song of Songs is about, in its literal sense and theologically relevant meaning. We may rejoice that Scripture includes such an explicit view among its varied witnesses to divine providence. But does the marvelous theological insight that the Song opens up have broader significance? Should we dismiss altogether the *Nachleben* of the text, the continuous though multi-faceted histories of its interpretation in both Judaism and Christianity? Having reappropriated the literal meaning, can we still give any credence to those who have heard the poetry speak eloquently of celibate love as well as connubial bliss, of divine-human covenant as well as male-female sexual partnership, of spiritual as well as physical rapture? It does not suffice to refute the Jewish and Christian interpretative traditions by pointing to arbitrary assumptions and improbable readings in the work of particular commentators and periods. Exaggerations, flawed premises, and outright errors in the exegetical quest to discover the Song's fuller theological significance can be admitted, and labelled counterproductive. Nevertheless, as modern expositors we should be open to the possibility that our predecessors, despite their foibles, may have caught a glimpse of theological reality that is not exhausted by the literal sense of the Song's poetry.[396] Why should we be enslaved by the very methodology that we claim has freed us from the tyranny of tradition?

If one grants that the consistent witnesses of earlier

---

396 While this is not the place to enter into broader discussions of recent developments in biblical interpretation and hermeneutics generally, there are increasing indications of scholarly recognition that historical-critical methodology does not in itself yield the exhaustive or final expository word: see, e.g., Walter Vogels, "Les limites de la méthode historico-critique," *Laval théologique et philosophique* 36 (1980) 173–94; and David Steinmetz, "The Superiority of Precritical Exegesis," *Theology Today* 37 (1980) 27–38. On the validity of a text's meaning beyond its "original" or "historical" sense, see Hans-Georg Gadamer, *Truth and Method* (ed. and tr. Garrett Barden and John Cumming; New York: Seabury, 1975) esp. 460–91 ["Supplement I: Hermeneutics and Historicism"]; for an assessment of Paul Ricoeur's hermeneutical contributions to interpretation of biblical texts, see John Dominic Crossan (ed.), *The Book of Job and Ricoeur's Hermeneutics* (Semeia 19; Chico: Scholars, 1981), with a select bibliography, 23–29. In the present commentator's judgment, the quest for the literal-historical sense of scriptural texts should not be abandoned, even though the results will only be proximate and need

generations of interpreters should challenge our exegetical methods and insights, as we have challenged theirs, then we take another step toward identifying the broader scope of the Song's theological significance in continuity with their perceptions. Within biblical traditions themselves, experiences of the world that comprise human knowledge and experiences of God that nurture faith are always interrelated.[397] Among the manifold ways this interrelationship comes to scriptural expression is the recognition that human love and divine love mirror each other.

Even if we cannot speak of 8:6 as the Song's climax, the verse is properly regarded by most interpreters as a high point. Here the power of "love" ('ahăbâ) is not only compared with the relentless force of death, it is identified in the final construction of the verse as "a flame of Yah" (šalhebet[-]yāh).[398] Tersely stated though it is, the insight is hermeneutically profound. It implies that the varied dimensions of human love described in the Song—the joy of presence and the pain of absence, yearning for intimate partnership with the beloved, and even erotic desire—can be understood, *mutatis mutandis*, as reflective of God's love.

The God of Israel transcended sex, but Israelite theology dared to use themes of human sexual love and marriage as metaphors in portraying the covenant relationship. The familiar formula of Leviticus 26:12—

"I will be your God, and you shall be my people"—parallels a bridegroom's wedding vow and may even have been so derived.[399] Certainly Hosea and other prophets depicted Yahweh as Israel's proper spouse, an often scorned but unyielding lover whose unrequited passion held open the promise of redemption. This imagery comes to especially bold expression in the salvation oracle of Isaiah 62:4–5, addressed to personified Zion:

> Never again shall you be called "Forsaken,"
>   nor shall your land any longer be called "Desolate";
> Rather, you shall be designated "I Delight in Her,"
>   and your land "Espoused."
> Indeed Yahweh takes delight in you,
>   and your land shall be espoused.
> As a young man espouses a virgin,
>   your ⟨Builder⟩ shall espouse you;
> As the bridegroom rejoices over the bride,
>   so shall your God rejoice over you.

God initiates and pursues a loving relationship with the community of faith. It is in terms of this grand metaphor that Jewish and Christian interpretative traditions understood the Song to express the communal "bride's" response, her memories of the divine love that had first claimed her, and her longing to experience always the joys of the lover's sublime presence.

---

not negate the value of traditional interpretation. The critical endeavor remains the surest means we possess that the topography of the text itself will not be overlooked in uncontrolled exegetical flights of fancy.

397 On this, see esp. the seminal remarks of Gerhard von Rad, "Some Aspects of the Old Testament World-View," *The Problem of the Hexateuch and Other Essays* (tr. E. W. Trueman Dicken; Edinburgh/London: Oliver & Boyd, 1965) 144–65.

398 For this reading of the construction, which is at least defensible, see the comments in the pertinent

sections of Notes and Interpretation below, pp. 191–92 and 197. Cf. also M. L. Ramlot, "Le Cantique des cantiques: 'une flamme de Yahve'," *RThom* 64 (1964) 239–59.

399 See Moshe Weinfeld, *Deuteronomy and the Deuteronomic School* (Oxford: Clarendon, 1972) 81–82, esp. n. 6 and the studies there cited. On the Song's view of sexual love in relationship to covenantal traditions, see Oswald Loretz, "Die theologische Bedeutung des Hohenliedes," *BZ* N.F. 10 (1966) esp. 39–43.

In the final analysis, then, what links the literal sense of the Song to the expository visions of synagogue and church is an exquisite insight: the love that forms human partnership and community, and that sustains the whole of creation, is a gift of God's own self.[400] But the biblical poet should have the last words in introducing the Song and its meaning (5:1b):

> Eat, friends, drink!
> Drink deeply of love!

---

[400] See, e.g., Lev 19:17–18; Deut 6:4–5; 7:6–11; 10:12–22; 1 Kgs 10:6–9; Jer 31:1–6; Ps 146:5–10; John 15:5–17; 1 Cor 13; 1 John 4:7–21.

A complete, sequential translation of the Song of Songs is provided here for the convenience of readers. The translation itself is relatively conservative, both stylistically and in its approach to the wording and syntax of the 𝔐 tradition. Words enclosed within parentheses ( ) amplify the sense of the literal Hebrew. Angle brackets ⟨ ⟩ are used to indicate places where the text of 𝔐 has been emended (for reasons discussed in the pertinent Notes to the individual commentary sections).

Major divisions represent sections of the work as they are treated in the commentary. These differ in many instances from the internal sectional divisions (*pārāšîyôt*) represented in 𝔐 as follows (*p = pĕtûḥâ; s = sĕtûmâ*): *p* 1:1–4; *s* 1:5–8; *s* 1:9–14; *s* 1:15—2:7; *s* 2:8–13; *s* 2:14; *s* 2:15–17; *s* 3:1–5; *s* 3:6–8; *s* 3:9–11; *s* 4:1–7; *s* 4:8–11; *s* 4:12—5:1; *s* 5:2—6:3; *s* 6:4–9; *s* 6:10; *s* 6:11—7:11; *s* 7:12—8:4; *s* 8:5–7; *s* 8:8–10; *p* 8:11–14.

Segments of the text which can be assigned with some certainty to specific speakers are indicated by capital letters in the left margin: M = the man; W = the woman; and D = the "Daughters of Jerusalem." To the right of the translation, references indicate important lexical and thematic correlations within the work itself.

1

1   The Song of Songs, by Solomon.

2 ■ W   Let him kiss me with the kisses of his mouth!
   Truly, more pleasing is your love than wine. 1:4; 4:10
The fragrance of your perfumes is pleasing, ... 4:10
   flowing perfume, your name;
   therefore the maidens love you.
Draw me after you! Let us run!
   The king has brought me to his chambers.
Let us exult and rejoice in you!
   Let us extol your love beyond wine! 1:2; 4:10
   Rightly do they love you.

Black am I, and beautiful, O Daughters of Jerusalem,
   like the tents of Qedar,
   like the pavilions of Solomon.
Do not stare at me because I am blackish,
   for the sun has burned me.
The sons of my mother were angry with me; 8:8–9
   they assigned me as keeper of the vineyards—   . . . . cf. 2:15; 7:13; 8:11–12
   my own vineyard I have not kept.

7 ■ W   Tell me, you whom my soul loves,
   where you pasture, where you rest at midday,
   lest I become as one who covers herself
   near the herds of your companions.

8 ■ M   If you do not know, O most beautiful of women, ... 5:9
   follow the tracks of the flock,
and pasture your kids
   near the tents of the shepherds.
To a mare of Pharaoh's chariots
   I compare you, my friend:
Lovely are your cheeks in pendants,
   your neck, in beads;
Pendants of gold we will make for you,
   along with silver ornaments.

12 ■ W   While the king was in his enclosure
   my nard gave forth its fragrance.
A sachet of myrrh is my lover to me;
   between my breasts he lies.
A cluster of henna is my lover to me,
   in the vineyards of Engedi.

15 ■ M   Ah, you are beautiful, my friend;
       ah, you are beautiful, your eyes are doves.   · · · · · · · · · 2:10,13; 4:1,7; 7:2,7
                                                           · · · · · · · · · · 4:1; 5:12

   ■ W   Ah, you are beautiful, my lover, most pleasing!
       Indeed our couch is verdant.
       The beams of our house, cedars;
         our rafters, cypresses.
2:1   I am a flower of Sharon,
         a lily of the valleys.

2 ■ M   As a lily among thorns,
       so is my friend among women.   · · · · · · · · · · 6:9–10

3 ■ W   As an apple tree among the trees of the forest,   · · · · · · · · · · cf. 8:5
       so is my lover among men.
       In his shadow I desire to remain,
         and his fruit is sweet to my taste.
       He has brought me to the wine house,
         and his banner over me is love.
       Strengthen me with raisin cakes,
         refresh me with apples,
         for I am sick with love.
       His left hand is under my head,   · · · · · · · · · · 6:8
         and his right hand embraces me.   · · · · · · · · · · 8:3
       I adjure you, O Daughters of Jerusalem,   · · · · · · · · · · 3:5; 5:8; 8:4
         by the gazelles and hinds of the fields:
       Do not arouse, do not stir up love,
         until it be ready!

8 ■ W   Hark, my lover!
       See, he comes:
       Springing over the mountains,
         leaping over the hills.
       My lover is like a gazelle,   · · · · · · · · · · 2:17; 8:14
         or a young stag.
       See, he stands behind our wall,
         looking through windows,
         peering through lattices.
       My lover responded to me:

   ■ (M)   "Arise, my friend,   · · · · · · · · · · 2:13; 7:12
       my beautiful one, and come!   · · · · · · · · · · 1:15; 4:1,7; 7:2,7
       See, the winter is past,
         the rains are over, gone.   · · · · · · · · · · cf. 5:6
       The blossoms appear in the land,   · · · · · · · · · · 6:11; 7:13
         the time for pruning has arrived;
       The song of the turtledove
         is heard in our land.
       The fig tree yields its figs;
         the vines, in bloom, give forth fragrance.
       Arise, my friend,   · · · · · · · · · · 2:10
       my beautiful one, and come!
       My dove, in the clefts of the rock,   · · · · · · · · · · 5:2; 6:9
         in the recesses of the cliff,
       Let me see your face   · · · · · · · · · · 8:13
         and hear your voice,
       For your voice is pleasant
         and your face lovely."

15 ■ W   **Catch us the foxes,**
     the little foxes
      that damage the vineyards, ...cf. 1:6; 7:13; 8:11–12
      when our vineyards are in bloom.

16   **My lover is mine**
      and I am his 6:3; 7:11
      who browses among the lilies. 4:5; 6:3
     Until the day breathes 4:6
      and the shadows flee,
     Turn, my lover;
      be like a gazelle or a young stag, ...2:9; 8:14
      upon the mountains of Bether.

3

1 ■ W   **Upon my bed at night** 5:2–8
     I sought him whom my soul loves,
     I sought him, but I did not find him.
   "I will rise and make the rounds of the city;
     in the streets and crossings
     I will seek him whom my soul loves."
   I sought him, but I did not find him.
   It was I the watchmen came upon
     as they made their rounds of the city.
   "Him whom my soul loves—have you seen him?"
   I had hardly left them
     when I found him whom my soul loves.
   I held on to him and would not let him go
     until I brought him to the house of my mother, ...8:2
     to the room of her who bore me. 6:9; 8:5
   I adjure you, O Daughters of Jerusalem, ...2:7; 5:8; 8:4
     by the gazelles and hinds of the fields:
   Do not arouse, do not stir up love,
     until it be ready!

6 ■ (?)   **What is this coming up from the desert,** 6:10; 8:5
     like a column of smoke?
   Perfumed with myrrh and frankincense
     from all kinds of exotic powders?
   This is Solomon's litter:
     sixty warriors surround it,
     of the warriors of Israel.
   All of them skilled with the sword,
     trained for war;
   Each with his sword ready
     against the terrors of the night.
   King Solomon made himself
     a carriage from Lebanon wood.
   Its columns he made of silver,
     its roof of gold;
   Its seat of purple,
     its interior woven with love.

⟨O Daughters of Jerusalem,⟩ go forth!
    Look, O Daughters of Zion!
Upon King Solomon
    in the crown with which his mother crowned him,
On the day of his marriage,
    on the day of the joy of his heart.

4

1 ■ M   Ah, you are beautiful, my friend, ... ■1:15; 2:10,13; 4:7; 7:2,7
    ah, beautiful.
Your eyes are doves 1:15; 5:12
    behind your veil.
Your hair is like a flock of goats 6:5
    that stream down Mount Gilead.
Your teeth are like a flock of sheep to be shorn, ...6:6
    that comes up from the washing,
All of them in pairs,
    and none of them missing.
Like a scarlet thread, your lips, ...4:11
    and your mouth, lovely;
Like a cut of pomegranate, your cheek 6:7
    behind your veil.
Like David's tower, your neck, ...7:5
    built in courses;
A thousand shields hang upon it,
    all the weapons of warriors.
Your breasts are like two fawns,
    the twins of a gazelle, ...7:4
    browsing among the lilies. 2:16; 6:3
Until the day breathes 2:17
    and the shadows flee,
I shall go to the mountain of myrrh
    and the hill of incense.
You are all beautiful, my friend, ...1:15; 2:10,13; 4:1; 7:2,7
    and there is no blemish in you.
With me from Lebanon, O bride, ...4:9–12
    with me from Lebanon shall you come!
Come down from the top of Amanah,
    from the top of Senir and Hermon;
From dens of lions,
    from ramparts of leopards.
You have ravished my heart, my sister, bride!
    You have ravished my heart with one (glance) of your eyes,
    with one bead of your necklace.
How beautiful is your love, my sister, bride!
    How much more pleasing is your love than wine, ...1:2,4
    and the fragrance of your perfumes, than any spices.. . . . . .1:3

Your lips drip honey, O bride; 4:3
  honey and milk are under your tongue. 5:1
The fragrance of your garments
  is like the fragrance of Lebanon.
A garden enclosed, my sister, bride, ... 4:9–12; 6:2
  a ⟨garden⟩ enclosed, a fountain sealed! 4:15
Your shoots, a paradise of pomegranates
  with choice fruits:
Henna with nard,
  nard and saffron;
Cane and cinnamon,
  with all scented woods;
Myrrh and aloes,
  with all finest spices.
A garden fountain, ... 4:12
  a well of fresh water,
  flowing from Lebanon!
Arise, north wind,
  and come south wind!
Blow upon my garden,
  that its spices may flow.

■ W Let my lover come to his garden 5:1; 6:2,11; 8:13
  and eat its choice fruits.

5

1 ■ M I have come to my garden, my sister, bride! 4:16; 6:2,11
  I gather my myrrh with my spices.
I eat my honeycomb with my honey; 4:11
  I drink my wine with my milk.

■ (?) "Eat, friends, drink! . . . . cf. 1:2; 4:10,15–16
  Drink deeply of love!"

2 ■ W I was sleeping, but my heart was awake: 3:1–5
  Hark! My lover knocking!

■ (M) "Open to me, my sister, my friend,
  my dove, my perfect one! 2:14; 5:2; 6:9
For my head is wet with the dew;
  my hair, with the moisture of the night."

3 ■ (W) "I have taken off my clothes;
  am I then to put them on?
I have washed my feet;
  am I then to soil them?"

4 ■W   My lover put his hand through the hole,
      and my heart trembled on account of him.
    I got up to open to my lover,
      and my hands dripped myrrh;
    My fingers, flowing myrrh 5:13
      on the handles of the lock.
    I opened to my lover,
      but my lover had turned, gone!
      I swooned when he left.
    I sought him but I did not find him; 3:1–2
      I called out after him, but he did not answer me.
    It was I the watchmen came upon,
      as they made their rounds of the city.
    They struck me, wounded me;
      they tore off the mantle I had on,
      the watchmen on the walls.

    I adjure you, O Daughters of Jerusalem:
      If you find my lover, what shall you say to him? 2:7; 3:5; 8:4
      That I am sick with love! 2:5

9 ■D   How does your lover differ from any lover,
      O most beautiful of women? 1:8
    How does your lover differ from any lover,
      that you adjure us so?

10 ■W   My lover is radiant and ruddy,
      outstanding among ten thousand.
    His head is gold, pure gold;
      his hair, palm fronds,
      black as a raven.
    His eyes, like doves 1:15; 4:1
      by the water streams.
    ⟨His teeth,⟩ washed in milk,
      set in place.
    His cheeks, like beds of spice
      that put forth aromatic blossoms.
    His lips, lilies
      that drip flowing myrrh. 5:5
    His arms, rods of gold
      adorned with Tarshish stones.
    His belly, a work of ivory
      covered with sapphires.
    His legs, columns of alabaster
      set in golden sockets.
    His stature, like Lebanon,
      select as the cedars.
    His mouth is sweetness;
      he is all delight.
    Such is my lover, such my friend,
      O Daughters of Jerusalem!

6

1 ■ D   Where has your lover gone,
　　　　O most beautiful of women?
　　　　Where has your lover turned,
　　　　that we may seek him with you?

2 ■ W   My lover has gone down to his garden, ... 4:16—5:1; 6:11; 8:13
　　　　to the beds of spice;
　　　　To browse in the garden,
　　　　and to gather lilies.
　　　　I am my lover's, ... 2:16; 7:11
　　　　and he is mine;
　　　　he browses among the lilies. 2:16; 4:5

4 ■ M   Beautiful are you, my friend, as Tirzah,
　　　　lovely as Jerusalem,
　　　　awe-inspiring as visions! 6:10
　　　　Turn your eyes away from me,
　　　　for they disturb me.
　　　　Your hair is like a flock of goats 4:1
　　　　that stream down from Gilead.
　　　　Your teeth like a flock of ewes 4:2
　　　　that come up from the washing,
　　　　All of them in pairs
　　　　and none of them missing.
　　　　Like a cut of pomegranate, your cheek 4:3
　　　　behind your veil.
　　　　Sixty are the queens,
　　　　eighty the concubines,
　　　　and maidens without number—
　　　　Unique is my dove, my perfect one! 2:14; 5:2
　　　　The unique one of her mother,
　　　　the chosen of the one who bore her. 3:4; 8:5
　　　　When women see her, they praise her;
　　　　queens and concubines, they bless her:
　　　　"Who is this that comes forth like the dawn, ... 3:6; 8:5
　　　　beautiful as the moon?
　　　　Pure as the sun,
　　　　awe-inspiring as visions?" 6:4

11 ■ W   To the nut-garden I came down   . . . . 4:16—5:1; 6:11
　　　　to see the fresh growth of the valley,
　　　　To see if the vines were budding, ... 2:12; 7:13
　　　　if the pomegranates were in blossom.
　　　　Before I knew it,
　　　　my heart made me
　　　　⟨the blessed one⟩ of the prince's people.

7

1[6:13] ■ (?) Turn, turn, O Shulammite;
     turn, turn, that we may gaze upon you!

  ■ W "Why do you gaze upon the Shulammite
     as upon the dance of the two camps?"

2[7:1] ■ M How beautiful your sandaled feet, ... 1:15; 2:10,13; 4:1,7; 7:7
     O noble daughter!
  The curves of your thighs, like rings,
     the handiwork of an artist.
  Your valley, a round bowl
     that is not to lack mixed wine.
  Your belly, a heap of wheat,
     surrounded with lilies.
  Your breasts like two fawns, ... 4:5
     twins of a gazelle.
  Your neck like a tower of ivory; 4:4
     your eyes, pools in Heshbon
     by the gate of Bath-rabbim.
  Your nose like the tower of Lebanon
     looking toward Damascus.
  On you, your head is like Carmel,
     and the hair of your head, like purple—
     a king is caught in tresses.
  How beautiful, and how pleasing, ... 1:15; 2:10,13; 4:1,7; 7:2
     O loved one, delightful ⟨daughter⟩!
  Your very stature is like a palm tree,
     and your breasts, clusters.
  I said, "I will climb the palm tree,
     I will take hold of its branches;
  Let your breasts be like the clusters of the vine,
     and the fragrance of your breath like apples;
  Your mouth like the best wine. . . ."

  ■ W Flowing smoothly for my lover,
     spreading over ⟨my lips and my teeth⟩.
  I am my lover's, ... 2:16; 6:3
     and towards me is his desire.
  Come, my lover, let us away to the field; 2:10
     let us spend the night in the villages.
  Let us be off early to the vineyards, ... cf. 1:6; 2:15; 8:11–12
     let us see if the vines have budded; 2:12; 6:11
  If the blossoms have opened,
     if the pomegranates are in bloom.
     There I will give you my love.
  The mandrakes give forth fragrance,
     and at our door are all choice fruits;
  New with the old,
     my lover, have I stored up for you.

8

1   Would that you were my brother,
     nursed at my mother's breasts!
  Were I to find you in public,
     I would kiss you
     and no one would despise me.
  I would lead you, bring you,
     to my mother's house 3:4
     (where) you would teach me.
  I would give you spiced wine to drink,
     my pomegranate juice.

   His left hand is under my head, ... 2:6
     his right hand embraces me.
  I adjure you, O Daughters of Jerusalem: 2:7; 3:5; 5:8
  Do not arouse, do not stir up love,
     until it be ready!

5   ■ (?)   "Who is this that comes up from the desert, ... 3:6; 6:10
     leaning upon her lover?"

     ■ (?)   "Under the apple tree I aroused you;   . . . . cf. 2:3
     there your mother conceived you,
     there the one who bore you conceived." 3:4; 6:9

6   ■ W   Place me as a seal on your heart,
     as a seal on your arm.
  Strong as Death is love;
     intense as Sheol is ardor.
  Its shafts are shafts of fire,
     a flame of Yah.
  Deep waters cannot quench love,
     nor rivers sweep it away.
  Were one to give all his wealth for love,
     he would be thoroughly despised.

8   ■ (W)   "We have a little sister
     and she has no breasts.
  What shall we do for our sister,
     on the day she will be spoken for?
  If she is a wall,
     we shall build upon her a silver turret.
  If she is a door,
     we shall board her up with a cedar plank."

   I am a wall,
     and my breasts like towers.
  Then I have become in his eyes
     as one who finds peace.

11 ■ (?) Solomon had a vineyard
              in Baal-hamon.
          He gave the vineyard to the keepers;
              one would pay for its fruit
              a thousand pieces of silver.
          My own vineyard is at my disposal—
              the thousand (pieces) for you, Solomon,
              and two hundred for the keepers of its fruit.

. . . . cf. 1:6; 2:15; 7:13

13 ■ M   You who dwell in the garden,
              friends are listening;
              let me hear your voice!

. . . . cf. 4:16—5:1; 6:11
. . . . 2:14

14 ■ W   Flee, my lover;
              be like a gazelle or a young stag
              upon the mountains of spices.

. . . . 2:9,17

Superscription:
Solomon's "Finest Song"?

1

1   **The Song of Songs, by Solomon.**

Notes

שִׁיר הַשִּׁירִים, which serves as the book's title in Jewish tradition (e.g., *b. Baba Batra* 146), is translated literally in 𝔊 (ᾆσμα ᾀσμάτων), 𝔖 (*tešbĕḥat tešbĕḥātāʾ*), and 𝔙 (*canticum canticorum*, whence ultimately derives the designation "Canticles"). The Hebrew idiom, comprised of singular and plural forms of the same noun in construct, is a typical expression of the superlative (*GHG* §133i; *HSyn* §§47, 80). Cf., for example, אֱלֹהֵי הָאֱלֹהִים וַאֲדֹנֵי הָאֲדֹנִים ("the God of Gods and the Lord of Lords") in Deut 10:17; הֲבֵל הֲבָלִים ("vanity of vanities") in Eccl 1:2 and 12:8, and Aramaic מֶלֶךְ מַלְכַיָּא ("the king of kings") in Ezr 7:12 and Dan 2:37.

The construction אֲשֶׁר לִשְׁלֹמֹה (so 𝔐 with the full support of the ancient versions) is quite intelligible as a relative clause attributing the work to Solomon. Use of the independent relative particle אֲשֶׁר sharply distinguishes the superscription from the text of the Song proper where the proclitic form ־שֶׁ is regularly employed (e.g., 1:6,12; 6:5). The preposition לְ is most easily taken to be the *lamed auctoris* (cf. *GHB* §130b). Just as many editorial superscriptions in the psalter exhibit לְדָוִד to claim Davidic authorship (e.g., Ps 3:1; 4:1; 5:1), so Solomon is named as the Song's author. Other senses of the preposition are possible if less likely here: "for/dedicated to Solomon" or "about/concerning Solomon" (cf. the use of לְ to introduce a topic in 1 Chr 24:20, וְלִבְנֵי לֵוִי הַנּוֹתָרִים ["and concerning the rest of the Levites"] and especially in Ugaritic literary rubrics, e.g., *lbʿl*, "About Baal," *CTA* 6.1.1 [= *UT* 49.1]).

The discrete superscription virtually disappears in the NEB, which construes v 2a as a purpose clause linked to v 1 and renders: "I will sing the song of all songs to Solomon that he may smother me with kisses." In addition to positing an awkward syntactical construction, this reading involves a textually unsupported emendation of 𝔐. The particle אֲשֶׁר is revocalized to yield אָשֵׁר, a first-person singular Qal imperfect of the verb שִׁיר ("to sing"); cf. L. H. Brockington, *The Hebrew Text of the Old Testament: The Readings Adopted by the Translators of the New English Bible* (Oxford University; Cambridge University, 1973) 172. This conjectural emendation, to yield indicative אָשִׁ(י)ר or subjunctive/cohortative אָשִׁירָה (cf. Ex 15:1), was proposed a generation ago by Gottfried Kuhn, *Erklärung des Hohen Liedes* (Leipzig: A. Deichert [Werner Scholl], 1926) 8: "Das Lied der Lieder will Ich singen dem Salomo"; cf. also Max Haller, "Das Hohe Lied," *Die Fünf Megilloth* (HAT 18; Tübingen: J. C. B. Mohr [Paul Siebeck], 1940) 26. But alteration of 𝔐 seems neither necessary nor productive of better sense.

Interpretation

In the superscription, an editor has supplied the work with a name and designated Solomon as its author. Although from a historical-critical perspective we may judge this information to be extraneous or secondary and unreliable, we must nonetheless reckon with its import. The superscription already constitutes an ancient, if not "original," frame of reference for interpretation of the poetry which follows.

Whether individually or as a collection, the poems which comprise the Song may have enjoyed an earlier existence in oral or written form. We can speculate about such matters and perhaps even reach some tenable conclusions regarding the precanonical setting, function, and intention of the poetry, especially with the help of comparable ancient Near Eastern sources now available to us. Yet the fact remains that an ancient editor labeled the work a "poem" or "song" (*šîr*). This is not a strict genre classification, necessarily meaning a lyric composition set to music or the like,[1] but it does indicate that the poetry was thought to constitute a singular literary creation. In this view, the unity is one of overall form and not merely of common authorship or coherent subject matter—such as is found in the various collections of proverbial "sayings" which make up the book of Proverbs (cf. 1:1; 10:1; 24:23; 25:1; 30:1; 31:1) or even the anthologies of a particular prophet's utterances (cf. especially Am 1:1).

As Audet has remarked, "the Song of Songs" is less an appropriate title for the work than an expression of great esteem for it.[2] In the editor's appreciative view, this particular song is the "greatest" or "finest" song. What is the probable frame of reference for this use of the superlative? According to Origen and the traditional Jewish Targum, the Song surpasses all divinely inspired hymnic compositions preserved in scripture which were authored before it, including the pentateuchal songs or poems attributed to Moses.[3] It is much more likely, however, that the editor had in mind the specific tradition of king Solomon's prolific literary productivity. Thus 1 Kings 5:12[4:32] reports that Solomon, with the superlative wisdom granted to him by God, ". . . uttered three thousand proverb(s) *[māšāl]*, while his song(s) *[šîrô]* were a thousand and five." If this is indeed the relevant context for the comparison, the editorial superscription deems the work to be "the greatest of *Solomon's* songs."

The editorial attribution of the work to Solomon no doubt represents a certain "historicizing" interest, comparable to that exhibited in many Psalm superscriptions. The assignment of individual Psalms to David reflects the traditional view that he was himself a skilled musician and composer as well as being a great patron of the hymnic arts.[4] In some cases, though, the headings are considerably more specific. For example, Psalm 63 is a lament with petition for deliverance from enemies; while the text itself displays no overt connection with particular persons or historical circumstances, it bears an editorial preface attributing its composition to David ". . . when he was in the Judaean wilderness," presumably

---

1   See above, p. 3.
2   Audet, "Love," 81: "It was a name which bore witness to the recognized merit of the composition, and to the affection for it, bred of long use or a long tradition. Canticle of Canticles is not the author's name for it, but that given it by an editor." Audet then suggests (82-83) that 1:2a ("May he kiss me with the kisses of his mouth") preserves the more ancient

designation of the work or the melody to which it was sung in the context of Israelite/Jewish marriage celebrations.
3   See above, p. 19 n. 81.
4   See, e.g., 1 Sam 16:14–23; 2 Sam 22; Am 6:5; 1 Chr 15:16; 16:7–36; 2 Chr 29:27; Sir 47:8–10. Cf. James L. Mays, "The David of the Psalms," *Int* 40 (1986) 143–155.

seeking refuge from king Saul.[5] Such redactional contributions to the Psalms appear to reflect scribal activity during the later Second Temple period, involving a kind of "inner-biblical" exegesis in which connections were sought between works of traditional hymnody and concrete events reported in narrative sources.[6] In the case of the Song, association with Solomon would have been obvious, given the description of his elaborate procession in 3:7–11 and other direct references (8:11–12; cf. 1:5) as well as possible allusions to him in the poetry.[7] Indeed, this line of reasoning may be supposed to have informed the "historical" interpretation of the Song attributed to Theodore of Mopsuestia, according to which the work celebrates Solomon's marriage to "the Shulammite" (7:1[6:13]) who is taken to be a dark-skinned Egyptian princess (cf. 1:5–6 and also 1 Kgs 3:1; 9:16,23).[8] Very similar are the hypotheses which have wanted to link the love poetry of the Song with one or another of Solomon's supposed amorous adventures—for example, a romantic liaison with the Queen of Sheba (though biblical tradition describes their friendly relationship only as based on mutual intellectual and commercial interests),[9] or a love affair with Abishag, the comely "Shunammite"

maiden who had tended David during his final days (1 Kgs 1:1–4,15) and had been sought as a wife by Adonijah, Solomon's chief rival for the throne (1 Kgs 2:17, 21–22).[10] Biblical tradition certainly remarks on Solomon's notoriety as a lover of women, both foreign and domestic (1 Kgs 11:1–8; cf. Deut 17:17); it is not difficult to imagine that ancient interpreters, no less than some moderns, speculated on possible connections between the Song's love poetry and Solomon's love life. But it seems futile to pursue this course, if only because the male protagonist of the Song is never identified with Solomon, either directly or by substantive allusion. More importantly, perhaps, the editorial superscription itself betrays no interest in such matters.

If, as seems most likely, the superscription alludes specifically to the tradition in 1 Kings 5:9–14[4:29–34], then ascription of the Song to Solomon involves a claim for the sapiential character or significance of the work. Both Audet and Childs have commented on the possible import of this.[11] They argue that the Song was supposed to exemplify Solomon's divinely granted insight into the nature of human affairs, attesting to the "wisdom" (*ḥokmâ*) which made him the envy of savants of the

5   Cf. also Ps 3:1; 7:1; 18:1; 34:1; 51:1; 54:1; 56:1; etc.
6   See Brevard S. Childs, "Psalm Titles and Midrashic Exegesis," *JSS* 16 (1971) 137–150; and also Elieser Slomovic, "Toward an Understanding of the Formation of Historical Titles in the Book of Psalms," *ZAW* 91 (1979) 350–380.
7   Cf. Loretz (61–62), who claims that all references in the Song to "king," as well as those to "Solomon" per se, are redactional touches, introduced in light of the late attribution of the work to Solomon. The mention of "King Solomon" in 3:9, 11 (cf. 3:7) does suggest a labored identification, but wholesale elimination of the term "king" would require substantial emendation of the text (see, e.g., 1:12).
8   See above, p. 22. Cf. the Jewish folkloristic traditions (among them the notion that the marriage occurred on the very day of the Jerusalem Temple's consecra-

tion) summarized by Louis Ginzberg, *The Legends of the Jews*, Vol. 4 (Philadelphia: Jewish Publication Society of America, 1913) 128–29; Vol. 6 (1928) 280–281.
9   1 Kgs 10:1–13. Cf. Josephus, *Jewish Antiquities*, 8.165–175; and also Louis Ginzberg, *The Legends of the Jews*, Vol. 4 (Philadelphia: Jewish Publication Society of America, 1913) 142–149.
10 Cf. Harold H. Rowley, "The Meaning of 'the Shulammite'," *AJSL* 56 (1939) 84–91.
11 Audet, "Le sens" and "Love," 79–81; Childs, *Introduction*, 573–576.

ancient world. For Childs, the superscription not only thus connects the Song with the larger corpus of biblical wisdom literature but also functions as a hermeneutical guide, establishing the "canonical context" within which the Song is to be interpreted. This, he argues, rules out an understanding of the love poetry as "secular songs" with only humanistic significance; in equal measure it calls into question allegorical efforts to construct a lofty spiritual sense, removed from the physical concreteness of the text's imagery, or to discover therein a broader view of salvation history (since the prophetic theme of God's love for the covenant people is alien to the sapiential corpus of scripture). Rather, Childs avers, "The Song is wisdom's reflection on the joyful and mysterious nature of love between a man and a woman within the institution of marriage."[12] The parsimony of Childs' approach to the Song is not unattractive. It has the merit of defining a context for interpretation which is at once observable in the biblical tradition as we have received it and relevant to issues of concern to contemporary theology and ethics.

---

12 Childs, *Introduction,* 575. See above, p. 99 n. 384.

**A Love More Pleasing
Than Wine**

1

2 ■ W   Let him kiss me with the kisses of his
      mouth!
    Truly, more pleasing is your love than
      wine.
3   The fragrance of your perfumes is pleasing,
    flowing perfume, your name;
    therefore the maidens love you.
4   Draw me after you! Let us run!
    The king has brought me to his chambers.
  Let us exult and rejoice in you!
    Let us extol your love beyond wine!
    Rightly do they love you.

5   Black am I, and beautiful, O Daughters of
    Jerusalem,
    like the tents of Qedar,
    like the pavilions of Solomon.
6   Do not stare at me because I am blackish,
    for the sun has burned me.
  The sons of my mother were angry with me;
    they assigned me as keeper of the
      vineyards—
    my own vineyard I have not kept.

Notes

2   𝔐 יִשָּׁקֵנִי (Qal jussive, נשׁק, plus pronominal suffix: "Let him kiss me") makes appropriate sense in context. Vocalization of the consonantal text to yield יַשְׁקֵנִי (Hipʿil jussive, שׁקה, plus pronominal suffix: "Let him give me to drink") is supported by Gordis (78) and apparently also NEB ("that he may smother me"); cf. the more radical emendation הַשְׁקֵנִי (Hipʿil imperative, שׁקה, plus pronominal suffix: "Make me drink" or "Drown me"), accepted by Karl Budde ("Das Hohelied" in E. Kautzsch and A. Bertholet [eds.], *Die Heilige Schrift des Alten Testament*, Vol. 2 [Tübingen: J. C. B. Mohr (Paul Siebeck), ⁴1923] 392), and Friedrich Horst (*BHK*, 1201 n. "a" to 1:2), and others. There is a wordplay on שׁקה ("drink") and נשׁק ("kiss") in 8:1–2; it may be that 1:2 already suggests this play (cf. also 5:1), but nothing is gained by alteration of 𝔐.

The preposition מִן in מִנְּשִׁיקוֹת ("with the kisses") is partitive (*GHB* §133e), and it contributes to the alliteration (יִשָּׁקֵנִי מִנְּשִׁיקוֹת).

The introductory כִּי ("truly") is to be taken as asseverative or emphatic, rather than causal (Albright, "Archaic Survivals," 2; cf. *HSyn* §449).

"Pleasing" is literally "good" (טוֹבִים). This word can mean "sweet" in relation to wine, as argued by Albright ("Archaic Survivals," 2) on the basis of the Ugaritic designations: *yn ṭb* is "sweet wine" in contradistinction to *yn d l ṭb*, "wine that is not sweet" (cf. *UT* 1084.1–23). But this distinction could depend on a quality other than sweetness. Here "good" need not be narrowed in meaning; cf. also 7:10[9].

Both 𝔊 and 𝔙 read consonantal דדיך as דַּדֶּיךָ, "your breasts" (cf. Ezek 23:21; Prov 5:19). But the vocalization of 𝔐 is preferable, deriving the noun from the root דוד. Thus one has דֹּדֶיךָ ("my love"), as the favorite term used by the woman of the man (1:13,14,16; etc.), and דּוֹדִים in the plural to designate acts or expressions of love (1:4; 4:10; 5:1; etc.).

The pronominal shift in v 2 with reference to the male lover, from third to second person ("his mouth . . . your love"), does not require emendation in the interest of consistency; such shifts (enallage) are well attested in Hebrew poetry (e.g., Ps 23:1–3,4–5,6), and elsewhere in the Song (1:4; 2:4; etc.).

3   The ל of 𝔐 לְרֵיחַ can be understood according to traditional Hebrew grammar as a kind of dative of reference (*GHB* §133d): "with respect to fragrance, your perfumes are pleasing." But there are other possibilities. The preposition ל can be taken as

asseverative or emphatic (*HSyn* §283), and thus parallel to כִּי in v 2: "indeed, more pleasing (than) the scent of your perfumes." This presupposes that the force of the comparative מִן carries over into v 3, and a parallel with v 2b emerges. Albright ("Archaic Survivals," 2 n. 4) and Pope (299–300) interpret the ל as comparative, on the basis of Ugaritic usage. The reading of 6QCant deserves notice: שׁמנים טובים; along with 𝔙 *(unguentis optimis)* it fails to represent the pronominal suffix "your," present in 𝔐. On this reading טוֹבִים can be interpreted as an attributive adjective, "fine/precious ointments" (cf. 2 Kgs 20:13=Isa 39:2). Hence one could translate: "Truly your love is finer than wine, indeed (finer than) the scent of precious ointments."

The repetition of שֶׁמֶן ("perfume") is particularly effective, and it forms a play on שֵׁם ("name"). However, "flowing" is a doubtful translation; תּוּרַק would seem to be the Hopʿal form of ריק ("pour out"), but it is not in agreement with שֶׁמֶן, which is always masculine. Hence changes have been suggested: תַּמְרוּק (used in Est 2:3,9,12 for oil of purification) or some form of מרק. None of the changes is advisable: 𝔊 (ἐκκενωθὲν) and 𝔙 *(effusum)* are guides to the meaning, "poured out." In his restoration of 6QCant, Baillet proposes מר[קחת מורקה] שמך (cf. *BHS*, 1325 n. "c–c" to 1:3), which is semantically cogent, since מִרְקַחַת means perfume or a mixture of aromatic herbs (cf. Exod 30:25; 1 Chr 9:30, and מֶרְקָחִים in Cant 5:13), but it is quite difficult to discern support for the reading in the published photograph (Maurice Baillet, J. T. Milik, and Roland de Vaux, *Les "petites grottes" de Qumran*, [DJD 3; Oxford: Clarendon, 1962] Vol. 1, 113; Vol. 2, pl. 23/6).

4   The woman addresses the man and perhaps associates him with herself when she cries "let us run." Again there is a transition, this time from second to third person, and the woman speaks of him as "king."

There is not sufficient reason to follow the NEB, which interprets הֱבִיאַנִי as "bring me" (so 𝔊 and σ'); this would also involve a change in the pronominal suffix at the end of the verse ("your" instead of "his" chambers). The plural חֲדָרָיו ("chambers") is a plural of generalization (*GHB* §136j), a frequent occurrence in Cant (1:17, etc.; cf. Joüon, 418 n. 4).

As in v 2, 𝔊 interpreted דֹּדֶיךָ as "breasts" and gave an *ad hoc* interpretation of the Hipʿil form נַזְכִּירָה: "We will love your breasts (more than wine)." Gordis (78), following Ibn Janah, proposed the meaning "inhale" on the basis of Lev 24:7; Isa 66:3; etc. This interpretation is reflected in NJV and in Pope (304–305). However, the Hipʿil of זכר ("remember") more commonly means "praise, celebrate," which seems equally appropriate here.

The final two words of v 4 have generated a variety of interpretations in the ancient versions and in modern translations. The reading of 𝔐 (מֵישָׁרִים אֲהֵבוּךָ) is presupposed but differently interpreted in 𝔙 ("the upright love you") and in 𝔊 ("righteousness loves you"), and in 𝔖 ("and more than the upright, your love"—continuing the thought of the previous line). A previously unattested variant appears in 6QCant: (מישרים) אהובים; perhaps this can be rendered, "more than the upright (are) loved." Gordis (78–79) and NJV interpret מֵישָׁרִים as a type of wine, because it is associated with wine in 7:10[9] and also in Prov 23:31. The present translation understands מֵישָׁרִים as an abstract adverbial accusative, "rightly" or "with right" (cf. Ps 58:2; 75:3, and *GHB* §126d).

5   שְׁחוֹרָה ("black") is a feminine singular adjective, indicating that the woman speaks. Here and elsewhere in biblical Hebrew it designates color, not race. In 5:11 it is used of the man's hair ("black as a raven"), and in Job 30:30 the cognate verb describes Job's blackened skin, which is paralleled with the heat that devours his body. That the woman's blackness is an effect of the sun becomes explicit in v 6. The woman continues describing herself: "and beautiful." It is not clear that she intends to institute a contrast, "black but beautiful," which is a possible translation of ו (adopted by 𝔙 *sed*). The comparisons that follow can be understood of both color and beauty.

The יְרִיעֹת ("pavilions") are fabric or animal skin, stretched out over poles to form the roof and walls of a tent (cf. Isa 54:2; Ps 104:2). The word is frequently parallel to אֹהֶל ("tent[s]"), e.g., Jer 4:20; Hab 3:7; in the singular form it is used in the Priestly tradition for the coverings of the tent-shrine (e.g., Exod 26:1–10).

Qedar (קֵדָר) designates a nomadic tribe of the Syro-Arabian desert, mentioned frequently in the Bible (Gen 25:13; Isa 21:16; Jer 49:28; etc.) and also in Assyrian records (*ANET*, 298). The tents of these Bedouin would have been made from black goat skins (cf. Exod 26:7).

The interpretation of consonantal שלמה as "Solomon" has the support of the ancient versions as well as the 𝔐 vocalization. In order to secure better parallelism (with "Qedar"), many modern translations

and commentators prefer to read שַׁלְמָה. This name ("Salmah," or NEB "Shalmah") designates a south Arabian nomadic tribe mentioned in ancient Near Eastern records and later Jewish sources (e.g., *Tg. Onq.* to Gen 15:19; Num 24:21).

6   Although the woman presumably addresses the Daughters, the verb תִּרְאוּנִי ("stare") is masculine plural in form; the second person feminine plural ending is rare and never is used before a pronominal suffix; cf. *GHB* §63a, §150a. This indifference to gender occurs several times in the Song (3:5,15; etc.). J. Cheryl Exum ("Asseverative *'al* in Canticles 1,6?" *Bib* 62 [1981] 416–419) has suggested that the initial אַל should be read as an emphatic rather than a negative particle, thus reversing the sense of the construction: "Look at me that I am black. . . ." However, neither syntax nor context commends such an interpretation.

"Black/blackish" is an attempt to preserve the play on words in vv 5–6: שְׁחוֹרָה/שְׁחַרְחֹרֶת; Exum ("Analysis," 71) calls attention to the chiastic use of אֲנִי with these two words, and also the chiastic placement of נטר and כרם in v 6.

In the only other places it occurs (Job 20:9; 28:7), the root שׁזף designates "see." The ancient versions had trouble with it (𝔊 παρέβλεψέν, "look across, despise (?)"; 𝔙 *decoloravit*, "discolor"). On the basis of a permutation of ר and ז, frequent in Aramaic, one can understand שׁזף as the equivalent of שׂדף, with the meaning of "burn" (cf. σ´ συνεκαυσε, θ´ περιεφρυξε, 𝔊 *d'wkmny*).

The Masoretic vocalization of נחרו (נִחֲרוּ) understands it as the Nipʿal of חרר, "burn, be angry"; cf. Isa 41:11. Vocalization as the Nipʿal of חרה, "be angry" (נֶחֱרוּ) is also possible.

The short form of the relative pronoun, שֶׁ, occurs thirty-two times in the Song, three times in this verse alone (rendered "because" in the first two instances). The final occurrence, שֶׁלִּי ("my own"), emphasizes the first person pronominal suffix in "my vineyard" (literally, "my vineyard which belongs to me").

Interpretation

The dialogue in vv 2–6 exhibits a bewildering shift in persons (enallage) which creates difficulty in establishing the identity of the speakers. There may even be two units: vv 2–4, with ʾăhēbûkâ "(they) love you," serving as an *inclusio* to bind vv 3–4 together), and vv 5–6, the discourse of the woman to the Daughters of Jerusalem. If the maidens of v 3 are to be understood as the Daughters of Jerusalem (v 5), one may regard dialogue as the bond among all these lines.

The genre of vv 2–4 is best classified as a "song of yearning": the woman yearns for the man's kisses ("let him kiss me") and his presence ("draw me"), and proclaims how lovable he is (fragrance, name, love). The genre of vv 5–6 is self-description.[1]

The life setting escapes us. Krinetzki identifies the maidens with the companions of the bride, and proposes that the setting is the bringing of the bride to the house of her betrothed.[2] Similarly, Würthwein understands vv 2–4 as a reply to the bridegroom's invitation to move to his house. But such reconstruction is too specific; nothing in the text really demands it. Verses 2–4 are best understood as a soliloquy by the woman; the physical presence of the man is not necessarily indicated. Verses 5–6 are directly addressed to the Daughters of Jerusalem who are present, either physically or in spirit.

■ **2** The woman expresses a desire to experience the signs of love. It is clear that mouth-kisses are meant, but nose-kissing is also known from Egyptian sources. The opening line certainly plunges *in medias res,* but this strong expression of the woman's desire is appropriate in view of the tenor of the rest of the work.[3]

The comparison of love to wine means that his caresses and affection provide her more pleasure than even the staple of Israelite life, wine. In 4:10 the man will return the compliment with the same comparison.

■ **3** "Perfume" is literally "oil," which was used along with spices by both males and females. The term suggests the ambience of love and the well-being of the man and woman.

Although the word "flowing" is problematical, the intention is to intensify in some way the compliment that has just been made; now his very "name," or person, is itself perfume.

The woman shows a generous and non-jealous attitude toward her lover. Although the reference to "maidens" is very general, it is possible that the "Daughters of Jerusalem" (v 6) are meant in the context. The love that other women have for the man is noted again in v 4.

■ **4** The woman has just addressed the man, and now the immediate use of the first plural leaves the scene in ambiguity. It is not certain whether she is associating the "maidens" with herself, or (more likely) speaking of only herself and the man she calls "king."[4] The transition

---

1   For these respective genre designations, cf. Horst, "Formen," 186 and 182.

2   L. Krinetzki, 85.

3   Bernard of Clairvaux has caught the spirit of this passionate opening of the Song: "The favors I have received are far above what I deserve, but they are less than what I long for. It is desire that drives me on, not reason. Please do not accuse me of presumption if I yield to this impulse of love. My shame indeed rebukes me, but love is stronger than all. I am well aware that he is a king who loves justice; but headlong love does not wait for judgement, is not

chastened by advice, not shackled by shame nor subdued by reason. I ask, I crave, I implore; let him kiss me with the kisses of his mouth" (*Sermon* 9.2 [tr. CFS 4, 54]).

4   See the discussion of the theme of the "king fiction" in the Introduction, above p. 83.

from imperative to indicative is sharp, but it highlights the intimacy which the lovers enjoy. The woman feels confident enough to involve the maidens ("let us exult") in her joyous praise of the man. The catch word for vv 3–4 is "love," as shown by the repetition of *'hbwk* at the end of each verse; noteworthy also is the repetition of *ddyk myyn*.

■ **5–6** These lines are bound together by the play on *šḥr* / *šḥrḥrt* ("black/blackish"). The genre is self-description, which leads into an admonition to the Daughters of Jerusalem. The mention of the brothers of the woman forms an *inclusio* for the whole work, since their words are quoted in 8:10. Although the Daughters of Jerusalem are addressed, they do not reply. They have hardly any role except to move the dialogue along; these lines could even be regarded as a soliloquy of the woman.

The comparison of the woman's color to the (black) tents of Qedar and Solomon/Salmah is somewhat exotic, but no more so than other comparisons in the Song. Her explanation is simply that she has been exposed to the harshness of the sun, incurred when her brothers appointed her as caretaker of the vineyards. There is no basis in the text for inferences about racial color.[5]

The effect of the sun upon the woman's body is an adequate explanation of her statement that she had failed to watch over her own vineyard, namely her own self. The term "vineyard" occurs again in 2:15 and 8:11–12. There seems to be a clear play on the word, which refers to the woman. This is also suggested by the emphatic *šellî* ("which is mine") in 1:6 and 8:12. One can detect two levels of meaning here. The woman has not protected herself from the sun, and neither has she kept her vineyard (herself) from her lover. She has given herself freely and responsibly to her lover. This meaning gains added support from the role played by the brothers, who are angry with her (1:6) and officiously decide about her future in 8:8–9. Her statement here, as also in 8:10, is a curt comment for her meddlesome brothers. Pope writes that "the well-attested sexual symbolism of vineyard and field strongly suggest [*sic*] that the purport of her statement is that she has not preserved her own virginity."[6] This hardly does justice to the delicacy of the text; it is doubtful that "guarding a vineyard," even if metaphorical, should be pressed so hard. Gerleman finds in the coquettish "depreciation" of her beauty a reminiscence of the Cinderella motif.[7] He interprets her failure to guard her own vineyard as a reference to the enforced labor which prevented her from caring for her beauty and protecting herself from the sun.[8]

---

5   The erudite and lengthy discussion on "black goddesses" offered by Pope (307–318) is simply wide of the mark; cf. Keel, 53–55. J. Cheryl Exum ("Asseverative *'al* in Canticles 1,6?" *Bib* 62 [1981] 416–419) points out that the only ostensibly unfavourable comment on the woman's appearance is found in 1:6; elsewhere her beauty is frequently praised. Hence Exum would look also for an expression of pride in the appearance of the woman in 1:6. In this regard, the comment of G. Krinetzki (9) merits consideration: "In the role of a vine-dresser, a young woman reinterprets in a teasing style and in favor of herself the reigning beauty concept of light colored skin which prevailed in the city ('you daughters of Jerusalem')."

6   Pope, 326.

7   Gerleman, 99.

8   Gerleman, 100–101.

A Dialogue Between the Lovers

1

7 ■ W Tell me, you whom my soul loves,
　　　　where you pasture, where you rest at
　　　　　midday,
　　　　lest I become as one who covers herself
　　　　near the herds of your companions.

8 ■ M If you do not know, O most beautiful of
　　　　　women,
　　　　follow the tracks of the flock,
　　　　and pasture your kids
　　　　　near the tents of the shepherds.

9　　　 To a mare of Pharaoh's chariots
　　　　I compare you, my friend:

10　　　Lovely are your cheeks in pendants,
　　　　your neck, in beads;

11　　　Pendants of gold we will make for you,
　　　　along with silver ornaments.

12 ■ W While the king was in his enclosure
　　　　my nard gave forth its fragrance.

13　　　A sachet of myrrh is my lover to me;
　　　　between my breasts he lies.

14　　　A cluster of henna is my lover to me,
　　　　in the vineyards of Engedi.

15 ■ M Ah, you are beautiful, my friend;
　　　　ah, you are beautiful, your eyes are doves.

16 ■ W Ah, you are beautiful, my lover, most
　　　　　pleasing!
　　　　Indeed our couch is verdant.

17　　　The beams of our house, cedars;
　　　　our rafters, cypresses.

2

1　　　 I am a flower of Sharon,
　　　　a lily of the valleys.

2 ■ M As a lily among thorns,
　　　　so is my friend among women.

3 ■ W As an apple tree among the trees of the
　　　　　forest,
　　　　so is my lover among men.
　　　　In his shadow I desire to remain,
　　　　and his fruit is sweet to my taste.

4　　　 He has brought me to the wine house,
　　　　and his banner over me is love.

5　　　 Strengthen me with raisin cakes,
　　　　refresh me with apples,
　　　　for I am sick with love.

6　　　 His left hand is under my head,
　　　　and his right hand embraces me.

7　　　 I adjure you, O Daughters of Jerusalem,
　　　　by the gazelles and hinds of the fields:
　　　　Do not arouse, do not stir up love,
　　　　until it be ready!

Notes

7 The phrase שֶׁאָהֲבָה נַפְשִׁי ("whom my soul loves"; cf. 1 Sam 20:17) is repeated in 3:1–4; the idea is that she loves him with her whole being (נֶפֶשׁ).

The literal translation of עֹטְיָה is "one who covers one's self" (so 𝕲 περιβαλλομένη), but the meaning is not obvious in the context. Commentators have interpreted the covering as a sign of mourning (2 Sam 15:30), or as the sign of a harlot (Gen 38:14–15). These references are not helpful in explaining the context of v 7, and in neither of the instances is the word עטה used. She seems rather to refer to some kind of covering or disguise she will be forced to use unless she knows where to find him. One can infer that the disguise will enable her to avoid being identified by his "companions," but no reason is given (perhaps she does not want them to know about the rendezvous?).

Many modern commentators (and NAB, NJV) presuppose a metathesis, reading the word as טעה (cf. Ezek 13:10), an Aramaizing form of the Hebrew תעה, "wander." Such a meaning is represented in 𝕲 ṭ'it', and σ' ρεμβομενη, and 𝕍 vagari. Another meaning, derived from the Arabic "delouse" (cf. Jer 43:12), is offered by the NEB, which reads "that I may not be left picking lice." Fuerst (171) suggests that "this rather humorous reading may in a vivid way suggest the weariness of being left alone."

חֲבֵרִים ("Companions") occurs again in 8:13, but in neither case are these people specified. In the context of vv 7–8 they seem to be the "shepherds" of v 8.

8 Three different terms have been used for the animals in vv 7–8: עֵדֶר, צֹאן, and גְּדִיָּה; both the men and the woman appear as shepherds, and רעה ("pasture") is the catch word binding the lines together. There is a play on יָצְאִי ("follow") and צֹאן ("flock").

9 סֻסָתִי ("mare") carries the *hireq compaginis* (*GHB* §931), a relic of the older genitive ending. 𝕲, 𝕾, and 𝕍 interpreted it as the first person pronominal suffix ("my").

רֶכֶב ("chariots") is mostly used in the singular to denote a collective plural; hence the plural form here (how would one mare be joined to several chariots?) has given rise to much discussion. *GHB* (§136j, note) interprets it as the plural of generalization, a phenomenon that occurs frequently in the Song. Despite 2 Sam 8:4, רֶכֶב designates chariotry (with horses), rather than horses. Another problem, pointed out by Pope (336–341), is that the evidence for (at least, military?) chariots in antiquity is that they were

drawn by stallions, not mares. Hence he likens the presence of a mare among the stallions of the cavalry to the episode in the Egyptian campaign against Qadesh: the prince of Qadesh released a mare in order to upset the Egyptian cavalry, but she was quickly slain by an Egyptian soldier (cf. *ANET*, 241). Thus Pope interprets the comparison as a reference to the sexual excitement generated by the woman. However, comparison of the woman to a mare can derive simply from her sex, and the vv 9–11 go on to elaborate the ornaments she wears, not primarily her sex appeal. Commentators generally note the widespread comparison of a woman to a horse, in a complimentary way, as in Theocritus' *Idylls*, 18.30 (see also Gerleman, 107).

רַעְיָתִי ("my friend," from רַעְיָה) is a special term of endearment for the woman, occurring only in the Song (1:9,15; 2:2,10,13; 4:1,7; 5:2; 6:4). רֵעַ "friend" (male) has a sexual nuance in Hos 3:1, and so also רַעְיָתִי. The woman calls the man רֵעִי ("my friend"), parallel to דּוֹדִי ("my lover") in 5:16.

10 נָאווּ ("lovely") is best understood as a Niṗʿal perfect of אוה (*GHG* §75x). 𝕲 and 𝕷 appear to have read מָה ("how!") before it, but more probably they have interpreted the line as an exclamation.

תֹּרִים ("pendants") designates something round (תור "go around"), such as a bangle or bracelet that would be an ornament for the woman's face.

חֲרוּזִים ("beads") indicates something formed by perforating and then stringing together, such as a necklace (cf. Syriac and Arabic ḥ(h)rz).

11 נְקֻדּוֹת ("ornaments") are literally "spots" or "points," and perhaps designate spangles or beads.

12 Although עַד־שֶׁ can mean "until" (cf. 2:7,17), it means "while" in v 12 (cf. *HELOT* 725, II.2).

מֵסַב derives from סבב and indicates something that is round, hence "environs," "circle," or the like. 𝕲 understood it in the sense of resting: ἐν ἀνακλίσει αὐτοῦ; similarly 𝕾 bsmkh, and 𝕍 in accubitu suo. Thus it is taken to be a couch or divan on which one reclined while eating. The word could indicate a group of people, such as entourage, but the intimacy of v 13 suggests a private place, an enclosure. If one understands vv 8–17 as a unit, the place is further specified in v 16 as a couch. L. Krinetzki (102) points out the notable alliteration of m, n, and r in v 12.

נֵרְדְּ ("nard") is an aromatic plant of Indian origin, which yields a precious perfume; cf. 4:13–14.

13 מֹר ("Myrrh") is an aromatic gum resin extracted from a tree, an import from Arabia and India. It was

a popular perfume in the ancient Near East.

דּוֹדִי ("my lover," literally "my love") is the woman's preferred term (27 times) to designate the man.

14 The flower of the cypress (כֹּפֶר) or henna shrub yields a strong and pleasant smell; it was cultivated in Egypt and Palestine.

יָלִין, if taken literally, means that the man "spends the night"; but the verb is used in a broad sense elsewhere (e.g., Job 19:4; Prov 15:31). The preposition בְּ in בְּכַרְמֵי can also be translated "from." But there may be a deliberate ambiguity here, in order to suggest that the vineyard represents the woman. In that case v 14b would be truly parallel to v 13b, and not merely a geographical note. Engedi (literally "the fountain of the kid") is a well-known oasis in the Judaean desert on the west bank of the Dead Sea.

15 הִנָּךְ has the effect of a strong affirmative: "indeed, you" (GHB §164a). The repetition is striking, and a melodious effect is achieved by the alliteration (n, k, y). This verse is repeated in 4:1, where it leads into a description of the woman's beauty.

16 אַף ("most" or "also") strengthens the affirmation. The woman deliberately picks up the הִנְּךְ יָפֶה, which the man used twice in reference to her in v 15.

17 𝔐 has the plural בָּתֵּינוּ ("our houses"), which is probably a plural of generalization (cf. GHB §136j). Nowhere else do either of them refer to "our" house (cf. "our door," 7:14[13]).

The translation follows the Qere', רַהִיטֵנוּ ("our rafters") as being better known (cf. also 7:6[5]) than the hapax, רַחִיטֵנוּ. The root רהט means "run" in Syriac and Aramaic.

בְּרוֹתִים ("cypresses") is the Aramaic form of בְּרוֹשִׁים; the precise type of cypress cannot be identified.

2:1 The ancient versions were vague about the identity of חֲבַצֶּלֶת ("flower"): 𝔊 ἄνθος; 𝔙 flos. It may be the asphodel or the narcissus, but there is no certainty. Cf. Pope (368) and Loretz (13 n. 2) for references to several studies on this flower.

הַשָּׁרוֹן: The proper name, "Sharon," rather than "the plain," seems indicated here; the reference would be to the fertile plain that extended north of Jaffa to Athlit.

שׁוֹשַׁנָּה ("lily") seems to be derived ultimately from the Egyptian word for the (blue) lotus or water-lily. Cf. Pope (367) and Loretz (13 n. 4) for references to studies on this flower.

3 The precise nature of תַּפּוּחַ ("apple tree"; cf. 𝔊 μῆλον; 𝔙 malus) has not been identified. The root etymology

(נפח, "breathe," "flow upon") suggests a fragrant fruit; cf. 7:9[8].

The literal meaning of חֵךְ ("taste") is "palate"; cf. 5:15; 7:10[9].

4 𝔊, 𝔖, and 𝔏 construed the verb הֱבִיאַנִי ("he has brought me") as an imperative (cf. v 5), as in 1:4. The direct address of dialogue is thus preserved. However, the transition to the third person address in 𝔐 and 𝔙 is not infrequent and can be easily understood in view of the third-person statement in v 6. The dialogue of vv 1–3 yields to the woman's description of her feelings.

בֵּית הַיַּיִן is "wine house." This serves as a trysting place (cf. 1:12, and the association of wine and love in 1:2,4), but the exact place is difficult to identify; the best solutions are "banquet hall" (cf. Est 7:8, בֵּית מִשְׁתֵּה הַיַּיִן, or "house of feasting" (Eccl 7:2, בֵּית מִשְׁתֶּה).

A traditional rendering of דִּגְלוֹ is "his banner." But there is no solid evidence that דָּגָל means "banner," despite the claims of dictionaries. The term often refers to a military unit (Num 2, passim), but a derived association "insignia," "emblem" or the like is highly tenuous. 𝔊 and 𝔖 read an imperative, in line with their general interpretation of v 4, with the meaning of "set" or "direct" (τάξατε); σ′ (ἐταξεν) and 𝔙 (ordinavit) read a finite form of the verb דגל. Any translation should be logically coherent with the preceding הֱבִיאַנִי. The best philological evidence links דגל with Akkadian dagālu, "to look." This understanding, yielding "his glance" or the like, is reflected by many modern commentators: cf. Eugenio Zolli, "In margine al Cantico dei Cantici," Bib 21 (1940) 273–282, especially 273–275; Robert Gordis, "The Root דגל in the Song of Songs," JBL 88 (1969) 203–204, and Pope (375–377, "intent").

5 סַמְּכוּנִי ("strengthen") is in the second-person masculine plural, but possibly without any gender intended (cf. 2:15, and especially 5:8); in context it can be considered as an appeal to the Daughters, who are addressed with masculine gender in v 7.

The exact meaning of אֲשִׁישׁוֹת ("raisin cakes") is hard to verify. The ancient versions went in different directions (e.g., 𝔙 "flowers"), and offer no help; cf. the discussion in Robert (104–105) and Pope (378–380). Jewish tradition interpreted the term in the light of 2 Sam 6:19 to mean a wine jug (cf. AV "flagons"). Modern commentators usually understand the word in the sense of "(raisin) cakes," a food of pressed dried grapes. These seem to have a (fertility) cult use in Hos 3:1, but not in 2 Sam 6:19 (1 Chr 16:3).

6 This verse is repeated in 8:3. As a nominal sentence it can be understood as a wish; then it proposes a remedy for the love-sickness.

7 Cf. 8:4 and also 5:8. The adjuration is certainly addressed to the Daughters despite the masculine pronominal suffix (אֶתְכֶם). The use of the masculine for the feminine is frequent in the Song (4:2; 5:8; 6:6,8).

בִּצְבָאוֹת אוֹ בְּאַיְלוֹת הַשָּׂדֶה ("by the gazelles and hinds of the fields") is rendered in 𝕲 "by the powers and forces of the field." This presupposes a different understanding, but not a different *Vorlage*. The mention of the gazelle and hind in the context of love has some support in Prov 5:18–19. But their appearance in an oath is strange. The best suggestion has been made by Gordis (28): that there is present a deliberate reluctance to use the divine name. The speaker ". . . replaces such customary oaths as *bĕʾlohei ṣĕbhāʾōth* or *bĕʾēl šaddai* by a similarly sounding phrase

biṣĕbhāʾōth ʾō bĕʾayĕlōth hassādeh 'by the gazelles or hinds of the field,' choosing animals, which symbolize love, for the substitutions."

For the adjuration ("do not arouse . . .") with אִם, see *GHB* §165a,d. The verbs derive from the same root (עור), and have the meaning of exciting or energizing (cf. Cant 4:16, where the north wind is told to "arise"). The verb does not mean "to disturb," although it can be used in the context of sleep from which one is awakened (Job 14:12). Sleep is not indicated in vv 6–7. Neither is there any indication of a prohibition to disturb the process of lovemaking.

הָאַהֲבָה (with the definite article) is to be taken as the abstract noun; many translations prefer "loved one," interpreting the abstract for the concrete (AV, NEB), but this is unnecessary. "Love" (personified) is the subject of the verb "be ready."

Interpretation

This section is separate from 1:6, where the woman addressed the Daughters. Now she speaks directly to the man ("whom my soul loves," v 7), and the following lines of admiration form a dialogue in direct address (vv 9–11, 12–14, 15–17; 2:1–3). The dialogue winds down with the change to the third person for the man in 2:4–6, and the unit ends, as in 1:6, with an address to the Daughters.

There seems to be a deliberate pattern of interlocking repetitions in 2:1–7: "lily," vv 1–2; "like . . . so," vv 2–3; "apple," vv 3,5; "love," vv 4,7.

The adjuration to the Daughters has the appearance of a refrain (2:6–7; 8:3–4; cf. 5:8). Except for the snatch of conversation in 1:5–6 and the dialogue in 5:2—6:3, it is always at the end of a section that the woman addresses the Daughters.

■ **7** The question spoken by the woman is at first sight clear: She wants to know her lover's whereabouts at noon time (the time of rest and relaxation). Apparently her purpose is to set up a rendezvous. She adds, with a certain air of threat and tease, that she must not become like one "covering" or disguising herself near the flocks of his companions.[1] The implication is that the covering would be necessary, but undesirable in her eyes. The reason for her covering is not clear; perhaps it is to avoid identification by the companions. Horst is correct in characterizing the genre of vv 7–8 as a teasing conversation.[2] Her question is nonetheless serious, in that the issue of the lover's presence/absence is a frequent theme in the Song. The tenderness of her question is underlined by the phrase "whom my soul loves" (cf. 3:1–4).

■ **8** Since the question of the woman was clearly directed to the man, the reply should be attributed to him and not to the companions, the Daughters of Jerusalem, a chorus, or the poet himself.[3] His reply is in the same teasing vein as her question. He tells her to go to the very place that she held out as a danger: the vicinity of the shepherds (the "companions" of v 7). He does not refuse her question; he teases her by telling her where to pasture her kids. This is the only reference to the woman as a shepherdess. Why she is so represented is not clear (poetic imagination?). Loretz takes up the suggestion of Haupt that the kids are symbols of love (Gen 38:17; Judg 15:1; Tob 2:13), but they have no such function in v 8. Verses 7–8 end with the designation of a place, suggesting that "companions" and "shepherds" are identical.[4]

■ **9–11** These lines are spoken by the man in admiration of his beloved's beauty. Horst designates the genre as a song of admiration.[5] In contrast to the *waṣf*, which emphasizes the physical beauty of successive parts of the body, this song focuses upon her adornment.

■ **9** The point of the comparison in v 9 is both the beauty and the finery with which the horses of Egyptian chariotry were adorned, as illustrated by the decoration of the chariot horses driven by Tut-ankh-Amon.[6] Gerleman and other commentators cite examples from Egyptian love poems in which the man is compared to a horse,[7] but the comparison is not relevant since it refers to the speed with which he comes to his beloved.[8]

■ **10** As indicated in the Notes, the specific nature of the ornaments cannot be determined. It is clear that they

---

1   See the Notes, p. 131 for the discussion of the difficult term ʿōṭɛyâ.
2   Horst, "Formen," 183.
3   These latter positions are represented respectively by Gordis (47; cf. also NEB); Bea (28) and Loretz (8); L. Krinetzki (94) and Robert (79); and Gerleman (102).
4   Note the preposition ʿal, "by," in both instances.
5   Horst, "Formen," 176.

6   *ANEP*, 60 (no. 190); cf. Keel, 60, 62–63, 66.
7   Gerleman, 106–107.
8   See Simpson, *Literature*, 321–322 (Chester Beatty Love Songs). For a different interpretation of v 9, see the Notes, p. 131.

adorn her face and neck, and that they enhance her beauty. One may derive some notion of this ornamentation from the Nimrud ivory carving of a woman's head and from the ivory plaque from Ugarit in which a woman seems to offer a jar of perfume (cf. Cant 1:3; 3:10) to her consort.[9]

■ **11** The "we" is explained as a plural of majesty by Würthwein, or as a literary fiction ("anonymous admirers, with whom the poet identifies himself") by Gerleman.[10] It is possible that the plural is suggested by the intimacy of the couple: she is to be the recipient of his gifts. Despite the plural, it is certain that the man speaks these lines, as indicated by his favorite term of endearment (ra'yātî, "my friend").

■ **12–14** These verses are spoken by the woman. The transition to the third person address is surprising but not unusual (cf. 2:4). Krinetzki identifies the genre as a "table-song," that develops into an expression of joy over the presence of the man.[11] But it can also be seen as a song of admiration describing the fragrance of his presence, and replying to the man's words in vv 9–11. Once again the man is portrayed by literary fiction as a king (cf. 1:4).

■ **12** Whatever be the precise meaning of "in his enclosure," the woman is speaking of an intimate scene with her lover (the "king"). Fragrance is once again the theme (cf. 1:3); the reference to precious and sweet perfumes is in character with the mood and language of the Song. The characters affect each other by means of fragrance: if she is nard (v 12), he is myrrh and henna (v 13). It is over-precise to say that the nard is a "sign of her devotion."[12] Rather, the perfumes symbolize the pleasure which their mutual presence brings to them. While the nard refers to her personal toilette, it stands implicitly for herself. In 4:13 he acclaims her as a garden with exotic plants, nard among them; hence she is a source of delights.

■ **13–14** In these lines the woman celebrates the intimacy and charm of the presence of the beloved to her, using the symbols of myrrh and henna. The man thus forms a counterpoint to herself (the "nard" of v 12). The similarity between vv 13a and 14a serves to underscore the apparent dissimilarity in vv 13b and 14b. After the personal and intimate note in v 13b (he rests between her breasts), it is odd to read of the vineyards of Engedi as the source of the henna. One wonders if there is not an implicit reference to the woman as a vineyard.[13] Henna could very well have grown in the oasis of Engedi, though the Song has a preference for exotic place names (Engedi, Heshbon, Baal-hamon, etc.).

■ **15** "My friend" (cf. 1:9) is a clear indication that the verse is spoken by the man; he will repeat the verse in 4:1. The admiratory tone of vv 12–14 is continued by him in what becomes a dialogue of mutual admiration (1:15—2:3). "Doves" is a metaphor, not a simile. To explain it, Gerleman has recourse to the conventional portraits done by the Egyptians in which the representation of the human eye suggests those of a bird.[14] Even if this usage is due to Egyptian influence—which is questionable—the point of the compliment is not evident.

■ **16** The woman returns the compliment to the man, and expands it with a reference to their trysting place. The description (bed in bloom, walls of cedar and cypress) differs from the "enclosure" mentioned in v 12. The king fiction has yielded to the rustic shepherd fiction; the room is now a leafy couch. The picture, which may be more evocative than locative, is in line with the rustic

---

9   *ANEP*, 343 (no. 782) and 351 (no. 818) respectively.

10   Würthwein, 42; Gerleman, 108.

11   L. Krinetzki, 104.

12   So Würthwein, 43.

13   See above, pp. 78–79. cf. 1:5.

14   Gerleman, 114; cf. Keel, 72–75.

imagery used throughout the Song. Here again, it is better not to be over-precise, as Rudolph is when he comments that the (bridal) bed is "green, because love is always fresh and young," and because from it "the future of the family will grow."[15] It is preferable to let the terms echo simply the atmosphere of intimacy.

■ **2:1** When the woman describes herself as a "flower," etc., she is not laying claim to any extraordinary beauty. There must have been many such flowers in the Sharon plain. She is "one among many," remarks Gerleman, who detects a modest and coquettish tone in this verse.[16]

■ **2** The man utilizes her own comparison, only in order to heighten it: "a lily among thorns." There will be more statements about her uniqueness (6:8–10).

■ **3** She returns his compliment with a similar comparison in his favor. Although the precise meaning of *tappûaḥ* ("apple tree") is uncertain, it offers shade and fruit.[17] The woman is able to expand her compliment by referring to her delight in his presence and loving attention. The metaphors of the "shadow" and "fruit" melt into the reality of their relationship, symbolizing the delights of love; cf. v 5. In a similar way she is a vineyard (1:5), a date-palm (7:8), and a garden (4:12–16).

■ **4** The transition from second to third person address has already begun in the dialogue of vv 2–3. Such changes have been noted already; cf. 1:4,12. But now the mood of the woman becomes heavier, and her words do not appear to be directly addressed to the man. She turns her attention more to the subjective experience of love. The atmosphere is similar to 1:12, and the place may be the same or at least similar ("enclosure," "wine house"). The choice of such trysting places is suggested by the natural and effective symbolism of wine (cf. 1:2; 4:10; 7:10).

Although "banner" is a doubtful translation of *degel*, the term may reflect the royal dignity associated with the man; he would then be presented as a king who has won the beloved. More important is the reflective nature in which love (*'ahăbâ*) is disclosed in the context. It is the central topic of v 7, where the Daughters are adjured not to arouse love. The same kind of reflection upon love (its strength) is found in the aphorism of 8:6. This sets the stage for the woman's avowal of love-sickness in the following verse.

■ **5** It is not clear to whom the request (imperative, second person masculine plural) is addressed. In context it can be regarded as directed to the Daughters (v 7), just as in 5:8 where the woman in an explicit adjuration to the Daughters again proclaims her love-sickness.[18]

The need for succor is explicitly stated: the woman's love has made her ill (expressed with delicacy and strength in 𝕍, *amore langueo*). Obviously raisin cakes and apples can have a nourishing effect, but no food can provide a remedy. Hence these two foods must have a

---

15   Rudolph, 128.

16   Gerleman, 116.

17   See Notes above, p. 132.

18   The seventh stanza of the "Songs of Extreme Happiness" in the Chester Beatty Love Songs expressly develops the theme of love-sickness (Simpson, *Literature*, 320–321):

> Seven days have passed, and I've not seen my lady love;
> a sickness has shot through me.
> I have become sluggish
> I have forgotten my own body.

> If the best surgeons come to me,
> my heart will not be comforted with their remedies.
> And the prescription sellers, there's no help through them;
> my sickness will not be cut out.

> Telling me "she's come" is what will bring me back to life.
> It's only her name which will raise me up.
> It's the coming and going of her letters
> which will bring my heart to life.

136

particular nuance, but it is difficult to capture this. Many commentators claim that they are symbolic of love,[19] or are to be associated with a love-spell.[20] But the bearing of the evidence for these associations on the text of the Song is quite uneven. We know that "cakes" (*kawwānîm*) were used in connection with the worship of Ishtar (cf. Jer 7:18; 44:19), but we do not know their precise role. It makes little sense for the woman to ask for an aphrodisiac here. Rather, the sense of the text is that she asks for food to cure her love-sickness. But it can be cured only by love, as paradoxical as that may be. The precise nuance of the apples and raisin cakes escapes us, but they seem to be exotic foods, fitting for a "winehouse" (v 4). The choice of "apples" may be due to the comparison of the man to a *tappûaḥ* in v 3.

■ 6 It makes little difference whether the lover is actually present or absent; the verse can be construed as a wish or as a simple fantasy. It expresses the intention stated in 2:3: "in his shadow I desire to remain." The physical presence of the man is not suggested by the next verse in which she (not the man) somewhat abruptly admonishes the Daughters. The juxtaposition of this verse with 2:7 in 8:3-4 suggests that these two verses are intended as a unity, perhaps a refrain. In 8:3-4 the presence of the man is secured by the woman's address to him in 8:2.

■ 7 This verse is practically repeated in 8:4, but with the omission of the "gazelles and hinds of the field." It seems to close the dialogue which began back in 1:7. The woman begins to relate a new episode in 2:8.

The reference to the gazelles and hinds seems to be an imitation of an invocation of God.[21] However, it is not without associations within the poem. Gazelles are mentioned in 2:8,17 (resemblance of the man); 4:5 (resemblance of the woman's breasts) and in 8:14 (echo of 2:17). The word "hind" is used of a wife in Prov 5:19. Also, the relationship between "gazelle" and "beauty" as meanings of *ṣěbî* should be remembered.

The woman's admonition prohibits (artificial) stimulation of love. Love is personified as a power, as in 8:6. The love about which she is speaking is the mutual love featured in the dialogue. Love has its own laws and is not to be achieved artificially. Only when it is truly present ("until it be ready") can the participants enjoy it. Other interpretations have been proposed: the union of the lovers is not to be disturbed until they have had enough;[22] the adjuration is supposedly spoken by the man, who admonishes the Daughters not to awaken the woman.[23]

To me the lady love is more remedial than any potion;
she's better than the whole Compendium.
My only salvation is her coming inside.
Seeing her, then I'm well.

When she opens her eyes my body is young,
when she speaks I'll grow strong,
when I embrace her she drives off evil from me.
But now the days of her absence amount to Seven.

Here, in contrast to the Song, it is the man who is love-sick, not the woman.

19 So, e.g., Würthwein, 44; and Rudolph, 131.
20 So Ringgren (in Helmer Ringgren and Artur Weiser, *Das Hohe Lied, Klagelieder, Das Buch Esther: Übersetzt und erklärt* [ATD 16/2; Göttingen: Vandenhoeck & Ruprecht, 1958] 11); cf. Pope (380), who suggests "aphrodisiacs."
21 So Gordis, 28; see the Notes, above p. 133.
22 Rudolph, 131.
23 So NEB; L. Krinetzki, 119; and others.

A Reminiscence Concerning
the Lover's Visit

2

8 ■ W Hark, my lover!
    See, he comes:
  Springing over the mountains,
    leaping over the hills.
9 My lover is like a gazelle,
    or a young stag.
  See, he stands behind our wall,
    looking through windows,
    peering through lattices.
10 My lover responded to me:

■ (M) "Arise, my friend,
    my beautiful one, and come!
11 See, the winter is past,
    the rains are over, gone.
12 The blossoms appear in the land,
    the time for pruning has arrived;
  The song of the turtledove
    is heard in our land.
13 The fig tree yields its figs;
    the vines, in bloom, give forth fragrance.
  Arise, my friend,
    my beautiful one, and come!
14 My dove, in the clefts of the rock,
    in the recesses of the cliff,
  Let me see your face
    and hear your voice,
  For your voice is pleasant
    and your face lovely."

15 ■ W Catch us the foxes,
    the little foxes
    that damage the vineyards,
    when our vineyards are in bloom.

16 My lover is mine
    and I am his
    who browses among the lilies.
17 Until the day breathes
    and the shadows flee,
  Turn, my lover;
    be like a gazelle or a young stag,
    upon the mountains of Bether.

Notes

8. "Hark" is literally "the voice of"; for this usage of קוֹל, cf. *GHB* §162e.

   הִנֵּה־זֶה ("See") is literally "this one," or "there." Cf. *GHB* §143a for the deictic character of זֶ; the idiom is repeated in v 9. Before the word "gazelle" is even mentioned the man is implicitly so described by the words מְדַלֵּג ("springing") and מְקַפֵּץ ("leaping"). Note the parallelism in the structure of vv 8–9, expressed by participles and prepositions.

9. מֵצִיץ ("peering") is the Hipʿil participle of צוץ, which normally means "blossom." As the parallelism and context demand, the ancient versions understood it in the general sense of "look": 𝕲 ἐκκύπτων, "peep"; 𝕾 *mrkn*, "bow (head)"; 𝕭 *prospiciens*, "gaze upon." Such a meaning appears also in the Talmud (*b. Yoma* 67a).

   הַחֲרַכִּים ("lattices") is hapax; along with הַחַלֹּנוֹת ("windows") this is a plural of generalization (cf. בָּתֵּינוּ in 1:17).

   צְבִי² means "gazelle," and צְבִי¹ means "beauty"; there seems to be a deliberate play on the word.

10. "Arise . . . and come" is repeated as an *inclusio* at the end of the man's invitation in v 13b.

    The noun כֹּתֶל ("wall") is a hapax, and perhaps an Aramaism (cf. כְּתַל in Dan 5:5). The "our" need not refer to the family of the woman; it can be understood in a mutual sense, as in 1:16–17 and 2:12.

11. הַסְּתָיו Qere' (הַסְּתָו) is a hapax and an Aramaism (cf. Wagner, *Aramaismen*, 79); it stands here for the winter rains. The asyndetic חָלַף הָלָךְ ("over and gone") is stylistically effective.

12. זָמִיר, a hapax, can be associated with two different roots: זמר² "cut"; זמר¹ "sing." Hence commentators vary between "pruning (the vine)" and "song." Lemaire argues that the term refers to the time of vintage, grapegathering: André Lemaire, "*Zāmîr* dans la tablette de Gezer et le Cantique des Cantiques," *VT* 25 (1975) 15–26. Pope (395) points to Isa 18:5 for the association of the blossoming of the vine and pruning.

13. חנט has to do with embalming in Gen 50:2,6; if it means "change color," "ripen," it can be understood in the present context.

    פַּגֶּיהָ ("its figs") is a hapax, but the word occurs in Aramaic and Arabic, and designates the first, unripe fruit.

14. מַרְאַיִךְ ("your face") is literally "your appearance." Note the ab/b'a' parallelism in v 14, preserved in the translation (face/voice).

15. "Foxes . . . foxes" is an example of "repetitive parallelism of the single-word type" (Albright, "Archaic Survivals," 3). The form אֶחֱזוּ ("catch") is plural imperative masculine, and the line seems to be spoken by a group ("us" is the indirect object).

16. This verse is repeated, with a slight variation in order, in 6:3; cf. 7:11. It is the refrain of "mutual belonging" (Feuillet, 28–29). הָרֹעֶה ("browses") is understood here intransitively, in the sense of "to feed oneself on," rather than transitively, in the sense of "pasture" (a flock). Both interpretations are possible.

17. עַד שֶׁ־ ("until") was rendered "when" in 1:12, which sense is preferred here by Rudolph (136) to indicate the time when the man is to return from pasturing his flock (v 16).

    The "breathing" of the day and the "fleeing" of the shadows have been interpreted in diametrically opposing ways: the end of the day or the end of night. In one case the words are understood to mean the afternoon breeze (Gen 3:8), and the lengthening of shadows, as night approaches. In the other, the reference would be to the morning wind, and the disappearance of darkness, as day dawns.

    סב is ambiguous; it could mean also "return" or "turn aside." Where the passage is almost repeated in 8:14, בְּרַח ("flee") is used. The context of the invitation suggests she means that he is to come to her, but it is not necessary to infer that he has been absent.

    Whereas in 2:9 the woman merely stated the comparison, now she urges him to be like a gazelle or stag; in 8:14 the imperative also occurs.

    Bether as a proper name is otherwise unknown; the identification with Bittir, southwest of Jerusalem, is quite uncertain. The etymology of בתר suggests "mountains of separation." Another possibility is to understand בֶּתֶר in the light of 8:14, where בְּשָׂמִים ("spices") occurs in its place. The "mountains of Bether" seem to be a symbol of the woman herself.

Interpretation

Tournay has pointed out a striking *inclusio* for 2:8–17.[1] The unit begins with mountains, gazelle, stag, and it ends in chiastic fashion with gazelle, stag, and mountains.

The abruptness, as well as the vividness, of this passage is striking. Nothing leads up to it (cf. the adjuration in 2:7), and the story of the woman's search in 3:1–5 is clearly a separate incident. The whole unit can be understood as a reminiscence; the woman recounts the visit of her lover and quotes his invitation to her (vv 8–13, with an *inclusio* for vv 10–13). Following upon this soliloquy is a conversation (vv 14–15), initiated by the man. In context, this seems to be a continuation of the reminiscence she began in v 8. Similarly, one may associate with the reminiscence the woman's proclamation of their mutual fidelity, and her invitation to her beloved (vv 16–17), who is present to her at least in the memory of the visit which she is evoking.

Horst sees that 2:8–9 marks the beginning of a "description of experience."[2] He also recognizes that the spring song is encased in an invitation that expresses yearning (2:10–13).

■ **8** The woman speaks these lines which describe the man's haste to reach her. She is in her house, presumably that of her parents ("our," v 9). Rudolph suggests that the time is early morning, because otherwise the invitation to enjoy the change in nature would be without purpose; it is certainly daytime.[3] Her description of his approach anticipates her description of him as a gazelle in v 9. The style is vivid; one feels the tension of the speaker as well as the desire of the man whose arrival and feverish activity are further described in the next verse.

■ **9** It is misleading to speak of a "peeping Tom" episode in v 9, or to say "the bride is preparing her toilet" and keeping her lover waiting outside.[4] The whole episode seems quite natural; note the comparison that the woman uses ("like a gazelle") and her awareness of his eager inquiry to see if she is there.[5] The theme of presence/absence of the beloved is illustrated in this passage in a slightly different manner than, say, in 3:1–5.

■ **10** "Arise . . . and come" is repeated in v 13b, ending the description of Spring, and thus forming an *inclusio* as well as chiastic structure (ab/b'a').

■ **11–13** The Song of the Spring in these verses has been called "the most beautiful song to nature in the Old Testament."[6] Only a few typical incidents of Spring are singled out, but they have great evocative power. The passage of winter is synonymous with the ending of the rainy season. A certain heightening effect characterizes the man's description: blossoms, pruning, and song of the birds, and then the actual budding of figs and vines.

■ **14–15** Although these verses include the enigmatic reference to the "little foxes" (v 15), they can be understood as a request and a reply. The larger issue is

---

1   Raymond Jacques Tournay, "Abraham et le Cantique des Cantiques," *VT* 25 (1971) 544–550, esp. 550 n. 22.

2   Horst, "Formen," 184.

3   Rudolph, 133.

4   Pope, 392.

5   The comparison of the man to a gazelle is found also in Egyptian love poetry (Simpson, *Literature*, 322):

> Please come quick to the lady love
> like a gazelle
> running in the desert. . . .

Here the speaker seems to be the poet, not the woman, and he elaborates on the pursuit of the wounded gazelle by the hunters. However, the gazelle is escaping speedily; so also the man hastens to the woman, as the concluding lines show:

> Before you have kissed my hand four times,
> you shall have reached her hideaway
> as you chase the lady love.

Cf. Keel, 94–96.

6   Rudolph, 134.

whether they are independent of the context. In vv 8–13 the woman occupied a home with lattices; now she is in an inaccessible rocky crevice. However, one need not be rigid about unity of place here. The inaccessibility of the beloved is a recognized topos of love poetry. Hence these words are to be understood as a new theme introduced by the man when he finishes his song about the Spring.

■ **14** The man uses the endearing term "dove" again in 5:2, 6:9; it is, of course, a frequent term for the female in many literatures and cultures. Pope remarks appropriately, "Doves make their nests in cliff-side clefts and caves; when frightened they are reluctant to emerge."[7] This summons of the man to the woman pictures her as inaccessible; in the context she is within the house. The theme of the inaccessibility of the beloved is universal; hence the desire expressed by the man to see and hear her is perfectly natural. Even if one were to judge vv 14–15 as a separate poem, they fit into the context neatly enough. His request (not the chiastic structure) seems to be echoed in 8:14.

■ **15** This verse has always been recognized as enigmatic. Though a reply by the woman to the man's request, it is addressed to a plural group (the speaker refers to "us" and to "our" vineyards). The meaning is obscure. One can understand the verse as an answer to his request to hear her voice; she now gives forth a ditty or song of some kind (in which the second person plural address is retained). But it is not clear what the threat of the foxes to the vineyards has to do with their situation. Would any snatch of words fit here, since she only intends to satisfy his request? Or must one look for pertinence in what she says? It may be possible to see some relevance if this is interpreted as a quotation by the woman. It can be seen as a saucy reply to the lover. He had just compared her to someone who is inaccessible in rocks and crevices. Let

him now know that she (the vineyard; cf. 1:6) is not as inaccessible as all that. There are always the little foxes who devastate the vineyards, young swain who lay siege to young women. In this view, then, the exchange in vv 14–15 can be classified as a tease. The original meaning of the verse would be this: the young women warn of the "danger" of the devastation of the vineyards (themselves), for the "little foxes" (young men) are on the prowl. But they are in fact practically inviting them by saying that "our vineyards" are in bloom! This little ditty is then employed by the woman in reply to v 14.

■ **16** This verse is echoed in 6:3 and partially in 7:11. Along with v 17, it appears to bring to an end the episode the woman began to relate in 2:8: the two lovers belong to each other.

The lover is described as one "who browses among the lilies" (also in 6:3). The meaning is not clear. As indicated in the Notes, there is an ambiguity in the word "browse" (*rʿh*). The translation understands him to be feeding on the lilies, which presumably are a symbol for the woman herself (2:1). However, Rudolph takes this to be merely a sign of Spring, as the man pastures his flock.[8] The similar phrase in 4:5 belongs to the same world of symbolism, but does not shed light on v 16; in 5:13 the man's lips are described as lilies, but the term should not be pressed in the context of v 16. Because the phrase seems so unruly, as the contrast between 2:16 and 4:5 shows, commentators are tempted to see poetic fantasy at work here. Krinetzki comments that the poet "likes such images just as he likes rare words in order to give thereby a peculiarly exotic character to his poetry. The artistic charm and attractiveness bring out all the more effectively the reality behind these images. What is not present in everyday life, what one can only dream of—this is to be found in a higher way in the realm of love!"[9] Gerleman likewise

7   Pope, 400.
8   Rudolph, 136.
9   L. Krinetzki, 138. For artistic representations, see   Keel, 106–111.

refuses to give a symbolic meaning to the lilies: "'Among the lilies' is not intended to characterize or individualize. Rather it serves as a formula for mere decoration and creation of atmosphere; it is an arabesque, a playful fiction of a poet who considers the life of a shepherd to be simply unreal."[10] While there is a certain truth in these views, it should not be exaggerated. In the case of v 16, it seems reasonable (cf. 2:1) to refer the "lilies" to the woman's person.

■ **17** As indicated in the Notes, the expressions about day and shadows could mean all night or all day. In this closing invitation the woman takes up the image of the gazelle (v 9). Whereas he was initially presented as a gazelle racing across the mountains to her (vv 8–9), he is now to be a gazelle upon the Bether mountains, which seem to be a symbol of her own person.[11] There is therefore a subtlety and poetic heightening in the *inclusio;* the comparison to the running of the gazelle on the mountains has now become a comparison to possession of her own person. Since there is no sign that the lover is absent, one should not regard v 17 as an appeal to one who has departed; he is present at least in spirit. The deliberate reprise of the symbols and phrases of vv 8–9 suggests that v 17 is her welcome to the visit which she began to relate in v 8.

10   Gerleman, 127–128.
11   Cf. the Notes, above p. 139. On Bether, cf. Sebastián Bartina, "Los montes de Béter (Cant 2,17)," *EstBib* 31 (1972) 435–444. Bartina's solution of 2:7—3:1 may not be convincing, but the discussion of the problems, and the survey of opinions, are helpful.

Loss and Discovery

3

1 ■ W   Upon my bed at night
      I sought him whom my soul loves,
      I sought him, but I did not find him.
2   "I will rise and make the rounds of the city;
      in the streets and crossings
      I will seek him whom my soul loves."
    I sought him, but I did not find him.
3   It was I the watchmen came upon
      as they made their rounds of the city.
    "Him whom my soul loves—have you seen
        him?"
4   I had hardly left them
      when I found him whom my soul loves.
    I held on to him and would not let him go
      until I brought him to the house of my
        mother,
      to the room of her who bore me.
5   I adjure you, O Daughters of Jerusalem,
      by the gazelles and hinds of the fields:
    Do not arouse, do not stir up love,
      until it be ready!

Notes

1 עַל־מִשְׁכָּבִי ("upon my bed") can be compared to עַל־מִשְׁכְּבוֹתָם ("on their beds") in Mic 2:1, which describes how the wicked make their plans early on—even in bed. The phrase then merely designates where the woman is. It does not necessarily indicate a dream (as many commentators claim); the parallel usage in Dan 2:28–29; 4:2; etc. is in a context in which dreams and visions are explicitly mentioned. The situation is left vague, perhaps deliberately (as in 5:1), so that one cannot be sure if this is a dream, a poetic idealization, or reality.

The plural בַּלֵּילוֹת ("in the nights") has a singular meaning, such as "during the night (watches)"; cf. GHB §136b.

A typical 𝔊 expansion occurs after v 1b with the addition of "I called him, but he did not answer me" from 5:6. Verse 1b should not be deleted. It enunciates the theme of the search which dominates this section. Its function in 5:6 is different from that which it has in v 2; here it anticipates the results of vv 1–3.

2 As she develops the episode, the woman quotes in v 2a the words that she proclaimed in her distress, giving vivid expression to her resolve to roam through the city to find him. L. Krinetzki (143–144) appropriately notes the intensive nuance (Polel form) in her "making the rounds," in contrast to the simple Qal form which describes the activity of the guardians in v 3.

The three cohortative forms of the verbs can be understood as a simple resolution of will, or one can recognize purpose in וַאֲסוֹבְבָה and אֲבַקְשָׁה. In any case, v 2b states the failure of her search; she is forced to have recourse to the guardians (v 3).

3 There is an ironic play on מצא ("found," to be understood here as "came upon"); the woman is unable to find her lover, but the guardians of the city find her.

She addresses a question to the watchmen (another vivid trait) couched in terms of her feelings ("whom my soul loves"), rather than in terms of any helpful sign of identification.

The repetition from v 2 (סבב בעיר) heightens the poetic effect. The quotation in v 2 ("I will rise . . .") is matched by the quotation of the question which she puts directly to the watchmen.

4 The propensity of the poet to repetition ("to the house . . ., to the room . . .") is obvious throughout the Song (e.g., cf. 3:11; 8:5). The house of the mother is mentioned again in 8:2, and the situation is not dissimilar; she meets him in public and leads him to the mother's home.

5 The adjuration to the Daughters is repeated from 2:7, where it also ends a unit. The way in which it is repeated here would seem to preclude the possibility that the verse is to be ascribed to the man.

Horst ("Formen," 185) describes the genre of this unit as a "description of an experience": the woman describes her anguished but successful search for the man in vv 1–4, and closes with an adjuration to the Daughters of Jerusalem. Many commentators (L. Krinetzki [141], Würthwein [48], Rudolph [155–156] and Lys [139], among the more recent) have interpreted the search as a dream. This approach is motivated mainly by the bizarre events: there would have been, supposedly, no freedom for a woman to roam the streets at night; the watchmen could not be presumed to know her lover; the details of the discovery are simply omitted. Moreover, the whole unit is paralleled by the events in 5:2–8, which are introduced by the statement that the woman is sleeping. However, it may be too much to insist that this is a dream. It is more like "daydreaming" than a dream, the fantasy of one who yearns to be with an absent lover. Psychologically, this may be only a slight degree removed from the expression of the unconscious in dream. The description internalizes an adventure, a quest, which is always going on within the woman when she is apart from the man. In any case, one is dealing with a literary topos: the search for and discovery of the beloved.

Interpretation

These verses are to be taken as a unit, because they are clearly separate from what precedes (a reminiscence about a past visit) and from what follows (a description of a procession). The lines are certainly spoken by the woman, and the repetition of the adjuration to the Daughters (cf. 2:7) makes it appear that these women are present to the speaker, at least in spirit and imagination.

The woman evokes an extraordinary scene in vivid language. The fourfold repetition of "whom my soul loves" (cf. 1:7), and the repeated emphasis on the theme of seeking/finding bind these verses together. Twice she quotes herself directly: to express her own thoughts and resolution (v 2) and to ask a question of the watchmen (v 3). The rhythm and sound of the lines is very attractive: the repetition of q/k, b, and s in v 1; the repetition of *sbb* ("make the rounds") for the woman and the watchmen (with the gracious alliteration of *haššōmĕrîm hassōbĕbîm* in v 3).[1]

■ **1** The woman is on her bed. Certainly, this is not as explicit as the parallel passage, 5:2, where she is said to be asleep. Hence whether this is a dream or not remains open. Verse 1a does not mean that she looked for him in bed. Rather, she is in bed, and yearns for his presence—this is expressed by the first of the four occurrences of *bqš* in this unit.

■ **2** This verse presents concretely her resolve to extend the search into the highways and byways of the city. The negative results are quickly summed up by the repetition without any details. There is no need to specify the unnamed city, but it is sizable, in view of the watchmen who patrol it.

■ **3** Almost every verse takes up a word or phrase from the preceding; here the description of the watchmen echoes the phrase in the woman's resolve (v 2). Little is known

about such guardians, and the poet merely sets down the woman's despairing question to them (cf. the puzzling difference in 5:7, where they beat and strip her).

■ **4** The description moves quickly to her discovery of the man, and her firm custody of him until she has brought him to her mother's house. The mention of the maternal home is emphasized by the parallel phrases at the end of the verse, a style characteristic of the song (cf. 4:8). It is a strange fact that the mother is so frequently referred to in the work: 1:6; 3:4; 6:9; 8:2,5. In 8:2 the house of the mother again plays a role as a haven to which the woman can bring the man. The mother is mentioned also in the Egyptian love poetry, but it is not clear why her role is so prominent.[2]

■ **5** The appearance of the adjuration (2:7; cf. 8:4) to the Daughters is sudden. In 2:7 and 8:4 it is paired with the formula of embrace (2:6; 8:3); here it simply follows upon the story of the loss and discovery. However, one can say that her possession of him ("and I did not let him go," v 4) is in harmony with the mention of the embrace that normally appears before the adjuration. Moreover, the contexts of 3:5 and 8:4 are similar in that the adjuration follows upon the mention of finding (8:1) and bringing the lover to the maternal home (8:2). It seems certain (contrary to NEB) that the words are to be attributed to the woman in 3:5, as well as in 2:7 and 8:4. Even Würthwein, who attributes 2:7 to the companions of the woman, is forced to say that in 3:5 she "quotes" the adjuration formula.[3]

In every instance the meaning of the adjuration to the Daughters remains the same, and translation must be consistent. I prefer the abstract meaning "stir up love" (*'ahăbâ*) rather than the concrete. In every instance the woman speaks of the man in the third person (2:6; 3:4; 8:3) before delivering the adjuration. In the context of

1   For details, see especially L. Krinetzki, 142–143.

2   Simpson, *Literature*, 317, 320 (Chester Beatty Love Songs).

3   Würthwein, 48.

3:1–5, the adjuration appears to be a lesson which the woman derives from her experience. She has just described her own anguish over the absence of the beloved, followed by her possession of him. Now she tells the Daughters that love is not to be trifled with; its arousal drives one into unanticipated and even unknown experiences. The adjuration is a refrain that deliberately ends a scene in three instances, but there is no evidence that it was a traditional literary "conclusion of a rendezvous description."[4] Finally, the adjuration to the Daughters does not demand their physical presence; they could be merely a foil for the woman. Only when they are clearly represented as speaking (as in 5:9; 6:1) is their physical presence necessary.

4   Gerleman, 133.

Solomon's Procession

3

6 ■ (?)   What is this coming up from the desert,
        like a column of smoke?
    Perfumed with myrrh and frankincense,
        from all kinds of exotic powders?
7   This is Solomon's litter:
        sixty warriors surround it,
        of the warriors of Israel.
8   All of them skilled with the sword,
        trained for war;
    Each with his sword ready
        against the terrors of the night.
9   King Solomon made himself
        a carriage from Lebanon wood.
10   Its columns he made of silver,
        its roof of gold;
    Its seat of purple,
        its interior woven with love.
    ⟨O Daughters of Jerusalem,⟩ 11/ go forth!
        Look, O Daughters of Zion!
    Upon King Solomon
        in the crown with which his mother
            crowned him,
    On the day of his marriage,
        on the day of the joy of his heart.

Notes

6 מִי זֹאת is literally "who is this?" The feminine זֹאת can be construed as neuter, and מִי can be translated as "what?" (*GHB* §142; §148b). This leaves open the identity of the person or thing being hailed by the speaker(s). The identical question occurs again in 8:5a, where the feminine participle (מִתְרַפֶּקֶת) indicates that the woman is meant, although no answer is given. A similar question in 6:10 is not quite analogous to 3:6 since it is a quotation of what the queens and concubines say about the woman, and terminates the man's praise of her which began in 6:2 (an inclusion). Again, no answer is given, but the context makes it clear that the woman is meant. This kind of question can receive an answer, as in Isa 63:1, or remain without one, as in Isa 60:8, and Cant 6:10; 8:5. The question in itself, from a form-critical point of view, can be considered as a cry of a watchman on the wall to the guards, or also as a challenge to an approaching party to offer some sign of identification. This would normally call for an answer. In the case of 3:6–7 it seems clear that the clause of v 7 is an explicit answer.

תִּימְרוֹת is another plural of generalization (*GHB* §136j); the noun occurs elsewhere only in Joel 3:3 [2:20], where it is also joined to עָשָׁן ("smoke"). Comparison with Judg 20:40 shows that "column of smoke" is meant here.

מְקֻטֶּרֶת ("perfumed") is the Puʿal feminine participle of קטר, which means in the intensive form "to send up a sacrifice (incense or animal) in smoke." Hence the participle here would mean "censed" or "smoked," therefore "perfumed," and refers back to זֹאת. The vocalization of 𝔐 should be retained, against 𝔙 and the Targum which understood the מ in מְקֻטֶּרֶת as the preposition "from."

לְבוֹנָה ("frankincense") receives its name from the white (לָבָן) color of the powdered gum resin that was imported from Arabia.

The phrase מִכֹּל אַבְקַת רוֹכֵל ("from all kinds of exotic powders") is literally "from all kinds of powder of a merchant." For the construction and meaning of מִכֹּל ("from all"), cf. *GHB* §133e, §139h. The meaning "powder" for the hapax אַבְקַת is secured by its masculine form (אָבָק), which is used with עָפָר ("dust") in Deut 28:26; cf. also Exod 9:9; Ezek 26:10.

7 The word translated by "litter" (מִטָּתוֹ), with the pronominal suffix having an articular and emphatic function; cf. *GHB* §131m,n) is the normal term for a bed; in this instance it is portable (cf. 1 Sam 19:15) as

the identification with אַפִּרְיוֹן "carriage" (v 9) also indicates.

8 Solomon's warriors are described literally as "held (fast)" (אֲחֻזֵי) by the sword; the nuance is that they are skilled, as the use of this root in Akkadian and Ugaritic suggests (cf. Pope, 435). The sword of each one is ready עַל־יְרֵכוֹ ("at his thigh"; cf. Exod 32:27). As in 3:1, the plural בַּלֵּילוֹת ("of the night") is a plural of generalization.

9 Solomon's אַפִּרְיוֹן ("carriage") is a hapax, and probably a loan word. There is no certainty whether it is originally Greek (φορεῖον in 𝔊), Sanskrit (*paryanka*), or Persian (*upari-yana*). Gerleman (139) derived it from Egyptian *pr* ("house"), and translated it as "Thronhalle." The person who had the carriage made is identified in 𝔐 as "king Solomon"; although the line is somewhat long, these words are not to be deleted.

10 Since the exact nature of the אַפִּרְיוֹן is unknown, the translation of the details in its description also remains uncertain. Thus it is not clear whether the "columns" served to hold up a canopy or were legs on which it rested. The mention of "silver" and "gold" probably refers to precious inlays or decorations. רְפִידָה ("roof") is a hapax; the meaning uncertain. The root, רפד, means "spread" or "stretch out" (Job 17:13; 41:42); hence the noun has been construed as "bed" (𝔊 *tšwyt*), "dais," "roof," etc. In Cant 2:5 the verb clearly means "support," and this meaning may be behind 𝔊 (ἀνάκλιτον) and 𝔙 (*reclinatorium*).

When the "seat" (a reasonable meaning for מֶרְכָּבוֹ) is described as "purple" (אַרְגָּמָן), this would mean that it is decorated with cloth or precious purple dye (from the murex shellfish). Such purple material is mentioned in connection with the vestments of the high priest (Exod 28:5,6,8; etc.).

The translation of רָצוּף אַהֲבָה ("woven with love") is uncertain. רָצוּף is hapax, but in the light of Akkadian (*raṣāpu*) and Syriac, it seems to mean "arrange, join," especially used of stones (cf. רִצְפָה, "pavement," in Ezek 40:17; and 𝔊 has λιθόστρωτον in Cant 3:10). "Love" is the rendering of a word that occurs several times in the song (אַהֲבָה); it can be taken as the adverbial accusative, to designate either the attitude of the worker or the loveliness of the work. It is less likely that it is in apposition to the previous object(s), as "a work of love." The emendation proposed by H. Graetz is accepted by many scholars: הָבְנִים ("ebony"); cf. Pope, 445. Others prefer אֲבָנִים ("stones"); e.g., Gerleman, 139, 142. All this is conjectural, as is also Driver's proposal, based on the Arabic, that אֲהָבָה means "leather" here (G. R. Driver, "Supposed Arabisms in the Old Testament," *JBL* 55 (1936) 101–120; so also NEB).

The last two words in v 10 (מִבְּנוֹת יְרוּשָׁלָ֫ם, "by/from the daughters of Jerusalem") are questioned by most commentators. As the text stands, 𝔐 implies that the Daughters of Jerusalem were involved in the making of the interior of the carriage (cf. NJV). It seems better to understand "Daughters of Jerusalem" in the vocative, parallel to the "Daughters of Zion" in v 11. The מ before בנות can be treated as the enclitic מ, and attached to the preceding אֲהָבָה; so NEB presumably, Pope (446), and other moderns.

11 As indicated in the previous note, "Daughters of Jerusalem" is taken over from v 10, and a chiastic structure, visible in the English translation, results.

חֲתֻנָּתוֹ ("his wedding/marriage") is a hapax, derived from חתן. Gordis (86) rightly observes that the pleonastic use of ו before "on the day of the joy of his heart" is correct (cf. Zech 9:9), and does not indicate an additional day.

This verse is filled with repetitions (daughters, crown, day), and with plays in sound: צְאֶינָה וּרְאֶינָה; and שְׁלֹמֹה . . . אִמּוֹ . . . לִבּוֹ (cf. L. Krinetzki [154–155] for details).

Interpretation

These verses describe a procession of "Solomon," which has nothing to do with the episode of the woman's search in vv 1–5. They are also separate from the words of the man in 4:1–7 (a *wasf* directed to the woman). The identity of the speakers is not clear, nor is the identity of the audience. Only v 11 is explicitly addressed to the "Daughters of Zion," but this is within the description itself, and does not necessarily mean that the previous lines are directed to them.

Gerleman has made three salient observations about 3:6–11. These verses contain a description of *things*—a striking shift in the tenor of the work. Secondly, there is a pronounced royal coloring to the passage. Thirdly, a boasting and hyperbolic tone is evident.[1] Further observations can also be made. Only in this unit is there a clear reference to a marriage setting (v 11), despite the alleged wedding traits which many commentators see in the entire work. There is a conspicuous mention of Solomon in three of the six verses, and although some scholars would remove the name, there is no compelling reason to do so. Finally, this section stands out from the rest of the Song which consists mainly of monologues or dialogues on the part of the lovers.

The setting suggested by the royal procession and the reference to the day of marriage in v 11 is that of Solomon's wedding. Gordis is quite specific: "This song is the oldest datable unit in the collection. It was written to mark the ceremonies connected with King Solomon's marriage to a foreign princess, perhaps from Egypt, across the desert. Another example of a royal wedding hymn, not connected with Solomon, is to be found in Psalm 45. Here the arrival of the princess' elaborate entourage is described by the court poets (3:6–11)."[2] It seems more likely, however, that the mention of Solo-

mon is to be interpreted in line with the king fiction that dominates the entire work (1:4,12; 6:8–9; 7:5,[4]; 8:11–12). Whatever may have been the pre-literary existence of these verses—and it is impossible to reconstruct this with any certainty—they are used here to extol the man.

There is a general agreement among commentators that 3:6–11 is a unit. But three parts can in fact be distinguished: a description of a procession from the desert (vv 6–8); a description of Solomon's carriage (vv 9–10); and an address to the Daughters (v 11). "King Solomon" dominates this passage, as no other in the entire Song. There are many ambiguities, in addition to the textual problem in vv 10–11. The text does not make clear if the man or the woman or both are in the procession that is hailed in v 6. Two awkward identifications of what comes from the desert are presented: Solomon's bed and bodyguard (vv 7–8), and his elaborate and rich carriage (vv 9–10). It is possible that these are two separate units, united here in order to form a continuous description of the procession from the desert. Finally, the identity of the speaker(s) is not clear; in v 11 the Daughters of Zion (to be identified with the usual Daughters of Jerusalem?) are addressed. Hence vv 6–11 can hardly be attributed to them—unless, perhaps, these verses are attributed to a spokesperson for the Daughters.[3]

■ **6** The question which begins this verse is repeated in 8:5 where it certainly refers to the woman. However, the context (v 7) means to identify "this" with Solomon's bed. The woman is never explicitly mentioned, and the *presence* of Solomon is not indicated until v 11. Commentators disagree on the identity of "this": Solomon, his bride (or both), or the bed. In view of the elaborate description of the bed/carriage which follows (vv 7–11), one may understand it as the referent.

It is clear that a procession is being described, but

---

1   Gerleman, 135.
2   Gordis, 56.
3   𝔊^A attributes 3:6–11 to "the bridegroom"

(*ho nymphios*), but this is not likely.

there is no apparent reason why it comes from the "desert." Pope points to the mythological background of *midbār* (desert or steppe-land, used as a term for the netherworld in Mesopotamian and Ugaritic myth), but this does not shed light on the function of *midbār* here.[4] Gerleman suggests the annual "beautiful feast of the desert valley," celebrated in Egypt, as the inspiration for the imaginative description of the Hebrew poet.[5] This suggestion also fails to explain *midbār*.

The comparison to the "column of smoke" is obscure. None of the solutions proposed by commentators is very convincing: the pillar of cloud mentioned in the Exodus story (Exod 13:21–22); the dust raised by the procession; the smoke from the torches in the procession; etc. The smoke may simply anticipate the mention of the burning of the incense. In any case, the point of the description is to underline the opulence and fragrance of this procession.

■ **7–8** More attention is given to the bodyguard, "sixty warriors," than to Solomon's litter. These heroes are celebrated in extravagant terms: "of the warriors of Israel" is in effect a superlative, and the number is twice that of David's "thirty" (2 Sam 23). Their military prowess is sufficient for any dangers in the night. Specific dangers are not mentioned, and the efforts of commentators to identify them, or the reasons for the bodyguard, have not been successful: demons, especially the wedding demon (cf. Tob 6:14–15); animals; or human marauders.[6] Ps 91:5 also leaves the "night terror" unspecified.

■ **9–10** The attention shifts from the bed and bodyguard to the carriage which Solomon had made for himself. The mention of gold, silver, and purple dye shows how precious it is. As indicated in the Notes, the significance of the word "love" is unclear, if it is not a mistake.

■ **11** The translation understands this verse as addressed to the Daughters of Jerusalem/Zion, urging them to view Solomon on his wedding day. This is the first and only mention of a wedding in the Song, and it appears abruptly. The fact that the woman is never mentioned could be sufficient reason to discount vv 6–10 as a *bridal* procession; only the king (Solomon) is the object of attention.

The reference to Solomon's crown raises questions. The text is to be understood as a command to look upon Solomon wearing his crown, not upon Solomon *and* upon his crown. This can be either a royal crown or some kind of wedding garland (cf. Isa 61:10). Nothing is known about any practice in which the queen mother would have crowned her son, whether at his coronation or on his wedding day. Hence there is no evidence to identify the crown as royal or not. Neither can one eliminate the possibility that this detail may be only a poetic flourish.

In the light of the above interpretation, 3:6–11 seems to be a somewhat foreign body within the Song. At least two levels of meaning are possible. These verses could represent a tradition concerning a royal wedding procession of a presumably Judaean king (Solomon or another), in which the full regalia and panoply of royalty are expressed. However, in the context of the Song the king fiction should be recognized here. The man who is the hero of the love songs is likened to Solomon, and the description of the glorious wedding procession is meant as a tribute to him.

---

4   Pope, 424–426.
5   Gerleman, 136.
6   Cf. the discussion in Pope, 436–440.

A Dialogue Between the Lovers

4

1 ■ M   Ah, you are beautiful, my friend,
    ah, beautiful.
Your eyes are doves
    behind your veil.
Your hair is like a flock of goats
    that stream down Mount Gilead.

2   Your teeth are like a flock of sheep to be
        shorn,
    that comes up from the washing,
All of them in pairs,
    and none of them missing.

3   Like a scarlet thread, your lips,
    and your mouth, lovely;
Like a cut of pomegranate, your cheek
    behind your veil.

4   Like David's tower, your neck,
    built in courses;
A thousand shields hang upon it,
    all the weapons of warriors.

5   Your breasts are like two fawns,
    the twins of a gazelle,
    browsing among the lilies.

6   Until the day breathes
    and the shadows flee,
I shall go to the mountain of myrrh
    and the hill of incense.

7   You are all beautiful, my friend,
    and there is no blemish in you.

8   With me from Lebanon, O bride,
    with me from Lebanon shall you come!
Come down from the top of Amanah,
    from the top of Senir and Hermon;
From dens of lions,
    from ramparts of leopards.

9   You have ravished my heart, my sister,
    bride!
    You have ravished my heart with one
      (glance) of your eyes,
    with one bead of your necklace.

10   How beautiful is your love, my sister, bride!
    How much more pleasing is your love than
      wine,
    and the fragrance of your perfumes, than
      any spices.

11   Your lips drip honey, O bride;
    honey and milk are under your tongue.
The fragrance of your garments
    is like the fragrance of Lebanon.

12   A garden enclosed, my sister, bride,
    a ⟨garden⟩ enclosed, a fountain sealed!

13   Your shoots, a paradise of pomegranates
    with choice fruits:
Henna with nard,

14   nard and saffron;
Cane and cinnamon,
    with all scented woods;
Myrrh and aloes,
    with all finest spices.

15   A garden fountain,
    a well of fresh water,
    flowing from Lebanon!

16   Arise, north wind,
    and come south wind!
Blow upon my garden,
    that its spices may flow.

■ W   Let my lover come to his garden
    and eat its choice fruits.

5

1 ■ M   I have come to my garden, my sister, bride!
    I gather my myrrh with my spices.
I eat my honeycomb with my honey;
    I drink my wine with my milk.

■ (?)   "Eat, friends, drink!
    Drink deeply of love!"

Notes

1   An inclusion binds together vv 1–7: הִנָּךְ יָפָה רַעְיָתִי; כֻּלָּךְ יָפָה רַעְיָתִי. Within the *wasf* there is a reprise in vv 5–6 of phrases occurring in 2:16–17, and a neat paronomasia in v 2.

The first seven words, down to יוֹנִים ("doves"), are a repetition of 1:15. There is no need to postulate haplography and translate "like doves." The mention of the veil, absent in 1:15, is widely regarded as a gloss from v 3; it does put the line out of balance.

The meaning of גלש, a hapax ("stream down," cf. 6:5), is uncertain. The ancient versions vary in their understanding, if they even read this word; cf. the discussion in Pope, 458–460. Verse 1b is repeated in 6:5b. Mount Gilead is not a single mountain; the reference is to the hilly area in Gilead, the Transjordan region to the east and south of the Sea of Galilee.

2   קצב is used elsewhere only in 2 Kgs 6:6, meaning "to cut off." There is evidence from the ancient Near East that lambs were washed before being shorn (see references in Robert, 441). Hence the translation "to be shorn"; cf. *GHB* §121i for this nuance of the passive participle. This verse is repeated in 6:6, except that רְחֵלִים ("ewes") replaces קְצוּבוֹת.

There is a remarkable paronomasia in v 2b: וְשַׁכֻּלָה / שֶׁכֻּלָּם ("all of them"/"missing"), and in chiastic sequence. As often in the Song, there is disagreement in gender: the pronominal suffixes (בָּהֶם ;) do not agree with their feminine antecedents; cf. *GHG* §135o. The point of the description is that the teeth are white, and also perfectly matched מַתְאִימוֹת ("in pairs," rendering the Hip̄ʿil participle of the denominative verb, תאם, "to be double").

3   מִדְבָּר can mean the organ of speech, but also the action of speaking, and hence "speech" (so 𝕲 λαλιά, and 𝕭 *eloquium*). Since the description deals with parts of the body, one may render it by "mouth."

רַקָּה means the "temple" (Judg 4:21–22), but it is not easy to see how this part would be singled out for beauty. Hence it is preferable to consider that the "temple" can include the jaw, and the veil would emphasize her cheeks rather than temples. Then the reference would be to their redness, the color of the interior of a pomegranate. On the other hand, one cannot rule out the possibility of "brow" (NJV; Pope, 464) which would be partially covered by her veil.

4   Nothing is known about David's tower, and it is mere guesswork to regard it as part of the Jerusalem fortifications, whether of David or a later time.

לְתַלְפִּיּוֹת ("in courses") is hapax, and the meaning is unknown. For the history of attempts to render this word, see Pope, 465–468. It seems reasonable to derive the word from the Aramaic root לפי, "to arrange in courses"; cf. A. Honeyman, "Two Contributions to Canaanite Toponymy," *JTS* 50 (1949) 50–51. But the particular aspect of the comparison is not clear (a graceful, arching neck?). The "courses" and "shields" might suggest decorations around the woman's neck; cf. also 7:5 ("tower of ivory").

The parallelism indicates that שְׁלָטֵי ("weapons") is something like a "shield" (מָגֵן), but the precise nature of שֶׁלֶט is not known. In light of Ezek 27:10–11 (cf. also 1 Macc 4:57), this may be a reference to warriors' shields placed upon fortification walls. Note the paronomasia: בָּנוּי ("built") and תָּלוּי ("hang").

5   This is repeated in the parallel description of the woman's physical charms in 7:4, except that "browsing among the lilies" is omitted there. The comparison made for her breasts suggests symmetry: תְאוֹמֵי ("twins"). Still, the point of the comparison is not obvious (color or form?), nor is it clear why the fawns are described as "browsing." The phrase הָרוֹעִים בַּשּׁוֹשַׁנִּים ("browsing among the lilies") describes the man in 2:16, in a context where he is likened to a gazelle (2:17; cf. 2:9; 8:14).

6   This verse is an echo of 2:17. Verse 6a is exactly the same as 2:17a, and the hill/mountain is reminiscent of the mountains of Bether. However, 2:17 is an invitation by the woman, whereas v 6 expresses the man's resolve, even if in words borrowed from the invitation. Furthermore, v 6 interrupts the description of the woman, which ends in 4:7. Perhaps the phrase, "who browses among the lilies" (2:16; 4:5) triggered the repetition of 2:17a here. There is not enough reason to change the order of vv 6–7, despite the obvious abruptness.

7   "All" is literally "the whole of you": כֻּלָּךְ. A similar use of כל is found in 5:16, where the woman concludes her *wasf;* the effect here is to recapitulate her beauty and bring the unit to a close. The English translation retains the chiasm.

8   𝔐 reads אִתִּי; the consonantal text can be vocalized differently (אֲתִי), as the ancient versions (𝕲, 𝕷, 𝕊, 𝕭) and many commentators (e.g., Robert, 168–169, and Pope, 474) have done: "Come from Lebanon. . . ." But 𝔐 ("with me") yields good sense, and has a chiastic form with repetitive parallelism: "come" is preceded by two phrases, and "come down" is followed by four phrases; cf. Albright, "Archaic

כַּלָּה ("bride") need not imply marriage here; it is parallel to אֲחֹתִי ("my sister"), a term of endearment in 4:9,10,12; 5:1.

תָּשׁוּרִי ("come down") can mean "look" (preferred by many commentators) or "travel"; the latter meaning is suggested by the parallelism with תָּבוֹאִי.

The Lebanon range embraces the two sections that run in a southwest–northwest direction, north of Palestine. The Amanah is probably to be identified with Jebel Zebedani in the Anti-Lebanon, rather than with the Amanus range near the Taurus mountains north of the Orontes river. Senir and Hermon are names for the same mountain (cf. Deut 3:9; 1 Chr 5:23), Jebel esh-Sheik, in the Lebanon range.

Lions and leopards are no longer associated with the Lebanon, but they have been witnessed in Palestine in various historical periods.

Albright ("Archaic Survivals," 3) finds an "obvious reference to Canaanite mythological literature" in v 8. It would supposedly refer to Adonis' invitation to his beloved to go hunting on the Lebanon. Pope (475–477) summarizes further discussion of the mythological background and concludes that "the difficulties commentators have found in this passage disappear when we see the lady as the goddess, Lady of the Steppe . . ., Mountain Mother, and Mistress of the Beasts. . . ." It is possible that v 8 reflects such background. But in the context, it suggests the inaccessibility of the woman, who is separated from the man by distance and danger.

9   לִבַּבְתִּנִי (a denominative verb from לֵבָב) can be interpreted in two directions: to hearten or dishearten. Probably it should be interpreted as the Piʿel privativum (GHG §52h). The "possibility" of sexual connotations of the noun, and hence of the verb, is explored by Pope, 478–480.

The use of the term "sister" has nothing to do with brother–sister marriage. The words "brother" and "sister" occur frequently in Egyptian love poems as terms of endearment; cf. Hermann, Liebesdichtung, 75–79. In the Song the woman never refers to the man as "brother." "Sister" also serves as a catchword (cf. 4:10,12; 5:1).

In בְּאַחַד מֵעֵינַיִךְ ("with one of your eyes") there is a grammatical disparity between the masculine numeral and the feminine "eyes." On the basis of Akkadian, Loretz (30, n. 4) argues that עַיִן ("eye") can mean a precious stone that is shaped like an eye; this

would give stricter parallelism but is hardly necessary. Pope raises the possibility that v 9 is a reflection of the goddess of multiple eyes, attested in the ancient world (481; and 456, fig. 9). The power of the eye is a common motif in love poetry: in 6:5, the man refers again to the spell of the woman's eyes, and in the Egyptian Nakht–Sobek cycle, the man writes, "with her eyes she catches me, with her necklace entangles me . . ."; cf. Simpson, Literature, 324.

עֲנָק ("bead") is used elsewhere only in the plural, indicating a decoration on the neck (Prov 1:9; Judg 8:26).

צַוְּרֹון is a hapax and found here only in the plural; its relationship to צַוָּאר ("neck," 4:4; 7:5) suggests the meaning of "necklace," as reflected in the ancient versions.

10 These words echo the compliments made by the woman in 1:2. There is an effective parallelism in מַה־טֹּבוּ דֹדַיִךְ and מַה־יָפוּ דֹדַיִךְ.

בֹּשֶׂם ("spice" or "balsam") is found in South Arabia; the perfume is yellowish and the scent is prized. The word is used repeatedly in the Song to designate the spice (4:14,15; 5:10) and the plant as well (5:13; 6:2; 8:14).

11 The alliteration is striking: נֹפֶת תִּטֹּפְנָה שִׂפְתוֹתַיִךְ. The usual word for honey, דְּבַשׁ, occurs in v 11b; נֹפֶת designates honey from the comb (Ps 19:11), hence liquid honey. Prov 5:3 provides a parallel to lips that drip honey; there the reference is to the seductive speech of an adulteress. However, kisses as well as words can be meant; cf. 1:2, and especially 5:13, where the woman describes the man's lips as dripping with myrrh.

The meaning of תַּחַת לְשׁוֹנֵךְ ("under your tongue") is that sweets are stored here, just as curses and mischief are found "under the tongue" of the wicked (Ps 10:7), where they can be savored (Job 20:12).

12 The translation presupposes that the גַּל should be changed to גַּן, with several Hebrew manuscripts, 𝕲, 𝕭, and 𝕾. גַּל is used to designate a heap of stones or waves of the sea, and many commentators render it here as "spring," or the like (Gordis [88], Lys [188], NJV) and achieve parallelism with the "fountain" (מַעְיָן). Pope (488–489) defends the meaning "pool," on the analogy of Ugaritic gl ("cup"), and the גֻּלָּה ("bowl") of Eccl 12:6; גַּל would then presumably mean bowl-shaped pool. The point of the comparisons (נָעוּל, "enclosed") is that the woman is reserved to the man; cf. 6:2. גַּן is repeated in 4:15,16;

156

5:1; cf. 6:2–11; like "vineyard" (1:6; 8:12), it is an appropriate symbol for the woman.

The change of metaphor picks up a theme, "fountain," that is explicit in Prov 5:16, where the same image, מַעְיְנֹתֶיךָ ("your fountains"), clearly indicates marital intimacy.

13 שְׁלָחַיִךְ ("your shoots") seems to continue the garden metaphor. The word itself, while certainly derived from the root שלח ("send"), is vague; cf. שִׁלְחוֹתֶיהָ (Isa 16:8), referring to branches. Other translators attempt to discover here a specific part of the body; cf. Pope (490–491) for discussion.

פַּרְדֵּס is a Persian loan word *(pairidaeza)* meaning "enclosures," "park" (cf. Eccl 2:5; Neh 2:9). The park is stocked with all kinds of exotic plants. The רִמּוֹן ("pomegranate"), already mentioned in 4:3, is a staple Palestinian fruit. The juxtaposition of "nard" (plural נְרָדִים in v 13, singular נֵרְדְּ in v 14) is unusual, but the frequent repetition within the Song counts against an emendation here. On nard, see 1:22, and on henna, 1:14.

14 Saffron (כַּרְכֹּם, a hapax) is indigenous to the Himalayas, but a local variety, *crocus sativus*, appears in Palestine. The flower is crushed to yield a spice.

קָנֶה ("cane") was imported (Jer 6:20), perhaps from central Asia where it was indigenous; it is an aromatic. קִנָּמוֹן ("cinnamon"), prized for its aroma (Prov 7:17), was also an import.

עֲצֵי לְבוֹנָה ("scented woods") is literally "trees of incense." These are indigenous to Arabia (Isa 60:6). מֹר וַאֲהָלוֹת ("myrrh and aloes," cf. Ps 45:9) are also imports, and are noted for their fragrance.

15 מַעְיַן גַּנִּים ("garden fountain") is literally "fountain of gardens," a fountain that irrigates gardens. The plural may be the plural of generalization, as גַּנִּים in 6:2 and 8:13, or possibly an interpretation of the original enclitic (גנן[י]־ם). The metaphor has now returned to the water symbol mentioned at the outset (v 12, "fountain"). This is intensified by the use of "well" בְּאֵר, used of one's wife in Prov 5:15. Grammatically, נֹזְלִים can be considered a noun or a participial adjective modifying מָיִם. "Lebanon" serves here as a kind of superlative expression for the best water, such as that which would have come from the heights in the Spring. The term also serves as a catchword with "Lebanon" in v 8 (cf. also v 11).

The entire sentence can be considered as independent (Robert, 185: "a sort of exclamation") or as a grammatical continuation of גַּן in v 12.

16 It is possible that the woman speaks v 16a; she is certainly the speaker in v 16b. But it is more likely the man, because the speaker refers to her as "my garden" (cf. 5:1). He is then inviting the winds to blow upon the garden so that its perfumes may waft (יִזְּלוּ, "flow" is cognate with the participle נֹזְלִים, which denotes "flowing" waters in v 15).

The North and South winds would be, respectively, cold and warm, but their function has to do with movement rather than temperature. Parallelism may account for their mention here. There is a certain cosmic style to this grand apostrophe. They are told to "arise"—the same word (עוּר) is used of stirring up love in 3:5—and to stir up the garden (the woman) for the aromatic scent.

5:1 This verse is dominated by the four main verbs, all in the perfect tense, with a series of double objects ("my myrrh with . . ."). The rendering in the present perfect tense seems appropriate, in view of the answer which the man now gives to the invitation (4:15b) which the woman has just uttered. The basic metaphor has changed once again; now it is a question of eating (not smelling, 4:16) the fruits of the garden. The man is present to the woman, enjoying the fruits which are a symbol of herself. The "myrrh" and the "spices" obviously recall the garden description. But the other objects to be eaten refer back to 4:12, where her lips are said to distill honey. Similarly, "wine" and "milk" were already mentioned in 4:10–11.

Verse 1b has been rendered in various ways, depending upon the interpretation of דּוֹדִים. (1) 𝕲, 𝕾, 𝖁, and many moderns (RSV, NIV) understand רֵעִים and דּוֹדִים as parallel expressions: "friends," "lovers." The speaker(s) cannot be identified with any certainty; it is the man and the woman who are addressed. However, the plural of דּוֹד elsewhere in the Song, and indeed in the rest of the Bible (e.g., Ezek 16:8), means love, signs of affection. This negates the argument drawn from 5:16, where דּוֹדִי and רֵעִי are parallel, in the *singular*. (2) דּוֹדִים, as elsewhere in the Song, is taken to mean "love," and parsed as an adverbial accusative: "drink deeply of love" (cf. 1:4; 4:10 for the association of דּוֹדִים with wine). In this view רֵעִים can refer to the man and the woman, and the line is addressed to them by some speaker(s) that cannot be identified with any certainty. Or conceivably רֵעִים might designate an unidentified group (such as the חֲבֵרִים; cf. 1:7; 8:13), and the speaker is the man, to whom 5:1a is certainly to be attributed.

Interpretation

A new section begins in 4:1, which has no connection with the preceding passage dealing with Solomon's procession, and finds a natural ending in the invitation of 5:1 to eat and drink of the fruits of the "garden." This unit is clearly separate from the woman's second description of her experience in seeking her lover (5:2–8//3:1–5).

From a form-critical point of view this section can be divided into separate poems: 4:1–7, the man's description of the woman's physical beauty; v 8, his invitation to her to come from Lebanon, which serves as a prelude to vv 9–11, a song of admiration; 4:12—5:1, the garden song. These divisions are based on genre and content. The dialogue pattern running through these verses is clear enough to give them a unity that should be honored: the man speaks of her beauty (vv 1–7), calls for her presence (v 8), and expresses his admiration (vv 9–16a); in v 16b she invites him to the garden, and in 5:1 he affirms his acceptance of the invitation. The section closes with a general exhortation to eat and drink (5:1b). Whatever may have been the origin of the individual poems, they now stand in a deliberate dialogical sequence.

It is certain that the man is the speaker of 4:9–16a. The catchword is *kallâ* ("bride," only in 4:8–12 and 5:1). The tendency of modern commentators has been to separate vv 9–11 from 4:12—5:1.[1] Horst agrees with this, but he also admits that 4:12—5:1 comes extraordinarily close to the genre of admiration poem.[2] That is quite true, and is a reason for taking them as a contin-

uation of vv 9–11. Albright calls attention to the repetitive parallelism: *bĕʾaḥad* ("with one of," v 9), *māh* ("how," v 10), and *rêaḥ* ("odor," vv 10–11).[3] The phrase *gan nāʿûl* occurs twice in v 12 (emended text). The play on Lebanon and incense occurs (vv 14–15); cf. vv 6,8. *ʾăḥōtî* is repeated in vv 9,10,12; 5:1; *bĕśāmîm* in vv 10,14,16; 5:1; and *gan* in vv 12,15,16; 5:1. These repetitions suggest that the lines are not to be fragmented. The admiration song comes to an end with invitations (4:16b; 5:1b), but there is an ambiguity in meaning in 5:1b.

■ **4:1** After a general exclamation about the woman's beauty, the man begins to single out specific parts of the body. Verses 1–7 constitute a classical example of the genre that has been given the Arabic name of *waṣf*, a description of the physical charms of the loved one.[4] The genre has a long history in the Near East, especially within Hebrew culture, as shown by the recently discovered Genesis Apocryphon, where Sarah's beauty is described.[5] The direct object of the praise is always the physical beauty of the beloved one (man or woman).

The description raises the question of interpretation; the comparisons sound strange to western ears. Are they to be taken as representing objective reality, or are they meant only to evoke sensations of a pleasurable scene? Are they representational, or only presentational? Perhaps this is not a simple either/or question. Soulen has argued that these comparisons are meant to convey the subjective delight of the beholder, the subject of the vision.[6] This does not seem adequate. It would imply that *any* pleasurable comparison would be satisfactory; then one could just as easily apply the vision of the goats

---

1   So, e.g., Gerleman, 154–158; Würthwein, 53–54; and Loretz, 30–31.
2   Horst, "Formen," 178.
3   Albright, "Archaic Survivals," 3–4.
4   Horst, "Formen," 180–182.
5   1QapGen, col. 20 ll. 1–8 (Joseph A. Fitzmyer and Daniel J. Harrington, *A Manual of Palestinian Aramaic Texts* [BibOr 34; Rome: Biblical Institute, 1978]

112–113). Cf. Moshe H. Goshen-Gottstein, "Philologische Miscellen zur den Qumrantexte," *RQ* 2 (1959–60) 46–48; and Wolfram Herrmann, "Gedanken zur Geschichte der altorientalischen Beschreibungslieder," *ZAW* 75 (1963) 176–197.
6   Richard Soulen, "The *Waṣfs* of the Song of Songs and Hermeneutic," *JBL* 85 (1967) 183–190.

(v 1b) or the pomegranate halves (v 3b) to the woman's mouth (v 3a). But the poet is not careless; he uses the image of a scarlet thread for the mouth. The intent is representational, even if the metaphors are unusual in western judgment. On the other hand, the descriptions are also highly symbolic and evocative. There is an inevitable personal reaction implied in "twin fawns, browsing among the lilies."

For v 1, see the comment on 1:15 concerning the comparison of the eyes to doves. The power of a woman's eyes is a familiar theme; cf. v 9 and 6:5; Prov 6:25; Sir 26:9. The veil serves to set off the beauty of her eyes, and is not necessarily a "marriage" veil.

The comparison of the hair to a flock of goats may be based on the color and the undulating flow of the hair from head to shoulders.

■ **2** The point of this verse is that the woman's teeth are white, and she has all of them, neatly arranged. The white color is elaborately developed by the reference to the sheep, clean and white after a washing. The sheep metaphor is continued ("in pairs") in order to indicate that the teeth are well matched and that none is missing.

■ **3** The woman's lips are red, and her mouth is attractive. It is not certain that *raqqâ* should mean "cheek." Gerleman retains the normal meaning of "temple," and understands the veil as creating two halves, one light, one dark (the part under the veil); this supposedly derives from an Egyptian artistic motif of representing sliced pomegranates with light and dark halves.[7]

■ **4** The comparison of the neck to the unknown tower of David bears on the ornaments worn by the woman. The shields and weapons hanging on the tower seem to suggest a necklace around her neck.

■ **5** The woman's breasts are compared to the twins of a gazelle, an animal noted for its beauty and grace. The

significance of young fawns "browsing among the lilies" is difficult to appreciate. The woman describes the man with this phrase in the formula of mutual possession in 2:16. Many excellent commentators betray an insensitive literalness here, as when the breasts are compared to a vision of the backsides of fawns nuzzling among flowers.[8]

■ **6** The man echoes the words of the woman in 2:17. There she invited him to the mountain; here he declares that he shall go to the mountain. One may surmise that there is a deliberate association between the two verses, almost as if "browsing among the lilies" (v 5; cf. 2:16) has acted as a catch phrase to resume an earlier thought. This resolution of the man to go to the mountain of myrrh appears to interrupt the *wasf*, which ends in v 7, and hence many propose the sequence vv 5,7,6.[9] This hardly seems necessary, since v 7 is quite general and serves as an *inclusio* to v 1. As the text stands, there is a deliberate echo of 2:16–17 in 4:5–6.

The meaning of the aromatic mountain/hill is left unspecified. The entire person of the woman seems to be meant, rather than a specific part of the body, as is suggested by the concluding summation in v 7, "all beautiful." Gerleman advises against any explicit identification of the mountain of myrrh and hill of incense. This is to be understood as stereotyped language that evokes wonderland (such as the region of Punt in the Egyptian love songs); one is moving in the unreal, make-believe world of love poetry.[10]

■ **8** This verse is widely held to be an interruption, with no continuity with what precedes or follows.[11] After the man states his resolve to go to the aromatic mountains (v 6), he is suddenly asking the woman to come away from Lebanon, a mountain wilderness where wild animals dwell. However, the geography of v 8 makes sense only if understood metaphorically. The Lebanon range is miles

7 Gerleman, 147–148.
8 Cf. Rudolph, 147; and Würthwein, 52. Budde (21) is quite clinical.
9 E.g., Rudolph, 145–146; and Loretz, 28.
10 Gerleman, 150 and esp. 152.
11 Cf. Gerleman, 151–152; Loretz, 29; and Rudolph,

distant from the Amanus and Hermon; these latter mountains are part of the Anti-Lebanon (if the Amanus is not to be situated much further away in the Taurus region!). The point of these geographical indications lies in their characterization as the lairs of wild animals. The woman is not physically present on these mountains, and the man could hardly call to her there. The metaphor stands for her inaccessibility, a theme that appeared already in 2:14 (crags and rocks). The animals are not threats to her, but to those who would try to reach her. A similar theme appears in the Cairo Ostracon 25218, where the lover is separated from his beloved by a crocodile.[12]

If v 8 is understood metaphorically, it follows easily enough upon the *wasf* in vv 1–7, and prepares for the outburst of admiration which begins with v 9. The man, who has been speaking since 4:1, continues throughout until v 16. There seems to be a catchword principle operating in vv 6–9: *lĕbônâ* ("incense") and *lĕbānôn* ("Lebanon")—the same sequence as in 4:14–15. As often, catchwords are ambivalent. Instead of being the principle for uniting disparate pieces, they could be in this case signs of a unitary composition.

■ **9** This is the first time that the woman is addressed as "my sister," a term frequently used of the beloved in Egyptian love poetry. "Bride" (which occurs six times and only in 4:8—5:1) locks vv 9–16 in with v 8. The designation need not be taken literally; it is used in anticipation, as a love-name.

Here eyes have a ravishing, enchanting effect upon the man (in contrast to 4:1). The ravishing of his heart is

paradoxically the danger which he wants to endure, just as when the woman calls out that she is love-sick, it is a sickness that she cannot do without. Both this verse and 6:5 have to be seen in the context of the love relationship between them. There is a certain heightening with the mention of "one bead" of the necklace she wears, which has an amulet quality. The role of the "heart" in affairs of love is of course well known; cf. 3:11 where the wedding day is "the day of the joy of his heart."

■ **10** The man is praising her caresses, the expression of her love for him. He couches his praise in terms derived from her description of his "love" in 1:2; a comparison to wine, and the mention of fragrance. The repeated reference to fragrance is deliberate; the topos of smell is common in love poetry, and will be further developed in the garden theme of 4:12—5:1.

■ **11** The reference to "lips" probably underscores the tenderness of her speech and kisses. Again fragrance is touched on, as he compares the scent of her garments to that of Lebanon. This is hardly a reference to the specific odor of cedar, since presumably there was also much vegetation there; Lebanon would be a symbol of all that is fragrant.

■ **12** The garden theme (4:12—5:1) is complex. The metaphor fluctuates between garden and water source (*maʿyān*, vv 12,15), but the major attention is focused upon the fruits and exotic perfumes of the garden. The peculiarity of the metaphor lies in the style of comparison, or better, the absence of comparison. The woman is almost forgotten in the full description of the exotic products. This garden is unreal, in the sense that no

---

148–149.

12   Simpson, *Literature*, 310:

The love of my sister lies on yonder side,
and the river is between [us];
a crocodile waits on the sandbank.
Yet I'll go down to the water,
I'll head into the waves;

my heart is brave on the water,
and the waves like land to my legs.

garden in the ancient Near East would have nourished such a wide variety of plants and trees. Gerleman rightly calls it a "utopian, fantasy-garden," that contains the precious aromatic plants of the ancient world.[13] One suspects that the terms are chosen for sound and exotic qualities, rather than for botanical reasons.[14]

The point of "garden enclosed" is that the woman belongs to the man alone. One is moving in the same world of thought as Prov 5:15–19. It is difficult to agree with Gordis when he regards v 12 as a complaint by the lover that the woman is sealed off from him, and v 15 as her denial of his charge by asserting that she is a well of flowing or fresh water.[15] Rather, both verses mean the same thing, although the metaphors (sealed fountain, well) differ. She is his exclusive water source, and also a

source in the garden which he describes.

■ **13-14** On these various plants, see the remarks in the Notes.[16] As already indicated, the variety of the plants is deliberately overwhelming and exaggerated.

■ **15** The man returns to the metaphor of water; the fountain is further defined as a well of flowing water, like the flow that cascades from Lebanon during the thaw. Presumably this waters the garden he has been describing.

■ **16** The summons to the winds to ventilate "my garden" can be attributed to either the man or the woman. But v 16b is certainly spoken by her. It seems better to attribute v 16a to him; it thus forms a climax to the garden description, and it serves to provoke an appropriate reply from her.

---

13   Gerleman, 159.
14   Jerrold S. Cooper ("New Cuneiform Parallels to the Song of Songs," *JBL* 90 [1971] 157–162, esp. 161–162) has compared the language of a Sumerian literary text (a description which a certain Ludingira presents of his mother) with Cant 4:12–15. He translates the relevant portion of the Sumerian text as follows:

> My mother is rain from heaven, water for the
>   finest seed,
> A harvest of plenty . . . ,
> A garden of delight, full of joy,
> A watered pine, adorned with pine cones,
> A spring flower, a first fruit,
> An irrigation ditch carrying luxuriant waters to
>   the garden plots,
> A sweet date from Dilmun, a date chosen from the
>   best.

Cooper comments (162): "Were it not for the words 'mother' in Ludingira, and 'sister, bride' in the Song of Songs, it would be difficult to detect any difference in the tenor of the two passages, and this tenor is decidedly erotic. While this is expected in the Song of Songs, it is problematic in the description of Ludingira's mother. Perhaps the author was using the only vocabulary he knew for describing a woman,

vocabulary drawn from erotic literature, where most descriptions of women would naturally be found." Cooper allows for a "certain amount of subjectivity" (162 n. 21) in the recognition of erotic imagery, but his main point is well taken. The erotic quality of the imagery of garden, fruit, waters, etc. is remarkable, and it is effective. It is interesting to note that Ludingira's description of his mother is given so that his messenger will be able to recognize her; the same device is used in Cant 5:9–16. On the symbolic aspect of the garden, see Francis Landy, "The Song of Songs and the Garden of Eden," *JBL* 98 (1971) 513–528; and also *idem*, *Paradoxes of Paradise: Identity and Difference in the Song of Songs* (BLS; Sheffield: Almond, 1983) 189–265. Cf. Keel, 158–164.

15   Gordis, 88.
16   Bibliography relevant to the plants and perfumes is given in Robert, 444; see also Michael Zohary, "Flora," *IDB* 2 (E–J), 284–302.

■ **5:1** The garden theme is continued as the man responds to the woman's invitation. There is a certain gravity to the four verbs (all in the perfect tense) and in the three-fold repetition of ʿim ("with," cf. 4:13–14).[17] In effect, he replies that he has taken possession of her, and he expresses this in metaphors (spices, honey, wine, milk) that were used in 4:10–14.

The varying interpretations of 5:1b have been discussed in the Notes. The translation understands the exhortation as addressed to "friends," i.e., either to the man and woman, or to a group associated with them.

Some commentators take v 1b to be a poetic aside by the author, who addresses the lovers with positive affirmation.[18] In a wedding context one or other of the lovers might address "friends" who are participating in the celebration. It seems preferable to interpret the imperatives as addressed to the lovers, and a fitting ending to the description of their love in the preceding dialogue emerges.

---

17 Robert, 187–188.
18 Cf. Würthwein, 55; and Gerleman, 162.

A Dialogue Between
the Woman and the Daughters

5

2 ■ W I was sleeping, but my heart was awake:
  Hark! My lover knocking!

  ■ (M) "Open to me, my sister, my friend,
    my dove, my perfect one!
  For my head is wet with the dew;
    my hair, with the moisture of the night."

3 ■ (W) "I have taken off my clothes;
    am I then to put them on?
  I have washed my feet;
    am I then to soil them?"

4 ■ W My lover put his hand through the hole,
    and my heart trembled on account of him.
5 I got up to open to my lover,
    and my hands dripped myrrh;
  My fingers, flowing myrrh
    on the handles of the lock.
6 I opened to my lover,
    but my lover had turned, gone!
  I swooned when he left.
  I sought him but I did not find him;
    I called out after him, but he did not
      answer me.
7 It was I the watchmen came upon,
    as they made their rounds of the city.
  They struck me, wounded me;
    they tore off the mantle I had on,
    the watchmen on the walls.

8 I adjure you, O Daughters of Jerusalem:
    If you find my lover, what shall you say to
      him?
    That I am sick with love!

9 ■ D How does your lover differ from any lover,
    O most beautiful of women?
  How does your lover differ from any lover,
    that you adjure us so?

10 ■ W My lover is radiant and ruddy,
    outstanding among ten thousand.
11 His head is gold, pure gold;
    his hair, palm fronds,
    black as a raven.
12 His eyes, like doves
    by the water streams.
  ⟨His teeth,⟩ washed in milk,
    set in place.

13 His cheeks, like beds of spice
    that put forth aromatic blossoms.
  His lips, lilies
    that drip flowing myrrh.
14 His arms, rods of gold
    adorned with Tarshish stones.
  His belly, a work of ivory
    covered with sapphires.
15 His legs, columns of alabaster
    set in golden sockets.
  His stature, like Lebanon,
    select as the cedars.
16 His mouth is sweetness;
    he is all delight.
  Such is my lover, such my friend,
    O Daughters of Jerusalem!

6

1 ■ D Where has your lover gone,
    O most beautiful of women?
  Where has your lover turned,
    that we may seek him with you?

2 ■ W My lover has gone down to his garden,
    to the beds of spice;
  To browse in the garden,
    and to gather lilies.
3 I am my lover's,
    and he is mine;
    he browses among the lilies.

Notes

5:2 עֵר ("awake") stands in deliberate contrast to יְשֵׁנָה ("sleeping"). Hence a dream or fantasy is a reasonable interpretation, even if the text is ambiguous. The woman proceeds to relate an experience she had while in this state.

קוֹל ("hark") is literally "the sound of "; cf. 2:8. The abruptness is in contrast to the detailed description of the man's approach in 2:8–9. The narrative style is made more vivid by the direct address in vv 2–3. The accumulation of the terms of endearment is further emphasized by the alliterative effect of the pronominal endings: תַּמָּתִי ,יוֹנָתִי ,רַעְיָתִי ,אֲחֹתִי.

"Hair" is a probable translation of the hapax קְוֻצּוֹתַי (cf. v 11). The lover urges that he be let in, adducing discomfort from the heavy Palestinian dew.

3 By כֻּתֹּנֶת ("clothes") is meant the main undergarment of both men and women, which reached to the knees or ankles. Its removal, and also the washing of feet, would indicate preparation to retire.

אֵיכָכָה is literally "how" (an emphatic and rare form of אֵיךְ; cf. Est 8:6). Note the repetitive parallelism: אֵיכָכָה אֶלְבָּשֶׁנָּה ("am I then to put them on?") . . . אֵיכָכָה אֲטַנְּפֵם ("am I then to soil them?").

4 מִן־הַחֹר is literally "from the hole"; the description of the action suggests that he inserts his hand into the latch or keyhole of the door from the outside, seeking entrance. Cf. the use of מִן, "from," in 2:9; מִן can possibly be translated "to" in the light of Ugaritic usage (cf. Pope, 518).

מֵעַי ("my heart") is literally "my innards." The verb הָמוּ ("trembled") designates a physical and emotional response, either in pain (Isa 16:11) or, as here, in joy (Jer 31:20).

It is also possible to translate עָלָיו as "for him." There is no reason to adopt עָלַי ("within me"), which is found in some Hebrew manuscripts but in none of the ancient versions.

5 The opening words of v 5 (קַמְתִּי אֲנִי) and v 6 (פָּתַחְתִּי אֲנִי) are emphatic. The pleonastic use of אֲנִי is frequent in Ecclesiastes (cf. GHB §146b).

It is not clear whence the מוֹר ("myrrh") comes, whether from the door latch or the woman's own hands. One may infer that the man had anointed the lock with myrrh; this was already a symbol of his presence in 1:13. The repeated mention of the myrrh on the woman's hands is deliberate and emphatic: the myrrh is "flowing" (עֹבֵר, a play on the word "gone," עָבָר, in v 6), as opposed to dry, resinous myrrh, reached by cutting into the wood (Robert, 202).

6 Chiasm characterizes the terse style: "I opened to my lover"; "my lover . . . gone." The asyndetic construction חָמַק עָבָר ("turned, gone") is striking and emphatic, as is the repetition of דּוֹדִי ("my lover").

"I swooned" is literally "my נֶפֶשׁ went out"; the phrase is used in the sense of physical death in Gen 35:18. While the situation is obviously not so dire here, her reaction is to faint from loss of breath at the departure of her lover.

The most obvious meaning of בְדַבְּרוֹ is "when he spoke." But this sense does not seem appropriate unless one moves the phrase to v 4b, a somewhat arbitrary solution. On the basis of cognate languages (Akkadian and Arabic), the root dbr/dpr can be understood as "turn" or "flee"; cf. LVTL, 201, with reference to CAD 3 (duppuru, 186–188) and AHW 1 (duppuru[m], 177).

The theme of seeking/finding is also found in the parallel scene, 3:1–5.

7 The exact meaning of רְדִיד ("mantle") is not clear; it could be a veil or an outer cloak. The severe reaction of the שֹׁמְרִים ("watchmen") is hard to fathom, as it contrasts with their role in 3:3–4. But the play on the word "find" remains (מְצָאֻנִי; cf. 3:2–3). She cannot find her lover, but the guardians of the town "find" her.

8 The adjuration to the Daughters is reminiscent of 2:7; 3:5; and 8:4; but it serves a different purpose here. It is nonetheless abrupt, even if it fits the woman's desolation. Her charge to the Daughters serves to set up the dialogue that follows. Lovesickness was featured already in 2:5.

9 The question posed by the Daughters is literally "What is your lover from (= more than) a lover?" For this use of מִן, see HSyn §473. The implication is that the Daughters need some way of identifying the lover. There is a striking similarity in the literary style of the questions raised by the Daughters (5:9; 6:1); they are characterized by repetitive parallelism (cf. Albright, "Archaic Survivals," 4).

10 The translation of צַח וְאָדוֹם ("radiant and ruddy") is adequate, but the red color has raised questions as to whether the reference is to true body color or a cosmetic. Gerleman (172–173), who inclines to the latter opinion, remarks that both adjectives may be considered symbolic, due to their inherent emotional tone, rather than concrete descriptions. The rest of the description of the man's body presents similar problems. Tournay has pointed out that David is described as אַדְמוֹנִי, "ruddy," in 1 Sam 16:12; 17:42 (in Robert, 445).

דָּגוּל (Qal passive participle, masculine singular) is of uncertain meaning; see the discussion of דגל at 2:4. The translation "outstanding" follows the sense of the versions: 𝕲 ἐκλελοχισμένος, "picked out of a military unit"; 𝖁 *electus*, "chosen"; and 𝕾 *gb*, "chosen." In context the man is singled out from everyone else because of his physical beauty. The same general meaning can be reached if the root meaning of דגל is "to look" (so Pope, 532: "conspicuous").

11   The construction כֶּתֶם פָּז ("gold, pure gold") is difficult; both terms designate some kind of refined gold. They are in apposition, or perhaps כֶּתֶם is to be read as a construct form; 𝕲 separates them with a conjunction (cf. Dan 10:5).

      The meaning of תַּלְתַּלִּים ("palm fronds"), a hapax, is uncertain. It seems to refer to the branches of the date palm (so 𝕲 and 𝖁, followed by Robert [212–213] and others), and presumably is used here to designate his full head of hair. Others prefer "curls" (cf. NJV), and derive the meaning from תֵּל ("small hill").

12   Cf. 1:15 and 4:1, for "doves." The point of the comparison here is not the eyes of the dove, but doves at a water pool. Thus far, the comparison would seem to bring out the glistening character of eyes. Presumably, the doves are wet with the water and their feathers shine. In 𝔐 the description of the doves continues in v 12b, according to which they wash in milk and sit by pools (?).

      The insertion of שִׁנָּיו ("his teeth"), for which there is no external textual evidence, follows the suggestion made by Alberto Vaccari ("Note critiche ed esegetiche," *Bib* 28 [1947] 399–401) and adopted by Rudolph (158–159) and others. There are solid reasons for the insertion: 1) v 12b is an apt description of the man's teeth, which are otherwise strangely left unmentioned (contrast 4:2; 6:6); 2) in 𝔐 the whole verse of two lines is given to the eyes, in contrast to other parts of the body which have one line each; 3) except for v 12b in 𝔐, each line begins with the mention of a particular part of the body. יֹשְׁבוֹת עַל־מִלֵּאת ("set in place") is literally "sitting in fullness." The translation understands this as a reference to the firmness of the teeth set in the gums. If one follows 𝔐, the reference would be to the place where the doves rest, such as water (so 𝕲 and 𝖁). The obscurity of this reference has not been resolved by emendation nor the ingenuity of commentators. Cf. the discussion in Pope, 538–539.

13   On the analogy of 6:2, it is likely that consonantal כערוגת should be vocalized as a plural, though 𝔐ᴸ reads it as singular; the plural reading is supported by some Hebrew manuscripts as well as the ancient versions. עֲרוּגוֹת ("beds") is thus a catchword, associating v 13 with 6:2; מוֹר עֹבֵר ("flowing myrrh") harks back to 5:5. The comparison seems to have in mind the man's perfumed beard; fragrance is a frequent topos in the poem.

      With support of the ancient versions (𝕲 φύουσαι; 𝖁 *consitae a*), consonantal מגדלות is preferably read as the Piʿel feminine plural participle of גדל (i.e., מְגַדְּלוֹת, "[that] put forth" or "grow"; cf. the Puʿal usage in Ps 144:12). 𝔐 vocalizes מִגְדְּלוֹת ("towers"), which Loretz (36) and Gerleman (175) interpret to refer to the shape of perfume bottles.

      שׁוֹשַׁנִּים ("lilies") are mentioned in 2:1,2,16; 4:5; 6:2 (v 13 may provide a catchword with this verse) and 7:3[2]. See the discussion at 2:1. The use of the flower here may have less to do with the color of the man's lips than with the delight they provide, because they drip myrrh just as her lips drip honey in 4:11; see also the role of the sachet of myrrh in 1:13, and the flowing myrrh in 5:5.

14   Hebrew יָד usually means "hand," but it can be used to indicate the forearm; cf. Gen 24:30,47; Jer 38:12.

      The root meaning of גְּלִילֵי is "roll" (גלל); hence the term should designate round objects, such as cylinders or "rods."

      תַּרְשִׁישׁ is literally "Tarshish," which stands for both the place (in the Mediterranean area?) and products that come from there, in this case apparently some kind of gemstones. The description of the man's arms centers on the ornaments they bear.

      Although מֵעִים ("belly") usually designates the interior of the body, the exterior is meant here; cf. Dan 2:32. See above, p. 72 n. 305.

      עֶשֶׁת ("work") is hapax; the meaning is uncertain. Robert (221) points out that translations and commentaries have hesitated between two meanings: a solid mass ("wrought metal" in rabbinical Hebrew), or something polished and shining (cf. Jer 5:28).

      In the ancient world סַפִּירִים ("sapphires") were lapis lazuli, a rich azure-blue stone. The description of the man's belly resembles that of a statue.

15   מַרְאֶה ("stature") is literally "appearance"; cf. 2:14, where the same word is used of the woman.

16   חֵךְ ("palate") is used to designate the mouth, both here and in 7:10[9]. Sweetness is associated with the mouth in v 13; cf. 4:11.

6:1   For the repetitive style, compare 5:9. The question

indicates that the description of the lover has enlisted the interest of the Daughters as to his whereabouts. בקש ("seek") harks back to 5:6.

2 For גן ("garden"), cf. 4:12 and 5:1, where it symbolizes the woman. Of itself, יָרַד ("go down") need not denote a descent to Sheol, as interpreted by the cultic school of thought (e.g., Meek, 131; cf. Ring-

gren, 26). עֲרוּגוֹת ("beds [of spice]") seems to be a catchword with 5:13.

"Browse" is the same word (רעה) that is used in v 3 as well as 2:16 and 4:5 ("browse among the lilies").

3 There is an inversion in v 3a, but the sentiment is the same as in 2:16; cf. 7:11.

Interpretation

There seems to be a clear break after the garden song ends in 5:1; the woman begins to relate an adventure in the style of 3:1–4. One may recognize "my sister" as a catchword (5:1,2), and perhaps also ʿûrî/ʿēr ("arise/awake") in 4:16 and 5:2. The man does not utter a word in this section; then he begins a new unit (6:4–10) with a description of the woman. Throughout, the woman does most of the talking, beginning with the description of her experience (5:2–8) and moving to a description of the man's beauty (5:10–16).

This section can be viewed as a unity because of the interplay between the woman and the Daughters of Jerusalem. After the description of her experience (5:2–7), the woman addresses the Daughters (v 8), who respond with a question (v 9) which provokes her description of the lover (vv 10–16). Thus far, there is a deliberate unity.[1] Moreover, 6:1–3 may be regarded as a natural continuation of the dialogue between the woman and the Daughters which began in 5:2.[2] One need not deny that the questions in 5:9 and 6:1 form the literary links between various genres. These questions can just as easily be attributed to the original author as to an editor. They point to a deliberate effort to unify the thought of 5:2—6:3, an effort which is not always so clearly shown in the rest of the work. The continuity of the whole is created by the theme of the absence of the lover, to which the question of the Daughters (v 9) naturally responds. The narrative then becomes a dialogue between the woman (5:10–16; 6:2–3) and the Daughters (6:1).

The scene in 5:2–7 is clearly parallel to 3:1–4, while deliberately different in details. The phrasing in v 2a is perhaps more suggestive of a dream sequence than is 3:1a, but even were this a dream, the whole unit is better classified in the genre of "description of an experience."[3] The woman is relating an episode, whatever the degree of the reality. But do vv 2–7 clearly describe a dream? They recall old motifs that appear in 3:1–4 (cf. also 2:8): the seeking and not finding (3:1–2; 5:6), the encounter with the watchmen of the city (3:3; 5:7), and the adjuration to the Daughters (3:5; 5:8). But none of these elements demands a dream context.[4]

Numerous parallels to the events described in 5:2–7 have been adduced by commentators. The *exclusus amator* in the *De rerum natura* of Lucretius can be said to resemble the man, in so far as "the excluded lover" does not gain entrance into the house of the woman. According to Lucretius, the lover weeps, and often covers the threshold with flowers and anoints the door.[5] The motif appears with considerable expansion and variation in several literary sources, and the description of the events in 5:2–7 is in harmony with the motif. One feature does not seem to be present in the Song, and that

1   Rudolph, 153; and Loretz, 34.
2   Cf. Ringgren, 26; and Würthwein, 59.
3   So Horst ("Formen," 184), who further identifies these lines as a "dream experience"; and similarly, e.g., Rudolph (155–156) and Würthwein (58).
4   See the comments on 3:1–4, p. 146 above.
5   *De rerum natura* 4.1177–1179 (W. H. D. Rouse, tr., *Lucretius: De Rerum Natura* [LCL; Cambridge, Harvard University; London: William Heinemann, ³1937] 330–332): "But the lover shut out, weeping, often covers the threshold with flowers and wreaths, anoints the proud doorposts with oil of marjoram, presses his love-sick kisses upon the door. . . ." (*at lacrimans exclusus amator limina saepa / floribus et sertis operit postisque superbos / unguit amaracino et foribus miser oscula figit*). Some contact with the practice of anointing the door of the beloved with myrrh cannot be excluded from 5:4, although myrrh in the Song (1:13; 3:6; 4:6,14; 5:1,5,13) may have its own independent and indefinable function. Considerable material relative to the "excluded lover" as literary motif is to be found in Frank O. Copley, *Exclusus Amator: A Study in Latin Love Poetry* (American Philological Monographs 17; Madison: American

is the *paraklausithyron,* or lament at the door.[6] Nowhere does the lover lament in 5:2–7. He is an "excluded lover"; he fails to gain entrance, undoubtedly a frequent experience among human beings. But the essence of the *paraklausithyron* is complaint, and this is totally absent. On the contrary, if there is a complaint, it seems to be perhaps implicit in the story as told by the woman, almost blaming herself for the trouble she had to undergo in her search for him. Again we are in the area of love topoi and love language, and we may expect the Song to reflect the typical experiences of people in love, just as the

theme of the *exclusus amator* also does.[7]

The *wasf* (5:10–16) is a description of physical attributes, the only such description of the male in the Hebrew Bible; it is similar to the style of enumeration in 4:1–7 and 7:2–10[1–9]. This poem is very symmetrical: one line for each part of the body (emended text in v 12). The comparisons are either by direct predicate nominatives or by means of the preposition "like."[8] The style is strange to our western taste, but it must be respected.[9]

■ **5:2** The woman's description of herself is at least ambiguous. Literally understood, her words support a dream

---

6 Philological Association, 1956).
   The attempts of both Pope (522–524) and Gerleman (165: *Türklagegedicht*) to adduce this parallel to our passage are unconvincing.

7 For the theme of the door in Egyptian love poetry, note the following lines from the Papyrus Harris (Simpson, *Literature,* 300–301):

   Back at the farmstead of my girl:
   the doorway in the center of the house,
   her door left ajar,
   her door bolt sprung;
   my girl is furious!
   If I were made the doorkeeper
   I could make her mad at me,
   then at least I'd hear her voice when she is angry,
   and I'd play the child afraid of her.

   In the Nakht–Sobek cycle, the following lines occur (Simpson, *Literature,* 324–325):

   See what the lady has done to me!
   Faugh! Shall I keep silent for her sake?
   She made me stand at the door of her house
   while she went inside.
   She didn't say to me, come in, young man,
   but deaf to me remained tonight.

   I passed by her house in the dark,
   I knocked and no one opened,
   What a beautiful night for our doorkeeper!

Open, door bolts!
Door leaves you are my fate, you are my genie.
Our ox will be slaughtered for you inside.
Door leaves do not use your strength.

It seems inevitable that such a theme would emerge in love poetry, and it is worth noting that the treatment of the door varies from poem to poem.

8 Although Gerleman (177) has exaggerated the influence of Egyptian pictorial art in these descriptions, his words have relevance for the treatment of the man, where the terms seem particularly appropriate for a statue or a picture (172): "The path to understanding the metaphorical language of the Song does not always lead through exterior appearance. The expressive power of these images is associated to a very high degree with their derivation from an erotic content that is bound up with feeling. Thanks to the emotional content, they are to be acknowledged as sensuous even when there is a minimum of reality expressed by them."

9 The description of Jerusalem's princes in Lam 4:7 is cut from the same cloth:

   Brighter than snow were her princes,
   Whiter than milk,
   More ruddy than coral,
   More precious than sapphires.

Cf. also the description of Simon, the high priest, in Sir 50:1–21, especially vv 5–10 (RSV):

interpretation, more than the vague mention of a bed in the parallel passage, 3:1–5. However, the reference to the knocking at the door and to the voice of the man can be taken to mean that she was thereby awakened from sleep.[10] As was stated above concerning 3:1–5, there is little to choose between a real dream and "daydreaming," in which love indulges its fantasy.[11] There are some differences in details between 3:1–4 and 5:2–7, but these have no particular exegetical significance. They can be understood as flowing from the freedom of fantasy.

The arrival of the lover is described suddenly, in contrast to the description of his visit in 2:8–9. The reason he gives for desiring to enter is relief from the night dew, which is assuredly heavy in Palestine. Yet there seems to be a deliberate exaggeration here; it is clear that this is not the real reason for seeking entrance.[12]

■ **3** The reply of the girl might suggest that she is bothered by her lover's request. But the context shows that this is not the case. Her remonstrations are to be interpreted as a tease, not as a refusal. His reactions in vv 4–5 show this; he attempts to open the door and she rises to let him in. This does not suggest a refusal. The tease is expressed in neat symmetrical lines, and it is as illogical as his excuse (the dew) to gain entrance.[13] It is off the mark to see in her reply and in his ensuing departure a "testing" of love. The literary motif of testing can hardly be exemplified by such an unreal, flimsy excuse.[14]

■ **4** The man apparently attempts to open the lock; the woman reacts with emotion and (v 5) rises to give him

---

How glorious he was when the people gathered round him
    as he came out of the inner sanctuary!
Like the morning star among the clouds,
    like the moon when it is full;
like the sun shining upon the temple of the Most High,
    and like the rainbow gleaming in glorious clouds;
like roses in the days of the first fruits,
    like lilies by a spring of water,
    like a green shoot on Lebanon on a summer day;
like fire and incense in the censer,
    like a vessel of hammered gold
    adorned with all kinds of precious stones;
like an olive tree putting forth its fruit,
    and like a cypress towering in the clouds.

10   Cf. L. Krinetzki, 179.

11   The very beginning of the woman's narrative gives one pause. The man is portrayed as knocking on her (presumably locked) door at night when she has retired. Gianfranco Nolli (*Cantico dei Cantici* [La Sacra Bibbia; Torino/Roma: Marietta, 1968] 112–113) asks some pertinent questions: Would he not have aroused the family of the woman? What would

they have said, had they heard her and become aware of her opening the door? Nolli concludes that the purpose of the song is to serenade the woman, as Romeo did under Juliet's balcony. These questions, reasonable in themselves, nevertheless "historicize" the situation in a manner foreign to the nature of the narrative. If the narrative had any basis in reality at one time, it has now become the vehicle of the woman's feelings about the presence/absence of her lover.

12   There is no room for Gerleman's suggestion (165) that the description of the dew-laden hair suggests the "majesty of youth."

13   If the "tease" interpretation is rejected, then the suggestion of Nolli (113–115) needs to be considered. He claims that the words are spoken by the man, and the genre is *serenata* ("serenade"). In this view, the man asks to come in (v 2) and indicates that he is prepared to spend the night with the woman, having taken off his tunic and cleansed his feet.

14   *Contra* L. Krinetzki, 179. Moreover, in order to understand the night visit of the lover, one cannot simply assume, as Krinetzki does, that the man and the woman are betrothed. Rather, the poetry moves in the realm of fantasy.

entrance. Despite the ambiguity of the term *ḥōr* ("hole"), there is not sufficient reason to see here a reference to sexual activity.[15] The symbolism of *ḥōr* may point in that direction, but the man remains always outside the woman's residence. If there is a double meaning here, it is muted, as throughout the Song. The scene prepares for the symbolism of the myrrh at the door (v 5).

■ **5** The myrrh on the lock comes either from the man or the woman; it seems more reasonable that the man is responsible. When she says that her fingers dripped myrrh, she means that she placed her hands on the anointed lock. The precise symbolism of the myrrh is not easy to determine. At the very least it is a sign from the lover. He put it there, perhaps as a token of his love and a tangible sign of his presence (cf. 1:13), even though he disappears.

■ **6** The narrative continues by way of taking up again previous words ("open," "my lover"), and describes again (cf. v 4) the woman's emotional state. But this time it is one of utter dismay over the departure of the man. The man's departure means, at the least, that he had interpreted the "tease" of v 3 as a refusal, and he leaves after putting his hand to the lock, apparently unsuccessful in gaining entrance. (Is his departure also to be taken as a tease in response to her words in v 3?). The sudden appearance of the seeking/(not) finding motif is due to a deliberate imitation of 3:1–2. The woman engages in a desperate, futile search.

■ **7** Again a detail ("the watchmen") from the scene in chapter 3 appears. But the harsh treatment meted out to the woman here is in sharp contrast to the encounter described in 3:3–4. Perhaps her failure to discover the man at once (as in 3:4) is enough to account for the addition of this graphic detail of physical beating. The result of the search is diametrically opposite to 3:4, and the loss

of his presence is pointed up by the pain of her own frantic wandering and the blows of the watchmen. Commentators usually report that her treatment suggests she was taken for a harlot (some Assyrian laws forbid harlots to wear veils); if so, the detail has no significance in the story.[16]

■ **8** The appearance of the Daughters of Jerusalem is sudden, for there has been no suggestion that the woman was relating this experience to them. Yet this seems to be allowed by the flexible role given to these characters within the Song; they appear with equal suddenness after 3:1–4. The adjuration to them is modeled on 2:7 and 3:5 (also 8:4), but the content is of course changed in view of a new context. In 3:4 the woman was able to enlist the watchmen in the search for the lover. Now she appeals to the Daughters; they are to tell him of her love-sickness (cf. 2:5). The function of the Daughters continues in a new and creative way, when they take up her address in v 9.

■ **9** The question addressed to the woman by the Daughters looks backward and forward: it responds to her implicit request for help in searching for him, but it also sets up the opportunity for her to launch into a description of the lover. Is this verse the work of an editor who wanted to join 5:2–8 with 5:10–16? This is plausible, but one cannot rule out the possibility that the experiences related in chapter 5 could have been composed as a unit. The answer to the question depends in part upon a final judgment concerning the function of the Daughters in the entire work. They seem to be original components, rather than editorial creations.

■ **10** The description of the youth begins with what seems to be a general statement about his color. It is possible that the adjectives are to be understood symbolically because of their inherent power to express feeling.[17]

15 *Contra* Pope, 519; Würthwein, 58; and others.
16 Cf. Pope, 527.
17 So Gerleman, 172.

The description proceeds from the top down, head to legs.

■ **11** A symbolic quality is particularly apparent in the adjectives used to describe the man's head ("gold, pure gold").[18]

■ **12** The eyes of the youth are compared to doves ("like," in contrast to 1:15 and 4:1, where the woman's eyes are said to *be* doves). It is the expansion of the comparison that creates the difficulty. The phrase "by the water streams" fills out the description of the doves, not the eyes. Verse 12b, according to 𝔐, is to be understood of the doves, and yet somehow as furnishing a point of comparison for the eyes. Hence it is usually explained as referring to the eyes set in white ("washing in milk") and in sockets ("sitting in fullness"). The comparison seems to have become an end in itself and is strikingly different from the other lines. There is no certain interpretation of this verse, as can be seen from the diversity among commentators.[19]

As indicated in the Notes, the conjectural insertion of "teeth" makes the metaphor of the milk bath and fullness more intelligible; the reference then would be to the white teeth set in firm gums.

■ **13** The description of the cheeks highlights the beard which is richly scented.[20] The comparison of lips to lilies may refer to their color, or also their shape. Moreover, they drip "choice myrrh," i.e., his kisses give delight; the

thought is akin to 4:11 (the woman's lips) and 5:5 (the theme of myrrh at the lock of the door).

■ **14** The man's arms are "rods of gold," decorated with precious stones. The description in vv 14–15 returns to metaphors that suggest a statue, as many commentators point out. There is no evidence in the Old Testament for such elaborate ornamentation of the male arm.[21]

The description of the belly as "ivory" may refer to the color of the skin or to smoothness.[22] Perhaps the intention is merely to bring out how precious his body is.

■ **15** Ben Sira describes the virtuous woman in similar terms: "Golden columns on silver bases are her shapely limbs and feet" (Sir 26:18). The sheen and whiteness of alabaster would seem to be the point of the comparison.

The statement in v 15b concerning the youth's stature (*mar'eh,* "appearance," cf. 2:14) attempts to capture a total impression. He is compared to the majestic cedars of Lebanon (cf. Am 2:9).

■ **16** The reference to the mouth is probably in view of the kisses which she receives from him (cf. 1:2). In 7:10[9] he returns the compliment to her.

When the woman calls him "my friend," she uses (only here) the masculine form of the term which he uses frequently of her (*rēʿî—raʿyātî*). With this the boastful description of his charms comes to an end.

■ **6:1** The reaction of the Daughters is clearly modeled on 5:9: both are questions, both repeat key phrases, both

---

18 Gerleman (173) appropriately refers to the *Odyssey* 6.232–234, where Athene pours charm on the head of Odysseus as a goldsmith pours out silver and gold.

19 E.g., Gerleman (174) understands "milk" and "fullness" as referring to the well-being and plenty the doves enjoy. L. Krinetzki (191) relates the "milk" to the whiteness of the doves and hence of the eyes. Pope (502, 538–539) sees the doves "Splashing in the milky spray, Sitting by brimming pools." Cf. also Keel, 187–189.

20 This is the appropriate sense, however the reading of 𝔐 ("towers") is to be explained; see the Notes, p. 166

above.

21 Gerleman (177) rightly rejects the suggestion of Rudolph (160) that the reference is to a tattoo, or to blue veins. Such interpretations exaggerate the representational aspect of the description.

22 Pope, 544. Gerleman (176) refers to the scene in the *Odyssey* 18.196 in which Athene brings it about that the sleeping Penelope is made whiter than ivory.

are designed to lead to an unstated but purposeful activity on the part of the Daughters. In v 1 they imply that her description of the man has caught their fancy—hence their offer to help her find him. The search motif has occurred already in the song (1:7–8; 3:1–5) and is intrinsic to love language. The search for Dumuzi or for Baal, while parallel to the motif, have quite different contexts.[23]

■ 2 The woman's response cuts off any hope the Daughters may have had concerning a possible relationship with the man. The point of vv 2–3 is that the lover was never really lost to her, even though he was absent according to the story she related in 5:2–7. This point is expressed in symbolic language in v 3: "his garden" is the woman; his going down to the garden means that he truly possesses the beloved. Although she implicitly appealed for help to the Daughters in 5:8 ("if you find him"), now she indicates the depths of their mutual presence and union.

The woman's triumphant cry, "my lover has gone down to his garden," is expanded by metaphors of browsing and gathering lilies. This symbolic language is reflected in 4:16 and 5:1, the conclusion of the "garden"

passage, and also in 6:11 and 7:12[11]. The activity in the garden is not that of horticulture but of love. Their union, despite the absences and searches, always perdures.

■ 3 The verse is a clear statement of mutual possession, and an unequivocal expression of the woman's claim that her lover was never really lost. The inversion of the first four words, in contrast to 2:16, does not seem to have any particular purpose, unless it is that the "I" is better expressed at once and clearly, after the veiled allusion ("garden") to herself in v 2.

One can conclude that the function of the Daughters (5:9; 6:1) has been to provide the woman with the opportunity of describing her lover's charms and affirming their mutual union. According to the thrust of these events, the structure of 5:2—6:3 forms a unit. It should also be noted that 5:1 and 6:1–3 have a certain correspondence: both speak of his going to the garden, and both bring a section to an end.

---

23   Cf. Pope, 553–554.

Praise of the Woman's
Unique Beauty

6

4 ■ M Beautiful are you, my friend, as Tirzah,
      lovely as Jerusalem,
        awe-inspiring as visions!
5   Turn your eyes away from me,
      for they disturb me.
    Your hair is like a flock of goats
      that stream down from Gilead.
6   Your teeth like a flock of ewes
      that come up from the washing,
    All of them in pairs
      and none of them missing.
7   Like a cut of pomegranate, your cheek
      behind your veil.
8   Sixty are the queens,
      eighty the concubines,
      and maidens without number—
9   Unique is my dove, my perfect one!
      The unique one of her mother,
      the chosen of the one who bore her.
    When women see her, they praise her;
      queens and concubines, they bless her:
10   "Who is this that comes forth like the dawn,
      beautiful as the moon?
    Pure as the sun,
      awe-inspiring as visions?"

11 ■ W To the nut-garden I came down,
      to see the fresh growth of the valley,
    To see if the vines were budding,
      if the pomegranates were in blossom.
12   Before I knew it,
      my heart made me
      ⟨the blessed one⟩ of the prince's people.

Notes

4 In a sudden appearance, the man addresses the woman in words that are very similar to 1:15 and 4:1,7 (cf. 2:10,13). The relationship to 4:1 is the most striking, since the succeeding lines turn to the topic of her eyes (4:1; 6:5). Because echoes of 4:1–3 appear in vv 4–7, Gerleman (181) describes this as an "abbreviated variant of 4:1ff., provided with a revised introduction."

It is a striking fact that 𝔊 (εὐδοκία), 𝔖 (ṣbyn'), and 𝔙 (suavis) did not recognize a proper name in תִּרְצָה ("Tirzah"), despite the parallelism with "Jerusalem"; they translate from the root meaning, רצה = pleasing. This has encouraged Pope (539) to propose "verily pleasing" for בְּתִרְצָה (asseverative בְּ), with the consequent deletion of "as Jerusalem." Tirzah was the name of the capital of the Northern Kingdom of Israel from Jeroboam to Omri (circa 920–880 B.C.E.); cf. 1 Kgs 14:17; 15:33; 16:23. The claim has been made that these lines must date back approximately to this time, since Samaria soon replaced Tirzah as the capital. The argument is not conclusive; indeed, it could be that at a later period the mention of Samaria might be deliberately avoided. Moreover, one can recognize a play on the word Tirzah, which derives from the root רצה, meaning "pleasing." Tirzah is probably to be identified with modern tell 'el-fâr'a; cf. Roland de Vaux, "Chronique archéologique: Tell el-Fâr'ah," *RB* 67 (1960) 245–247.

Jerusalem is called "lovely" in Jer 6:2 (נָוָה, a *Nebenform* of נָאוֶה), and in Lam 2:15 it is described as "the all beautiful city, the joy of the whole earth"; cf. Ps 48:3.

The masculine form of אֲיֻמָּה ("awe-inspiring") is used in Hab 1:7 of the fearsome Chaldeans (Neo-Babylonians); the noun (אֵימָה) is associated with war (Deut 32:25), and with theophany (Gen 15:12). This is clearly a bold description of the woman, in view of the tenderness which is elsewhere expressed. The context (v 5) supports the disquieting effect which the sight of the woman produces. It is simply too convenient to treat the entire phrase as an addition from v 10, where it is more in context (a solution urged by Loretz, 38, n. 2).

נִדְגָּלוֹת ("visions") is the Nip'al feminine plural participle of דגל. This is often understood as a verb derived from the noun דֶּגֶל ("banner"); hence the translation "bannered troops" (NEB) or "bannered hosts" (NJV). As noted at 2:4, this meaning is very uncertain. The ancient versions attributed a military

sense to נִדְגָּלוֹת: 𝔊 τεταγμέναι, "drawn up"; 𝔙 *castrorum acies ordinata*, "camps in battle array." As in the case of 2:4, another meaning can be conjectured from the Akkadian *dagālu*, "to look." "Things seen" (feminine for neuter) would then be the general sense. Hence "trophies" (Pope, 560–562) and, due to the mention of the sun and moon in the context, "starry heavens" (NEB) and "heavenly bodies" (Rudolph, 162) have been suggested as specific connotations of the term.

5 The masculine pronoun, הֵם, refers back to "eyes," which are feminine; the fluctuation of gender occurs throughout the Song; cf. הֵמָּה in 6:8, and the verbs in 6:9b. The word הִרְהִיבֻנִי ("disturb me") was interpreted by 𝔊, 𝔖, and 𝔙 in the sense of "fly away," due perhaps to the man's disappearance in chapter 5 (cf. 4:9). The root is associated by some with Arabic *rahaba*, "to fear" (cf. L. Kopf, "Arabische Etymologien und Parallelen zum Bibelwörterbuch," *VT* 9 [1959] 273–276); but the use of the Qal form in Isa 3:5 and Prov 6:3 suggests "oppress" or "assault." The Hip'il of רהב occurs elsewhere only in Ps 138:3, where it refers to divine action in the נֶפֶשׁ of the psalmist: God effects "strength" (עֹז) in him.

Except for an insignificant variant (omission of הַר, "mount"), v 5b is a repetition of 4:1b.

6 This is another repetition; 4:2 appears with a minor variant. The הַקְּצוּבוֹת ("shorn") of 4:2 are explicitly identified here as הָרְחֵלִים ("ewes").

7 A repetition of 4:3b.

8 The masculine pronoun, הֵמָּה, is used as the copula with the feminine plural noun מְלָכוֹת ("queens"). Grammarians justify this as a rarity (*GHB* §149c); less likely is the correlation with the Ugaritic *hm*, a particle of emphasis.

9 אַחַת ("unique," "one") is in emphatic position and an alliteration (cf. 5:2) follows. The point is the uniqueness of the woman, not that she is an only child (against NEB).

The root ברר means "pure," which has developed into "chosen" (1 Chr 7:40) and "purified" or "shining" (as it can be rendered in 6:10). The stylistic repetition of the mother is reminiscent of 3:4.

The women are בָּנוֹת (literally "daughters"), but there is no reason to identify them specifically with the Daughters of Jerusalem. They seem to be identical with the עֲלָמוֹת ("maidens") of v 8, and members of the royal harem, as the parallelism with מְלָכוֹת ("queens") indicates. In 2:2–3 "daughters" and "sons" indicate the whole range of females and males with whom the woman and man are compared.

10   This question appears in 3:6 and 8:5; here it is certain that the reference is to a female, in contrast to 3:6.

נִשְׁקָפָה ("comes forth") means literally "looks out," as from a mountain or from heaven (Ps 14:2), or from a window (Judg 5:28). The context, however, suggests the picture of the rising of the dawn or the sun; hence the woman's beauty rises, or comes forth. In Sir 26:16 a woman's beauty is compared to "the sun rising in the Lord's heavens."

The words rendered "moon" and "sun" are [הַ]לְּבָנָה ("the white") and [הַ]חַמָּה ("the hot"), a poetic usage that is found also in Isa 24:23; 30:26.

For the phrase אֲיֻמָּה כַּנִּדְגָּלוֹת ("awe-inspiring as visions"), see the remarks on 6:4.

11   אֱגוֹז ("nut-garden") is a hapax and of uncertain origin (cf. Pope, 574–579, for an extended discussion; and also Wagner, *Aramaismen,* 18). The association of the nut-garden with the valley is not clear. The garden could hardly include a valley. It must be a vantage point from which to see the valley in bloom, which occurs in the Spring as a result of the winter rains. But perhaps we are simply confronted with a profusion of images (garden, valley, vines, pomegranates) that have no spatial connection. There is no need to interpret נחל (with Ricciotti [256] and Rudolph [166]) in the light of an Arabic root as "palm-tree." Echoes of this verse appear in 7:13[12]; 𝕲 has added ἐκεῖ δώσω τοὺς μαστούς μου σοί ("there I will give you my breasts") from v 13b.

12   This is a famous *crux interpretum;* the proper reading has never been successfully discovered. 𝔐 is certainly corrupt, and is hardly susceptible of translation. A literal rendering might be: "I did not know; my soul/life set me; chariots of Ammi-nadib." The ancient versions provide no help. 𝕲 reads οὐκ ἔγνω ἡ ψυχή μου· ἔθετό με ἄρματα Αμιναδαβ ("my soul did not know; it made me chariots of Aminadab"); 𝕾 is similar, but represents the final phrase as "chariots of the people that is prepared *[dmtyb]*"; 𝖁 has *nescivi anima mea conturbavit me propter quadrigas Aminadab* ("I did not know; my soul disturbed me [reading שׁמם for שׂים] because of the chariots of Aminadab"). It appears that all had basically the same corrupt text found in 𝔐. None of the many emendations pro-

posed by scholars is really convincing. (See the discussion in Pope, 584–592). With full justification this verse might be left untranslated. Instead, an emendation (suggested by Kuhn [40, 42] and underlying the NAB rendering) is adopted here: מְבֹרֶכֶת (Puʿal feminine singular participle of ברך, "blessed one"; cf. Deut 33:13) for 𝔐 מַרְכְּבוֹת ("chariots"); cf. *BH³,* 1208, n. "b" to 6:12. (NAB renders the clause "the blessed one of my kinswomen." The relevant textual note ["Confraternity" edition, Vol. 3 (Paterson, New Jersey: St. Anthony Guild, 1955) 689] posits בְּנוֹת עַמִּי for 𝔐 עַמִּי־נָדִיב, suggesting that the latter involves dittography of 7:2[1]. But this further departure from the consonantal text of 𝔐 seems unnecessary as well as textually unwarranted.) One may find an echo here of the praise of the woman in 6:9; cf. also the "blessing" of Jael in Judg 5:24: "the blessed one of my people."

לֹא יָדַעְתִּי ("before I knew it") is literally "I did not know," which is to be understood as an almost parenthetical remark, equivalent to "unawares" or "suddenly."

נַפְשִׁי שָׂמַתְנִי ("my heart made me") is literally "my soul placed me." The verb שִׂים is often used idiomatically to express making a thing (first object) into something else (second object, sometimes introduced with a preposition); e.g., Gen 21:13,18; Isa 28:17. One cannot properly translate 𝔐 as "placed me on" without a preposition (although Pope [586] maintains that "chariots" is an adverbial accusative); hence "made me" seems indicated. Another problem lies in the reference to "Ammi-nadib," who like Satan in the *Cantico Espiritual* of San Juan de la Cruz (where he is called "Aminadab"), has resisted all efforts at solution. If the phrase is not a proper name, it can be rendered "the people of (the) prince," with עַמִּי containing the paragogic י (so Ginsburg; cf. *GHB* §931). Pope (589–590) accepts this interpretation of the final *yod* and reads עם as the preposition "with," yielding עִמִּי נָדִיב ("with [the] prince"). For a discussion of old and new translations and interpretations, see Raymond Tournay, "Les chariots d'Aminadab (Cant. vi 12): Israël, peuple théophore," *VT* 9 (1959) 288–309, esp. 288–292 (reprinted in *idem, Études,* 73–81).

Interpretation

A new section clearly opens at 6:4 when the man addresses the woman. He had been the object of her futile search in the previous section, but now he speaks as if appearing out of nowhere. His words of admiration and boasting end at v 10. The connection of vv 11–12 with his address is uncertain. If, as understood in this translation, the woman now speaks, she seems to remind him of a previous tryst.

There are mixed genres in vv 4–10. The man begins with a song of admiration (vv 4–5a), and enters into a *wasf* (vv 5b–7, repeating lines from 4:1–3). There is no obvious explanation of the repetition; it serves to develop the praise of the woman's beauty that opens 6:4. He concludes with a song of admiration that boasts of her incomparability and excellence. The genre of the obscure vv 11–12 seems to be the description of an experience.

■ **4** The woman is addressed by the man, who compliments her on her beauty in the style of 1:15 and 4:1,7. The comparison of a woman to a city gives trouble to many commentators.[1] However, it should be recalled that cities are typically personified as females (Isa 60:1–12; Ezek 23:4–5; etc.), which seems sufficient to justify the simile here. Not only is the woman compared to cities, but her appearance is described as inspiring fear or awe. This line should not be expunged as a gloss influ-

enced by v 10b. The lover feels the dangerous and threatening aspect of the woman. This is a well known topos in love literature.

The imagery may have mythological overtones, suggesting goddesses who inspire terror.[2] A prime candidate among the latter is ʿAnat, the Ugaritic goddess of love and war, with whom Inanna, Ishtar, Isis, and others are also to be associated. It is reasonable to conclude that such a model has influenced the growth of the theme of the dangerous woman. This does not mean, however, that the poem in 6:4–10 refers to the goddess; it is simply that the love language may have been influenced by this concept of deity. It is perhaps difficult for the modern to hold together the traits of love and war in the beloved, but this was apparently no problem to the ancient. The description in v 4 is meant as a compliment to the woman and as testimony to the attractive but frightening mystery which the male finds in her. The poet obviously sees no conflict between attraction and fear; they can coexist. Both 4:1–2 and 6:4–5 are alike in that they begin with a compliment concerning the woman's beauty and end with a remark about her hair. Within this envelope, her eyes are characterized as doves (4:1), and also seen as upsetting. The mystery and danger of the woman's eyes remain, paradoxically, what the man wishes to experience.

■ **5a** The theme of fear instilled by the woman is con-

---

1   Pope, 558–559.
2   Pope, 560–563. A particular value of the erudite commentary of Marvin Pope is that he has supplied the mythological background to Hebrew love poetry. His treatment demonstrates the background of the sentiments in 4:9 and 6:5. However, the myth is background only: the intent of the poet is something quite different. One can compare the use of the myth of *hêlēl ben šaḥar* ("morning star, son of dawn") in Isa 14 to describe the fall of the king of Babylon. The intent, or level of meaning, of the poet deals with the king of Babylon, not the mythical figure. The extent

to which the background story has been "demythologized" in the Song is very difficult to determine. However, the obvious emphasis on the attraction and love which the man and the woman feel for each other in the Song suggest that the myth has been considerably tamed.

tinued in v 5. The power of her eyes over the man has already been expressed in 4:9. Now he pleads that she avert her gaze from him because of the tumult he feels. But no matter how disturbing be the effect of her eyes upon him, he still yearns for her, to gaze upon her, as the entire Song makes evident.

■ **5b** See the commentary on 4:1.

■ **6-7** See the commentary on 4:1–3. The transition in v 5b to the genre of *wasf*, and in practically the same words found in chapter 4, is sudden and inexplicable, save as a continuation of the praise in 6:4.

■ **8** After the digression concerning the physical charms of the woman, the man begins what Horst has called a "boasting song" (vv 8–10).[3] The royal background is noteworthy. The woman is contrasted with the royal harem, which can be explained from the king fiction which appears elsewhere in the Song (cf. 1:4, 12).

The harem is classified on three levels: "queens . . . concubines . . . maidens." The official status of the concubine was below that of the formal wife or queen.[4] The ever increasing number is a stylistic device that serves to underline the claim made for the beloved in v 9: "Sixty . . . eighty" represents three score . . . four score; the woman is being compared to an unlimited number.[5]

■ **9** After the mention of the high numbers in v 8, the repeated use of 'aḥat ("unique, one") underscores how

incomparable and superior this woman is. Such a tribute is a commonplace in love poetry. In the Egyptian love poems, for example, the woman boasts that the man has made her "as first of the girls," and the man boasts similarly: "She turns the head of every man, all captivated at the sight of her; everyone who embraces her rejoices, for he has become the most successful of lovers. When she comes forth, anyone can see that there is none like that One."[6]

The various classes of royal consorts mentioned in v 8 are represented as praising the man's beloved; the point is that all women, including especially the foremost, acknowledge her superiority.

■ **10** This verse is put in quotations to indicate that it is the exclamation uttered by the women designated in the preceding verse. It is the sort of question that would be asked as a beautiful woman approaches the speakers.

Comparison to the dawn, moon, and sun suggests the radiant beauty of the woman. These metaphors are common coin to describe female beauty.[7] The rendering "visions" for *nidgālôt* is uncertain, but in the present context the term may refer to celestial phenomena, such as stars.[8]

■ **11** Verses 11–12 represent a sudden break with the preceding song of admiration. It is difficult to determine who is the speaker. Since the woman is the garden to which the man comes in 5:1, the verse might be attrib-

---

3   Horst, "Formen," 183.
4   Cf. Roland de Vaux, *Ancient Israel: Its Life and Institutions* (tr. John McHugh; New York/Toronto/London: McGraw-Hill, 1961) 117, where it is noted that Cant 6:8 is the only place in the Old Testament that uses the term "queen" *(malkâ;* plural *mĕlākôt)* to refer to Israelite or Judaean royal consort(s).
5   The numerical pattern of sixty/eighty/unlimited is not to be correlated with 1 Kgs 11:3 (Solomon's harem). Gordis (94) thinks that "60 and 80, which are three and four score, respectively, represent the 'ascending numeration' common in Biblical and

Semitic poetry for designating a large and indefinite quantity." The progression "seventy/eighty" is well attested in Ugaritic. Cf. Albright, "Archaic Survivals," 1; and the discussion in Pope, 567–568.
6   Simpson, *Literature*, 305, 316.
7   See, e.g., the first stanza of the Egyptian "Songs of Extreme Happiness" (Simpson, *Literature*, 315–316):

     One, the lady love without duplicate,
     more perfect than the world,
     see, she is like the star rising
     at the start of an auspicious year.
     . . .

uted to him. On the other hand, the blooming of the vine and blossoming of the pomegranates are repeated in an invitation uttered by the woman in 7:13. The difficulty is compounded by the obscurity of v 12. One may draw a parallel with chapter 7, where the man's resolve to be united with the woman follows a song of admiration (7:8–9[7–8], after 7:2–7[1–6]). So also, 6:11–12 might represent his coming to the woman after the praise of her beauty in the previous verses. However, v 11 can also be understood as spoken by the woman who recalls a former tryst with the man. She gives a specific purpose to her visit to the garden: to see if the flowers are in bloom, etc. In the language of the Song, this sign is associated with love. The man spoke of the awakening of nature in the famous Spring song of 2:11–13, and it has been

pointed out that phrases of 6:11 are repeated in 7:13 (spoken by the woman). The visit to the garden may be intended as a real visit to a real garden by the woman; the language about the blossoms would then suggest that the purpose is a rendezvous with the lover. In this view, the woman would also speak the lines in v 12.[9]

■ **12** The Notes indicate how problematical any rendering of this verse must be. The translation suggests that v 12 completes a reminiscence on the part of the woman: a visit to the nut-garden, where she had a rendezvous with the man, and where she fell suddenly and completely in love, being made "the blessed one of my people" (conjectural emendation).

When she comes forth, anyone can see that there is none like that one.

8   See the Notes to 6:4, p. 175 above.

9   For possible mythological associations of the nut, and also the fertility background to the 'ēb ("fresh growth") and the naḥal ("valley"), see Pope, 574–583.

The Union of Lovers

7

1[6:13] ■ (?) Turn, turn, O Shulammite;
 turn, turn, that we may gaze upon you!

■ W "Why do you gaze upon the Shulammite
 as upon the dance of the two camps?"

2[7:1] ■ M How beautiful your sandaled feet,
 O noble daughter!
 The curves of your thighs, like rings,
 the handiwork of an artist.

3 Your valley, a round bowl
 that is not to lack mixed wine.
 Your belly, a heap of wheat,
 surrounded with lilies.

4 Your breasts like two fawns,
 twins of a gazelle.

5 Your neck like a tower of ivory;
 your eyes, pools in Heshbon
 by the gate of Bath-rabbim.
 Your nose like the tower of Lebanon
 looking toward Damascus.

6 On you, your head is like Carmel,
 and the hair of your head, like purple—
 a king is caught in tresses.

7 How beautiful, and how pleasing,
 O loved one, delightful ⟨daughter⟩!

8 Your very stature is like a palm tree,
 and your breasts, clusters.

9 I said, "I will climb the palm tree,
 I will take hold of its branches;
 Let your breasts be like the clusters of the
 vine,
 and the fragrance of your breath like
 apples;

10 Your mouth like the best wine. . . ."

■ W Flowing smoothly for my lover,
 spreading over ⟨my lips and my teeth⟩.

11 I am my lover's,
 and towards me is his desire.

12 Come, my lover, let us away to the field;
 let us spend the night in the villages.

13 Let us be off early to the vineyards,
 let us see if the vines have budded;
 If the blossoms have opened,
 if the pomegranates are in bloom.
 There I will give you my love.

14 The mandrakes give forth fragrance,
 and at our door are all choice fruits;
 New with the old,
 my lover, have I stored up for you.

8

1 Would that you were my brother,
 nursed at my mother's breasts!
 Were I to find you in public,
 I would kiss you,
 and no one would despise me.

2 I would lead you, bring you,
 to my mother's house
 (where) you would teach me.
 I would give you spiced wine to drink,
 my pomegranate juice.

3 His left hand is under my head,
 his right hand embraces me.

4 I adjure you, O Daughters of Jerusalem:
 Do not arouse, do not stir up love,
 until it be ready!

Notes

7:1[6:13] שׁוּבִי ("turn") can mean: "[do it] again" or "return." It is hardly the word that would serve as an invitation to dance. Rather, the woman is asked to face the speaker(s).

הַשּׁוּלַמִּית has not been explained with any certainty. It is probably an epithet, not a proper name, with the definite article indicating the vocative (*GHG* §126e). The following are among the solutions that have been proposed: 1) The name goes back to *Šulmānîtu*, a goddess of love and war known from Mesopotamian sources (cf. William F. Albright, "The Syro-Mesopotamian God Šulmân-Ešmûn and Related Figures," *AfO* 7 [1931–1932] 164–169; and *idem*, *Yahweh and the Gods of Canaan: A Historical Analysis of Two Contrasting Faiths* [Garden City: Doubleday, 1968] 150). 2) The term is to be understood as a feminine gentilic, equivalent to "Shunammite," designating a woman of Shunem, a town in the eastern part of the Esdraelon plain (e.g., Josh 19:18; 1 Sam 28:4). Hence association has often been made with Abishag, the beautiful "Shunammite" woman of 1 Kgs 1:3,15; 2:17–22 (cf. Budde, 36; Delitzsch, 119–120; Ringgren, 31). While an interchange of "l" and "n" in these epithets is unobjectionable, the proposed equation cannot claim support from the ancient versions (𝔊 ᴬ etc. Σουλαμῖτις; 𝔊 ᴮ σουμανειτις; 𝔙 *Sulamitis*; cf. Rudolph, 170. 3) The word is derived from "Solomon" and/or שָׁלוֹם ("peace"), and hence the sense is something like "the Solomoness" (H. H. Rowley, "The Meaning of 'the Shulammite,'" *AJSL* 56 [1939] 84–91) or "the peaceful one" (Robert, 250; cf. Fox, 157–158). For an extended review of interpretations given to the term, cf. Pope, 596–600.

The identity of the speakers in v 1a is also uncertain. One might infer that they are males, in view of the gender used in the reply in v 1b; so NEB reads "companions" of the bridegroom. But there have been other instances where the masculine plural seems to be used in a general sense (2:5,15). Hence the command has been attributed to the Daughters of Jerusalem.

The reply to the summons is itself a question, "Why . . .?" This should be attributed to the Shulammite; it is less likely that it is an explanatory intervention by the man (so NEB). Although 𝔊, 𝔖, and 𝔙 translate מָה ("why") as the accusative pronoun "what," this can be taken as the adverbial accusative (*GHB* §144e).

𝔐ᴸ exhibits בְּמֹחֹלַת, but in other manuscripts the initial preposition is בְּ ("in"); cf. σ′ ἐν τρώσεσιν. Both 𝔊 (ὡς Χοροὶ) and 𝔖 (*'yk ḥdwt'*) support 𝔐ᴸ, and understand the preposition as comparative; so also, implicitly, 𝔙 (*nisi choros*). Pope (605) remarks that "The *k*-may also be taken as having temporal meaning, on the occasion of the dance, i.e., as she dances." However, the preposition can convey simple comparison: Why do you gaze upon the Shulammite (as you would gaze upon) . . . ? There is no grammatical difficulty in the omission of כ (notice the נֶחֱזֶה־בָּךְ in v 1a); see *GHB* §133h. Cf. Roland E. Murphy, "Dance and Death in the Song of Songs," *Love and Death in the Ancient Near East: Essays in Honor of Marvin H. Pope* (ed. John H. Marks and Robert M. Good; Guilford, Conn.: Four Quarters, 1987) 117–119.

There has been much discussion of the root of מחלה (חוּל, "turn," "dance"; or חלל, "celebrate," "sing"), but "dance" is the generally accepted interpretation. Cf. the summary of opinions in Pope, 601–603. Mayer I. Gruber ("Ten Dance-Derived Expressions in the Hebrew Bible," *Bib* 62 (1981) 341–345) derives מָחוֹל from חלל/חיל, "perform a whirling dance"; he points out that the term comes to denote joy (Ps 30:12) and is also associated with safe return from battle (Judg 11:34) and with accompanying song (1 Sam 18:6–7; 12:12; 29:5). Gruber suggests that the "dance of the two camps" celebrated a military victory and translates the crucial line in 7:1 as follows (343): "'What,' (she asks), 'will you see in the Shulamite?' (They answer), 'Of course, the dance of the two camps.'" And the dance begins. הַמַּחֲנָיִם could refer to the well-known place, "Mahanaim," in the Transjordan near the Jabbok (2 Sam 17:24); but evidence is lacking to associate a particular dance with the site (cf. Delitzsch, 120–121; Loretz, 42). The term is dual in form, literally meaning "the two camps"; it has been interpreted by many commentators as referring to the manner in which the dance was presented: the grouping of the spectators, men and women, about the dancer (cf. NEB: "as she moves between the lines of dancers!"). All this is very hypothetical; the nature of "the dance of the two camps" remains unknown.

2[1] The precise nuance of נָדִיב ("noble," "prince") is disputed; it can refer to her generous character, but more likely it is a compliment in keeping with the king fiction in the Song. If the royal harem praises her (6:9–10), she deserves royal distinction. There may be some association between נָדִיב here and in the enigmatic 6:12, at least as a catch word.

חַמּוּקֵי ("curves") is hapax, although the word appears in 5:6 in the sense of "turn"; it could designate the movement, or the actual contour, of the thigh.

חֲלָאִים ("rings") is the plural of חלי/חלא; in Prov 25:12 and Hos 2:12 this root is associated with נֶזֶם ("ring"). 𝔊 understood it to be a "necklace" (ὁρμίσκος). אָמָּן ("artist") is hapax, but the meaning is not in doubt (cf. Wagner, *Aramaismen*, 26).

3[2] שָׁרְרֵךְ (rendered here as "your valley") is used in Ezek 16:4 (שָׁרֵּךְ) for the umbilical cord, and hence the translation "navel" or the like has been widely accepted for שֹׁר here also; so already 𝔊 (ὀμφαλος), 𝔙 (*umbilicus*), and 𝔖 (*šrky*). In defending this interpretation, Nolli (131) and Gerleman (63–72, esp. 70) call attention to the standards of Egyptian artistic taste (cf. Keel, 214–215). But unless one accepts other instances of the influence of Egyptian art on the *wasf*, as Gerleman does, the argument is not very convincing. Moreover, the sequence in which שֹׁר appears does not suggest the woman's navel; it occurs between references to her thighs and belly. Hence many commentators have suggested a relationship to Arabic *sirr*, meaning "secret," and then "pudenda" or "vulva": e.g., Ricciotti, 264; Würthwein, 62; Pope, 617–618. (Cf. Ernst Vogt, "Einige hebräische Wortbedeutungen," *Bib* 48 [1967] 69–72, who argues that שֹׁר must mean "Schoss"; similarly, e.g., Miller, 63; Ringgren, 28.) But this has philological difficulties; one cannot simply assume a like development from "secret" in Hebrew. The Arabic word *surr* matches the Hebrew; it means "umbilical cord," "navel," or "valley." Doubtless, "valley" is an extension of the first meaning, "navel." In 7:3, "valley" preserves something of the original meaning of שֹׁר, and also provides a term that fits better into the context. In the third stanza of "In praise of his Mistris," Thomas Carew, the seventeenth-century English poet, used "valley" in just this sense:

> Hills of Milk with Azure mixd
>   Swell beneath,
> Waving sweetly, yet still fixd
>   While she doth breath.
> From those hills descends a valley
> Where all fall, that dare to dally.

(Rhodes Dunlap, ed., *The Poems of Thomas Carew* [Oxford: Clarendon, 1949] 122.) The translation adopts this rendering as a metaphor for the euphe-mism and double meaning that seem intended.

אַגָּן ("bowl") is used elsewhere in the Bible only in Exod 24:6, to describe the container for the blood to be poured out, and in Isa 22:24, where it is a generic term to include everything "from cups to flagons." The bowl is described by the term הַסַּהַר (with the article, oddly), which is a hapax. 𝔊 rendered it τορευτὸς ("worked in relief") and 𝔙 has *tornatilis* ("turned"). The sense of the comparison is probably not the size but the shape of the bowl ("round" or the like). What it holds is מֶזֶג. This is also hapax, and seems to be an Aramaism for Hebrew מֶסֶךְ, "mixed wine," found only in Ps 75:9; the verb מסך is attested in the sense of "mix" (e.g., Isa 19:14; Ps 102:10). (Cf. Wagner, *Aramaismen*, 73–74.) The mixture could be wine and water, or wine and spices. אַל with the imperfect ("not to lack") can designate an emphatic denial (*GHB* §144k) or even a prohibition.

The sense of the comparison of the woman's abdomen (בִּטְנֵךְ ["your belly"]) to עֲרֵמַת חִטִּים ("a heap of wheat") is obscure; shape or color could be meant (Delitzsch, 125). Some commentators (e.g., Ricciotti, 265; and Nolli, 132) interpret the likeness as a symbol of fertility.

סוּגָה ("surrounded") is the Qal feminine singular passive participle of סוג; it is possibly an Aramaism (cf. Wagner, *Aramaismen*, 86). There is no other reference in ancient sources to surrounding wheat with lilies. Perhaps the metaphor is prompted by a garment or decoration worn by the woman (cf. Pope, 624; and Keel, 216–217).

4[3] This is a repetition of 4:5, except that "browsing among the lilies" is omitted, "probably because there was question of lilies at the end of the preceding verse" (Robert, 261). 𝔊 does attest the phrase here.

5[4] In 4:4, the woman's צַוָּאר ("neck") was compared to "David's tower"; here it is likened to מִגְדַּל הַשֵּׁן ("a tower of ivory"), about which nothing is otherwise known (although ivory inlay was used for decoration [cf. Am 6:4]). This description stands as an isolated line (v 5a), in contrast to the poem's prevailing pattern of bicola. Thus there is reason to suspect that a parallel colon has been lost or misplaced (so, e.g., Robert, 262; Würthwein, 62; Loretz, 42; cf. Lys, 262). To fill the ostensible gap, Nolli (132–133) transposes to this place v 6aα ("On you, your head is like Carmel"). Other, more hypothetical solutions include reconstructing a colon on the basis of 5:15aβ: מְיֻסָּד עַל־אַדְנֵי־בָהַט ("set in sockets of porphyry"); cf. *BHS*, 1333, n. "a" to 7:5.

בְּרֵכוֹת בְּהֶשְׁבּוֹן ("pools in Heshbon") is to be understood as metaphor, not simile, despite the "like" found in 𝕲 and 𝔙. The comparison of eyes to doves has been made by both the man and the woman (4:1; 5:12). This verse is reminiscent of 5:12 where the doves are associated with water—a natural image, since water refracts light. Heshbon is the famous biblical city (cf. Num 21:26–30), located about twelve kilometers north of Madaba.

בַּת־רַבִּים literally means "daughter of many" and was so translated by both 𝕲 (θυγατρὸς Πολλῶν) and 𝔙 (filiae multitudinis). But the construction is parallel to Heshbon and should be kept as a proper name, although the site cannot be identified.

As Robert (264) points out, אַפֵּךְ ("your nose") cannot be "face," since the form is singular, not dual. But this hyperbole about the nose has been questioned by commentators.

Nothing is known about מִגְדַּל הַלְּבָנוֹן ("tower of Lebanon"), but it presumably means a towering mountain. Because it "faces" (צוֹפֶה) Damascus, some commentators (e.g., Ricciotti, 266; and Robert, 265) speculate that Mount Hermon is meant.

6[5] The comparison of the woman's רֹאשׁ ("head") to Carmel, the famous mountain range that juts into the Mediterranean near Haifa, would suggest stateliness. Because of the parallelism with "hair" which follows, commentators mention the luxuriant growth on Carmel. But Pope (629) points out the possibility of a play on the word "Carmel" and the color כַּרְמִיל ("purple" or "crimson") of the woman's hair.

דַּלָּה ("hair") derives from דלל ("hang") and is found elsewhere only in Isa 38:12, where it designates the thread of the loom. The comparison to purple indicates that her hair is dyed.

Some commentators (e.g., Gerleman, 194) follow the lead of α', σ', 𝕲, and 𝔙 and join מֶלֶךְ ("king") with אַרְגָּמָן ("[royal] purple"). But this is not necessary; the reference to the king fits well with the king fiction which has already been noted.

The translation of רְהָטִים (cf. also 1:17) as "tresses" is doubtful. The root רהט means "run" in Aramaic and Syriac, and רְהָטִים in Gen 30:38,41 means "watering trough." Both 𝔙 (canalibus) and 𝕲 (Παραδρομαῖς) suggest the meaning "courses." The translation "tresses" rests on the idea that her wavy hair evokes the image of running water (cf. also 4:1); for another interpretation, see Eugenio Zolli, "In Margine al Cantico dei Cantici," *Bib* 21 (1940) 273–282, esp. 276.

7[6] The compliment to her beauty takes up terms (יפה, נעם) which the woman used of the man in 1:16.

אַהֲבָה ("loved one") is literally "love." The abstract can be used for the concrete; it is also possible to vocalize the word as the passive participle, אֲהֻבָה.

"Delightful daughter" rests upon a correction of 𝔐, which reads בַּתַּעֲנוּגִים ("with delights"; so NJV, "with all its rapture"). However, it seems better to recognize haplography here and read בַּת תַּעֲנוּגִים, "O daughter of delight(s)" (with the support of 𝕲 and α').

8[7] זֹאת קוֹמָתֵךְ ("your very stature") is literally "this your stature"; cf. *GHB* §143f for the adjectival use of the demonstrative pronoun.

אַשְׁכֹּלוֹת ("clusters") normally designates clusters of grapes (as explicitly in v 9). But here it must mean the date clusters of the palm tree (cf. also 1:14).

9[8] סַנְסִנָּיו ("its branches") is hapax, but is to be related to Akkadian *sissinnu*, "the upper branches of the date palm." It probably designates the fruit along with the branch (Robert, 272). σ' (βάϊον) and 𝕲 (swbwhy) support the translation "branches."

אַף ("breath") normally means nostrils or nose (cf. v 5); it designates the organ for breathing (root, אנף). Both Mitchell Dahood ("Canticle 7,9 and UT 52, 61. A Question of Method," *Bib* 57 [1976] 109–110) and Pope (636) cite the Ugaritic "Birth of the Gracious Gods" (*CTA* 23[= *UT* 52].61), in which the gods are said to suck *b'ap dd*, "on the nipple of the breast." Hence Dahood reads "nipple," but Pope, understanding אַף as an aperture, takes it to mean "vulva" in 7:9.

10[9] חֵךְ ("mouth") is literally "palate" (cf. 5:16); kisses are meant.

As vocalized in 𝔐, כְּיֵין הַטּוֹב ("like the best wine") is literally "like the wine of the good," an expression of the superlative. The man's statement of his desires ends abruptly at this point, unless one rewrites the text by omitting לְדוֹדִי (with Pope [639] and the RSV) or changing it to לְחִכִּי (as do Budde [40] and Miller [66]); then the entire verse is spoken by the man. The translation adopted here follows 𝔐. In a sudden transition, the woman continues in the words that follow, returning the compliment, a device that has occurred before (1:15–16; 4:16b).

The rendering of מֵישָׁרִים as "smoothly" can be justified from Prov 23:31; cf. Gordis (97) for another, less likely, interpretation.

דּוֹבֵב ("spreading") is hapax; it is probably to be derived from דוב דום meaning "flow" (rather than רבב, which seems to mean "murmur"; cf. 𝔙 *ruminandum*).

There is no evidence that it is a transitive verb, so perhaps the final ב in דּוֹבֵב should be attached to or duplicated before the next word as preposition ("over"); cf. the ancient versions, and Rudolph, 174.

שִׂפְתֵי יְשֵׁנִים M is rendered literally "the lips of sleepers" in NJV (with a note that the meaning is uncertain). No convincing explanation of the phrase has been given. Delitzsch (132) understands this as a reference to talking in one's sleep under the influence of good wine. For Pope (641), the "sleepers" are the dead whose lips move (דּוֹבֵב) in the grave; he suggests that the phrase in context alludes to libations offered to ancestors in a common funerary meal. Robert (274–275) regards יְשֵׁנִים ("sleepers") as the plural of generalization, designating the woman (as in 5:2, יְשֵׁנָה); thus, the verse expresses the reciprocity of love (symbolized by wine), which "goes" to the man but is returned upon the lips of the sleeping woman.

The basic question is, who are the sleepers? It seems arbitrary to identify these with the lovers, yet they cannot (against Pope) reasonably be identified with anyone else. It seems better to emend the text, reading [שְׂפָתַי וְשִׁנָּי[ם ("my lips and my teeth") with the support of 𝕲, 𝕾, and 𝖁, as well as the majority of commentators. The only consonantal change is from י to ו (and these are frequently confused) before שׁנים; the final ם may be regarded as enclitic.

11[10] תְּשׁוּקָה ("desire") has sexual connotation; cf. Gen 3:15, where it refers to the woman's desire.

12[11] כְּפָרִים can mean either "villages" (from the singular כְּפָר¹, or *כָּפָר [so the ancient versions and a majority of commentators]) or "(bushes of) henna" (from כֹּפֶר³ [so Rudolph (175), Pope (645), and others]).

13[12] The mention of "vines" and "pomegranates" seems to be a deliberate echo of 6:11.

14[13] The Mediterranean mandrake plant served as an aphrodisiac (note the similarity between the name of the plants, דּוּדָאִים, and דּוֹדִים, "love") and is associated with fertility; see Gen 30:14–15, and also *CTA* 3 (= *UT* 'nt).3.12. Cf. Keel, 235–237, 239.

פְּתָחֵינוּ ("our door") is literally "our doors," a plural of generalization (*GHB* §136j). The broad use of "our" is characteristic; cf. 1:16; 2:9. In context, the door is probably to be associated with the "house" in 8:2.

8:1 כְּאָח לִי is literally "like a brother to me." The preposition "like" seems superfluous and is not reflected in 𝕲 and 𝖁; it is possibly dittography of the preceding pronominal suffix (ךְ). Gordis (98) understands it as the asseverative כְּ ("indeed"). מצא ("meet") evokes the search of 3:1–4 and 5:6–8, which leads the woman "into the streets" (3:2).

יָבוּזוּ ("despise") serves as a catchword with 8:7.

2 Other examples of asyndetic style ("lead you, bring you") are found in 2:11 and 5:6.

תְּלַמְּדֵנִי in M is ambiguous. In context, it could also be rendered "(the house of my mother) who taught me" (L. Krinetzki, 232), or "where you would teach me to give you to drink," or "were you to teach me, I would give you to drink" (Gerleman, 208). There is a play on אשׁקך; in v 1 it means "I would kiss you" (נשׁק), and in v 2, "I would give you to drink" (שׁקה).

Many commentators emend the text in the light of some support from the ancient versions. Instead of תְּלַמְּדֵנִי, 𝕲 and 𝕾 reflect the final clause of 3:4 (cf. 6:9; 8:5): "to the chamber of the one who conceived me." The omission of ם in תלמדני would yield תֵּלְדֵנִי ("who bore me"); see the comments of Kuhn (50–51), Rudolph (178), Pope (658–659), and Würthwein (66).

In M, הָרֶקַח stands in apposition to יַיִן ("wine"). רָקַח ("spiced") means to mix or blend with perfume.

There is no reason to emend M רִמֹּנִי in order to read the plural "pomegranates"; the suffix "my" affects the genitival phrase, "my pomegranate juice."

4 M here varies slightly from the wording of 2:7 and 3:5; the mention of the gazelles and hinds is omitted (although some ancient versions preserve it). The מָה of negation replaces אִם (cf. *GHB* §144h; and *HSyn* §§128, 428). The omission of the reference to the gazelles and hinds of the fields "is appropriate to the change from adjuration to prohibition, since there is no place in the prohibition for reference to the objects by which an adjuration is made" (Pope, 661).

Interpretation

Because of the uncertainty of the text in 6:12, it is almost imperative to recognize that a new section begins at 7:1. Here the identity of the speaker(s) is left vague. The *wasf* in vv 2–7 is spoken by an individual, whether the leader of an unidentified group (v 1) or the man. It is certainly the man who continues in vv 8–10 with an expression of yearning. He is answered by the woman in 7:10—8:3.

This section contains several literary genres that can be tied together by the sequence of the dialogue. A *wasf* is found in 7:2–7; in vv 8–10 aα, the man expresses his yearning for union with the woman, and she replies in vv 10aβ—11; she continues with an invitation and a promise to him in 7:12—8:2, and a statement of mutual possession and an adjuration (8:3–4).

The setting of 7:1–7 is usually considered to be a dance. But there are difficulties with this interpretation. In 7:1a an unidentified group issues a command to the Shulammite to "(re)turn" (*šûbî*). There is nothing specified that she can turn or return from; the context suggests that she is to turn around so that the speakers may gaze upon her beauty. Her reply in v 1b does mention the "dance of the two camps," or the "*mahănāyim*-dance." However, she uses this as a term of comparison; she does not necessarily refer to herself as performing in a dance. With more imagination than truth, the so-called sword dance has been read into this scene, on the basis of *modern* Near Eastern customs.[1] A characteristic *wasf*, this time proceeding from feet to head, follows the puzzling v 1.

The next section, vv 8–10aα, contains the man's yearning for physical union with the woman. If the previous *wasf* was spoken by him, these lines follow naturally upon his description of her beauty. There is an unusual switch in the speakers in v 10, when she replies

to him and continues in a relatively long declamation to 8:4.

■ **7:1[6:13]** The purpose of the address to the woman, here called "the Shulammite", is to persuade her to face the group that is speaking.

Her reply (v 1b) is in a rather teasing mood. She is hardly ignorant of the reason they wish to look upon her. Both the question and the answer serve to introduce the following description of her beauty. Why she compares herself to the "dance of the two camps" is not clear, since the phrase refers to something unknown. In any case, she compares the interest of the onlookers to the interest that such a dance would inspire. She does not say that she is dancing or intends to dance.

In the context of v 1 it is possible to ascribe the *wasf* that follows to the onlookers or to their spokesperson. Elsewhere the *wasf* is spoken by the man (4:1–7; 8:5–7), and hence it is reasonable to attribute vv 2–7 to him.

■ **2[1]** The *wasf* begins with the feet, in contrast to previous descriptions, and goes up to her head. The woman is called "noble daughter," in complimentary style, but there is apparently no intent to suggest royalty in the proper sense. Any attempt to explain the appellation by reference to Aminadab (6:12) is to explain *obscurum per obscurius*.[2] The comparison of the woman's thighs to an ornament, such as a ring, is not obvious; perhaps the point is the roundness.

■ **3[2]** As indicated in the Notes, "valley" is meant as a euphemism for the pudenda. The presence of "mixed wine" in this anatomical vessel has been understood as a reference to fecundation, or even to "love water."[3] But

---

1   See the Introduction, pp. 39 and 59. Cf. also the discussion in Pope, 604.
2   *Contra* Gerleman, 192–194.
3   Cf. Pope (620), who, however, adopts "punch" as his rendering of the hapax *mezeg*. Lys (255, 260) translates the term as "cocktail"!

the line may merely be intended to convey the richness of the comparison.[4]

It must have been, and still is, common to see heaps of grain after the winnowing. Many commentators attempt to find an indication of color in the comparison. But the description of the belly may not be so much in the interest of beauty as of fertility. At least, the grain would suggest this; it is a recognized symbol of female fertility. In practice, some kind of hedge could have surrounded the grain. Here the lilies serve this purpose: this may be a reference to an ornamental girdle she is wearing.[5]

■ **4[3]** The description of the woman's breasts repeats 4:5, but there is no apparent reason why "browsing among the lilies" should be omitted here (unless it is a gloss in 4:5?).

■ **5[4]** The four proper names (only Bath-rabbim is unknown) are used deliberately in this short description of the woman's neck, eyes, and nose. The comparison of the neck to a tower of ivory echoes 4:4 (the tower of David), perhaps indicating color and smoothness. Whereas in 4:1 (cf. 5:12) the eyes were "doves," here they are compared to Heshbon's pools (about which nothing is known), perhaps for limpidity or brightness.[6] In Hebrew ʿayin means both eye and water source; water is a natural reflector. The nose is compared to something that is simply unknown, and unclear in itself: is it a tower built on Lebanon, or a formation of the terrain that resembles

a tower? Either is possible. From such an uncertain comparison one can hardly conclude anything about her nose, although it is doubtless a compliment.

■ **6[5]** The comparison of the woman's head to Carmel, the prominent mountain range between the Mediterranean and the plain of Esdraelon, evokes majesty. Her hair is compared to purple, apparently because it is dyed (the ʾargāmān being the purple dye that comes from the murex shellfish).

In the final line the speaker departs from the *wasf* to inject a personal note, if he is to be identified with the lover or "king." This is the only instance of such a personal reference in a *wasf*, and the line has been rejected by many commentators. The meaning of *rĕhāṭîm* is uncertain; "tresses" is arrived at more from the context than from etymology.

■ **7[6]** It is better to regard this line as a conclusion of the preceding *wasf*, with *mah-yyāpît* serving as the *inclusio* to *mah-yyāpû* of v 2. But recent commentators begin a new unit here, opening with a general cry of admiration which quickly becomes an expression of the man's desire for physical union with the woman.[7]

■ **8[7]** The man begins by singing the praises of the woman's figure, which he compares to a palm-tree. Such a comparison is a common one in various cultures to suggest grace and elegance,[8] and may have a bearing on the common Hebrew feminine name, Tamar ("palm"). In

---

4 Gerleman (198) regards it as a witty remark (*witzigen Einfall*) that interrupts the description.

5 However, Gerleman (198) would regard the lilies as having merely stylistic effect, for emotional—not visual—purposes.

6 In this connection, commentators refer to Ovid, *Ars amatoria* 2.721–722 (J. H. Mozley, tr., *Ovid*, Vol. 2: *The Art of Love, and Other Poems* [LCL; Cambridge: Harvard University; London: William Heinemann, ²1979] 114–115): "You will see her eyes shooting tremulous gleams, as the sun often glitters in clear water" (*Aspicies oculos tremulo fulgore micantes, / Ut sol a*

liquida saepe refulget aqua).

7 So Gerleman, 201; Rudolph, 173–175; and Loretz, 44.

8 Cf. the *Odyssey*, 6.162–169. Cf. also the illustration and discussion in Keel, 224–230.

context, the palm-tree metaphor is important, and is developed in v 9.

The comparison of her breasts to clusters of dates (presumably two clusters are meant) is unusual. Perhaps it is due to the rigid adherence to the metaphor of the palm with which he began.

■ **9[8]** The importance of the palm metaphor is seen in the manner in which the man expresses his resolve to have physical union: he will climb the palm. Now her breasts become grape clusters which he will enjoy.

"The fragrance of your breath" would refer to the physical delight of kissing. The term rendered "breath" (*'ap*) usually designates the nostrils and is translated "nose" in 𝕲. The reference is to the Egyptian "nose-kiss," which involved more the sense of smell than of taste.[9]

The precise nature of the *tappûaḥ*, usually identified as "apple,"[10] is disputed; this fragrant fruit has already been associated with the lovers in 2:3,5.

■ **10[9]** The man's address concludes with the comparison of her mouth to wine; he is interrupted by the woman who continues the metaphor—a wine that flows smoothly for "my lover." While this interruption is sudden, the ancient versions support the understanding of 𝔐, which should be retained. The woman affirms that her kisses, like wine, are tasty and full.

■ **11[10]** The formula of mutual possession (cf. 2:16; 6:3) is deliberately inverted. The emphasis on sexual desire is paramount. In allusion to Gen 3:16, the word *tĕšûqâ*, which indicated the woman's desire for her husband, is now used of his desire for her. This fits neatly into the present context in which he has expressed his desire so vividly.[11]

■ **12[11]** Most of the explicit invitations issued in the Song are made by the man (2:10; 4:8). Here, and probably also in 4:16b, the woman invites him into the fields for a tryst.

■ **13[12]** "Let us be off early" does not mean a second stage in their activity; the verb is parallel to "let us away" (v 12).[12] Reference to the blossoming of the vines and the blooming of the pomegranates is a deliberate repetition of 6:11. The association of the awakening of nature with a love tryst is familiar from 2:11–13. At the same time, there is a clear undertone of symbolism or double meaning: the woman is herself the garden where exotic plants grow (4:12–16); she has called herself the "vineyard" (1:6).

■ **14[13]** This verse continues the pastoral scene of the tryst that was evoked in v 13. But the scenery has become more symbolic of the woman herself, who is the "choice fruits."

The scent of the mandrake is very penetrating. It was considered to be an aphrodisiac (cf. Gen 30:14–16).[13]

The reference to "our door" is rather sudden. In context, the man and woman have been out in the fields

---

9   Cf. Hermann, *Liebesdichtung*, 94–95. Gerleman (203) appropriately cites a line from an Egyptian love poem collected by Hermann (*Liebesdichtung*, 94): "it is the breath of your nose that keeps me alive."

10   Cf. John Trever, "Apple," *IDB* 1 (A–D), 175–176; and Fox, 107, who understands the fruit to be the "apricot."

11   In light of the contrast between Genesis and the Song, Phyllis Trible (*God and the Rhetoric of Sexuality* [OBT 2; Philadelphia: Fortress, 1978] 160) comments on Cant 7:11: "In Eden, the yearning of the woman for harmony with her man continued after

disobedience. Yet the man did not reciprocate; instead, he ruled over her to destroy unity and pervert sexuality. Her desire became his dominion. But in the Song, male power vanishes. His desire becomes her delight. Another consequence of disobedience is thus redeemed through the recovery of mutuality in the garden of eroticism. Appropriately, the woman sings the lyrics of this grace: 'I am my lover's and for me is his desire.'"

12   So Gerleman, 207.

13   For the history of the literary use of the mandrake, see Pope, 647–650; cf. also the comments and

(v 12), so perhaps the door anticipates their return to the "mother's house" (8:2). But it is not clear why the fruits are at the door, which does not seem to be a normal place for them.

"New with the old" is best taken as an idiomatic expression to express a totality, "all kinds of."[14] It would not make much sense to take this literally (cf. Lev 26:10), as if she had stored up *old* fruits for him. The "choice" fruits recall the use of *mĕgādîm* (which occurs elsewhere only in Deut 33:13,16) in 4:13,16, where the woman herself is meant.

■ **8:1–2** These verses are a song of yearning. The lines are tied together by *'immî* ("my mother") and by the deft word-play of *'eššāqĕkā* ("I would kiss you," v 1b) and *'ašqĕkā* ("I would give you to drink," v 2b).

The woman fantasizes about her lover as a brother (of the same mother—a point of emphasis) whom she might kiss in public without having to meet the disapproval of others. The clear implication is that public demon-stration of affection, unless among members of the immediate family, is contrary to social mores. Yet this remark is puzzling: the woman has not betrayed any concern about social opinion previously, where it might have been a factor (3:1–4; 5:6–8; 7:12–13). More importantly, public demonstration of affection is accepted in Gen 26:8 (Isaac and Rebekah); 29:11 (Jacob and Rachel); and Est 15:12–15(𝔊). We are rather in the dark as to what was or became socially acceptable in this matter. It seems best to prescind from the social implications and accept the woman's yearning as an intense desire for intimacy and privacy which would allow for signs of tenderness. Rudolph has noted "the charming lack of logic" in the desire that he might be her brother in order that she can act as more than a sister.[15]

As has already been noted, the woman's mother is mentioned with striking frequency in the work, and here twice in two verses. According to the translation adopted above for v 2, the woman wishes to bring him into her

---

illustrations in Keel, 236–239.

14   Gerleman (211) appropriately compares Deut 29:18, "the watered soil and the parched ground"; cf. also Matt 13:52, "new and old." He refers also to the Egyptian poem of the little sycamore in the "Songs of the Orchard" (Simpson, *Literature*, 315):

> These servants of yours
> come with their stuffs,
> bringing beer of every sort,
> all kinds of kneaded dough for beer,
> heady wine of yesterday and today,
> all kinds of fruit for enjoyment.

Here "yesterday and today" connote totality, "every sort of" or the like.

15   Rudolph, 179. This passage from the Song deserves comparison with one of the Chester Beatty Love Songs, entitled "The Beginning of the Songs of Extreme Happiness." The sixth stanza is spoken by the woman (Simpson, *Literature*, 319–320):

> I passed by the precinct of his house,
> I found his door ajar,

the lover standing by his mother,
with him his brothers and sisters.

Love of him captures the heart
of all who walk the road.
Handsome guy, no one like him,
a lover of perfect taste.

He stares me out when I walk by,
and all alone I cry for joy;
how happy in my delight
with the lover in my sight.

If only mother knew my wish,
she would have gone inside by now.
O, Golden Goddess, place him in her heart too,
then I'll rush off to the lover.

I'll kiss him in front of his crowd,
I'll not be ashamed because of the women.
But I'll be happy at their finding out
that you know me this well.

188

mother's home, where he would "teach" her to prepare for him a drink of wine and pomegranate. Obviously such potions in this context must symbolize the delights of love, as the word-play "kiss"/"drink" indicates. The intensity of the yearning has increased from v 1 to v 2.

In some respects vv 1–2 remind one of the fantasy in 3:1–5 and 5:2–8. The occurrence of *mṣ'* ("come upon") seems to be an echo of *mṣ'* in 3:2–4 and 5:6–8. Also, *baḥûṣ* ("in public") is the equivalent of the "streets" in 3:2. Finally, the search in 3:1–3 is climaxed by discovery, and the woman leads her lover into the house of her mother (3:4; cf. 8:2).

■ **3–4** These verses are a reprise of 2:6–7, with some insignificant variations (e.g., the omission of the gazelles and hinds in v 4); the prohibition is also reflected in 3:5

and 6:8. The meaning of vv 3–4 is the same as that of 2:6–7. The woman expresses her satisfaction in his embrace, and delivers a statement about the proper circumstances for arousing love. As with 2:6–7, the refrain is preceded by mention of a rendezvous in a given place ("house of wine," 2:4; and cf. 3:4, "house of my mother," 8:2). The refrains in 8:4 and 3:5 are both followed by the same question: Who is this that comes up from the desert? However, in 3:6–7 the response is Solomon's "litter," while 8:5 certainly refers to the woman. These tie-ins are very tantalizing, but they yield no sure conclusions about the structure of the work, or the nature of the individual units (differences due to oral recital?).

I'll make festivals for my Goddess,
my heart trembles to come forth,
and to let me look over the lover tonight.
How happy, how happy is this passing by.

Appendices

8

5 ■ (?) "Who is this that comes up from the desert,
leaning upon her lover?"

■ (?) "Under the apple tree I aroused you;
there your mother conceived you,
there the one who bore you conceived."

6 ■ W Place me as a seal on your heart,
as a seal on your arm.
Strong as Death is love;
intense as Sheol is ardor.
Its shafts are shafts of fire,
flames of Yah.

7 Deep waters cannot quench love,
nor rivers sweep it away.
Were one to give all his wealth for love,
he would be thoroughly despised.

8 ■ (W) "We have a little sister
and she has no breasts.
What shall we do for our sister,
on the day she will be spoken for?

9 If she is a wall,
we shall build upon her a silver turret.
If she is a door,
we shall board her up with a cedar plank."

10 ■ W I am a wall,
and my breasts like towers.
Then I have become in his eyes
as one who finds peace.

11 ■ (?) Solomon had a vineyard
in Baal-hamon.
He gave the vineyard to the keepers;
one would pay for its fruit
a thousand pieces of silver.

12 My own vineyard is at my disposal—
the thousand (pieces) for you, Solomon,
and two hundred for the keepers of its
fruit.

13 ■ M You who dwell in the garden,
friends are listening;
let me hear your voice!

14 ■ W Flee, my lover;
be like a gazelle or a young stag,
upon the mountains of spices.

Notes

5 מִתְרַפֶּקֶת ("leaning") is a hapax, and the translation is only approximate. The general meaning of "support" is attested for the root רפק in other Semitic languages (cf. Joüon, 308).

In v 5b, 𝔐 vocalizes the second person singular pronominal suffixes ("you," "your") as masculine, and hence attributes these lines to the woman. This understanding is retained by many commentators (e.g., Miller [69]; Ringgren [34]; Gordis [13]; Gerleman [214–215]; Pope [663]). Against it one may argue that there has been no previous reference to the woman arousing the man to love under the apple tree. (Throughout the Song, עור is used in this sense, except in 4:16; it does not in any case refer to arousal from sleep.) Moreover, except for the reference to the mother of Solomon in 3:11, the "mother" is always the mother of the woman. A change in vocalization of the suffixes, to read feminine forms, would be a very minor emendation; but among the ancient versions only 𝔊 ('rtky, ḥbltky 'mky, yldtky) attests such a reading against 𝔐. (Pope [663] rightly points out that the vocalization in 𝔐 does not support the mainstream of Jewish allegorical interpretation, and thus may constitute a solid, earlier tradition.) In any case, no matter who speaks these lines, the allusions remain obscure. Why is the arousal to love now associated with the place where the mother had once conceived or given birth?

It is not certain whether the verbs חִבְּלַתְךָ and חִבְּלָה in v 5b refer to the mother's conception or travail in childbirth; forms of the root חבל can be used to express both of these activities (cf. Ps 7:15; Isa 13:8; 26:17). 𝔙 (corrupta, violata) and α' (διεφθάρη) seem to have read Puʿal perfect forms, חֻבְּלָה ("was ruined"); but both 𝔊 (ὠδίνησέν σε) and 𝔖 (ḥbltky) support 𝔐.

Previously the woman compared the man to an apple tree, whose fruit and shade delighted her (2:3); and in her love-sickness, she sought refreshment from apples (2:5). This fruit also appears in 7:9[8], with reference to its fragrance. But the significance of the apple tree in 8:5b is not immediately apparent, though it may reflect the motif of "love under the trees" which is found in Egyptian love songs (Gerleman, 215; cf. Simpson, *Literature*, 312–315).

6 חוֹתָם ("seal") is an Egyptian loanword. Such objects could be worn on strings about the neck (Gen 38:18) and thus lie over the "heart"; they were also worn as rings on the hand (Jer 22:24). Seals were used for identification (Gen 38:18) and signature purposes. (זְרוֹעַ, literally "arm," may be interchangeable here with יָד ["hand"], just as in 5:14 "hand" was understood as "arm.") The practice of wearing something that belongs to one's beloved is of course widespread, in the ancient and modern worlds alike.

The כִּי which introduces v 6b is asseverative, not causal (cf. *GHB* §164b), and is better left untranslated.

The parallelism of מָוֶת with "Sheol" suggests that "Death" is personified here as a dynamic power. Ugaritic mythological texts provide abundant testimony to such a personification, and it was also quite common in ancient Hebrew thought (cf. Christoph Barth, *Die Errettung vom Tode in den individuellen Klage- und Dankliedern des Alten Testaments* [Zollikon: Evangelischer Verlag, 1947]; Nicholas J. Tromp, *Primitive Conceptions of Death and the Nether World in the Old Testament* [BibOr 21; Rome: Pontifical Biblical Institute, 1969]; and Pope, 668–669). Here love is compared to death with respect to strength.

In this context, "ardor" is a better translation of קִנְאָה than "passion" (so, e.g., Pope, 669) which might be interpreted too narrowly as only sexual in character. The use of the root קנא with respect to Yahweh (Deut 4:24, referring to divine "ardor" and "fire") and to the prophet Elijah (1 Kgs 19:10, "with zeal I have been zealous") illustrates its broad meaning; cf. Hendrik A. Brongers, "Der Eifer des Herrn Zebaoth," *VT* 13 (1963) 269–284, esp. 278.

The construction רְשָׁפֶיהָ רִשְׁפֵּי אֵשׁ and its parallelism with שַׁלְהֶבֶתְיָה (see below) indicates that the regnant idea has to do with fire. In Ps 76:4, רִשְׁפֵי־קֶשֶׁת is used to indicate "fiery arrows." The term may also be associated with the name of a deity, "Rešep"; see William Fulco (*The Canaanite God Rešep* [AOS 8; New Haven: American Oriental Society, 1976] 60) who takes the plural forms in 8:6 to represent a common noun, while noting that "its roots in mythology are unmistakable."

The construction שַׁלְהֶבֶתְיָה is quite unusual and difficult. The noun שַׁלְהֶבֶת occurs in Ezek 21:3 and Job 15:30, meaning "flame." The vocalization in 𝔐 suggests that the final two letters, יה, represent an abbreviation or short form of the sacred name, "Yahweh." The short form occurs in several psalms (e.g., Ps 118:5) and in other poetic texts, but usually exhibiting *mappîq* in the letter ה (cf. Robert, 302; and Fox, 170). 𝔊 (φλόγες αὐτῆς ["its flames"]) presupposes the same consonants as 𝔐, but understood the final

יה to be a third feminine singular pronominal suffix (referring to אַהֲבָה, "love"); cf. also 𝕲 (wšlhbyt') and 𝕼 (atque flammarum). Most commentators and modern translations assimilate the reading of 𝔐 to an idiom for the superlative, which elsewhere uses אֵל or אֱלֹהִים to express the greatness of divinity (e.g., Ps 36:7; 80;11); cf. David Witton Thomas, "A Consideration of Some Unusual Ways of Expressing the Superlative in Hebrew," *VT* 3 (1953) 209–227, esp. 221. So understood, the sense here would be "a most vehement flame" (RSV), "blazing flame" (NJV), or the like. Some commentators have questioned the integrity of the text, but without substantial support from the ancient versions. Although the colon is short, with only four syllables, one need not conclude that the construction is a gloss (against Pope, 670–671). It is possible that the text has suffered haplography; perhaps its original reading was שַׁלְהֶבְתְיָה שַׁלְהַבְתֶּיהָ ("flames of Yah are its flames"). After the preceding plurals (רְשָׁפֶיהָ רִשְׁפֵּי), a plural vocalization of שלהבת makes better sense (so 𝕲). This reading is adapted by Rudolph (179–180) and others. Tournay (in Robert, 453) points out that the rhythm of the verse (3+2) would demand separation of יה from שלהבת. Those who claim that the sacred name does not occur in the Song obviously do not accept the expression in this sense.

7 מַיִם רַבִּים ("mighty waters") occurs some twenty-eight times in the Old Testament. The expression has a mythological background: it is associated with the deity Yamm, Ba'l's opponent in Ugaritic lore; in biblical tradition it connotes the powers of chaos, which only God can dominate (Gen 1; Isa 51:9–10; Ps 76:12–14). Cf. Herbert G. May, "Some Cosmic Connotations of *Mayim Rabbîm*, 'Many Waters,'" *JBL* 74 (1955) 9–21. This verse thus heightens the description of the power of love, which has been compared to the strength of "Death" (v 6) and is now likened to the strength of the mythical waters of chaos. (Pope [673] has argued that v 7a and v 6b have the same meaning: the waters are the waters of Death/Sheol, not the waters of chaos. But this view unnecessarily restricts the sense of the metaphor. Cf. Roland E. Murphy, "Dance and Death in the Song of Songs," *Love and Death in the Ancient Near East: Essays in Honor of Marvin H. Pope* [ed. John H. Marks and Robert M. Good; Guilford, Conn.: Four Quarters, 1987] 119: "The appropriateness of the water metaphor is twofold: it contrasts with fire, and it represents the powers of chaos which only the Lord

can dominate. Love refuses to be conquered even by such strength as the *mayim rabbîm* represent.") Robert (304) points to the remarkable verbal similarity between v 7a and Isa 43:2.

For the phrase כָּל־הוֹן בֵּיתוֹ ("all his wealth" [literally "the whole value of his house"]), cf. Prov 6:31. For the sense of the preposition ב in בָּאַהֲבָה ("in exchange for love"), cf. *GHB* §133c; and *HSyn* §246.

The impersonal plural-active construction בּוֹז יָבוּזוּ לוֹ (literally "they would thoroughly despise him/it") is best rendered passively: "he would be thoroughly despised." The verb יָבוּזוּ forms a catchword with 8:1b. The antecedent of the third masculine singular pronominal suffix (לוֹ) is uncertain; it may refer to אִישׁ ("one") in the preceding colon (so NJV, NAB, and the translation adopted above) or to "all his wealth" (so RSV and NEB ["it would be utterly scorned"], following AV). There is not sufficient reason to interpret the phrase as a question (cf. Pope, 676).

8 By implication vv 8–9 were originally spoken by the brothers of the woman (cf. 1:6) and thus are put in quotation marks. NEB ascribes the words to "companions," apparently identifying them as rival suitors for the woman; cf. Fuerst, 198: ". . . suitors who now follow a time-honoured ritual of making one last attempt teasingly to woo the bride (who herself is the *little sister*) away from the bridegroom." Rather, it would appear that the woman recalls the concerns expressed by her brothers about her eventual marriage. It is evident from Gen 24:29–60 and Judg 21:22 that brothers had a role in the marriage of a sister. The woman quotes them directly, in the vivid style effected by the Song. Their point is that the "sister" is not yet physically mature. There is no reason to interpret the "little sister" as a younger sister of the woman. The reference in the final phrase is to marriage, as the expression ב יְדֻבַּר ("speak for") in 1 Sam 25:39 makes clear; cf. Joüon, 321–322. (It is not probable that in v 8 שֶׁיְדֻבַּר־בָּהּ means "speak against" in a hostile sense; cf. Pope, 678.)

9 The metaphor of the חוֹמָה ("wall") in itself suggests something that encloses and protects. Hence the supposition is that the little sister is inaccessible, and closes herself off from something.

טִירָה ("turret") means an enclosure of some kind (Ezek 46:23). This could be protective or delimiting, but also decorative. Since here it is made of "silver," one may infer that an ornamental structure is meant.

Commentators who interpret מִגְדָּל as a protective buttress, something to defend the woman, find the reference to its construction of "silver" difficult to explain.

The metaphor of the דֶּלֶת ("door") is ambiguous, suggesting both entrance and closure. Accordingly, this word can be taken to stand in either antithetic or synonymous parallelism to "wall." Both interpretations have some support: either the little sister is open, yielding, and not closed off; or else closed, firm, and impregnable. Gordis (33, 100) cites with approval the Akkadian incantation advanced by Tur-Sinai: "If he is a door, I will open thy mouth; if he is a bar, I will open thy tongue." But this charm does not "demonstrate" the synonymous parallelism alleged for v 9.

In the expression נָצוּר עָלֶיהָ ("we shall board her up"), the verb is most easily related to the root צור[II] (HELOT 848: "confine, bind, besiege"; cf. צרר[I]), which is often construed, as here, with the preposition עַל (e.g., 2 Sam 11:1; 2 Kgs 6:24,25; Isa 29:3). Less likely is the interpretation represented in 𝕲 (διαγράψωμεν) and 𝕭 (conpingamus), which derives the verb from צור[IV] (HELOT 849: "fashion, delineate"; cf. יצר). Accordingly, the following accusative of specification לוּחַ אָרֶז ("[with] a cedar plank") should symbolize the strength of the defense intended by the brothers, rather than its ornamental character.

From the above it is clear that the proposal of the brothers can be understood in two ways, involving either synonymous or antithetic parallelism of the metaphors. 1) If their sister resists whatever they have in mind (synonymous parallelism of wall/door), then they will act to overcome this resistance (turret/plank). 2) If the sister resists (wall), they will treat her in one way (turret); but if she yields (door), they will treat her in another way (plank). It is not enough to claim that the door, in relation to the wall, necessarily indicates a weak point that makes a breach possible, and therefore the parallelism is antithetic. The translation adopts antithetic parallelism on the basis of the course of action followed by the brothers. Specifically, the boarding up with a cedar plank suggests aggressive action against a yielding door. In addition, this interpretation of the metaphor enables one to understand these lines in the context of the brothers' attitude and the sister's reply.

10 The woman, now fully mature and responsible, reflects upon her brothers' designs for their "little sister" by taking up the metaphor of the "wall,"

thereby affirming her independence. In comparing her breasts to "towers" (כַּמִּגְדָּלוֹת) she also gives a sharp response to their manner of describing her physical immaturity. She is now indeed nubile, and there seems to be a note of pride in the comparison.

אָז ("then") is to be taken in the sense of "in that case," or "thus," and not in a strictly temporal sense.

There is no explicit antecedent to the third masculine singular pronominal suffix in the phrase בְּעֵינָיו ("in his eyes"). In the context of the whole work, it must be understood to refer to the woman's lover. However, the lack of an antecedent is a good reason for regarding these lines as a fragment.

The preposition כְּ before מוֹצֵאת is either comparative or asseverative ("indeed"); cf. GHB §133g (kaph veritatis), and HSyn §261. מוֹצֵאת can be derived either from מצא ("find," Qal feminine singular active participle) or from יצא ("go out," Hipʿil feminine singular participle: "one who brings out, produces"). The ambiguity makes any translation uncertain. The woman could mean that she found שָׁלוֹם ("peace") or that she offers terms of peace (cf. Deut 20:10–11), in the sense that she surrenders herself to the man. However, a different idiom is used in Deut 20:10–11: קָרָא שָׁלוֹם or עָנָה שָׁלוֹם. Hence it is better to derive מוֹצֵאת from מצא, understanding the expression to mean that the woman "finds peace." In the context, the woman affirms that the man's loving acceptance of her—in contrast to the distrustful attitude of the brothers—has brought peace, well-being, and fulfillment. There is probably a deliberate play here on the name of Solomon (שְׁלֹמֹה, שָׁלוֹם; cf. Shulammite).

11–12 These verses seem to comprise a separate unit, in which the topic is vineyards, one belonging to Solomon and the other to the speaker. The unit does not continue the "little sister" theme of vv 8–10, and is apparently unrelated to vv 13–14, in which the man and the woman exchange words in a conversation. The verses could be spoken either by the man or the woman.

11 Like בַּת־רַבִּים (7:5), בַּעַל הָמוֹן seems to be the name of a place; it means "lord of a multitude" (cf. 𝕭 ea quae habet populos ["that which has people"]) or possibly "lord of wealth" (so Gordis, 101). The place in question has not been securely identified, although some have associated it with Balamon near Dothan (on the basis of Jdt 8:3). For discussion of these and other interpretations, see Robert, 317–318; and Pope, 686–688.

The indefinite "one" (אִישׁ) does not refer to the guardians, but to "anyone," and the emphasis of the statement bears on the price of the vineyard's fruits.

Isaiah 7:23 speaks of vineyards, each with a thousand vines and worth a thousand pieces of silver, which may give an idea of the size and value of Solomon's "vineyard." The speaker does not have in mind an actual transaction to purchase the vineyard's produce for אֶלֶף כָּסֶף ("a thousand pieces of silver"); the intent is only to suggest how valuable the property is. The stated price may well include an allusion to the "thousand" wives and concubines in Solomon's harem (1 Kgs 11:3). The symbolism of vineyard representing the woman is essential to an understanding of these lines.

12 כַּרְמִי שֶׁלִּי ("my own vineyard") is found on the lips of the woman in 1:6; hence many commentators attribute vv 11–12 to her. On the other hand, it is possible that the man uses her phrase of 1:6 to describe her in 8:12. In any event, this second "vineyard" is set in deliberate contrast to that of Solomon (v 11).

"At my disposal" is literally "before me" (לְפָנָי). The vineyard belongs only to the possessor, who can do as he/she pleases with it. (For this usage of לְפָנַי, cf. Gen 13:9; 24:51; 34:10; etc.).

הָאָלֶף ("the thousand [pieces]") must refer to the silver of v 11. Only here is "Solomon" addressed by name in the Song. The "keepers" refer back to the keepers to whom the vineyard was given (v 11). The "two hundred" silver pieces are allotted to them as some kind of payment.

13–14 In keeping with the disparate character of 8:5–14, the last two verses of the work have no obvious connection with the immediately preceding lines, but seem to attest portions of conversation.

13 The Qal active feminine singular participle הַיּוֹשֶׁבֶת ("you who dwell") indicates that the woman is being addressed, presumably by the man, who voiced a similar wish in 2:14. The variants reflected in 𝕲 and 𝕾 are not significant enough to modify the reading in 𝔐. 𝕲 understood the participle as masculine (ὁ καθήμενος); and 𝕾 read the plural ('ylyn dytbyn ["those who dwell"]).

גַּנִּים ("gardens") is the plural of generalization (GHB §136j; HSyn §7) and should be taken literally, rather than as a metaphor for the woman (cf. 4:12; 5:1; 6:2).

"Friends" is literally "companions" (חֲבֵרִים). These are not further identified, but the word is used in 1:7 to indicate those who are associated with the "shepherd" in pasturing the flocks.

The accentuation in 𝔐 joins לְקוֹלֵךְ to the preceding Hip'il masculine plural participle מַקְשִׁיבִים ("[friends] are listening to your voice"). The translation above follows the syntax of 𝖁 (fac me audire vocem tuam ["make me hear your voice"]) in making קוֹלֵךְ the object of הַשְׁמִיעִינִי (cf. the man's request in 2:14).

14 The woman issues an invitation to the man couched in language that is a reprise of 2:17. בְּרַח ("flee") is not to be understood as a rejection, but in the sense of שׁוּב ("turn"), as in 2:17. Here she invites him to the הָרֵי בְשָׂמִים ("mountains of spices"), apparently to be identified with the obscure "mountains of Bether" mentioned in 2:17. In both cases, of course, the mountains are a metaphor for the woman.

Interpretation

The continuity and coherence of the text seem to break down in 8:5–14, which may be a collection of disparate poems or fragments of poems.[1] Five separate units can be distinguished: vv 5; 6–7; 8–10; 11–12; and 13–14. These units are not united by dialogue, although dialogue occurs within them. They include many echoes of lines appearing in earlier parts of the Song.

Verse 5 has no apparent connection with 8:4, and its relationship to 8:6 is equally problematical. The woman is hailed as coming from the desert with her lover (v 5a). In v 5b she speaks (so 𝔐) to the man, referring to her arousal of his love in the very place where his own mother conceived him. Our translation changes the vocalization so that v 5b is spoken by the man to the woman. But in either case, the import of the verse remains obscure. It is hard to escape the impression that the verse is a mere fragment.[2]

Verses 6–7 clearly belong together as a unit. The woman's plea to be inseparably united with her lover (v 6a) is followed by a poem celebrating the power of love (vv 6b–7).[3]

Verses 8–10 consist of a reminiscence on the part of the woman, recalling her brothers' plans for her (vv 8–9), followed by her own statement of independence from them (v 10). There is no apparent connection with the immediately preceding or following verses, but the reference to the "brothers" can be seen as a kind of *inclusio* with 1:6.

Verses 11–12 deal with the vineyard, and can probably be attributed to the woman, but again there is no

immediate context for interpretation of these lines.

Verses 13–14 are apparently a conversation between the man and the woman, drawing on earlier lines in the Song.

The disparate nature of these units gives one greater appreciation for the dialogical unity that prevails through most of the chapters in the Song. If the word "anthology" is used for any part of the work, it is particularly suitable for 8:5–14.

■ **5** Although the question in v 5a ("Who is this . . . ?") is a reprise of 3:6, a different answer is now given. Here it is clearly the woman who "comes up from the desert"; there it was a procession bearing Solomon's litter (3:7). In both instances the question follows upon the same appeal to the Daughters of Jerusalem, and in both instances a new unit appears to begin. It is impossible to say with any certainty who speaks these words, which are intended to hail the approach of the woman. The significance of the allusion to the desert escapes us here, as it does also in 3:6 and 6:10.

The translation sets v 5b in quotation marks to indicate a direct statement by the man or, according to the vocalization of 𝔐, the woman. Presumably this statement represents a snatch of conversation between the two. The words about love under the apple tree could be spoken by either party.[4] The association of love and fruits, flowers, etc. is common elsewhere in the Song (5:1; 6:2; 7:13) as well as in Egyptian love poetry. It must be admitted that the emphatic reference to the place ("there"—under the apple tree) where the mother conceived remains very obscure.[5]

---

1   Robert (308) characterized 8:8–14 as "appendices"; the label can just as easily apply to 8:5–7.
2   So Gerleman, 215; and Würthwein, 67.
3   Cf. Horst, "Formen," 185; similarly Loretz, 49; and Robert, 300.
4   G. Krinetzki (25–26) suggests that the reference to the apple tree in 8:5b is meant to recall the comparison of the man to an apple tree in 2:3; if it is he

who now speaks, the sense is: "with me, through my body and my tenderness have I aroused you." In this case, the man would also be drawing a comparison between the woman and her mother (cf. 3:4).
5   In contrast to the uncertainty registered above, Albright ("Archaic Survivals," 7) writes: "There can be little doubt that the mother of the beloved was a mythical figure, possibly a girl who had escaped to

■ **6** Verses 6–7 may be described as a climactic point in the Song, in the sense that they neatly summarize what the poems are about: the desire of the lovers for abiding union. One may note parallels in Egyptian love poetry and elsewhere, but the beauty of these biblical lines remains unsurpassed.

The 𝔐 vocalization of the pronominal suffixes in v 6a correctly attributes the verse to the woman.[6] The comparison of the seal ring points to the inseparability of the couple.[7] This is further developed by v 6b, which is concerned with the awesome power of love.[8] In what sense is love here compared to Death and Sheol? Behind the biblical metaphor of death as a personified force lies the Canaanite mythology of Mot, god of Death, who

the desert after having become pregnant by a god. A somewhat similar situation is described in the Poem of the Beautiful and Gracious Gods, where the two infants born of El and two unnamed women are reared in the 'Desert of Kadesh'." Even if such a mythological association could be proved, however, one is still left with the question of how this would be understood in the context of Hebrew love poetry. Could the reference be taken as a compliment to the beloved, adumbrating his/her supposedly divine origins? There is simply no analogy for such a notion elsewhere in the literature of the Hebrew Bible.

6   *Contra* Robert, 298–299.

7   In one of the Cairo Love Songs, the man expresses his desire to be a seal ring on his lover's hand (Simpson, *Literature*, 311):

> I wish I were the seal ring,
>   the guardian of her [fingers],
> then [. . .].

Moreover, because no obstacle is too great for love to overcome, the Egyptian lover expresses himself in terms similar to those of 8:7 (Simpson, *Literature*, 310):

> The love of my sister lies on yonder side,
>   and the river is between [us];
> a crocodile waits on the sandbank.
> Yet I'll go down to the water,
> I'll head into the waves,
> my heart is brave on the water,
> and the waves like land to my legs.

8   The power of love has, of course, been celebrated in other ancient literature. Especially noteworthy is the hymn to Eros (comprised of strophe and antistrophe) in Sophocles' *Antigone*, 781–800 (F. Storr, tr.,

Sophocles, Vol. 1 [LCL; Cambridge: Harvard University; London: William Heinemann, 1912] 376–377):

> Love resistless in fight,
>   all yield at a glance of thine eye,
> Love who pillowed all night
>   on a maiden's cheek dost lie,
> Over the upland folds thou roam'st,
>   and the trackless sea.
> Love the gods captive holds.
>   Shall mortals not yield to thee?
> Mad are thy subjects all,
>   and even the wisest heart
> Straight to folly will fall,
>   at a touch of thy poisoned dart.
> Thou didst kindle the strife,
>   this feud of kinsmen with kin,
> By the eyes of a winsome wife,
>   and the yearning her heart to win.
> For as her consort still,
>   enthroned with Justice above,
> Thou bendest man to thy will,
>   O all invincible Love.

([strophe, lines 781–790] Ἔρως ἀνίκατε μάχαν, Ἔρως, ὃς ἐν κτήμασι πίπτεις, ὃς ἐν μαλακαῖς παρειαῖς νεάνιδος ἐννυχεύεις, φοιτᾷς δ᾽ ὑπερπόντιος ἔν τ᾽ ἀγρονόμοις αὐλαῖς· καί σ᾽ οὔτ᾽ ἀθανάτων φύξιμος οὐδεὶς οὔθ᾽ ἁμερίων ἐπ᾽ ἀνθρώπων, ὁ δ᾽ ἔχων μέμηνεν. [antistrophe, lines 791–800] Σὺ καὶ δικαίων ἀδίκους φρένας παρασπᾷς ἐπὶ λώ-

engages in struggle with Baʿl, only to be eventually overcome. A personification of death can be recognized in Hos 13:14: "Shall I deliver them from the power of the nether world? Shall I redeem them from death? Where are your plagues, O death! Where is your sting, O nether world!" Similarly, "Death" and "Sheol" are also used in parallelism in Pss 18:6; 49:15; 89:48. Thus "Death/Sheol" was thought to be a dynamic force that pursues every human being. This pursuit goes on as long as one lives, until "the hand [power] of death" ostensibly prevails (Ps 49). The psalmist describes distress, any degree of nonlife, as being in Sheol (Ps 30:4). To the extent that good is absent in life, "Death" is exerting its influence. It is this dynamic view of death and its power that is the point of comparison in 8:6. But here the emphasis is not upon the threat which "Death/Sheol" undoubtedly constitutes for humans, but upon its sheer force and relentlessness. So it is with love. Love will not give up, but will pursue the loved one just as persistently as the great and fearful power of "Death." The parallel word for love, "ardor" (qin'â), is not to be understood in the narrow sense of (sexual) passion, or in the sense of jealousy; it has to do with intense devotion, dedication to the loved one.

Note well that v 6 does not "emphasize Love's power over against that of Death."[9] Love is compared to Death as regards strength, but it is not presented as being locked in battle with Death. The point of the comparison is the quality of love in its relationship to the beloved; in this respect it is comparable to Death and its relationship to a human being. Both attain their objects.

Another forceful dimension appears in the comparison of love to "flames of Yah[weh]" (šlhbtyh). The sense of the latter term is admittedly ambiguous. In view of the parallel expression, "shafts of fire," most commentators are inclined to interpret this as a reference to lightning (Yahweh's "flames"). Already Ginsburg remarked that the comparison suggests not merely the vehemence of the fires of love, but that they "emanate from the Eternal."[10] One may doubt if this meaning was intended by the original writer. Nevertheless, the received text can bear such an interpretation. Human love has or resembles the flame of divine love; both can be compared in intensity (and perhaps even in origin, in the sense of 1 John 4:7?). A perspective on human love is taken here that calls for theological evaluation.[11]

βα· σὺ καὶ τόδε νεῖκος ἀν-
δρῶν ξύναιμον ἔχεις ταράξας·
νικᾷ δ' ἐναργὴς βλεφάρων
ἵμερος εὐλέκτρου
νύμφας, τῶν μεγάλων
πάρεδρος ἐν ἀρχαῖς θεσ-
μῶν· ἄμαχος γὰρ ἐμπαί-
ζει θεὸς Ἀφροδίτα.)

Cf. also Ovid, *Ars amatoria*, 1.19–23.

9   Pope, 667.
10   Ginsburg, 188.
11   L. Krinetzki (244) remarks as follows: "It [love], as participating in divine qualities (6f.), is victor over the floods of chaos, as God himself who conquered the primeval waters at the beginning of the world." Yet it is the "flames" of love, not explicitly the power of love, that participates "in divine qualities." See also Leo Krinetzki, "Die Macht der Liebe," *MTZ* 13 (1962) 256–279. Nicholas J. Tromp ("Wisdom and the Canticle. Ct 8,6c–7b: text, character, message and import," *La Sagesse de l'Ancien Testament* [ed. Maurice Gilbert; BETL 51; Gembloux: J. Duculot, 1979], 94) provides a slightly different perspective: "The implication of these remarks is that Love is represented here as a force which is able to overcome the negative forces which threaten the very existence of the world and mankind. In other words, Love gains the victory over chaos and creates wholesome order and life. Very likely the dark powers are personified in God. That means that Love is brought on the stage as a person as well. Consequently, Love is a personified creative power in these lines, and the partition here between Love and God is extremely

The mention of flames in v 6 appropriately evokes the image of its opposite, water. The epithet *mayim rabbîm* ("mighty waters") stands for the waters of chaos, a formidable threat to life. But not even this primordial power is stronger than love. The "rivers" serve merely as a parallel to *mayim rabbîm* but are no less significant as a symbol of stark, overwhelming power.

Disdain is surely the proper reaction to one who would attempt to purchase love. This judgment may seem somewhat anticlimactic after the preceding lines, but in the biblical world, where the *mōhar*, or bride-price, played a significant role, the reference was appropriate. Moreover, the practices associated with the bride-price seem to figure in the background of vv 8–12.

■ **8-12** These verses introduce a vignette that has no obvious connection with the immediate context, but, as already indicated, the episode forms a kind of *inclusio*, echoing the reference to "brothers" of 1:6. Actually, the lines of vv 8–12 are to be attributed to the woman, who first quotes directly words spoken about her, when she was younger, by her brothers (vv 8–9) and then replies to them (v 10) from the viewpoint of a mature woman.

There is a rather solemn air about the announcement of the brothers concerning their little sister, whom they formally introduce as a child in v 8a. But she becomes the "problem" in v 8b. What will be their responsibility to her when she reaches marriageable age? There is an almost riddle-like quality to the solution (v 9) which the brothers propose to their own question. They offer two alternatives, whose meaning depends upon the interpretation of "wall" and "door." These terms are most likely to be understood as standing in antithetic, rather than synonymous parallelism.[12]

The force of the "wall" metaphor has to be ascertained. A wall encloses; it also protects and defends. How is this to be understood in context? Gordis judges that the sister is obdurate, and refuses her suitors' offers of marriage.[13] Other commentators derive the sense from v 10, where "wall" seems to be a symbol of physical maturity ("breasts like towers"); hence they understand "wall" to refer to the ripe maturity of the girl.[14] The more usual interpretation sees in the wall a symbol of the sister's chastity: she has never been known by a man, and is to remain so.[15] Accordingly, the *ṭîrâ* which the brothers build upon (or against) her is variously interpreted as a means to overcome her obduracy or as an adornment, such as a silver crown, a bridal crown, or a high bride-price.[16]

The ambiguity of the "door" metaphor leads to several possible interpretations. Some commentators understand "door" in opposition to "wall" (cf. v 10), and hence take it to symbolize the woman's physical immaturity; in this case, the brothers intend to protect their young sister from an early marriage.[17] But if the door is understood

---

thin indeed." Tromp claims that these verses are the "proper end" of the Song; he adopts Tournay's point that the term *'ahăbâ* ("love") in 8:6 forms an *inclusio* with 1:3–4.

12   See the Notes above, and now also R. Lansing Hicks, "The Door of Love," *Love and Death in the Ancient Near East: Essays in Honor of Marvin H. Pope* (ed. John H. Marks and Robert M. Good; Guilford, Conn.: Four Quarters, 1987) 153–158.

13   Gordis, 100.

14   So Würthwein, 70; and Loretz, 51.

15   Rudolph, 183; Gerleman, 220; and L. Krinetzki, 250–251.

16   So, respectively, Loretz, 51 *(Silberkranz);* Würthwein, 70 *(Brautkranz);* and Rudolph, 183 *(hohen Brautpreis).*

17   Cf. Würthwein, 70; and Loretz, 51.

as a symbol for yielding, the supposition may be that should she fail to keep her chastity, the brothers will sequester her.[18] Or the supposition may be that should she give up her obduracy and yield to one of her suitors, he (or the brothers) will reward her with gifts.[19]

The translation adopted here supposes that the brothers mean to take harsh measures if necessary to protect their sister. If she fails to remain chaste, they will take steps to board her up. Obviously the other interpretations mentioned above would yield different translations.

■ **10** The girl gives answer to the plans of the brothers which she has just quoted. The answer presupposes a period of time has elapsed since the brothers announced their plans. She reverts back to the brothers' words in order to give a triumphant reply, affirming the first of the alternatives which they proposed. "Wall" in v 10 must have the same meaning given to it by the various interpretations of v 9. Hence she is saying that she is unyielding to "unwelcome suitors," because she already belongs to her lover.[20] Or she states that she is now physically mature and ready for marriage.[21] In either case, she is to be understood as affirming her chastity, in the sense of her fidelity to her lover; she is the "enclosed garden" of 4:12, who belongs totally to him.

The woman again takes up a significant term from the brothers' words ("breasts"), in order to emphasize her maturity and beauty, and the distance from the days when they had thought to supervise her.

The male lover is very much present in this discussion of the woman's future, as the sudden reference to "his eyes" indicates. With him she has found welcome or well-being (the precise meaning of "peace" is hard to determine here), a totally satisfying relationship that goes far beyond the protective designs of her brothers.

In summary, the plan of the brothers is twofold, depending upon their sister's reaction. She will be rewarded if she observes their restrictions, but she will be constrained if she disobeys them. Her reply disregards their plan, even while it takes up their language, and affirms her readiness for marriage, her independence and chastity, and the fact that she has been accepted by her lover. This vignette is best seen as a boast, made by the woman against her meddlesome brothers. It has a certain humor and irony, but it speaks against the disposition of the woman as mere family property.

■ **11–12** These verses are a boasting song, comparable to 6:8–9, in which the man prizes his beloved beyond the entire harem of Solomon.[22] This interpretation supposes that the man is speaking of her in the phrase "my own vineyard," in contrast to Solomon's vineyard. The style is unusual; it begins as a story about the vineyard of Solomon, then suddenly Solomon is being addressed by someone speaking of another "vineyard."

No matter who the speaker is in v 11, there is clear reference to King Solomon. There is no reason to see the king fiction at work. Solomon is meant literally here, because he was rich enough to possess such a valuable "vineyard." Similarly, the reference to "vineyard" can be taken literally here, but in view of the metaphorical meaning of vineyard in v 12, with which Solomon's vineyard is contrasted, the term may also be a metaphor for Solomon's harem.[23]

There is no obvious reason why "keepers" of the vineyard are mentioned. This reference does not seem to have any relationship to the role assigned to the woman by her brothers in "keeping" the vineyards in 1:6. However, it is worth noting that several themes in chapter 1 reappear in the last part of chapter 8 (vineyard, keepers, brothers). The mention of the keepers here also provides

---

18 Rudolph, 183.
19 So Gordis, 100.
20 Gordis, 100–101.

21 Loretz, 51; and Würthwein, 69–70.
22 So Horst, "Formen," 183.
23 Regarding Solomon's harem, see 1 Kgs 11:1–3; and

the occasion for a pointed and emphatic reference in v 12. Similarly, the indication of the value of the vineyard ("a thousand pieces of silver") is given in view of the use that will be made of it in v 12.

The phrase "my own vineyard" is clearly emphatic, and is in contrast to Solomon's vineyard in v 11. Because this is the exact phrase which occurs on the lips of the woman in 1:6, it is possible that she speaks these words. She would be referring to her own independence, when she characterizes "my vineyard" as "before me," or at my disposal. Thus if she speaks these lines, she affirms her free gift of herself—an affirmation that is in accord with the disdain expressed for the bride-price in 8:7b. However, the situation in v 12 is not the same as in 1:6; hence this verse need not be assigned to the woman. There she explained her appearance ("my own vineyard I have not kept") in terms of the menial work in the vineyard to which her brothers had assigned her. Here the stakes are greater; the speaker is contrasting a vineyard with the "vineyard" of no less a personage than king Solomon. Hence it is also possible to understand these lines as spoken by the man about the woman, in the spirit of his praise of her in 6:8–9, as surpassing the royal harem itself. The vineyard of Solomon in v 11 now seems to have the aura of the royal harem; the speaker could be comparing his vineyard to that of Solomon, that is, his beloved to the harem of Solomon. This is perhaps indicated by what follows.

If the woman addresses Solomon, she seems to be saying that his vineyard has merely monetary value. If this is spoken by the man, he is telling Solomon that he can keep his vineyard (the royal harem), which cannot compare in value to his beloved (cf. 6:8–20). With a kind of satirical panache, the speaker specifies a sum (two hundred pieces) for the vineyard keepers.

■ **13-14** The concluding verses epitomize the tantalizing shifts of person and scene that are characteristic of the Song as a whole. Now the man addresses the woman, who is present in the garden, and she replies.[24]

The man expresses the same desire he uttered in 2:14—to hear her voice. The desire is sharpened by the reference to the "friends." Who are these *ḥăbērîm?* This term is used to describe the "companions" of the man in 1:7, where he is portrayed as a shepherd: the woman expressed a fear of being misled and straying "near the herds of your companions." It is hardly necessary to insist on a marriage context and to interpret the companions as part of the wedding party. They are simply the friends of the lover, whom he associates with his own desire to hear her voice.

The reply (v 14) is an echo of 2:17, which was also spoken by the woman. Hence it should be understood here also as spoken by her in reply to the request of v 13. She responds with a snatch of verse modeled on 2:17 (cf. also 2:9; 4:6). She invites him to "flee" to the mountains of spice, i.e., to herself. Her reaction is, first of all, just what he asks for: she lets her voice be heard. Secondly, her words can be anything, as long as she speaks. When he asked to hear her voice in 2:15, she replied with the enigmatic lines about the little foxes (2:16). But now her answer is more cogent: she invites him to join her.

---

cf. p. 178 above (on 6:8–9).

24 Gerleman (223) considers v 14 to be a continuation of v 13, in the sense that the concluding words are those which the man asks to hear. But on the analogy of 2:17, it is more likely that the verses are to be read as dialogue, with v 14 assigned to the woman. It has been suggested that the original setting of this exchange is a lovers' game of "hide and seek"

(Marcus Antonius van den Oudenrijn, *Het Hooglied* [BOT 8/3; J. J. Romen & Zonen, 1962] 44).

**Bibliography
Indices**

Bibliography

1. Commentaries to the Song of Songs (chronological listing)

The list of commentaries given here is selective, especially for works written before the nineteenth century. For more extensive listings of earlier works, see the following (in section **b/** below): Rosenmüller (1830) 280–301; Joüon (1909) 96–109; Ricciotti (1928) 172–192; and Pope (1977) 236–251.

a / Pre-Nineteenth Century

Hippolytus of Rome [d. 235 C.E.]
Fragmenta in Canticum canticorum in *PG* 10, 627–630; and Gottlieb Nathanael Bonwetsch and H. Achellis (eds.), *Hippolytus Werke*, Vol. 1: *Hippolyts Kommentar zum Buche Daniel und die Fragmente des Kommentars zum Hohenliede* (GCS; Leipzig: J. C. Hinrichs, 1897) 341–374. Cf. also Gottlieb Nathanael Bonwetsch, *Hippolyts Kommentar zum Hohenlied auf Grund von N. Marrs Ausgabe des grusinischen Textes* (TU 23/2c [N.F. 8]; Leipzig: J. C. Hinrichs, 1902); and the Latin translation in Gérard Garitte (tr.), *Traités d'Hippolyte* (CSCO 264; Louvain: Secretariat du CorpusSCO, 1965).

Origen [185–254]
Homiliae in Canticum canticorum and *Commentarium in Canticum canticorum* in W. A. Baehrens (ed.), *Origenes Werke*; Vol. 8 (GCS 33; Leipzig: J. C. Hinrichs, 1925) 20–241 = *Origen: The Song of Songs. Commentary and Homilies* (tr. R. P. Lawson; ACW 26; Westminster, Maryland: Newman; London: Longman/Green, 1957).

Gregory of Nyssa [335–394]
Commentarius in Canticum canticorum in *PG* 44, 755–1120; and Hermannus Langerbeck (ed.), *Gregorii Nysseni in Canticum canticorum* (Gregorii Nysseni Opera 6; Leiden: E. J. Brill, 1960).

Ambrose of Milan [339–397]
Commentarius in Cantica canticorum in *PL* 15, 1945–2060.

Jerome [c. 340–420]
Interpretatio homiliarum duarum Origenis in Canticum canticorum in *PL* 23, 1173–1196.

Theodoret of Cyrus [c. 393–466]
Explanatio in Canticum canticorum in *PG* 81, 27–214.

Procopius of Gaza [d. 538]
In Cantica canticorum, selectarum expositionum epitome in *PG* 87, 1545–1780.

Gregory the Great [540–604]
Expositiones in Canticum canticorum in Patricius Verbraken (ed.), *Sancti Gregorii Magni* (CCSL 144; Turnholti: Brepols, 1963) 3–46.

Isidore of Seville [c. 600]
Expositio in Cantica canticorum Salomonis in *PL* 83, 1119–1132.

Canticles Rabbah (*Midrāš ḥāzîtā*) [c. 600]
"Song of Songs" in H. Freedman and Maurice Simon (eds.), *Midrash Rabbah*, Vol. 9 (tr. Maurice Simon; London: Soncino, 1930).

Targum *Šîr haššîrîm* [c. 700]
"Targum to Canticles" in Alexander Sperber (ed.), *The Bible in Aramaic, Based on Old Manuscripts and Printed Texts*, Vol. 4A: *The Hagiographa: Transition from Translation to Midrash* (Leiden: E. J. Brill, 1968) 127–141. Translations: Wilhelm Riedel, *Die Auslegung des Hohenliedes in der jüdischen Gemeinde und der griechischen Kirche* (Leipzig: A. Deichert, 1898) 9–41; Hermann Gollancz, *The Targum to the Song of Songs* (London: Luzac, 1908); Paul Vulliaud, *Le Cantique des cantiques d'après la tradition juive* (Paris: Universitaires de France, 1925) 67–103.

Beda *Venerabilis* [673–735]
In Cantica canticorum allegorica expositio in *PL* 91, 1065–1236; and D. Hurst (ed.), *Bedae Venerabilis Opera*, Part II/2B (CCSL 119B; Turnholti: Brepols, 1983) 165–375.

'*Aggādat šîr haššîrîm* (*Šîr haššîrîm zûṭā'*) [c. 1000]
Solomon Schechter (ed.), אגדת שיר השירים (Cambridge: Bell, 1896); and Salomon Buber (ed.), מדרש זוטא על שיר השירים, רות, איכה וקהלת (Berlin, 1894; Wilno, ²1925).

Midrāš šîr haššîrîm [c. 1000]
Lazar Grünhut (ed.), מדרש שיר השירים (Jerusalem/Jaffa, 1897).

Anselm of Laon [d. 1117]
Enarrationes in Cantica canticorum in *PL* 162, 1187–1228.

Bruno of Asti [1049–1123]
Expositio in Cantica canticorum in *PL* 164, 1233–1288.

Rupert of Deutz [1070–1129]

Commentaria in Cantica canticorum in *PL* 168, 837–962.

William of Saint Thierry [c. 1085–1148]

Expositio altera super Cantica canticorum in *PL* 180, 473–546. Translations: J.–M. Déchanet and M. Dumontier, *Guillaume de Saint-Thierry: Exposé sur le Cantique des Cantiques* (SC 82; Paris: Cerf, 1962); *The Works of William of St. Thierry*, Vol. 2: *Exposition on the Song of Songs* (tr. Columba Hart; CFS 6; Spencer, Massachusetts: Cistercian Publications, 1970).

Bernard of Clairvaux [c. 1091–1153]

Sermones in Canticum in Jean Leclerq, Henri M. Rochais, and Charles H. Talbot (eds.), *Sancti Bernardi Opera*, Vols. 1–2 (Rome: Editiones Cistercienses, 1957, 1958) = [*The Works of*] *Bernard of Clairvaux: On the Song of Songs*, 4 Vols. (tr. Kilian Walsh and Irene M. Edmonds; CFS 4, 7, 31, 40; Spencer, Massachusetts/Kalamazoo, Michigan: Cistercian Publications, 1971–80); also *Canticum Canticorum: Eighty-six Sermons on the Song of Songs by Saint Bernard* (tr. S. J. Eales; London: Stock, 1895).

Gilbert of Hoyland [d. 1172]

Sermones in Canticum Salomonis ab eo loco ubi B. Bernardus morte praeventus desiit in *PL* 184, 11–252 = *The Works of Gilbert of Hoyland: Sermons on the Song of Songs*, 3 Vols. (tr. Lawrence C. Braceland; CFS 14, 24, 26; Kalamazoo: Cistercian Publications, 1978–79).

Ioannis de Forda [c. 1190]

Super extremam partem Cantici canticorum sermones = *John of Ford: Sermons on the Final Verses of the Song of Songs*, 7 Vols. (tr. Wendy Mary Beckett; CFS 29; Kalamazoo: Cistercian Publications, 1977, 1982–84).

Luther, Martin

In Cantica Canticorum brevis, sed admodum dilucida enarratio in *D. Martin Luthers Werke. Kritische Gesamtausgabe*, Vol. 31/2 (Weimar: Hermann Böhlaus, 1914) 586–769 [with George Rorer's transcription of the lectures delivered in 1530–31 as well as the text of the edition printed in 1539] = [printed edition only] "Lectures on the Song of Solomon: A Brief but Altogether Lucid Commentary on the Song of Songs by Dr. Martin Luther" (tr. Ian Siggins) in Jaroslav Pelikan and Hilton C. Oswald (eds.), *Luther's Works*, Vol. 15 (Saint Louis: Concordia, 1972) 189–264.

Clarius

Canticum Canticorum Salomonis, ad hebraicam veritatem nunc demum emendatum, adjectis scholiis ex arcanis hebraeorum erutis, quae tamen in primis Christi et Ecclesiae misteria breviter explicant (Venice, 1544).

Genebrard, Gilbert

Observationes in Canticum Canticorum (Paris, 1579, ²1585 [*Canticum Canticorum versibus jambicis et Commentariis explicatum, adversus trochaicam Theod. Bezae paraphrasin*].

Leon, Luis de [Luysius Legionensis]

In Canticum Canticorum Solomonis explanatio (Salamanca, 1580) = *El Cantar de los Cantares* (ed. Jorge Guillen; Salamanca: Sigueme, 1980).

Théodore de Bèze

Sermons sur les trois premiers chapitres du Cantique des Cantiques de Salomon (Fleuron, 1586) = *Master Bezaes Sermons upon the Three First Chapters of the Canticle of Canticles* (tr. John Harmer; Oxford: Joseph Barnes, 1587).

Ghislerius, Michael [Pius V]

Canticum Canticorum Salomonis, juxta lectiones Vulgatam, Ebraeam et Graecas, tum Septuaginta, tum aliorum interpretum (Rome, 1609; Venice, 1613).

Brightman, Thomas

Scholia et analysis in Canticum canticorum (Basel, 1614) = [revised and abridged] "A Commentary on the Canticles, or the Song of Salomon. Wherein the Text is Analised, the Native signification of the Words Declared, The Allegories Explained, and the Order of times whereunto they relate Observed . . ." in *The Workes of that Famous Reverend, and Learned Divine, Mr. Tho. Brightman* (London, 1644).

Sanctius [Sanchez], Caspar

Commentarius in Canticum canticorum (Lyon, 1616).

Ainsworth, Henry

Solomons Song of Songs, in English Metre: With Annotations and References to Other Scriptures, for the Easier Understanding of It (London, 1639).

Cotton, John

Explicatio Cantici Canticorum (London, 1642) = *A Brief Exposition of the Whole Book of Canticles; or, Song of Solomon* (London, 1648 [reprinted in Nichol's Series of Commentaries (Edinburgh/London, 1868)]).

Salazar, Ferdinand Quirini de

Expositiones in Canticum Canticorum (Lyon, 1642).

Grotius, Hugo
"Ad Canticum Canticorum" in *Annotationes ad Vetus Testamentum*, Vol. 1 (ed. G. I. L. Vogel; Halle, 1644, [2]1775) 449–454.

Lapide, Cornelius à
In Canticum Canticorum in *Commentarii in Scripturam Sacram*, Vol. 4: *In Ecclesiasten, Canticum Canticorum, in Librum Sapientiae* (Antwerp, 1657; Lyon/Paris, 1875) 357–750.

Coccejus, Johannes
Cogitationes de Cantico Canticorum Salomonis ut Icone regni Christi (Amsterdam, 1665 [reprinted: *Opera omnia theologica, exegetica, didactia, polemica, philologica*, Vol. 2: *Commentarius in Librum Ijobi, Psalmos, Proverbia, Ecclesiasten et Canticum Canticorum* (Amsterdam, [3]1701) 565–623]).

Bossuet, Jacques Bénigne
"In Canticum Canticorum" in *Libri Salomonis: Proverbia, Ecclesiastes, Canticum Canticorum, Sapientia, Ecclesiasticus, cum notis* (Paris, 1693 [reprinted: *Oeuvres complètes de Bossuet*, Vol. 3 (Paris, 1863) 412–428]).

Clericus, Joannis
Canticum Canticorum Salomonis in *Veteris Testamenti Libri Hagiographi* (Amsterdam, 1731) 717–750.

Lowth, Robert
De Sacra Poesi Hebraeorum Praelectiones (London, 1753) = *Lectures on the Sacred Poetry of the Hebrews* (tr. G. Gregory; London, 1787 [287–308, "Lecture 30: The Song of Solomon Not a Regular Drama"; 309–344, "Lecture 31: Of the Subject and Style of Solomon's Song"]).

Jacobi, Johann Friedrich
Das durch eine leichte und ungekünstelte Erklärung von seinen Vorwürfen gerettete Hohe Lied; nebst einem Beweise, dass selbiges für die Zeiten Salomons und seiner Nachfolger sehr lehrreich und heilsam, und eines heiligen Dichters würdig gewesen (Celle, 1772).

Herder, Johann Gottfried von
Lieder der Liebe: Die ältesten und schönsten aus dem Morgenlande (1778 [reprinted: J. G. Müller [ed.], *J. G. von Herders sammtliche Werke*, Vol. 39 (Sammlung der vorzüglichsten deutschen Classiker 138; Carlsruhe, 1828) 1–156]).

Lessing, J. T.
Eclogae regis Salomonis (Leipzig, 1779).

Hufnagel, Wilhelm Friedrich
Salomos Hohes Lied, geprüft, übersetzt, erläutert (Erlangen, 1784).

Velthusen, Johann Caspar
Catena Cantilenarum in Salomonem. Duplici interpretatione, restrictiore altera, altera liberiore, expressit, et modulationis hebraicae notas (Helmstadt, 1786).

Beyer, Johann Franz
Sammlung von Liedern der Liebe im Geschmack Salomos, neu übersetzt und mit Anmerkungen (Marburg, 1792).

b / Nineteenth and Twentieth Centuries

Good, John Mason
Song of Songs: or, Sacred Idyls. Translated From The Original Hebrew with Notes Critical and Explanatory (London, 1803).

Hug, Johann Leonhard von
Das Hohe Lied in einer noch unversuchten Deutung (Freyburg/Constanz, 1813).

Ewald, Heinrich Georg Augustus
Das Hohe Lied Salomos übersetzt und mit Einleitung, Anmerkungen und einem Anhang (Göttingen, 1826, [2]1867 ["Das Hohe Lied übersetzt" in *Die Dichter des Alten Bundes*, Vol. 2, 333–426]).

Döpke, Johann Christian Carl
Philologisch-kritischer Commentar zum Hohen Lied Salomos (Leipzig, 1829).

Rosenmüller, Ernst Friedrich Carl
Salomonis regis et sapientis quae perhibentur scripta, Vol. 2: *Ecclesiasten et Canticum continens* (Scholia in Vetus Testamentum 9/2; Leipzig, 1830).

Magnus, E. J.
Kritische Bearbeitung und Erklärung des Hohen Liedes Salomos (Halle, 1842).

Delitzsch, Franz
Hoheslied und Koheleth (BC 4/5; Leipzig, 1851, [2]1875) = *Commentary on the Song of Songs and Ecclesiastes* (tr. M. G. Easton; CFTL 4/54; Edinburgh: T. & T. Clark, 1891).

Hahn, H. A.
Das Hohe Lied von Salomo übersetzt und erklärt (Breslau, 1852).

Hengstenberg, Ernst Wilhelm
Das Hohelied Salomonis ausgelegt (Berlin, 1853 [cf. "Prolegomena to the Song of Songs" in *idem, Commentary on Ecclesiastes with Other Treatises* (tr. D. W. Simon; Philadelphia: Smith/English, 1860) 264–305]).

Meier, Ernst
Das Hohe Lied in deutscher Übersetzung, Erklärung, und kritischer Textausgabe (Tübingen, 1854).

Hitzig, Ferdinand
Das Hohe Lied (KEH 16; Leipzig, 1855).

Ginsburg, Christian David
The Song of Songs, Translated from the Original Hebrew with a Commentary, Historical and Critical (London, 1857 [reprinted in *The Song of Songs and Coheleth* (LBS; New York: Ktav, 1970)]).

Vaihinger, J. G.
Der Prediger und das Hohe Lied (Stuttgart, 1858).

Weissbach, F. E.
Das Hohe Lied Salomos (Leipzig, 1858).

Weiss, Benjamin
The Song of Songs Unveiled: A New Translation and Exposition (Edinburgh, 1859).

Renan, Ernest
Le Cantique des Cantiques, traduit de l'hébreu avec une étude sur le plan, l'âge et le caractère du poème (Paris, 1860).

Withington, Leonard
Solomon's Song: Translated and Explained (Boston: J. E. Tilton, 1861).

Zöckler, Otto
Das Hohelied (Theologische-homiletische Bibelwerk 13; Bielefeld/Leipzig, 1868) = *The Song of Solomon* (tr. W. H. Green; A Commentary on the Holy Scriptures: Critical, Doctrinal, and Homiletical 10; New York: Charles Scribner, 1870).

Stuart, A. Moody
The Song of Songs: An Exposition of the Song of Solomon (Philadelphia: Wm. S. Rentoul, 1869).

Graetz, Heinrich Hirsch
Schir Ha-Schirim oder das Salomonische Hohelied (Wien, 1871; Breslau: W. Jacobsohn, ²1885).

Schäfer, Bernhard
Das hohe Lied (Münster: Theissing, 1876).

Reuss, Eduard
Le Cantique (La Bible 5; Paris: Sandoz et Fischbacher, 1879).

Stickel, J. G.
Das Hohelied in seiner Einheit und dramatischen Gliederung (Berlin, 1888).

Oettli, Samuel
"Das Hohelied" in Wilhelm Volck and Samuel Oettli, *Die poetischen Hagiographen (Buch Hiob, Prediger Salomo, Hohelied und Klagelieder* (KK A/8; Nördlingen: C. H. Beck, 1889) 155–198.

Gietmann, Gerardus
Commentarius in Ecclesiasten et Canticum Canticorum (Paris: Lethielleux, 1890).

Bruston, Charles
La Sulammite, mélodrame en cinq actes et en vers, traduit de l'hébreu avec des notes explicatives et une introduction sur le sens et la date du Cantique des Cantiques (Paris: Fischbacher, 1891).

Rothstein, Johann Wilhelm
Das Hohelied (Halle, 1893).

Reuss, Eduard
Das Alte Testament übersetzt, eingeleitet und erläutert, Vol. 5: *Die hebräische Poesie* (Braunschweig, 1893) 315–394.

Adeney, Walter F.
The Song of Solomon and the Lamentations of Jeremiah (The Expositor's Bible; New York: A. C. Armstrong, 1895).

Baethgen, Friedrich
"Das Hoheslied" in Ernst Kautzsch (ed.), *Die Heilige Schrift des Alten Testaments* (Freiburg/Leipzig: J. C. B. Mohr, ²1896) 854–860.

Budde, Karl
"Das Hohelied erklärt" in Karl Budde, Alfred Bertholet, and D. G. Wildeboer, *Die fünf Megillot (Das Hohelied, Das Buch Ruth, Die Klagelieder, Der Prediger, Das Buch Esther)* (KHC 6; Freiburg/ Leipzig/Tübingen: J. C. B. Mohr [Paul Siebeck], 1898) IX–48. [See also Budde (1910).]

Siegfried, Carl
"Hoheslied" in Wilhelm Frankenberg and Carl Siegfried, *Die Sprüche, Prediger und Hoheslied, übersetzt und erklärt* (HK 2/3; Göttingen: Vandenhoeck & Ruprecht, 1898) 78–126.

Harper, Andrew
The Song of Solomon, with Introduction and Notes (The Cambridge Bible for Schools and Colleges; Cambridge: Cambridge University, 1902, ²1907).

Haupt, Paul
The Book of Canticles: A New Rhythmical Translation with Restoration of the Hebrew Text (Chicago: University of Chicago, 1902).

Haupt, Paul
Biblische Liebeslieder: Das sogenannte Hohelied Salomos unter steter Berücksichtigung der Übersetzungen Goethes und Herders (Leipzig: J. C. Hinrichs, 1907).

Zapletal, Vincenz
Das Hohelied kritisch und metrisch untersucht (Freiburg, 1907).

Hontheim, Joseph
Das Hohe Lied übersetzt und erklärt (Biblische Studien 13/4; Freiburg im Breisgau: Herder, 1908).

Martin, George Currie
  Proverbs, Ecclesiastes and Song of Songs (The Century Bible 13; London: Caxton, 1908).
Joüon, Paul
  Le Cantique des Cantiques: Commentaire philologique et exégétique (Paris: Gabriel Beauchesne, [2]1909).
Budde, Karl
  "Das Hohelied" in Ernst Kautzsch and Alfred Bertholet (eds.), *Die Heilige Schrift des Alten Testament*, Vol. 2 (Tübingen: J. C. B. Mohr [Paul Siebeck], [3]1910, [4]1923) 390–407. [See also Budde (1898).]
Staerk, Willi
  Lyrik (Psalmen, Hoheslied und Verwandtes) (SAT 3/1; Göttingen: Vandenhoeck & Ruprecht, 1911, [2]1920).
Cannon, William Walter
  The Song of Songs, Edited as a Dramatic Poem (Cambridge: Cambridge University, 1913).
Ehrlich, Arnold B.
  "Das Hohelied" in *Randglossen zur hebräischen Bible: Textkritisches, Sprachliches und Sachliches*, Vol. 7 (Leipzig: J. C. Hinrichs, 1914) 1–18.
Dussaud, René
  Le Cantique des Cantiques: Essai de reconstitution des sources du poème attribué à Salomon (Bibliothèque historique des religions; Paris: Ernest Leroux, 1919).
Mowinckel, Sigmund
  Sangenes Sang (Kristiania, 1919). [See also Mowinckel (1962).]
Jastrow, Morris, Jr.
  The Song of Songs, Being a Collection of Love Lyrics of Ancient Palestine: A New Translation Based on a Revised Text, together with the Origin, Growth, and Interpretation of the Songs (Philadelphia: J. B. Lippincott, 1921).
Thilo, Martin
  Das Hohelied, neu übersetzt und ästhetisch-sittlich beurteilt (Bonn: A. Marcus/E. Webers, 1921).
Breuer, Raphael
  Lied der Lieder übersetzt und erläutert (Frankfurt am Main: A. J. Hofmann, 1923).
Kuhn, Gottfried
  Erklärung des Hohen Liedes (Leipzig: A. Deichert [Werner Scholl], 1926).
Wittekindt, Wilhelm
  Das Hohe Lied und seine Beziehungen zum Ištarkult (Hannover: Orient-Buchhandlung [Heinz Lefaire], 1926).

Miller, Athanasius
  Das Hohe Lied übersetzt und erklärt (HS 6/3; Bonn: Peter Hanstein, 1927).
Ricciotti, Giuseppe
  Il Cantico dei Cantici: Versione critica dal testo ebraico con introduzione e commento (Torino: Società editrice internazionale, 1928).
Gebhardt, Carl
  Das Lied der Lieder: Übertragen mit Einführung und Kommentar (Berlin: Philo, 1931).
Gemser, Berend
  Spreuken, Vol. 2: *Prediker en Hooglied van Salomo* (Tekst en uitleg; Groningen: Wolters, 1931).
Kalt, Edmund
  Das Hohe Lied (Paderborn, 1933).
Pouget, Guillaume; and Jean Guitton
  Le Cantique des Cantiques (ÉtB; Paris: Librairie Lecoffre [J. Gabalda], 1934, [2]1948) = *The Canticle of Canticles* (tr. Joseph L. Lilly; The Catholic Scripture Library; New York: Declan X. McMullen, 1948).
Hazan, Albert
  Le Cantique des Cantiques enfin expliqué (Paris: Librairie Lipschatz, 1936).
Oesterley, W. O. E.
  The Song of Songs: The Authorized Version together with a New Translation, an Introduction and Notes (London: Golden Cockerel, 1936).
Haller, Max
  "Das Hohe Lied" in Max Haller and Kurt Galling, *Die fünf Megilloth* (HAT 18; Tübingen: J. C. B. Mohr [Paul Siebeck], 1940) 21–46.
Buzy, Denis
  "Le Cantique des Cantiques, traduit et commenté" in Louis Pirot and Albert Clamer (eds.), *La Sainte Bible*, Vol. 6 (Paris: Letouzey et Ané, 1941) 281–363. [See also Buzy (1950).]
Lehrmann, Simon Maurice
  "The Song of Songs" in Abraham Cohen (ed.), *The Five Megilloth* (Hindhead: Soncino, 1946, [2]1952).
Butte, A.
  Le Cantique des Cantiques (Paris: Pierre Seghers, 1947).
Waterman, Leroy
  The Song of Songs, Translated and Interpreted as a Dramatic Poem (Ann Arbor: University of Michigan, 1948).
Fischer, Johann
  Das Hohe Lied (Echter-Bibel 10; Würzburg: Echter, 1949, [2]1952).

Bettan, Israel
The Five Scrolls (Cincinnati: Union of American Hebrew Congregations, 1950).

Buzy, Denis
Le Cantique des Cantiques (Paris: Letouzey et Ané, 1950). [See also Buzy (1941).]

Vaccari, Alberto
"La Cantica" in *I Libri Poetici* (La Sacra Bibbia 5/2; Firenze: Salani, 1950) 111–129.

Robert, André
Le Cantique des Cantiques (La sainte Bible 18; Paris: Cerf, 1951, ²1953). [See also Robert (1963).]

Aalders, Gerhard Charles
Het Hooglied vertaald en verklaard (COT 19; Kampen: N. V. Uitgeversmaatschappij [J. H. Kok], 1952).

Ambroggi, P. de
Cantico dei Cantici—dramma dell'amore sacro (Rome: Paoline, 1952).

Bea, Augustinus
Canticum Canticorum Salomonis quod hebraice dicitur Šîr Haššîrîm (SPIB 104; Rome: Pontifical Biblical Institute, 1953).

Chouraqui, André; and Lucien-Marie de Saint-Joseph
Le Cantique des Cantiques (Paris: Brouwer, 1953). [See also Chouraqui (1970).]

Feuillet, André
Le Cantique des Cantiques: Étude de théologie biblique et réflexions sur une méthode d'exégèse (LD 10, Paris: Cerf, 1953).

Saydon, P. P.
"The Canticle of Canticles" in Bernard Orchard *et al.* (eds.), *A Catholic Commentary on Holy Scripture* (London: Thomas Nelson, 1953) 496–503.

Gordis, Robert
The Song of Songs: A Study, Modern Translation and Commentary (Texts and Studies 20; New York: Jewish Theological Seminary of America, 1954 [revised in *The Song of Songs and Lamentations: A Study, Modern Translation and Commentary* (New York: Ktav, 1974]).

Knight, George A. F.
Esther, Song of Songs, Lamentations (TBC; London: SCM, 1955).

Siegel, Abraham M.
The Sublime Songs of Love: A New Commentary on the Song of Songs and Related Essays (New York: Exposition, 1955).

Bruno, Arvid
Das Hohe Lied, Das Buch Hiob: Eine rhythmische und textkritische Untersuchung nebst einer Einführung in das Hohe Lied (Stockholm: Almquist & Wiksell, 1956).

Meek, Theophile J.
"The Song of Songs: Introduction and Exegesis" in George Arthur Buttrick *et al.* (eds.), *The Interpreter's Bible*, Vol. 5 (Nashville: Abingdon, 1956) 89–148.

Schmökel, Hartmut
Heilige Hochzeit und Hoheslied (Abhandlungen für die Kunde des Morgenlandes 32/1; Wiesbaden: Deutsche Morgenländische Gesellschaft [Franz Steiner], 1956).

Saussure, Jean de
Le Cantique de L'Église (Genève: Labor et Fides, 1957).

Ringgren, Helmer
"Das Hohe Lied" in Helmer Ringgren and Artur Weiser, *Das Hohe Lied, Klagelieder, Das Buch Esther: Übersetzt und erklärt* (ATD 16/2; Göttingen: Vandenhoeck & Ruprecht, 1958) 1–37.

Dhorme, Édouard
"Cantique des Cantiques" in *La Bible de la Pleiade*, Vol. 1/2 (Paris: Gallimard, 1959).

Schonfield, Hugh J.
The Song of Songs, Translated from the Original Hebrew with and Introduction and Explanations (London: Elek, 1959).

Winandy, Jacques
Le Cantique des Cantiques: Poème d'amour mué en écrit de sagesse (Bible et vie chrétienne; Tournai: Castermann [Maredsous], 1960).

Murphy, Roland E.
The Book of Ecclesiastes and the Canticle of Canticles with a Commentary (New York: Paulist, 1961). [See also Murphy (1968) and (1990).]

Lamparter, Helmut
Das Buch der Sehnsucht (BAT 16/2; Stuttgart: Calwer, 1962).

Mowinckel, Sigmund
Salomos høysang: Gammelhebraiske kjaerlighetsdikte (Oslo: O. Falch, 1962). [See also Mowinckel (1919).]

Oudenrijn, Marcus Antonius van den
Het Hooglied uit de grondtekst vertaald en uitgelegd (BOT 8/3; Roermond: J. J. Romen & Zonen, 1962).

Rudolph, Wilhelm
Das Buch Ruth, Das Hohe Lied, Die Klagelieder (KAT 17/1–3; Gütersloh: Gütersloher Verlagshaus [Gerd Mohn], 1962).

Schneider, Heinrich
Die Sprüche Salomos, Das Buch des Predigers, Das Hohelied (HB 7/1; Freiburg/Basel/Wien: Herder, 1962).

Herbert, A. S.
"The Song of Solomon" in Matthew Black and H. H. Rowley (eds.), *Peake's Commentary on the Bible* (London: Thomas Nelson, 1963) 468–474.

Robert, André; and Raymond Tournay, with André Feuillet
Le Cantique des Cantiques: traduction et commentaire (ÉtB; Paris: Librairie Lecoffre [J. Gabalda], 1963). [See also Robert (1951).]

Krinetzki, Leo [= Günter]
Das Hohe Lied: Kommentar zu Gestalt und Kerygma eines alttestamentlichen Liebesliedes (KBANT; Düsseldorf: Patmos, 1964). [See also Krinetzki (1980) and (1981).]

Rylaarsdam, J. Coert
The Proverbs, Ecclesiastes, The Song of Solomon (The Layman's Bible Commentary 10; Richmond: John Knox, 1964).

Gerleman, Gillis
Ruth, Das Hohelied (BKAT 18; Neukirchen-Vluyn: Neukirchener, 1965).

Tournay, Raymond; and M. Nicolaÿ
Le Cantique des Cantiques: Commentaire abrégé (Paris: Cerf, 1967).

Lys, Daniel
Le plus beau chant de la création: Commentaire du Cantique des Cantiques (LD 51; Paris: Cerf, 1968).

Murphy, Roland E.
"Canticle of Canticles" in Raymond E. Brown *et al.* (eds.), *The Jerome Biblical Commentary* (Englewood Cliffs: Prentice-Hall, 1968) 1/506–510. [See also Murphy (1961) and (1990).]

Nolli, Gianfranco
Cantico dei Cantici (La Sacra Bibbia; Torino/Roma: Marietti, 1968).

Alonso Schökel, Luis
El Cantar de los Cantares (Los Libros Sagrados 10/1; Madrid: Ediciones cristiandad, 1969).

Würthwein, Ernst
"Das Hohelied" in Ernst Würthwein, Kurt Galling, and Otto Plöger, *Die fünf Megilloth* (HAT 18²; Tübingen, J. C. B. Mohr [Paul Siebeck], 1969) 25–71.

Chouraqui, André
Le Cantique des Cantiques suivi des Psaumes (Paris: Presses Universitaires, 1970). [See also Chouraqui (1953).]

Grad, A. –D.
Le véritable Cantique de Salomon: Introduction traditionelle et kabbalistique au Cantique des Cantiques avec commentaires verset par verset précedés du texte hébreu et de sa traduction (Paris: G. –P. Maisonneuve et Larose, 1970).

Bunn, J. T.
"Song of Solomon" in *The Broadman Bible Commentary*, Vol. 5 (Nashville: Broadman, 1971) 128–148.

Dentan, Robert C.
"The Song of Solomon" in Charles M. Laymon (ed.), *The Interpreter's One-Volume Commentary on the Bible* (Nashville/New York: Abingdon, 1971) 324–328.

Loretz, Oswald
Studien zur althebräischen Poesie 1: Das althebräische Liebeslied. Untersuchungen zur Stichometrie und Redaktionsgeschichte des Hohenliedes und des 45. Psalms (AOAT 14/1; Kevelaer: Butzon & Bercker; Neukirchen-Vluyn: Neukirchener, 1971).

Fuerst, Wesley J.
The Books of Ruth, Esther, Ecclesiastes, The Song of Songs, Lamentations: The Five Scrolls (CBC; Cambridge: Cambridge University, 1975).

Pope, Marvin H.
Song of Songs: A New Translation with Introduction and Commentary (AB 7; Garden City: Doubleday, 1977).

Krinetzki, Günter [= Leo]
Hoheslied (NEchB; Würzburg: Echter, 1980). [See also Krinetzki (1964) and (1981).]

Krinetzki, Günter [= Leo]
Kommentar zum Hohenlied: Bildsprache und Theologische Botschaft (BET 16; Frankfurt am Main/Bern: Peter D. Lang, 1981). [See also Krinetzki (1964) and (1980).]

Mannucci, Valerio
Sinfonia dell' Amore Sponsale: Il Cantico dei Cantici (Torino: Elle Di Ci, 1982).

Salvaneschi, Enrica
Cantico dei cantici: Interpretatio ludica (Genova: Melangolo, 1982).

Reese, James M.

The Book of Wisdom, Song of Songs (OTM 20; Wilmington: Michael Glazier, 1983).

Carr, G. Lloyd

The Song of Solomon: An Introduction and Commentary (TOTC; Leicester/Downers Grove: Inter-Varsity, 1984).

Fox, Michael V.

The Song of Songs and the Ancient Egyptian Love Songs (Madison: University of Wisconsin, 1985).

Ravasi, Gianfranco

Cantico dei Cantici (ed. David M. Turoldo; Milan: Paoline, 1985, ²1986).

Davidson, Robert

Ecclesiastes and the Song of Solomon (Daily Study Bible; Philadelphia: Westminster, 1986).

Goulder, Michael D.

The Song of Fourteen Songs (JSOTSup 36; Sheffield: JSOT, 1986).

Keel, Othmar

Das Hohelied (ZBAT 18; Zürich: Theologischer Verlag, 1986).

Falk, Marcia

"Song of Songs" in James L. Mays *et al.* (eds.), *Harper's Bible Commentary* (San Francisco: Harper & Row, 1988) 525–528.

Murphy, Roland E.

"Canticle of Canticles" in Raymond E. Brown *et al.* (eds.), *The New Jerome Biblical Commentary* (Englewood Cliffs: Prentice-Hall, 1990) 462–465. [See also Murphy (1961) and (1968).]

2. Books, Monographic Studies, and Articles (alphabetical listings in categories)

a / Overviews and General Treatments of the Song

Broadribb, Donald

"Thoughts on the Song of Solomon," *Abr-Nahrain* 3 (1961–62 [Leiden: E. J. Brill, 1963]) 11–36.

Buzy, Denis

"Un chef-d'oeuvre de poésie pure: le Cantique des Cantiques" in L.-H. Vincent (ed.), *Mémorial Lagrange* (Paris: Librairie Lecoffre [J. Gabalda], 1940) 147–162.

Childs, Brevard S.

Introduction to the Old Testament as Scripture (Philadelphia: Fortress, 1979) 568–579 ["Song of Songs"].

Eissfeldt, Otto

The Old Testament: An Introduction (tr. Peter R. Ackroyd; New York/Evanston: Harper and Row, 1965 [*Einleitung in das Alte Testament* (³1964)]) 483–491 ["The Song of Songs"].

Feuillet, André

"Le Cantique des cantiques et la tradition biblique," *La nouvelle revue théologique* 74 (1952) 706–733.

Fohrer, Georg

Introduction to the Old Testament, Initiated by Ernst Sellin (tr. David E. Green; Nashville/New York: Abingdon, 1968 [*Einleitung in das Alte Testament* (¹⁰1965)]) 299–303 ["The Song of Solomon"].

Friedländer, Moritz

"The Plot of the Song of Songs," *JQR* 6 (1894) 648–655.

Gordis, Robert

"A Wedding Song for Solomon," *JBL* 63 (1944) 263–270.

Idem

"The Song of Songs" in Moshe Davis (ed., *Mordechai M. Kaplan Jubilee Volumes*, Vol. 2 (New York: Jewish Theological Seminary of America, 1953) 281–325; reprinted in *idem, Poets, Prophets, and Sages: Essays in Biblical Interpretation* (Bloomington/London: Indiana University, 1971) 351–398.

Gottwald, Norman K.

"Song of Songs," *IDB*, Vol. 4 (R–Z), 420–426.

Haupt, Paul

"The Book of Canticles," *AJSL* 18 (1902) 193–245; 19 (1902) 1–32.

Hulst, Alexander R.

"Hoheslied, I. Das at. Buch," *RGG*³, Vol. 3, 428–430.

Lesêtre, Henri

"Cantique des cantiques," *DB*, Vol. 2 (C–F), 185–199.

Murphy, Roland E.

"Song of Songs," *IDBSup*, 836–838.

Idem

"Towards a Commentary on the Song of Songs," *CBQ* 39 (1977) 482–496.

Rothstein, Johann Wilhelm

"Song of Songs" in James Hastings (ed.), *A Dictionary of the Bible*, Vol. 4 (Pleroma-Zuzim) (New York: Charles Scribner's; Edinburgh: T. & T. Clark, 1907) 589–597.

Schoville, Keith N.; and Bathja Bayer

"Song of Songs," *EncJud*, Vol. 15 (Sm–Un), 144–152.

Segal, Morris [Moshe] Hirsch
"The Song of Songs," *VT* 12 (1962) 470–490; rev.
in *idem, The Pentateuch, its composition and its
authorship, and other Biblical Studies* (Jerusalem:
Magnes/Hebrew University, 1967) 221–241.

Tournay, Raymond Jacques
*Quand Dieu parle aux hommes le langage de l'amour.
Études sur le Cantique des cantiques* (CRB 21; Paris: J.
Gabalda, 1982) = *Word of God, Song of Love* (tr. E.
Crowley; New York: Paulist, 1989).

b / Text and Language

Albright, William Foxwell
"Archaic Survivals in the Text of Canticles" in D.
Winton Thomas and W. D. McHardy (eds.),
*Hebrew and Semitic Studies Presented to Godfrey Rolles
Driver* (Oxford: Clarendon, 1963) 1–7.

Bloch, Joshua
"A Critical Examination of the Text of the Syriac
Version of the Song of Songs," *AJSL* 38 (1921–22)
103–139.

Delcor, Matthias
"Le Texte Hébreu du Cantique de Siracide LI et
ss. et les Anciennes Versions," *Textus* 6 (1968) 27–
47.

Driver, Godfrey Rolles
"Supposed Arabisms in the Old Testament," *JBL*
55 (1936) 101–120.

Idem
"Hebrew Notes on 'Song of Songs' and 'Lamentations'" in Walter Baumgartner *et al.* (eds.), *Fest-
schrift für Alfred Bertholet zum 80. Geburtstag*
(Tübingen: J. C. B. Mohr [Paul Siebeck] 1950)
134–146.

Idem
"Lice in the Old Testament," *PEQ* 106 (1974)
159–160.

Emerton, John A., and D. J. Lane (eds.)
"Song of Songs" in *The Old Testament in Syriac
According to the Peshitta Version*, Vol. II/5 (Leiden:
E. J. Brill, 1979).

Euringer, Sebastien
"Die Bedeutung der Peschitto für die Textkritik
des Hohenliedes" in O. Bardenhewer (ed.),
Biblische Studien, Vol. 6 (Freiburg im Breisgau:
Herder, 1901) 115–128.

Idem
"Ein unkanonischer Text des Hohenliedes (Cnt
8:15–20) in der armenischen Bibel," *ZAW* 33
(1913) 272–294.

Idem
"'Schöpferische Exegese' im äthiopischen Hohenliede," *Bib* 17 (1936) 327–344, 479–500; 20
(1939) 27–37.

Idem
"Ein äthiopisches Scholienkommentar zum
Hohenliede," *Bib* 18 (1937) 257–276, 369–382.

Gordis, Robert
"The Root דגל in the Song of Songs," *JBL* 88
(1969) 203–204; reprinted in *idem, The Word and
the Book: Studies in Biblical Language and Literature*
(New York: Ktav, 1976) 311–312.

Hamp, Vincenz
"Zur Textkritik am Hohenlied," *BZ* N.F. 1 (1957)
197–214.

Hirschberg, Harris H.
"Some Additional Arabic Etymologies in Old
Testament Lexicography," *VT* 11 (1961) 373–385.

Hurwitz, Avi
"The Chronological Significance of 'Aramaisms' in
Biblical Hebrew," *IEJ* 18 (1968) 324–340.

Köbert, Raimund
"Syrische Fragmente eines griechischen Kommentars zum Hohen Lied," *Bib* 48 (1967) 111–
114.

Oudenrijn, Marcus Antonius van den
"Scholia in locos quosdam Cantici canticorum," *Bib*
35 (1954) 268–270.

Sigwalt, C.
"Das Lied der Lieder in seiner ursprünglichen
Textordnung," *BZ* 9 (1911) 27–53.

Vaccari, Alberto
"Note critiche ed esegetiche," *Bib* 28 (1927) 394–
406 [398–399, "Cant 4,8"; 399–401, "Cant 5,12"].

Idem
"Latina Cantici canticorum versio a s. Hieronymo
ad Graecam Hexaplarem emendata," *Bib* 36 (1955)
258–260.

Idem
"Cantici Canticorum latine a s. Hieronymo
recensiti emendatio," *Bib* 44 (1963) 74–75.

Vattioni, Francesco
"Bricole di versioni latine del Cantico dei Cantici,"
RCT 3 (1978) 353–358.

Wagner, Max
*Die lexikalischen und grammatikalischen Aramaismen
im alttestamentlichen Hebräisch* (BZAW 96; Berlin:
Alfred Töpelmann, 1966).

Wilmart, A.
"L'ancienne version latine du Cantique I–III,"
Revue bénédictine 23 (1911) 11–36.

Zolli, Eugenio
"In margine al Cantico dei Cantici," *Bib* 21 (1940) 273–282.

c / Canonization and History of Interpretation

Baer, Y.
"Israel, the Christian Church, and the Roman Empire, from the time of Septimus Severus to the Edict of Toleration of c.e. 313" in A. Fuks and I. Halpern (eds.), *Studies in History* (SH 7; Jerusalem: Magnes/Hebrew University, 1961) 79–149.

Bardy, Gustave
"Les traditions juives dans l'oeuvre d'Origène," *RB* 34 (1925) 217–252.

Idem
"Marie et le Cantique chez les Pères," *BVC* 7 (1954) 32–41.

Bentzen, Aage
"Remarks on the Canonization of the Song of Solomon" in *Studia Orientalia Ioanni Pedersen* (Hauniae: Einar Munksgaard, 1953) 41–47.

Beumer, Johannes
"Die marianische Deutung des Hohen Liedes in der Frühscholastik," *ZKT* 76 (1954) 41–439.

Bonsirven, Joseph
Exégèse rabbinique et exégèse paulinienne (Paris: Beauchesne, 1939).

Bonwetsch, Gottlieb Nathanael
Studien zu den Kommentaren Hippolyts zum Buche Daniel und zum Hohenlied (TU 16/2 [N. F. 1]; Leipzig: J. C. Hinrichs, 1897).

Bonnardière, A. M. la
"Le Cantique des cantiques dans l'oeuvre de saint Augustin," *Revue des études Augustiniennes* 1 (1955) 225–237.

Bornkamm, Heinrich
Luther und das Alte Testament (Tübingen: J. C. B. Mohr [Paul Siebeck], 1948) = *Luther and the Old Testament* (tr. Eric W. and Ruth C. Gritsch; ed. Victor I. Gruhn; Philadelphia: Fortress, 1969).

Brot, Isaäk
De Allegorische Uitlegging van het Hooglied voornamelijk in Nederland (Zuijderduijn-Woerden, 1971).

Brunet, A. M.
"Théodore de Mopsueste et le Cantique des cantiques," *Études et recherches* 9 (1955) 155–170.

Buzy, Denis
"L'allégorie matrimoniale de Jahvé et d'Israël et le Cantique des cantiques," *RB* 52 (1944) 77–90.

Cambe, M.
"L'influence du Cantique des cantiques sur le Nouveau Testament," *RThom* 62 (1962) 5–26.

Cantwell, Laurence
"The Allegory of the Canticle of Canticles," *Scr* 16 (1964) 76–93.

Carr, G. Lloyd
"The Old Testament Love Songs and Their Use in the New Testament," *JETS* 24 (1981) 97–105.

Cavallera, F., A. Cabassut, and M. Olpe-Galliard
"Cantique des cantiques. II: Histoire de l'interprétation spirituelle" in Marcel Viller *et al.* (eds.), *Dictionnaire de Spiritualité*, Vol. 2 (Paris: Beauchesne, 1953) 93–109.

Chappuzeau, Gertrud
"Die Auslegung des Hohenliedes durch Hippolyt von Rom," *JAC* 19 (1976) 45–81.

Idem
"Die Exegese von Hohelied 1, 2a.b und 7 bei den Kirchenvätern von Hippolyt bis Bernhard," *JAC* 18 (1975) 90–143.

Chênevert, Jacques
L'église dans le commentaire d'Origène sur Cantique des cantiques (Studia, Travaux de recherche 24; Paris: Brouwer; Montreal: Bellarmin, 1969).

Cohen, Gershon D.
The Song of Songs and the Jewish Religious Mentality (The Samuel Friedland Lectures; New York: Jewish Theological Seminary of America, 1966); reprinted in Sid Z. Leiman (ed.), *The Canon and Masorah of the Hebrew Bible* (New York: Ktav, 1974) 262–282.

Dubarle, André-Marie
"Le Cantique des Cantiques dan l'exégèse récente" in Charles Hauret (ed.), *Aux grands carrefours de la révélation et de l'exégèse de l'ancien testament* (Recherches bibliques 8; Paris: Brouwer, 1967) 139–152.

Habersaat, Karl
"Glossare und Paraphrasen zum Hohenlied: Ein Beitrag zur Geschichte der jüdisch-deutschen Hohelied–Uebersetzungen," *Bib* 17 (1936) 348–358.

Hanson, R. P. C.
Allegory and Event: A Study of the Sources and Significance of Origen's Interpretation of Scripture (London: SCM; Richmond: John Knox, 1959).

Herr, Moshe David
"Song of Songs Rabbah," *EncJud*, Vol. 15 (Sm–Un), 152–154.

Herde, Rosemarie

Das Hohelied in der lateinischen Literatur des Mittelalters bis zum 12 Jahrhundert (Münchener Beiträge zur Mediävistik und Renaissance-Forschung [Estratto da "Studi medievali" 3/8 (1967) 957–1073]; Spoleto: Centro italiano di studi sull' alto medioeva, 1968).

Kamin, Sarah

"A Thirteenth Century Latin Version of Rashi's Commentary to the Song of Songs" [Hebrew] *Tarbiz* 55 (1985–86) 381–411.

Kimelman, Reuven

"Rabbi Yoḥanan and Origen on the Song of Songs: A Third-Century Jewish-Christian Disputation," *HTR* 73 (1980) 567–595.

Kuhl, Curt

"Das Hohelied und seine Deutung," *TRu* 9 (1937) 137–167.

Lachs, Samuel Tobias

"Prolegomena to Canticles Rabba," *JQR* N.S. 55 (1964–65) 235–255.

Idem

"The Proems of Canticles Rabba," *JQR* N.S. 56 (1965–66) 225–239.

Lacocque, André

"L'insertion du Cantique des Cantiques dans le Canon," *RHPR* 42 (1962) 38–44.

Lauterbach, Jacob Z.

"Shir ha-Shirim (Canticles) Rabbah," *JE*, Vol. 11, 291–292.

Leclercq, Jean

The Love of Learning and the Desire of God: A Study of Monastic Culture (tr. Catherine Misrahi; New York: Fordham University, 1961).

Idem

Monks on Marriage: A Twelfth-Century View (New York: Seabury, 1982).

Lerch, David

"Hoheslied, II. Auslegungsgeschichtlich," *RGG³*, Vol. 3, 430–431.

Idem

"Zur Geschichte der Auslegung des Hohenliedes," *ZTK* 54 (1957) 257–277.

Littledale, Richard Frederick

A Commentary on the Song of Songs From Ancient and Medieval Sources (London, 1869).

Loewe, Raphael

"Apologetic Motifs in the Targum to the Song of Songs" in Alexander Altmann (ed.), *Biblical Motifs: Origins and Transformations* (Philip W. Lown

Institute of Advanced Studies, Brandeis University, Studies and Texts 3; Cambridge: Harvard University, 1966) 159–196.

Lubac, Henri de

Méditation sur l'Église (Collection "Theologique," Études publiées sous la direction de la Faculté de Théologie S.J. de Lyon-Fourvière 27; Paris: Montaigne, 1953).

Idem

The Sources of Revelation (tr. Luke O'Neill; New York: Herder & Herder, 1968).

Margolis, Max L.

"How the Song of Songs Entered the Canon" in Wilfred H. Schoff (ed.), *The Song of Songs: A Symposium* (Philadelphia: The Commercial Museum, 1924) 9–17.

Marocco, Giuseppe

"Alcun studi recenti sul Cantico dei Cantici," *RivB* 35 (1987) 69–77.

McNeil, Brian

"Avircius and the Song of Songs," *Vigiliae Christianae* 31 (1977) 23–34.

Montgomery, James A.

"The Song of Songs in Early and Mediaeval Christian Use" in Wilfred H. Schoff (ed.), *The Song of Songs: A Symposium* (Philadelphia: The Commercial Museum, 1924) 18–30.

Murphy, Roland E.

"Recent Literature on the Canticle of Canticles," *CBQ* 16 (1954) 1–11.

Idem

"Patristic and Medieval Exegesis—Help or Hindrance?" *CBQ* 43 (1981) 505–516.

Idem

"History of Exegesis as a Hermeneutical Tool: The Song of Songs," *BTB* 16 (1986) 87–91.

Ohly, Friedrich

Hohelied-Studien. Grundzüge einer Geschichte der Hohenliedauslegung des Abendlandes bis um 1200 (Schriften der wissenschaftlichen Gesellschaft an der Johann Wolfgang Goethe-Universität Frankfurt am Main, Geisteswissenschaftliche Reihe 1; Wiesbaden: Franz Steiner, 1958).

Parente, Paschal P.

"The Canticle of Canticles in Mystical Theology," *CBQ* 6 (1944) 142–158.

Perella, Nicholas James

The Kiss Sacred and Profane: An Interpretative History of Kiss Symbolism and Related Religio-Erotic Themes (Berkeley/Los Angeles: University of California, 1969).

Phipps, William E.
"The Plight of the Song of Songs," *JAAR* 42 (1974) 82–100.

Pirot, Louis
L'oeuvre exégétique de Théodore de Mopsueste, 350–428 après J.–C. (SPIB; Rome: Pontifical Biblical Institute, 1913).

Riedel, Wilhelm
Die Auslegung des Hohenliedes in der jüdischen Gemeinde und der griechischen Kirche (Leipzig: A. Deichert, 1898).

Riedlinger, Helmut
Die Makellosigkeit der Kirche in den lateinischen Hoheliedkommentaren des Mittelalters (Beiträge zur Geschichte der Philosophie und Theologie des Mittelalters. TU 38/3; Münster: Aschendorf, 1958).

Rowley, Harold H.
"The Interpretation of the Song of Songs," *JTS* 38 (1937) 337–363; rev. in *idem, The Servant of the Lord and Other Essays on the Old Testament* (Oxford: Basil Blackwell, ²1965) 195–245.

Rudolph, Wilhelm
"Das Hohe Lied im Kanon," *ZAW* 59 (1942–43) 189–199.

Salfeld, Siegmund
Das Hohelied Salomos bei den jüdischen Erklärern des Mittelalters (Berlin: Benzian, 1879).

Scheper, George L.
The Spiritual Marriage: The Exegetic History and Literary Impact of the Song of Songs in the Middle Ages (Ph.D. dissertation; Princeton University, 1971).

Idem
"Reformation Attitudes towards Allegory and the Song of Songs," *PMLA* 89 (1974) 551–562.

Shmueli, E.
"Song of Songs Exegesis—Worlds of Symbols" [Hebrew] *BMik* 23 (1978) 272–288.

Sibinga, J. Smit
"Une citation du Cantique dans la Secunda Petri," *RB* 73 (1966) 107–118.

Simke, Heinz
"Cant. 1, 7f. in altchristlicher Auslegung," *TZ* 18 (1962) 256–267.

Smalley, Beryl
The Study of the Bible in the Middle Ages (Oxford: Basil Blackwell, 1952).

Staerk, Willi
"Warum steht das Hohe Lied im Kanon?" *Theologischer Blätter* 16 (1937) 289–291.

Schwarz, Leo W.
"On Translating the 'Song of Songs'," *Judaism* 13 (1964) 64–76.

Timm, Hermann (ed.)
Das Hohe Lied Salomos: Nachdichtungen und Übersetzungen aus sieben Jahrhunderten (Insel Taschenbuch 600; Frankfurt: Insel, 1982).

Urbach, Ephraim E.
"The Homiletical Interpretations of the Sages and the Expositions of Origen on Canticles, and the Jewish–Christian Disputation" in Joseph Heinemann and Dov Noy (eds.), *Studies in Aggadah and Folk-Literature* (SH 22; Jerusalem: Magnes/Hebrew University, 1971) 247–275.

Vaccari, Alberto
"Il Cantico dei Cantici nelle recenti publicazioni," *Bib* 9 (1928) 443–457.

Vajda, Georges
L'amour de Dieu dan la théologie juive du Moyen Age (Études de Philosophie médiévale 46; Paris: Librairie philosophique [J. Vrin], 1957).

Vulliaud, Paul
Le Cantique des cantiques d'après la tradition juive (Paris: Universitaires de France, 1925).

Welserheimb, L.
"Das Kirchenbild der griechischen Väterkommentare zum Hohen Lied," *ZKT* 70 (1948) 393–449.

Winandy, Jacques
"Le Cantique des Cantiques et le Nouveau Testament," *RB* 71 (1964) 161–190.

Würthwein, Ernst
"Zum Verständnis des Hohenliedes," *TRu* 32 (1967) 177–212.

d / Near Eastern Sources and Comparative Studies

Carr, G. Lloyd
"Is the Song of Songs a 'Sacred Marriage' Drama?" *JETS* 22 (1979) 103–114.

Cooper, Jerrold S.
"New Cuneiform Parallels to the Song of Songs," *JBL* 90 (1971) 157–162.

Davis, Virginia L.
"Remarks on Michael V. Fox's 'The Cairo Love Songs'," *JAOS* 100 (1980) 111–114.

Dornseiff, Franz
"Ägyptische Liebeslieder, Hohes Lied, Sappho, Theokrit," *ZDMG* 90 (1936) 588–601.

Ebeling, Erich
"Ein Hymnenkatalog aus Assur," *Berliner Beiträge zur Keilschriftforschung* 1/3 (1923) 1–9.
Idem
"Das Hohelied im Lichte der assyrischen Forschungen," *ZDMG* 78 (1924) LXVIII–LXIX.
Idem
Liebeszauber im alten Orient (Mitteilungen der Altorientalischen Gesellschaft 1/1; Leipzig: E. Pfeiffer, 1925).
Foster, John L.
Love Songs of the New Kingdom (New York: Charles Scribner's Sons, 1974).
Fox, Michael V.
"The Cairo Love Songs," *JAOS* 100 (1980) 101–109.
Idem
"'Love' in the Love Songs," *JEA* 67 (1981) 181–182.
Idem
"The Entertainment Song Genre in Egyptian Literature" in Sarah Israelit Groll (ed.), *Egyptological Studies* (SH 26; Jerusalem: Magnes/Hebrew University, 1982) 268–316.
Idem
"Love, Passion, and Perception in Israelite and Egyptian Love Poetry," *JBL* 102 (1983) 219–228.
Idem
"Four Ancient Egyptian Love Songs" [Hebrew] *Shnaton: An Annual for Biblical and Ancient Near Eastern Studies* 7–8 (Jerusalem/Tel Aviv: Israel Bible Society [M. Newman], 1983–84) 187–215.
Halévy, Joseph
"Le Cantique des cantiques et le mythe d'Osiris-Hetep," *Revue sémitique* 14 (1922) 248–255.
Held, Moshe
"A Faithful Lover in an Old Babylonian Dialogue," *JCS* 15 (1961) 1–26; 16 (1962) 37–39 ["Addenda et Corrigenda"].
Hermann, Alfred
"Beiträge zur Erklärung der ägyptischen Liebesdichtung" in Otto Firchow (ed.), *Ägyptologische Studien* (Deutsche Akademie der Wissenschaften zu Berlin, Institut für Orientforschung 29; Berlin: Akademie-Verlag, 1955) 118–139.
Idem
Altägyptische Liebesdichtung (Wiesbaden: Otto Harrassowitz, 1959).
Hyde, Walter Woodburn
"Greek Analogies to the Song of Songs" in Wilfred H. Schoff (ed.), *The Song of Songs: A Symposium* (Philadelphia: The Commercial Museum, 1924) 31–42.
Jacobsen, Thorkild
The Treasures of Darkness: A History of Mesopotamian Religion (New Haven/London: Yale University, 1976) 23–73 ["Fourth Millennium Metaphors. The Gods as Providers: Dying Gods of Fertility"].
Idem
The Harps That Once . . .: Sumerian Poetry in Translation (New Haven/London: Yale University, 1987).
Kramer, Samuel Noah
"The Biblical 'Song of Songs' and the Sumerian Love Songs," *Expedition* 5 (1962) 25–31.
Idem
"Cuneiform Studies and the History of Literature: The Sumerian Sacred Marriage Texts," *PAPS* 107 (1963) 485–516.
Idem
The Sacred Marriage Rite: Aspects of Faith, Myth, and Ritual in Ancient Sumer (Bloomington/London: Indiana University, 1969) 85–106 ["The Sacred Marriage and Solomon's Song of Songs"].
Lambert, W. G.
"Divine Love Lyrics from Babylon," *JSS* 4 (1959) 1–15.
Idem
"The Problem of the Love Lyrics" in Hans Goedicke and J. J. M. Roberts (eds.), *Unity and Diversity: Essays in the History, Literature, and Religion of the Ancient Near East* (Baltimore: Johns Hopkins University, 1975) 98–135.
Meek, Theophile J.
"Canticles and the Tammuz Cult," *AJSL* 39 (1922–23) 1–14.
Idem
"Babylonian Parallels to the Song of Songs," *JBL* 43 (1924) 245–252.
Idem
"The Song of Songs and the Fertility Cult" in W. H. Schoff (ed.), *The Song of Songs: A Symposium* (Philadelphia: The Commercial Museum, 1924) 48–69.
Müller, W. Max
Die Liebespoesie der alten Ägypter (Leipzig: J. C. Hinrichs, 1899).
Neuschotz de Jassy, Oswald
Le Cantique des Cantiques et le mythe d'Osiris-Hetep (Paris: C. Reinwald, 1914).

Perugini, Cesare
"Cantico dei Cantici e lirica d'amore sumerica," *RivB* 31 (1983) 21–41.

Ringgren, Helmer
"Hoheslied und hieros Gamos," *ZAW* 65 (1953) 300–302.

Sasson, Jack M.
"A Further Cuneiform Parallel to the Song of Songs?" *ZAW* 85 (1973) 359–360.

Schmidt, Nathaniel
"Is Canticles an Adonis Litany?" *JAOS* 46 (1926) 154–164.

Schmökel, Hartmut
"Hoheslied und altorientalische Götterhochzeit," *Forschungen und Fortschritte* 27 (1953) 110–113.

Schoff, Wilfred H.
"The Offering Lists in the Song of Songs and their Political Significance" in *idem* (ed.), *The Song of Songs: A Symposium* (Philadelphia: The Commercial Museum, 1924) 80–120.

Schott, Siegfried
Altägyptische Liebeslieder (Zürich: Artemis, 1950) = *Les chants d'amour de l'Égypte ancienne* (tr. Paul Krieger; L'orient ancien illustré; Paris: A. Maisonneuve, 1956).

Schoville, Keith N.
The Impact of the Ras Shamra Texts on the Study of the Song of Songs (Ph.D. dissertation; University of Wisconsin, 1969).

Seiple, William G.
"Theocritean Parallels to the Song of Songs," *AJSL* 19 (1902–03) 108–115.

Shashar, M.
"Song of Songs and Bedouin Love Poetry" [Hebrew] *BMik* 31 (1985–86) 360–370.

Stephan, Stephen H.
"Modern Palestinian Parallels to the Song of Songs," *JPOS* 2 (1922) 199–278.

Suys, Émile
"Les chants d'amour du papyrus Chester Beatty I," *Bib* 13 (1932) 209–227.

Wetzstein, J. G.
"Die syrische Dreschtafel," *Zeitschrift für Ethnologie* 5 (1873) 270–302 [cf. also "Appendix. Remarks on the Song by Dr. J. G. Wetzstein" in Delitzsch, 162–176].

White, John Bradley
A Study of the Language of Love in the Song of Songs and Ancient Egyptian Literature (SBLDS 38; Missoula: Scholars, 1978).

Yamauchi, Edwin M.
"Tammuz and the Bible," *JBL* 84 (1965) 283–290.

e / Literary Structure, Genre, Character, and Aesthetics

Alonso Schökel, Luis
Estudios de Poética Hebrea (Barcelona: Flors, 1963).

Angénieux, Joseph
"Structure du Cantique des Cantiques en chants encadrés par des refrains alternants," *ETL* 41 (1965) 96–142.

Idem
"Les trois portraits du Cantique des Cantiques. Étude de critique littéraire," *ETL* 42 (1966) 582–596.

Idem
"Le Cantique des Cantiques en huit chants à refrains alternants. Essai de reconstitution du texte primitif avec une introduction et des notes critiques," *ETL* 44 (1968) 87–140.

Buzy, Denis
"La composition littéraire du Cantique des cantiques," *RB* 49 (1940) 169–194.

Carniti, Cecilia
"L'unità letteraria del Cantico dei Cantici," *BeO* 13 (1971) 97–106.

Exum, J. Cheryl
"A Literary and Structural Analysis of the Song of Songs," *ZAW* 85 (1973) 47–79.

Falk, Marcia
Love Lyrics from the Bible: A Translation and Literary Study of the Song of Songs (BLS 4; Almond: Sheffield, 1982).

Freedman, David Noel
"Prolegomenon" in George B. Gray, *The Forms of Hebrew Poetry* (LBS; New York: Ktav, 1972) vii–lvi; reprinted in *idem*, *Pottery, Poetry, and Prophecy: Studies in Early Hebrew Poetry* (Winona Lake: Eisenbrauns, 1980) 23–50.

González, Angel
"El lenguaje de la naturaleza en el Cantar de los Cantares," *EstBíb* 25 (1966) 241–282.

Grober, S. F.
"The hospitable lotus: A cluster of metaphors. An inquiry into the problem of textual unity in the Song of Songs," *Semitics* 9 (1984) 86–112.

Horst, Friedrich
"Die Formen des althebräischen Liebesliedes" in *Orientalistische Studien, Enno Littmann zu seinem 60.*

Geburtstag überreicht (Leiden: E. J. Brill, 1935) 43–54; reprinted in *idem, Gottes Rechte: Gesammelte Studien zum Recht im Alten Testament* (ed. Hans Walter Wolff; TB 12; München: Chr. Kaiser, 1961) 176–187.

Keel, Othmar
Deine Blicke sind Tauben: Zur Metaphorik des Hohen Liedes (SBS 114–115; Stuttgart: Katholisches Bibelwerk, 1984).

Kessler, R.
Some Poetical and Structural Features of the Song of Songs (Leeds University Oriental Society, Monograph Series 8; Leeds, 1957).

Landsberger, Franz
"Poetic Units Within the Song of Songs," *JBL* 73 (1954) 203–216.

Landy, Francis
"The Song of Songs and the Garden of Eden," *JBL* 98 (1979) 513–528.

Idem
"Beauty and the Enigma: An Enquiry into Some Interrelated Episodes of the Song of Songs," *JSOT* 17 (1980) 55–106.

Idem
Paradoxes of Paradise: Identity and Difference in the Song of Songs (BLS; Sheffield: Almond, 1983).

Müller, Hans-Peter
Vergleich und Metapher im Hohenlied (OBO 56; Freiburg Schweiz: Universitätsverlag; Göttingen: Vandenhoeck & Ruprecht, 1984).

Murphy, Roland E.
"The Structure of the Canticle of Canticles," *CBQ* 11 (1949) 381–391.

Idem
"Form-Critical Studies in the Song of Songs," *Int* 27 (1973) 413–422.

Idem
"The Unity of the Song of Songs," *VT* 29 (1979) 436–443.

Idem
Wisdom Literature: Job, Proverbs, Ruth, Canticles, Ecclesiastes, and Esther (FOTL 13; Grand Rapids: William B. Eerdmans, 1981).

Ringgren, Helmer
"Die Volksdichtung und das Hohe Lied," *UUÅ* 5 (1952) 82–118.

Robert, André
"Le genre littéraire du Cantique des Cantiques," *RB* 52 (1944) 192–213.

Segert, Stanislav
"Die Versform des Hohenliedes" in Felix Taver *et al.* (eds.), *Charisteria Orientalia praecipue ad Persiam pertientia: Ioanni Rypka sacrum* (Prague: Československé Akademie, 1956) 285–299.

Shea, William H.
"The Chiastic Structure of the Song of Songs," *ZAW* 92 (1980) 378–396.

Snaith, Norman
"The Song of Songs: The Dances of the Virgins," *AJSL* 50 (1933–34) 129–142.

Soulen, Richard N.
"The *Wasfs* of the Song of Songs and Hermeneutic," *JBL* 86 (1967) 183–190.

Webster, Edwin C.
"Pattern in the Song of Songs," *JSOT* 22 (1982) 73–93.

f / Meaning and Theological Significance

Adinolfi, Marco
"La coppia nel Cantico dei Cantici," *BeQ* 22 (1980) 3–29.

Audet, Jean-Paul
"Le sens du Cantique des cantiques," *RB* 62 (1955) 197–221 [summary: "The Meaning of the Canticle of Canticles," *Theology Digest* 5 (1957) 88–92].

Idem
"Love and Marriage in the Old Testament" [tr. F. Burke] *Scr* 10 (1958) 65–83.

Buzy, Denis
"Le Cantique des Cantiques. Exégèse allégorique ou parabolique?" *RSR* 39 (1951) 99–114.

Cook, Albert Spaulding
The Root of the Thing: A Study of Job and the Song of Songs (Bloomington: Indiana University, 1968).

Dubarle, André-Marie
"L'amour humain dans le Cantique des cantiques," *RB* 61 (1954) 67–86.

Freehof, Solomon B.
"The Song of Songs: A General Suggestion," *JQR* N. S. 39 (1948–49) 397–402.

Feuillet, André
"Le drame d'amour du Cantique des cantiques remis en son contexte prophétique," *Nova et Vetera* 62 (1987) 81–127; 63 (1988) 81–136.

Gaster, Theodor H.
"What the Song of Songs Means," *Com* 13 (1952) 316–322.

Gollwitzer, Helmut

Das hohe Lied der Liebe (Kaiser Traktate; München: Chr. Kaiser, 1978) = *Song of Love: A Biblical Understanding of Sex* (tr. Keith Crim; Philadelphia: Fortress, 1979).

Grelot, Pierre

"Le sens du Cantique des cantiques," *RB* 71 (1964) 42–56.

Kearney, Peter J.

"Marriage and Spirituality in the Song of Songs," *BT* 25 (1987) 144–149.

Krinetzki, Leo [= Günter]

Die Liebe hört nie auf (Werkhefte zur Bibelarbeit 4; Stuttgart: Katholisches Bibelwerk, 1964).

Idem

"Die erotischen Psychologie des Hohen Liedes," *TQ* 150 (1970) 404–416.

Idem

"'Retractationes' zu früheren Arbeiten uber das Hohelied," *Bib* 52 (1971) 176–189.

Laurin, Robert B.

"The Life of True Love: The Song of Songs and Its Modern Message," *Christianity Today* 6 (1962) 1062–1063.

Leahy, F. S.

"The Song of Solomon in Pastoral Teaching," *Evangelical Quarterly* 27 (1955) 205–213.

Loretz, Oswald

"Zum Problem des Eros im Hohenlied," *BZ* N.F. 8 (1964) 191–216.

Idem

"Die theologische Bedeutung des Hohenliedes," *BZ* N.F. 10 (1966) 29–43.

Lys, Daniel

"Le Cantique des cantiques: Pour une sexualité non-ambiguë," *Lumière et Vie* (1979) 39–53.

Maccoby, Hyam

"Sex According to the Song of Songs: Review of Marvin Pope, *The Song of Songs*," *Com* 67 (1979) 53–59.

Müller, Hans-Peter

"Die lyrische Reproduktion des Mythischen im Hohenlied," *ZTK* 73 (1976) 23–41.

Murphy, Roland E.

"Interpreting the Song of Songs," *BTB* 9 (1979) 99–105.

Idem

"A Biblical Model of Human Intimacy: The Song of Songs" in Andrew Greeley (ed.), *The Family in Crisis or in Transition: A Sociological and Theological Perspective* (Concilium 121; New York: Seabury, 1979) 61–66.

Nowell, Irene

"A Celebration of Love," *BT* 25 (1987) 140–143.

Oudenrijn, Marcus Antonius van den

"Vom Sinne des Hohen Liedes," *Divus Thomas* 31 (1953) 257–280.

Pope, Marvin H.

"Response to Sasson on the Sublime Song," *Maarav* 2 (1980) 207–214.

Ramlot, M. L.

"Le Cantique des cantiques: 'une flamme de Yahve'," *RThom* 64 (1964) 239–259.

Raurell, Frederic

"El plaer eròtic en el Càntic dels Càntics," *RCT* 6 (1981) 257–298.

Sadgrove, M.

"The Song of Songs as Wisdom Literature" in E. A. Livingstone (ed.), *Studia Biblica 1978, I: Papers on the Old Testament and Related Themes* (JSOTSup 11; Sheffield: JSOT, 1979) 245–248.

Sasson, Jack M.

"On M. H. Pope's *Song of Songs* [AB 7c]," *Maarav* 1 (1979) 177–196.

Idem

"Unlocking the Poetry of Love in the Song of Songs," *Bible Review* 1 (1985) 10–19.

Schmökel, Hartmut

"Zur kultischen Deutung des Hohenliedes," *ZAW* 64 (1952) 148–155.

Segal, Benjamin J.

"The Theme of the Song of Songs," *DD* 15 (1986–87) 106–113.

Trible, Phyllis

God and the Rhetoric of Sexuality (OBT 2; Philadelphia: Fortress, 1978) 144–165 ["Love's Lyrics Redeemed"].

Zolli, Israele

"Visionen der Liebe im Hohenlied," *Wiener Zeitschrift für die Kunde des Morgenlandes* 51 (1948) 34–37.

g / Particular Passages and Issues

Bar Ilan, Meir

"Text Criticism, Erotica and Magic in the Song of Songs" [Hebrew] *Shnaton: An Annual for Biblical and Ancient Near Eastern Studies* 9 (Jerusalem/Tel-Aviv: Israel Bible Society [M. Newman], 1985) 31–53 [English summary: xvi–xvii].

Bartina, Sebastián
"Los cuatro vientos del Cantar y los cuatro ríos del
Paráiso (Cant 4,16)," *EstBib* 31 (1972) 337–342.
Idem
"Los montes de Béter (Cant 2,17)," *EstBib* 31
(1972) 435–444.
Bishop, Eric F. F.
"Palestiniana in Canticulis," *CBQ* 29 (1967) 20–30.
Brenner, Athalya
"Aromatics and Perfumes in the Song of Songs,"
JSOT 25 (1983) 75–81.
Idem
"*dôdî ṣaḥ wĕ'ādôm* (Cant 5:10–11)" [Hebrew] *BMik*
27 (1981–82) 168–173.
Charbel, A.
"Come tradurre ''*eškōl hak-kōfer*' (Cant. 1,14)?" *BeO*
20 (1978) 61–64.
Crim, Keith R.
"'Your neck is like the Tower of David': The
Meaning of a Simile in the Song of Solomon 4:4,"
BTr 22 (1971) 70–74.
Dahood, Mitchell
"Canticle 7,9 and UT 52,61: A Question of
Method," *Bib* 57 (1976) 109–110.
Exum, J. Cheryl
"Asseverative '*al* in Canticles 1,6?" *Bib* 62 (1981)
416–419.
Feuillet, André
"Le Cantique des Cantiques et l'Apocalypse," *RSR*
49 (1961) 321–353.
Idem
"La formule d'appartenance mutuelle (II,16) et les
interprétations divergentes du Cantique des
Cantiques," *RB* 68 (1961) 5–38.
Idem
"Einige scheinbare Widersprüche des Hohen-
liedes," *BZ* N.F. 8 (1964) 216–239.
Fox, Michael V.
"Scholia to Canticles (*i 4b, ii 4, i 4ba, iv 3, v 8, vi
12*)," *VT* 33 (1983) 199–206.
Garbini, Giovanni
"La datazione del 'Cantico dei Cantici'," *RSO* 56
(1982) 39–46.
Gaster, Theodor H.
"Canticles i.4," *Expository Times* 72 (1960–61) 195.
Gerleman, Gillis
"Die Bildersprache des Hohenliedes und die
altägyptische Kunst," *ASTI* 1 (1962) 24–30.
Görg, Manfred
"Die 'Sänfte Salomos' nach HL 3,9f.," *Biblische*

Notizen: Beiträge zur exegetischen Diskussion 18 (1982)
15–25.
Goitein, Shlomo Dov
"Ayummā Kannidgālōt (Song of Songs VI.10)
'Splendid like the Brilliant Stars'," *JSS* 10 (1965)
220–221.
Goodspeed, Edgar J.
"The Shulammite," *AJSL* 50 (1933–34) 102–104.
Goshen-Gottstein, Moshe H.
"Philologische Miszellen zu den Qumrantexten,"
RQ 2 (1959–60) 43–51 [46–48, "4. Die Schönheit
Saras (*1 Q Genesis Midrasch* und der *waṣf* im
Hohenliede"].
Grossberg, Daniel
"Canticles 3:10 in the Light of a Homeric
Analogue and Biblical Poetics," *BTB* 11 (1981) 74–
76.
Gruber, Mayer I.
"Ten Dance-Derived Expressions in the Hebrew
Bible," *Bib* 62 (1981) 328–346.
Heitzmann, Alfonso Alegre
"El Cantar de los Cantares: Poesía y Ritual de la
Pascua (Cant. I,4.—VIII,5.)," *EstBib* 43 (1985)
321–330.
Herrmann, Wolfram
"Gedanken zur Geschichte der altorientalischen
Beschreibungslieder," *ZAW* 75 (1963) 176–197.
Hicks, R. Lansing
"The Door of Love" in John H. Marks and Robert
M. Good (eds.), *Love and Death in the Ancient Near
East: Essays in Honor of Marvin H. Pope* (Guilford:
Four Quarters, 1987) 153–158.
Honeyman, Alexander M.
"Two Contributions to Canaanite Toponymy," *JTS*
50 (1949) 50–52.
Isserlin, B. S. J.
"Song of Songs IV,4: An Archaeological Note,"
PEQ 909 (1958) 59–60.
Krauss, Samuel
"Die 'Landschaft' im biblischen Hohenliede,"
MGWJ 78 (1934) 81–87.
Idem
"Die Rechtslage im biblischen Hohenliede," *MGWJ*
80 (1936) 330–339.
Idem
"The Archaeological Background of Some Pas-
sages in the Song of Songs," *JQR* N.S. 32 (1941–
42) 115–137; 33 (1942–43) 17–27; 35 (1944–45)
59–78.

Krinetzki, Leo [=Günter]

"Die Macht der Liebe: Eine ästhetisch-exegetische Untersuchung zu H1 8,6–7," *MTZ* 13 (1962) 256–279.

Lee, G. M.

"Song of Songs V 16, 'My Beloved is White and Ruddy'," *VT* 21 (1971) 609.

Lemaire, André

"*Zāmīr* dans la tablette de Gezer et le Cantique des Cantiques," *VT* 25 (1975) 15–26.

Luciani, F.

"L'ultima parola di Ct 5,11a nei LXX e nelle versioni derivati," *RivB* 36 (1988) 73–78.

Lys, Daniel

"Notes sur le Cantique" in *Congress Volume: Rome 1968* (VTSup 17; Leiden: E. J. Brill, 1969) 170–178.

Müller, Hans-Peter

"Poesie und Magie in Cant 4,12—5,1," *ZDMG* Supplement 3/1 (1977) 157–164.

Murphy, Roland E.

"Dance and Death in the Song of Songs" in John H. Marks and Robert M. Good (eds.), *Love and Death in the Ancient Near East: Essays in Honor of Marvin H. Pope* (Guilford: Four Quarters, 1987) 117–119.

Idem

"Cant 2:8–17—A Unified Poem?" in André Caquot *et al.* (eds.), *Mélanges bibliques et orientaux en l'honneur de M. Mathias Delcor* (AOAT 215; Kevelaer: Butzon & Bercker; Neukirchen: Neukirchener, 1985) 305–310.

Paul, Shalom M.

"An Unrecognized Medical Idiom in Canticles 6,12 and Job 9,21," *Bib* 59 (1978) 545–547.

Pope, Marvin H.

"A Mare in Pharaoh's Chariotry," *BASOR* 200 (1970) 56–61.

Robert, André

"La description de l'Époux et de l'Épouse dans Cant., V,11–15 et VII,2–6" in F. Lavallée (ed.), *Mélanges E. Podechard* (Lyon: Facultés catholiques, 1945) 211–223.

Idem

"Les appendices du Cantique des cantiques (VIII, 8–14)," *RB* 55 (1948) 161–183.

Rowley, Harold H.

"The Meaning of 'the Shulammite'," *AJSL* 56 (1939) 84–91.

Saviv, S.

"The Antiquity of the Song of Songs" [Hebrew] *Beth Mikra* 26 (1981) 344–352 [Song of Songs and the Book of Isaiah]; 29 (1983–84) 295–304 [The Song of Song's Influence on Isaiah and Jeremiah].

Segal, Benjamin J.

"Four Repetitions in the Song of Songs," *DD* 16 (1987–88) 32–39.

Idem

"Double Meanings in the Song of Songs," *DD* 16 (1987–88) 249–255.

Tournay, Raymond Jacques

"Les affinités du Ps. xlv avec le Cantique des Cantiques et leur interprétation messianique" in *Congress Volume: Bonn 1962* (VTSup 9; Leiden: E. J. Brill, 1963) 168–212.

Idem

"Les chariots d'Amminadab (Cant vi 12): Israël peuple théophore," *VT* 9 (1959) 288–309.

Idem

"Abraham et le Cantique des cantiques," *VT* 25 (1975) 544–552.

Idem

"The Song of Songs and Its Concluding Section," *Immanuel* 10 (1980) 5–14.

Tromp, Nicolas J.

"Wisdom and the Canticle. Ct 8,6c–7b: text, character, message and import" in Maurice Gilbert (ed.), *La Sagesse de l'Ancien Testament* (BETL 51; Gembloux: J. Duculot, 1979) 88–95.

Vogt, Ernest

"Einige hebräische Wortbedeutungen," *Bib* 48 (1967) 57–74 [69–72, "Der Mischkrug im A. T. und der Vergleich in H1 7.3"].

Waldman, Nahum M.

"A Note on Canticles 4:9," *JBL* 89 (1970) 215–217.

Waterman, Leroy

"דודי in the Song of Songs," *AJSL* 35 (1918–19) 101–110.

Idem

"The Role of Solomon in the Song of Songs," *JBL* 44 (1925) 171–187.

Winandy, Jacques

"La litière de Salomon (Ct. III 9–10)," *VT* 15 (1965) 103–110.

1. Texts

a / Hebrew Bible

2. Hebrew Words

אב (’ēb) 179

אבקה (’ăbāqâ) 75, 149

אגוז (’ĕgôz) 75, 176

אגן (’aggān) 182

אדום (’ādôm) 165

ארמוני (’admônî) 165

אהב (’hb) 127, 128, 131

אהבה (’ahăbâ) 82, 99, 104, 133, 136, 146, 149, 183, 198(n.11)

אהלות (’ăhālôt) 67(n.292), 157

אז (’az) 193

אח (’āḥ) 184

אחד (’aḥad) 156, 158, 175, 178

אחות (’āḥôt) 81, 158, 165

אחז (’ḥz) 139

אחזים (’ăḥūzîm) 149

איככה (’êkākâ) 165

אילות (’ayyālôt) 133

אילים (’ayyālîm) 78

אימה (’ăyūmâ) 70, 175

איש (’îš) 194

אל (’al) 126, 182

אלך (’elep) 194

אם (’ēm) 188

אמן (’āmmān) 75, 182

אף (’ap) (conj.) 132

אף (’ap) (noun) 73, 183, 187

אפריון (’appiryôn) 75, 149

ארגמן (’argāmān) 149, 183, 186

ארז (’erez) 193

אש (’ēš) 191

אשישות (’ăšîšôt) 132

אשכלות (’aškōlôt) 183

אשר (’ăšer) 74, 75, 87(n.346), 119

את (’t) 9, 87(n.346)

ב (bĕ) 132

באר (bĕ’ēr) 157

בוא (bw’) 125, 132, 156

בוז (bwz) 184, 192

בטן (beṭen) 182

בית (bayit) 132, 192

בנה (bnh) 155

בנות (bĕnôt) 83(n.336), 150, 175, 176

בעל (ba‘al) 193

בקש (bqš) 79, 145, 146

ברותים (bĕrôtîm) 75, 132

ברח (brḥ) 194

ברית (bĕrît) 93

ברכות (bĕrēkôt) 182

ברר (brr) 175

בשם (bōśem) 156

בשמים (bĕśāmîm) 158, 194

בת (bat) 82, 183

בתר (bāter) 76, 93, 139

גדיה (gĕdîyâ) 131

גדית (gĕdiyyōt) 75

גל (gal) 156

גלילים (gălîlîm) 166

גלש (glš) 76, 155

גן (gan) 78, 156, 158, 167

גנים (gannîm) 157, 194

דבר (dbr) 165, 192

דבש (dĕbaš) 156

דגל (degel) 132, 136

דגול (dāgûl) 76, 166

דדוהו (Dōdāwāhû) 96(n.369)

דובב (dôbēb) 75, 183, 184

דוד (dôd) 9, 40, 82, 95, 125, 128, 131, 132, 156, 165

דודאים (dûdā’îm) 184

דודים (dôdîm) 157, 184

דלה (dallâ) 183

דלת (delet) 193

דמה (dāmâ) 71

הון (hôn) 192

הלך (hlk) 139

המה (hmh) 165

המה (hēmmâ) 175

המון (hāmôn) 193

הנה (hinnēh) 132, 139

הר (har) 78

הרים (hārîm) 76, 78, 93, 194

ו (wĕ) 126

זמיר (zāmîr) 75, 89, 139

זרוע (zĕrôa‘) 191

חבל (ḥbl) 191

חבצלת (ḥăbaṣelet) 132

חברים (ḥăbērîm) 64, 67(n.292), 131, 157, 194, 198

חדרים (ḥădārîm) 125

חומה (ḥômâ) 192

חוץ (ḥûṣ) 189

חותם (ḥôtām) 191

חטים (ḥiṭṭîm) 182

חך (ḥēk) 166, 183

חכמה (ḥokmâ) 121

חלאים (ḥălā’îm) 182

חלונות (ḥallōnôt) 139

חלף (ḥlp) 139

חמה (ḥammâ) 176

חמוקים (ḥammûqîm) 75, 182

חנט (ḥnṭ) 76, 139

חר (ḥôr) 165, 170

חרה (ḥrh) 126

חרוזים (ḥărûzîm) 75, 131

חרכים (ḥărakkîm) 75, 139

חרר (ḥrr) 75, 126

חתנה (ḥătūnnâ) 75, 150

טוב (ṭwb) 156

טוב (ṭôb) 70, 183

טובים (ṭôbîm) 70, 125

טירה (ṭîrâ) 192, 198

טנף (ṭnp) 75

יד (yad) 166

ידע (yd‘) 176

יונה (yônâ) 81, 165

יונים (yônîm) 155

יושבת (yôšebet) 4, 194

יין (yayin) 128, 132, 183, 184

יום (yôm) 78

יפה (yph) 156, 186

יפה (yāpeh / Yāpâ) 70, 81, 183

יצא (yṣ’) 131

ירד (yrd) 167

יריעות (yĕrî‘ôt) 85, 126

ירך (yārēk) 149

ישבות (yōšĕbôt) 166

ישנה (yĕšēnâ) 165

ישנים (yĕšēnîm) 183

כ (kĕ) 70, 181, 184, 193

כונים (kawwānîm) 137

כי (kî) 125

כל (kōl) 149, 155, 192

כלה (kallâ) 60, 81, 156, 158

כפר (kōper) 76, 132

כפרים (kĕpārîm) 76, 184

כרכם (karkōm) 75, 157

כרם (kerem) 74, 85, 194

כרמיל (karmîl) 183

כתל (kōtel) 75, 139

כתם (ketem) 67(n.292), 166

כתנת (kuttōnet) 165

228

ל-/לְ (lĕ) 74, 119, 125	נאוה (nā'weh/nāwâ) 70, 131	פגה (paggâ) 75, 139
לבב (lbb) 156	נדגלות (nidgālôt) 76, 175, 178	פז (paz) 166
לבונה (lĕbônâ) 149, 157, 158	נדיב (nādîb) 82, 176, 181	פילגשים (pîlagĕšîm) 83
לבנה (lĕbānâ) 176	נוזלים (nōzĕlîm) 157	פרדס (pardēs) 157
לבנון (lĕbānôn) 158, 183	נחל (naḥal) 176, 179	פתח (petaḥ) 184
לוח (lûaḥ) 193	נעול (nā'ûl) 156, 158	
לילות (lêlôt) 145, 149	נעם (n'm) 183	צאן (ṣō'n) 131
לין/לון (lwn/lyn) 132	נעם (nā'îm) 70	צבאות (ṣĕbā'ôt) 133
למד (lmd) 184	נפש (nepeš) 131, 165, 176	צבי (ṣĕbî)
לפני (lipnê) 194	נפת (nōpet) 156	(="beauty") 139
לשון (lāšôn) 156	נצנים (niṣṣānîm) 75	צבי (ṣĕbî)
	נקדית (nĕquddôt) 75, 131	(="gazelle") 78, 137, 139
מברכת (mĕbōreket) 176	נרד (nērĕd) 131	צואר (ṣawwā'r) 182
מגדים (mĕgādîm) 188	נרדים (nĕrādîm) 157	צופה (ṣopê) 183
מגדל (migdāl) 182, 183	נשים (nāšîm) 81	צור (ṣwr) 193
מגדלות (mĕgaddĕlôt) 166, 193	נשיקות (nĕšîqôt) 125	צורון (ṣawwārôn) 75, 156
מגן (māgēn) 155	נשק (nšq) 125, 184, 188	צח (ṣaḥ) 165
מדבר (midbār) 151, 155	נשקפה (nišqāpâ) 176	צללים (ṣĕlālîm) 78
מדלג (mĕdallēg) 139		צמה (ṣmh) 9
מה (māh) 158, 181	סבב (sbb) 139, 145	
מוהר (mōhâr) 198	סהר (sahar) 75, 182	קדר (Qedar) 126
מוצאת (môṣē't) 193	סובבים (sōbĕbîm) 146	קול (qôl) 139, 165, 194
מור/מר (mōr/mŏr) 131, 157, 165, 166	סוגה (sûgâ) 75, 182	קוצות (qĕwwūṣôt) 165
	סוסה (sûsâ) 75, 131	קומה (qômâ) 183
מות (mawet) 191	סמדר (semādar) 76	קנאה (qin'â) 191, 197
מזג (mezeg) 75, 182	סמך (smk) 132	קנה (qānâ) 157
מחלה (mĕḥōlâ) 181	סנסנים (sansinnîm) 75, 183	קנמון (qinnāmôn) 157
מחנים (maḥănāyim) 185	ספירים (sappîrîm) 72(n.305), 166	קצב (qṣb) 155
מטה (miṭṭâ) 74, 149	סתיו (סתו) (sĕtāw) 75, 139	קצובות (qĕṣûbôt) 155
מי (mî) 149		
מים (mayim) 192, 198	עבר ('obēr) 165, 166	ראה (r'h) 126
מישרים (mêšārîm) 126, 183	עד ('ad) 75, 131, 139	ראש (rō'š) 183
מלאת (millē't) 75, 166	עדר ('ēder) 131	רבים (rabbîm) 183, 192, 198
מלך (melek) 83	עור ('wr) 133, 157, 168, 191	רבץ (rbṣ) 83
מלכות (mĕlākôt) 83, 175	עין ('ayin) 156, 186, 193	רדיד (rĕdîd) 165
מן (min) 125, 149, 165	עיר ('ir) 145	רהטים (rĕhāṭîm) 183, 186
מסב (mēsab) 131	עטיה ('ōṭĕyâ) 131, 134(n.1)	רהב (rhb) 175
מעה (m'h) 72	על ('al) 165	רוכל (rôkēl) 149
מעים (mē'îm) 166	עלמות ('ălāmôt) 83, 84, 175	רחיט (rāḥîṭ) 75, 132
מעה (mē'ê) 165	עם ('am) 176	רחלים (rĕḥēlîm) 175
מעין (ma'yān) 157, 158	עם ('im) 71, 162, 176	רחצה (raḥṣâ) 76
מעינות (ma'yānôt) 157	ענק ('ănāq) 156	ריח (rêaḥ) 158
מעלפת (mĕ'ullepet) 72(n.305)	עפר ('ōper) 76, 78	רכב (rekeb) 131
מצא (mṣ') 145, 183, 189	עפרים ('ŏpārîm) 76	רמון (rimmôn) 157, 184
מקטרת (mĕquṭṭeret) 76, 149	עצים ('ēṣîm) 156	רע (rē(a)') 82, 131
מקפץ (mĕqappēṣ) 75, 139	ער ('ēr) 165, 168	רעה (r'h) 83, 131, 139, 167
מקשיבים (maqšîbîm) 194	ערב ('ārēb) 70	
מראה (mar'eh) 139, 166, 172	ערוג(ו)ת ('ărûgôt) 166, 167	רעה (rō'eh) 82, 139
מרכב (merkāb) 149	ערמה ('ărēmâ) 182	רעי (rĕ'î) 83, 172
מרקחים (merqaḥîm) 75	עשת ('ešet) 72(n.305), 75, 166	רעיה (ra'yâ) 76, 81, 131, 135, 165, 172
משכב (miškāb) 145		
משל (māšāl) 120	עשן ('āšsn) 149	רעים (rē'îm) 157
מתאימות (mat'îmôt) 155		רעים (rō'îm) 83, 155
מתוק (mātôq) 70		רפידה (rĕpîdâ) 75, 149
מתרפקת (mitrappeqet) 75, 149, 191		רקה (raqqâ) 155, 159

3. Subjects

In the design of the visual aspects of *Hermeneia*, consideration has been given to relating the form to the content by symbolic means.

The letters of the logotype *Hermeneia* are a fusion of forms alluding simultaneously to Hebrew (dotted vowel markings) and Greek (geometric round shapes) letter forms. In their modern treatment they remind us of the electronic age as well, the vantage point from which this investigation of the past begins.

The Lion of Judah used as visual identification for the series is based on the Seal of Shema. The version for *Hermeneia* is again a fusion of Hebrew calligraphic forms, especially the legs of the lion, and Greek elements characterized by the geometric. In the sequence of arcs, which can be understood as scroll-like images, the first is the lion's mouth. It is reasserted and accelerated in the whorl and returns in the aggressively arched tail: tradition is passed from one age to the next, rediscovered and re-formed.

"Who is worthy to open the scroll and break its seals. . . ."

Then one of the elders said to me

"weep not; lo, the Lion of the tribe of David,
the Root of David, has conquered,
so that he can open the scroll and
its seven seals."

Rev. 5:2, 5

To celebrate the signal achievement in biblical scholarship which *Hermeneia* represents, the entire series will by its color constitute a signal on the theologian's bookshelf: the Old Testament will be bound in yellow and the New Testament in red, traceable to a commonly used color coding for synagogue and church in medieval painting; in pure color terms, varying degrees of intensity of the warm segment of the color spectrum. The colors interpenetrate when the binding color for the Old Testament is used to imprint volumes from the New and vice versa.

Wherever possible, a photograph of the oldest extant manuscript, or a historically significant document pertaining to the biblical sources, will be displayed on the end papers of each volume to give a feel for the tangible reality and beauty of the source material.

The title-page motifs are expressive derivations from the *Hermeneia* logotype, repeated seven times to form a matrix and debossed on the cover of each volume. These sifted-out elements will be seen to be in their exact positions within the parent matrix. These motifs and their expressional character are noted on the following page.

Horizontal markings at gradated levels on the spine will assist in grouping the volumes according to these conventional categories.

The type has been set with unjustified right margins so as to preserve the internal consistency of word spacing. This is a major factor in both legibility and aesthetic quality; the resultant uneven line endings are only slight impairments to legibility by comparison. In this respect the type resembles the handwritten manuscripts where the quality of the calligraphic writing is dependent on establishing and holding to integral spacing patterns.

All of the type faces in common use today have been designed between A.D. 1500 and the present. For the biblical text a face was chosen which does not arbitrarily date the text, but rather one which is uncompromisingly modern and unembellished so that its feel is of the universal. The type style is Univers 65 by Adrian Frutiger.

The expository texts and footnotes are set in Baskerville, chosen for its compatibility with the many brief Greek and Hebrew insertions. The double-column format and the shorter line length facilitate speed reading and the wide margins to the left of footnotes provide for the scholar's own notations.

Kenneth Hiebert

236

Category of biblical writing,
key symbolic characteristic,
and volumes so identified.

1
Law
(boundaries described)
  Genesis
  Exodus
  Leviticus
  Numbers
  Deuteronomy

2
History
(trek through time and space)
  Joshua
  Judges
  Ruth
  1 Samuel
  2 Samuel
  1 Kings
  2 Kings
  1 Chronicles
  2 Chronicles
  Ezra
  Nehemiah
  Esther

3
Poetry
(lyric emotional expression)
  Job
  Psalms
  Proverbs
  Ecclesiastes
  Song of Songs

4
Prophets
(inspired seers)
  Isaiah
  Jeremiah
  Lamentations
  Ezekiel
  Daniel
  Hosea
  Joel
  Amos
  Obadiah
  Jonah
  Micah
  Nahum
  Habakkuk
  Zephaniah
  Haggai
  Zechariah
  Malachi

5
New Testament Narrative
(focus on One)
  Matthew
  Mark
  Luke
  John
  Acts

6
Epistles
(directed instruction)
  Romans
  1 Corinthians
  2 Corinthians
  Galatians
  Ephesians
  Philippians
  Colossians
  1 Thessalonians
  2 Thessalonians
  1 Timothy
  2 Timothy
  Titus
  Philemon
  Hebrews
  James
  1 Peter
  2 Peter
  1 John
  2 John
  3 John
  Jude

7
Apocalypse
(vision of the future)
  Revelation

8
Extracanonical Writings
(peripheral records)